PENGUIN BOOKS

DAZZLER

Darren Gough is the most popular English cricketer since Ian Botham's heyday. He was a Wisden Cricketer of the Year in 1999, the same year as his spectacular hat-trick in the final test against Australia, and he remains the linchpin of England's strike force, having proved his worth again during the summer of 2000, when he was named England's Man of the Series in their remarkable victory over West Indies. He was England's leading wicket taker in the 2001 Ashes series against Australia.

David Norrie has been cricket correspondent of the *News of the World* for many years. He is the author of a number of books, including *Athers*, a biography of Michael Atherton. He lives in Surrey with his family.

D1368953

Dazzler

The Autobiography

DARREN GOUGH

with David Norrie

PENGUIN BOOKS

PENGUIN BOOKS

Published by the Penguin Group
Penguin Books Ltd, 80 Strand, London WC2R ORL, England
Penguin Putnam Inc., 375 Hudson Street, New York, New York 10014, USA
Penguin Books Australia Ltd, 250 Camberwell Road, Camberwell,
Victoria 3124, Australia
Penguin Books Canada Ltd, 10 Alcorn Avenue, Toronto, Ontario, Canada M4V 3B2
Penguin Books India (P) Ltd, 11 Community Centre, Panchsheel Park,
New Delhi – 110 017, India
Penguin Books (NZ) Ltd, Cnr Rosedale and Airborne Roads,
Albany, Auckland, New Zealand
Penguin Books (South Africa) (Pty) Ltd, 24 Sturdee Avenue,
Rosebank 2196, South Africa

Penguin Books Ltd, Registered Offices: 80 Strand, London WC2R ORL, England

www.penguin.com

First published by Michael Joseph 2001
Published in Penguin Books 2002
2

Copyright © Darren Gough, 2001
Statistical Appendix copyright © Paul Dyson, 2001
Revised Statistical Appendix copyright © Paul Dyson, 2002
All rights reserved

The publishers wish to thank the following copyright holders for the use of their
photographs: Patrick Eagar, Allsport, Graham Morris and Action Images.

The moral right of the author has been asserted

Set in Monotype Bembo
Printed in England by Clays Ltd, St Ives plc

CONTENTS

For Mum and Dad, for all their sacrifices in the early years,
and for Anna and our two boys, Liam and Brennan,
who are my inspiration for the future.

ACKNOWLEDGEMENTS

My thanks to all those who have offered a helping hand over the past thirty years. I've tried to give the important ones, Yorkshire and otherwise, their rightful place in my book. My grateful thanks to my 'ghost' of the past seven years, *News of the World* cricket correspondent David Norrie, who has helped put the words in the right order and made sure my memory hasn't played too many tricks. To Clifford Bloxham and Sian Masterton at Octagon, who have looked after me since 1995, and Rowland White and the team at Penguin for making this book such a fine production. And, finally, to all those cricketers I've played with and against in a thoroughly enjoyable cricket career, which I hope still has some way to run.

FOREWORD: Walking on Sunshine

Darren Gough, 1970 to the present day. The life-story of a Yorkshire fast bowler, who has had the great good fortune to play for his country at cricket. It has not always been the best of times for either Yorkshire or England. From 'Guzzler' to 'Dazzler', I have tried to give my story straight, with little soft-soaping. Soft-soaping is not my style. In any competitive environment there are bound to be a few harsh words and actions along the way. Such incidents are all part of the story. I have not glossed over them. In some cases I have been the offender; in others, I have not been at fault and have not been afraid to point the finger of blame.

This has been a time of dramatic change in English cricket. Some sections of the England set-up wanted success first, so as to justify the new structure. It did not work that way. It was never going to work that way. I'm convinced that it took Lord MacLaurin longer to get things moving than he had anticipated. I am equally sure that without him England cricket would still be whistling into the wind. By the summer of 2000 many changes were in place: central contracts, two divisions and the new international schedule. Lo and behold, England enjoyed a vintage season, winning two Test series – against Zimbabwe and the West Indies – and the new triangular tournament. Do not tell me the two are not related. England finished the year in style with a first win in Pakistan for 39 years.

Getting England off the bottom of the Test pile has been a battle, both on and off the field. The more interesting and significant battles are recounted here. I have described events as honestly and as fairly as I can from a player's viewpoint. We take the brunt of the fame and the shame for what happens on the field. I may smile a lot and seem happy but there have been plenty of bad days. I struggled to hold down a first-team spot at Yorkshire for several seasons. 'Gough the Scoff' burst on to the international scene in

1994, but my England career was interrupted repeatedly because of injuries and lack of fitness or form. At one stage I had missed as many Tests as I had played.

I have never given up or lost hope, never thought for a second that my England career was over. That is the way I have always played my cricket. That is the reason I have enjoyed such a great rapport with cricket fans all over the country and around the world. The simple truth is, I love playing cricket, especially when the result of a Test match rests on one wicket, one catch or a few runs – as it did at Lord's against the West Indies in 2000. That is why there is always a smile on my face, even in the heat of battle. I would not have swapped one second of my cricket career. The highs are much more enjoyable because I have also known periods of doubt and despair. I have never found cricket a chore. I may often have moaned about tour itineraries, England fees and officials' insensitivity to our needs, but I am not one for keeping quiet if I feel there is an injustice. Not for one second, though, have any of those disputes affected my commitment to England's cause. By the time that cricket decides it has had enough of me, or vice versa, I want to have been the eighth Englishman to take 200 Test wickets. That is only natural. We all love the personal-glory bit. Yet I would swap it all – the congratulations from Harold Larwood and Ray Lindwall in Sydney on the 1994/5 Ashes trip, beating the Aussies at Edgbaston ('97) and Melbourne ('98), the Sydney hat-trick, sealing England's first major-series win for 12 years against South Africa, hitting the winning runs at Centurion Park, batting with Corkie when we won at Lord's, destroying the West Indies in two days on my home ground of Headingley and those 2000/1 wins in Karachi and Kandy – to be part of an England team that wins the Ashes. That's how much playing for England's cricket team means to me. I hope you enjoy reading about my career half as much as I have enjoyed taking part.

1. Long Day's Journey

'You're going to hit the winning runs.'

'Thanks, Nas, but no thanks.' Or words to that effect.

That was my wake-up call on the morning of 1 July 2000 – a day I knew only too well would decide this West Indies series. More than that: this was the last chance for my generation of England cricketers to prove we were anything other than hit-and-miss merchants, collective failures who had taken England to the bottom of the cricket pile. The clock was ticking and our time was almost up.

Glory was certainly not on the Gough agenda. I planned a day of leisure in the home dressing-room at Lord's. No strapping-on of pads in anger. That might seem strange: Darren Gough happy to keep in the background. I have never been slow to grab centre stage, but this was one time when I wanted no part of the action. I had already played my part, along with Caddie (Andrew Caddick) and Corkie (Dominic Cork).

I still had to pinch myself that England were actually in with a shout of winning this hundredth Test at Lord's. When we'd walked out to bowl for a second time the previous afternoon, we trailed by 133 runs. England had lost the first Test – a terrible drubbing at Edgbaston – so our main aim now was to try to restore some damaged pride.

Let me make it clear: we had not given up, but even an elementary knowledge of arithmetic would tell you our situation was dire. Although Nasser's broken thumb had forced him to hand over the captaincy to Alec Stewart, he still gave the 'backs to the wall' battlecry. Brave words, full of hope and passion, but I had heard them all before. Playing for England as long as I have – since 1994 – hopeless situations requiring mission-impossible solutions have been a common occurrence. It is fair to say that I strolled on to Lord's that

Friday with some hope in my heart but with little doubt in my head that England were heading for another embarrassing defeat.

When I woke up on Saturday morning, everything had changed. It was 'game on'. Still, I had to switch on the TV and check in the newspapers to make sure that we really had rolled the West Indies over for 54 runs – only twice before had the cricketers from the Caribbean been dismissed for a lower total.

England's victory target was only 188 runs when it could have been 300-plus. Only 188 runs! How easily that total rolled off the tongue. Four of our top six had been in a similar situation six years before at Port of Spain, when England needed 194 to win. On that occasion Curtly Ambrose made sure the tourists did not get a quarter of the way towards their target, as England were demolished for 46. Having been part of an attack that had just bowled out the Windies out for 54, I appreciated how special that was. They say that time is a great healer. Not in the West Indies' case. The Trinidad tormentor, Ambrose, was still leading the West Indies attack and still at the top of his game. Ambrose was approaching 400 wickets, although it was his long-time partner-in-crime, Courtney Walsh, who had overtaken Kapil Dev and was now the leading wicket-taker in Test history and heading for 500.

The Lord's Friday had been fantastic, pure adrenalin, pure emotion. The crowd got carried away even more than we did. The Windies were always going to have second go at us, and the side that had been dismissed for 54 were still the favourites to win the match and go 2–0 up in the series. If England could bowl the Windies out for that score, what would Walsh and Ambrose do to us? Why had we given them so many runs in the first innings? Why couldn't we have scraped together a few more ourselves? One thing was certain: unless the weather intervened, all matters would be decided on this Saturday.

If you are going to have a day of cricket drama, where better than at Lord's and when better than the hundredth Test match at the home of cricket? I love playing there. I love the history of the place, I love my special spot in the dressing-room and, believe it or not, this Barnsley lad loves making his way through the egg-and-bacon ties and toffs in the Long Room. They were as keen to see me bat as I was to get my pads on. If Darren Gough, England's No. 10, was walking through them on his way out to bat, it meant that the home side were in all sorts of trouble.

I like to get into the dressing-room early. So do Nasser (Hussain), Stewie (Alec Stewart) and Athers (Michael Atherton). We all have our own places at Lord's. Looking down the ground, I'm in the right-hand corner by the window. I hate sitting on the balcony; instead, I can watch the action through the window. Stewie has the left-hand corner by the balcony, Nasser sits on the back bench, looking out. Caddie changes next to me, so do Chalky (Craig White) and Corkie. The bowlers' corner. Athers has the Old Father Time armchair in the middle of the room, as befits his status.

Nobody needed any reminding that this was a huge day, there was enough tension around. In those circumstances, you try to keep everything as normal as possible, with all the usual mickey-taking. Athers had his head buried in the *Racing Post* as usual. After studying the form, he'd be on the phone to his Lancashire colleague, Graham Lloyd, son of former England coach David, with his nap of the day. Before you start worrying, let me make it clear that they have a bet with each other, not with the bookies. Once that's done, Athers switches off his mobile. Papers are read, gear is examined and a fair amount of tea is drunk.

Then it is across the field to the Nursery End for nets. No more fielding in this Test, so everyone was keen to get some batting practice in, even me. Normally I never have a net during a game, just a few throw-downs. Today was different. Better safe than sorry.

The mood in the dressing-room was positive. In the past, I have felt that some players have merely paid lip-service to being positive. Not this time. That was down to the previous day's amazing turnaround. Not so much for what we did . . . more for the way we destroyed the West Indies.

We had decided to go down fighting. Why not? We had no other option. Defeat was inevitable. Still, we wanted to rough up the Windies, give them a taste of their own medicine, get them dancing to some English 'chin music', maybe make a statement for the rest of the series, which was going to be a hard slog for us. That is exactly what happened. Shake, rattle and roll. We peppered them. It was short, sharp, aggressive bowling. You had to hit the deck hard but, if it landed in the right spot, it would fly. Caddie might have been a pussycat on the first day. However, once he got his length right on Friday, he was unplayable, someone that tall – as tall as Ambrose or Walsh – and Caddie's quicker than them. We needed Caddie firing on all cylinders. He didn't in the first innings. Sometimes he needs a kick start or a kick up the arse.

We all needed something to fire us up on that Friday. The spark came when Sherwin Campbell flashed at a wide delivery. It flew in my direction at wide third man. That's such a strange position in which to be fielding. I never feel I'm going to get a catch there. You start to move when you see the batsman play a full off-side shot. A split second later, you know whether it's coming anywhere near you. Fortunately, there was no time to panic because the ball was moving low and fast. My first reaction was 'Oh, ★★★★!' I knew it was travelling and was going to my right. I started to move. When the ball flies straight at you, there's only its speed and height to worry about. Now I had to hare to my right. I had my sunglasses on, we'd just come out, I had bowled my first over and was thinking about how it had gone. I had no option. Death or glory. Whether it was a half-chance, quarter-chance, or whether I failed to get there didn't matter. Because of our hopeless position, I had to go for the catch.

It stuck. Relief. This might not be the catch that wins us the Test, but I was certain as hell that if I had dropped it we were going to lose the match and the series. I don't think I've ever caught a cricket ball better. The ball went straight into my hands; I don't think I even felt it. And it was never going to pop out.

England had given themselves nothing more than a sniff, but I knew this was the lift we needed. It was the perfect start. Caddie, especially, needed it. I saw his eyes light up. A few hours earlier, we had walked off the Lord's pitch together and he was really down, wondering where his next wicket would come from. Caddie hadn't bowled well against Zimbabwe at Trent Bridge or at

Edgbaston against the Windies. On Thursday at Lord's, his rhythm still wasn't there.

My catch perked him up. Suddenly a procession of West Indies batsmen were making their way to the middle and back again. Caddie was on fire from the Nursery End, finishing up with 5–16. After taking a couple of wickets, I took a rest, not realizing that the action would soon be over. Corkie came on to claim three. What did surprise me was how quickly the Windies fell apart. They looked shell-shocked. Franklyn Rose, who performed well throughout the series with the bat, came in like a startled rabbit and prodded the ball straight back to Corkie; I had never seen him play a defensive shot before. We didn't give them time to regroup. New batsmen got peppered. That was our plan from the start: we might be going down, but the Windies were coming with us. That was the strategy for the rest of the summer. England weren't going to lie down.

In a couple of hours England had gone from no hope to a real chance of squaring the series. The crowd, which had been getting noisier and noisier, went wild as we came off the field. Now there was the small matter of those 188 runs. Our batting plan was easy: sit in against Walsh and Ambrose, attack King and Rose. Another strategy that applied all summer.

'Sit in' the dressing-room was my own plan for the Saturday; sit in my corner, watch the cricket out of the window, the TV and my DVD player. Leave my bat undisturbed in my cricket coffin.

Play started fifty minutes late because of the rain. Overcast conditions and uncertain weather were not what we had ordered with Walsh and Ambrose about. Ramps (Mark Ramprakash) and Athers were our opening duo. No shortage of pressure there. Athers has been England's anchor ever since Goochie (Graham Gooch) quit. The Windies and England knew that Athers was the key to wrapping the game up quickly. His early departure would be a body-blow to our chances.

Ramps knew that his Test place was on the line. Unhappy at batting at No. 6 and having to try to protect and nurture the tail, Ramps had seen an opportunity as opener, now that Alec was back as wicket-keeper. His success had been limited so far. More crucially, despite Lord's being his home ground, this was not a happy Test hunting-ground for Ramps. He failed again. It wasn't the start we wanted, but I was more concerned for him personally as he walked back. Ramps is a huge talent and I am a huge fan. He knew he needed runs at Lord's. A second failure meant it was back to county cricket, and who knows how long it might be before Ramps would get another chance? All around the country, people ask me why the selectors keep bothering with Ramps. I tell them that I find him one of the hardest batsmen to bowl at. Like them, I do not understand why he cannot hack it or crack it at Test level. Ramps has the ability; there's something else missing or not right. I wish I knew what it was. If I were a selector I would persevere with him, but that's not my choice. Maybe it was a mistake for him to open, but I have always thought he was too good a player for No. 6. Maybe he should have stayed there; after all, with Chalky, Corkie and Caddie, England's tail is not as fragile as it once was.

Back to Lord's. England 3–1, and my Yorkshire colleague, Michael Vaughan, went out to join Athers.

Nobody's had a Test baptism like Vaughanie. He had been earmarked for stardom for a long time, but had to wait for the 1999/2000 South Africa tour for his chance. I'm not sure, when that proud moment finally came for Vaughanie to walk out for his first England Test innings, that it was quite what he expected. On the way out, he passed his captain, Nasser, who had just bagged a duck. Out in the middle, there was time for a quick chat with his batting partner, Mark Butcher. It was the end of the over, so Vaughanie was now at the non-striker's end. Before he had faced a ball, 'Butch' departed, Stewie appeared briefly and another debutant, Chris Adams, strode to the wicket. Welcome to Test cricket, Vaughanie. Two new boys who had not faced a single ball between them, with the scoreboard showing England 2–4 on the first morning of a Test series against South Africa.

But Vaughanie survived and showed a real appetite for cricket at Test level. A broken finger kept him out of the early Tests in the summer of 2000. Only Nasser's cracked thumb gave him this Lord's chance. Had our captain been fit, he would not have played.

Vaughanie and Athers kept Walsh and Ambrose at bay until the rain came at about 12.30. After 11.1 overs, England were 13–1. It was nerve-racking stuff. We might only have nibbled at our target but we had not lost any more wickets, and that was crucial. These rain breaks weren't helping England much; they kept giving Walsh and Ambrose a breather, delaying the introduction of the Windies second-string bowlers.

The bacon sandwiches had appeared around eleven o'clock. Still, we were ready for the early lunch; it's a strange how sitting around can make you so hungry. Our mood was still positive. Nothing had been settled yet. I felt that one of the two England batsmen at the wicket could provide the platform for victory.

Halfway through the afternoon, England were coasting. Ambrose came off after bowling 13 overs for 13 runs, Walsh's spell was 1–25 off nine overs. There was plenty of playing and missing, but who cared? Our pair rode their luck and hit the bad balls. Ambrose was relentless, so good. Too good – that's my opinion. 'Ambie' bowls unplayable deliveries, lots of them. But he won't bowl a ball for you to hit. He's too miserly to try the magic ball: here it is, have a go. Courtney isn't. That's why he picked up twice as many wickets (34) as Ambrose in the series.

I should have known better than to relax. England had passed half way when Vaughanie was caught behind . . . 95–2. It was a great effort, as he showed the ideal temperament for the Test match scene.

Hickie was the new batsman in. The Windies had been making his life a misery for almost a decade. He started positively. At 119–2 – 69 runs short with eight wickets left – I sensed the tension lifting, especially after Hickie was dropped in the slips by Chanderpaul. The tourists were running out of runs.

Not so fast. Hickie edged one to Lara. Athers was trapped l.b.w. England 120–4. All four wickets to Walsh, who was on fire. All bets were off again as the England dressing-room became a quieter place once more. At least Stewie and Nick Knight, our two new batsmen, were experienced campaigners.

I was beginning to fiddle with my kit, making sure my pads,

gloves and bat were where they should be. When several wickets
have fallen, the dressing-room becomes a different place; some
players have finished taking part, while others are waiting to go in.
There's not much passing on of information. It was pretty obvious
to all of us what was going on out there. Guys coming back get 'Well
done,' 'Bad luck' or 'That was close.' Most returning batsmen don't
want to chat straight away and they are given time and space. Usually,
the dismissed batsmen just take their pads off, go out and sit on the
balcony, so as to be out of the way of those getting ready, as well as
offering visible support to those out in the middle. Coach Duncan
Fletcher and physio Dean Conway had spent most of the day on the
balcony. One of the great cricketing superstitions is: when partnerships start to develop – and even when they don't – nobody
moves. Many a promising partnership has ended apparently because
someone in the dressing-room has got up and gone for a pee.

The day certainly had not gone the way Ramps wanted, yet he
still came over to chat to me about my batting. He had been very
supportive all summer. 'Just play your natural game.'

'Why? You don't think I'm going to bat, do you?'

Ramps just looked at me. I think that's when I realized for the
first time that Nasser's prediction might come true. I should have
known. At Centurion Park, earlier in the year, our skipper had said
the same thing. 'You're going to hit the winning runs.' And I did.
Lightning doesn't strike twice, does it?

Stewie and Nick reduced the target to 48 runs, with six wickets
remaining. I shut my coffin lid again, only for another West Indian
one-two: Stewie was l.b.w. and Chalky went for a duck. Both to
Walsh, who now had six wickets. England 140–6.

This was getting serious. A state of confusion always ensues when
wickets fall in bunches. Now the final batsmen, Oggie (my county
team-mate, Matthew Hoggard, on his debut) and I, were clam-
ouring to get our gear on. Like it or not, it looked as if I was going
to have to bat today, and the winning target seemed to be getting
further away. Oggie was wicketless on his debut, but he had taken
the catch that started the Windies' first-innings collapse. When
we batted together, Oggie tried to stare out Ambrose. Nothing

intimidates this lad, I thought. Wrong again. You should have seen him in the dressing-room. I've never seen anyone chew most of the rubber off a bat handle the way he did that day. The lads started taking the mick as the rubber began to disappear.

Rose ended Walsh's run of wickets. Nick Knight was caught behind. 149–7 – 39 runs still needed. By this stage I was pacing the dressing-room in my helmet. One of the advantages of Lord's is that you've got time to put your pads on when the last wicket falls. I wasn't taking any chances with being timed out today. It's a nightmare most sportsmen have: a lace snapping at a vital moment, you've forgotten to pack your boots, your fingers are not working properly. It was at Lord's on his debut that David Steele got lost and ended up in the toilets when he went out to bat. I knew my way, but it was still a bit of a rush job when Caddie was l.b.w. to Ambrose. 160–8 – 28 runs needed for victory.

'Good luck, Gough!' 'Piece of cake.' 'Go and grab the glory.' Plenty of words of encouragement, but for ages my batting had been nothing to write home about. After some promising scores at the start of my England career, my batting has got worse as my bowling improved. My knock of 23 at Edgbaston in the previous Test was the first time I had reached 20 in over five years of Test cricket!

England's hopes for salvation now rested on Corkie (playing his first Test innings for nearly 20 months), Goughie (for batting record, see above) and Oggie, who at this precise moment was facing the reality that it could be his batting prowess that would decide the destiny of this West Indies series.

Coach Duncan Fletcher had chatted to me a bit earlier, and so had Nasser. They offered comfort and assurance. 'You can do it.' I nodded. I wanted to believe it. Frightening. Yet, believe it or not, I wouldn't have swapped that painful knot in my stomach for anything. There was nowhere else in the world I would rather have been at that precise moment. Situations like that are why I play cricket, international cricket, Test cricket for my country. I was only too well aware of the consequences of failure on this day: another summer of cricketing defeat and shame. Perhaps the last chance of this team staying together, of achieving something, anything.

My newspaper column after the three-day Edgbaston defeat expressed the doubts I had as to whether I would ever be part of a great England team. After reading it, the lads had ribbed me about it. But I was serious. It's all very well chalking up Test caps and wickets, but I wanted *collective* cricket success, *England* success. We had enjoyed the odd success here and there. The biggest achievement of my career so far had been coming back to beat the South Africans at Headingley in 1998. More Ashes failure followed that. We had been inept in the first World Cup on home soil for 16 years. A home loss to New Zealand followed, before another defeat in South Africa. Even our victory in the final Test at Centurion Park had been tarnished: bookmakers' money had influenced Hansie Cronje's decision to make a game of it.

'Cronjegate' dominated the early summer in 2000. It became clear that match-fixing and betting were a real problem in international cricket. Corruption, it was claimed, was rife. The spotlight even turned on England, when it was revealed that Chris Lewis had passed on the names of three England cricketers who were alleged to have taken money. I was furious: it was a slur on England, it was a slur on me, and I felt not enough was being done to clear our names. Playing the game took a back seat. There were arguments about our new central contracts, the new two-division county championship, the new international England summer with seven Tests and a triangular trophy in the middle.

Fortunately, none of this baggage was anywhere near my thoughts as I made my way through the Long Room. Although the place was packed, the mass of people divided, leaving a clear path to the doors. Down the steps, through the little wooden gates and on to the most famous sporting turf in the world. I felt totally in control. The mental buzz was incredible. Who better to find waiting for me than Corkie? We went back a long way. There's no better man for a crisis.

One of the great tactical conversations of all time followed.

'We can get these runs,' he said.

'That's what I was thinking. You carry on batting the way you have been, keep thumping the bad ball. I'll take the singles. I'm not going to get out. Trust me. I'll block it. I won't do anything silly. You play your shots.'

That was the game-plan. Nothing earth-shattering. But we took our time about it, trying to give the impression of confidence and being casual. The Windies, normally the kings of cool, were the ones under pressure. This Test had been in the bag, their bag. Their carelessness and our fighting spirit had brought it back to life. We needed 28 runs to win. At that stage, it seemed like 128. Runs had been like gold dust all day. On our reckoning and at that rate, it would take us about an hour. We couldn't last that long. Corkie, ten not out, had to chance his arm.

Then something remarkable happened. Ambrose had removed Caddick at the end of his first over back. Rose had been bowling from the Nursery End. Walsh had not had much of a rest, but surely Adams would bring him back now. He didn't. I looked at Corkie. This was our chance. How Corkie took it, hitting 12 runs off Rose's over, including a hooked six towards the new members' stand and a slogged boundary over mid-on.

Rose bowled another over and, when Walsh finally came on, the target was ten runs. We were living on scraps again, scampering singles. Ambrose conceded a single in his final three overs. Now I was encouraging Corkie to be more careful. There was nearly a run-out. Corkie played a couple of airy shots. I had to wander down and tell him: 'Don't throw it away. We can win this. Wait for the bad ball and hit it.'

It was almost seven o'clock. The light was dodgy. Three lights came on. No chance of us going off; this had to be finished tonight. Can you imagine trying to sleep with six runs needed to win and Ambrose and Walsh resting up? No way.

Three overs brought three runs, and Walsh began his 24th over, with England wanting three to win and two to tie. We chased for two leg-byes off the first ball. One to win. Three dot balls, then Lord's erupted as Corkie hit the ball through the covers to the Tavern boundary. Corkie punched the air, then we completed the single just in case and went for the stumps as souvenirs.

Lord's went mad. I've always felt that the home of cricket, even at its most enthusiastic and excited, is a restrained place. Too much of a show of emotion is not English or cricket, old boy. What have I got to say to that? Bollocks! If this didn't make you want to jump about and shout, nothing would. The outpouring from all parts of the ground and all sections of the crowd, even the egg-and-bacon-tie-wearing members in the pavilion, was remarkable. I could see Nasser, Athers, Stewie and Fletcher embracing one another on the balcony, with Oggie looking even more relieved than me and Corkie.

I only had time to dump my stuff before the endless round of press conferences and interviews began. There never seems to be enough time for the team to have a few minutes together to savour the moment on these occasions. Even if we're bowling, the crowd invasions here mean you're scampering for the pavilion the second it's all over. I love those initial shows of emotion. They are the special ones because the adrenalin is still pumping. It's never the same once you start coming down from that high. I was away from the dressing-room for almost an hour, satisfying the increasing demands of the media. When I returned, the place was empty. Everyone had packed up and left.

The consolation was that we had all promised to attend Mark Ramprakash's benefit dinner that night at the Landmark Hotel in Marylebone. The theme was a Caribbean evening, but none of the West Indies turned up. I can't blame them; I wouldn't have felt like being sociable if England had lost a Test match like that. The tourists had been within a few runs and even fewer wickets of securing the series. I can't begin to imagine what would have happened to this England team if we had gone 2–0 down in the series. We kept looking at one another all night and shaking our heads. We could not quite believe what had happened. The previous day, this bunch of cricketers had been heading for the knacker's yard. Was this a stay of execution, or had England found a way back? It did not seem important that Saturday night. I was intent on savouring this moment. Chalky (White) and I carried on from the dinner. Where to, I'm not too certain. All that does linger in the memory is that I will never get used to London prices.

I was in no fit state to drive home the next morning. Michael Vaughan and his girlfriend Nicola came back with me, and I handed the car keys to my Yorkshire colleague. He stopped at the first M1 services station for me to be sick. (Incidentally, I was to use the same services station for the same purpose after England won the triangular series.) The rest of the journey was spent sleeping in the back of the car. Vaughanie was picked up at a junction, just before home. I was still half asleep and ended up driving back down the motorway for three junctions, wondering why Leeds had disappeared from the road-signs, to be replaced by 'London'.

2. Long Live the Legend

18 September 1970. A sad day for the Flower Power culture and rockers of that era: legendary guitarist Jimi Hendrix was found dead at the age of 27 in his London flat. I am not sure there was a Monk Bretton Chapter of the Hendrix fan club. The residents of that small Yorkshire town had other things on their mind that Friday. That date in 1970 may have been a bad day for rock'n'roll, but for the Gough family, and the cricket world in general, the more important event of the day was the arrival of Trevor and Christine's first son, Darren. I didn't find out about the Hendrix connection until much later, and my response was apparently: 'One legend goes. Another arrives.' I can't quite remember saying that, but it sounds a typical Gough sound-bite. I'm not the least bit musical but, in true Hendrix fashion, I've always been something of a showman.

I was the newest member of a typically Yorkshire family. Both my grandads worked down the pit. Dad never did, although he worked in the pit offices on leaving school. After spells in the Barnsley Council planning department, as a milkman, working in a warehouse, my dad has been in the pest control business for the past 20 years, first as a service technician for Rentokil and now with Terminex. That led to me being described as the 'son of a Barnsley rat catcher' by one of the big national dailies when I made my debut for Yorkshire. Neither my dad nor I was best pleased. I loved it when he was a milkman because I'd go out and help on the rounds. Mum, the last of eight, has always been a midwife. I have always been closer to my dad's side of the family, mainly because Mum's people come from further away, in the mining community of Grimethorpe. That's my background, good Yorkshire stock, working class.

I had a privileged upbringing. Privileged, because most of my waking time was spent playing sport. Privileged, because I enjoyed a freedom and an environment that is denied to today's kids, even to my own, however much my wife Anna and I want to spoil them. I started life in a council house in King Edward's Street in Monk Bretton, but we soon moved to an estate called Hanbury Close which was full of young married couples with kids. The place was enclosed, so we could play cricket, tennis and football on the streets in safety.

The street was our playground. I would come back from school, dump my stuff, grab a cheese sandwich and rush out again. I lived on cheese. I'd have crackers and cheese before going to bed. Even now, it's my big weakness. Full-fat and full-strength cheddar. A real healthy diet, with crisps, Tizer and Sugar Puffs. All the things I won't let my kids have. Bacon sandwiches were a treat at weekends. Sunday lunches was at Grandma Gough's, with huge Yorkshire puddings.

Occasionally, Mum and Dad would look out of the window to check we were okay. I would be out there until it got dark. Total freedom. Sadly, those days are gone for ever. It hurts me that my kids can't walk out of the house and play with loads of other kids. At our last house in Yorkshire we put in a 'magic gate' to next door's garden, so that my kids Liam and Brennan felt they could wander unsupervised. In fact, they were enclosed; we knew both gardens were secure. I feel for them. They go to school and their play time is at school. When Liam and Brennan are at home and want to play, then it's me they get. If I got fed up with playing football or skateboarding or riding my chopper bike, we'd all barge into one of the houses and play on our Spectrum computer or with Scalextric. The street and the buildings were just one big playground as far as we were concerned. Our only no-go area was one woman's garden; she was a real pain and her boys were a couple of softies. She would make a big play out of threatening to keep our footballs. I didn't waste time arguing; I sent my dad round, and he always came back with the ball.

My brother Adrian appeared three years after me. Our relationship did not get off to the best of starts. Adrian was premature and initially I was not allowed to see him. When we eventually went to bring him home from hospital, Mum and Dad, sensing trouble, had bought me a big Rupert Bear toy. When we got to the hospital, I threw it away. 'I don't want it,' was the start of the tantrum. 'And I don't want him to come home with us.' I was as jealous as hell because of all the attention he was getting. Ever since then, whenever I was going out, Mum would shout: 'Why don't you take Adrian with you?' I'm sure I'm not the only person who hated having to drag his younger brother around. At least he was someone to play with and, like me, he hated being inside. He used to borrow my golf set, even though he was left-handed and I'm right. I say golf set; actually, it was a single seven-iron, as that was all we could afford. Adrian was always a good sportsman and was the sprint champion at school. He's always been the more complete footballer, while I was more skilful. Adrian captained Yorkshire Schools and played once for England Schools. I was always the better cricketer. Adrian has been unlucky with injuries and once needed a back operation.

There's a 12-year gap between me and my sister, Andrea. I was the one who had to take her to school, dress her, put her hair in a ponytail and pick her up in the afternoon. Andrea always had to be touching you as a baby – but not now. One of the most vivid memories of my childhood is when Andrea caught measles when she was six. Andrea had had such a bad reaction to the first vaccination that she was advised not to have the second. She recovered, then got ill again a week later. One night as my dad came home from work at about ten o'clock, Andrea woke up and started having a fit. Even now, it is vivid in my memory. I had never seen anything like it: she turned blue, and I thought she was dying. Fortunately, my mum was there. While reviving her, she shouted for me to phone for an ambulance. I went outside to wait for them, sure that my sister was dead. It was terrifying. She was taken to hospital. Whether it all looked a lot worse than it was (the convulsion fits were a combination of the measles and her high temperature) I don't know. She still lives with my mum and dad.

My sporting prowess probably comes from my dad's side. Mum

was a ballet dancer, while Dad was a sprint champion at school. The talented footballer was his brother, my uncle Alan, and I played with him a lot. He's about ten years older than me and played football and opened the bowling for Barnsley. He might have had better prospects if contact lenses had been around then, as he wore glasses. I'm not sure whether he was a keen student. He's the one I blame for my lack of qualifications. His favourite trick was to kick the ball as high as he could – and make me head it. Uncle Alan's also responsible for the scar inside my right cheek. With Mum outside, we were playing on an old mattress and I was trying to do somersaults. Unfortunately, one of the springs popped out and went through my cheek. Not that my mum was able to say much; she had pulled my left shoulder out of its socket, swinging me around, when I was very young. It still clicks.

Even school did not spoil my idyllic life. The fun carried on, although you had to be able to take care of yourself. When I left St Helen's Primary School for the Priory Comprehensive, that's when the trouble started. Three primary schools fed into the secondary. St Helen's was the one in 'posh' Monk Bretton, so we were the ones identified as such by the other two, which were both in mainly council estate areas. The school's biggest claim to fame came when it was used as the backdrop for Ken Loach's 1970 film *Kes*. It was a sort of *Billy Elliot*, only replacing ballet with a kestrel. The film poster was memorable, with this scruffy youngster offering a V-sign to the world. That attitude has remained.

Our big soccer clashes were with Honeywell. If you didn't go to Priory, you went there. I'd been one of the football stars at St Helen's, in the first team for my last three years at primary school. The lads from St Helen's who went to Honeywell would make sure I was a marked man, with threats made both on and off the field. They must have thought I wouldn't turn up. I remember, after one rugby sevens tournament, I was chased the three and a half miles home. They were on bikes and cut through the woods. Luckily, I was fit and made it home safely.

Not that I escaped the odd scrap. My best mate, Chris Lycett, has been my best mate ever since the second of our two scraps at school. The first one lasted one punch. When we were 13 I knocked him down. A year and a half later, he was the cock of the school. He was a hard bugger and had suddenly got big. We had a more serious scrap after another football match. Fortunately, others piled in and pulled us apart. No arguments; he was winning. We've been best mates ever since. When I went to Rotherham United on leaving school, Chris played for Scarborough.

Priory may have not been a fashionable school, but we were a fairly fashion-conscious lot. At the time, we had punks and mods. We had our own group – the Farrah boys. Most of us were Jam fans. There was no school uniform, so our desire to look the part cost our folks a fortune. Trainers, like Thedora Gold or Adidas Los Angeles, meant no change from £50. The Farrah trousers we thought so trendy are worn mainly by old men now. Our tops would have to show the Pringle or Lyle & Scott logos. And, of course, we would wear the corduroy jackets with hoods. Other groups at school included rockers, and there were lots of guys with Mohican haircuts. We were the cool group. I can handle myself, but I've never been attracted to trouble; I never even wanted to join the smokers' corner. My mum smokes quite a lot, as does my sister. Dad doesn't.

My days growing up were filled with sport which, at the time, I just saw as play. I had masses of energy. It was others who pointed the way. My first sports teacher, Mr Rogerson at St Helen's, got me to join the local cricket club at Monk Bretton. Our next-door neighbour, Kevin Gaskell, was the first-team captain. Kevin, Roger Glover, Trevor Link, Herbert Jones, who is still playing in his seventies, all come and watch me whenever they can.

The two teachers who had a big influence on me at the Priory were Mr Hague and Mr Bunting. Although Mr Hague had played for Manchester United as a youngster, there was no trace in him of the memorable character played by Brian Glover in *Kes*, who turned out in a Manchester United strip and re-took penalties if they were saved. I saw Mr Bunting at the Old Trafford Test match last year, when he brought some kids down from a Cumbria school.

Another great help was Mr Clarke, who was in charge of Barnsley

Schools. He took us everywhere by bus and train. He was the Barnsley representative at Yorkshire Schools. He used to say it was hard work getting us in. So much depended on which school you went to and what kind of upbringing you had had. I always knew it mattered. I came from a working-class background and from a school with not the best of reputations.

I remember turning up at the Yorkshire Under-14 cricket trials in the back of Dad's work van; other lads were getting out of very posh cars. I felt a bit out of place because it was clear that your school and social circle mattered. And you could see some parents sucking up to those in charge. My dad would never do that; like me, he believes in getting there on your own merits. I had no problems with getting out of my dad's van; I wasn't embarrassed. What did make me feel uncomfortable was the thought that this might affect my chances of getting in the team – and with good reason. I used to open the batting and bowling for Barnsley schools side, but I couldn't get in Yorkshire's starting XI at Under-14 or Under-15 level. I was in the Under-15 second team. Playing for the Under-14 county side earned you a badge and a sweater. Under-15 brought you a Yorkshire Schools cap. Luckily I was brought in for a tour of the Taunton area at the end of the Under-15 season and got my cap in the second-to-last game.

And the following year I opened the bowling for the Under-16 and Under-19 sides. What led to this amazing transformation? Might it have had something to do with the fact that selection went from the Yorkshire Schools system to the Cricket Association system? No more schoolteachers. Proper cricket coaches, now, run by the county. In a way, I hate to admit that it has always bugged me that I couldn't get into that Under-15 side straight away and had to sneak in for a few games at the end – a reserve player filling in against crap teams. A year later, I was turning out for Yorkshire Seconds. Don't tell me the system wasn't bent.

What did concern me most when I was growing up were my ears: they were rather pointed. That's why my hair in all my early pictures is at least halfway down my ears. My next-door neighbour cut my hair once when I was 14, exposing the offending appendages, and I did not go out for a week. Luckily, I grew out of worrying about them. Anyway, after meeting Andrew Caddick, I realized that I was in the minor league as far as ears go. One of my early nicknames was Spock; the other was Spit the Dog, because of my surname. After the short haircut, I had a perm. My musical tastes were, and still are, rock'n'roll, especially Elvis, a preference I inherited off Uncle Alan. Even at my wedding I showed off my rock'n'roll dancing skill. I just love dancing that way. Growing up, my favourite records were Adam Ant's 'Prince Charming', the Jam's 'Going Underground', various Wham discs and Bros's 'When Will I Be Famous'. Paul Weller was my pop hero. Dad's a big Western fan. I like the big epics like *Ben Hur*, *The Ten Commandments*, *Bridge on the River Kwai*, *The Guns of Navarone*, *The Great Escape* and *Spartacus* – nothing in black and white. The first film I saw at the cinema was *Superman* and I ran about like him for a week afterwards. My comic heroes were the 'Bash Street Kids' and 'Desperate Dan', along with 'Roy of the Rovers'.

My sporting heroes were Glenn Hoddle and Ian Botham. Hoddle was such a skilful player, a man who could change a game with one pass. That's the way I liked to play my football, and that was my downfall – a bit like his. It was an era of the work rate, running around at 100 m.p.h. If you had combined my brother's speed and my skill, I would have made a good footballer. I met Hoddle in Portugal during a cricket camp. I saw him and went all gooey, didn't know what to do. He had obviously read that I was a fan. He walked over to me and said, 'Hello. Nice to meet you.' Hoddle's the reason I'm a Tottenham fan. Not the other way around.

Botham was simply brilliant; all my era remembers the 1981 Ashes and his heroics. My first bat was a Duncan Fearnley Attack with a choo-choo train on the back, like he had. It was miles too heavy for me, but that didn't matter. Botham was such a star, but he had character with it, a sporting hero whom everyone wanted to watch. Now, Beefy's someone I have a chat and a beer with; I still can't believe it. I remember enjoying a drink in his room in Faisalabad in the winter of 2000. I have to pinch myself that I'm sitting down with the Legend. I've played with and against the likes of Gooch, Gower and Gatting, but it's Botham who gives me the tingle. No matter how many Test wickets I take, he'll always be the man. My hero.

There was never any danger of my wasting time on further education or it interfering with my sporting aspirations. Two 'O' levels and five C.S.E.s was a fair reflection of the effort I had put in . . . more than fair. My sporting prowess might offer some sort of a way out. Nobody, as yet, was beating a path to my door. The future looked less certain when the family decided to move to Caister-on-Sea, near Norwich. My mum's brother lived nearby in Great Yarmouth, where we had often been on holiday. We lived in a caravan while the house was being built. I had left school, but Adrian had to move schools. Barnsley had arranged for the Norfolk Cricket Union to look at me, and I was to have a trial with Norwich City Football Club. We had been in the caravan three weeks when we heard that I had been picked by Yorkshire Schools Under-19s. That was a big step, so I went back to Yorkshire and lived with my grandma in Grimethorpe. I never got into the new house and nor did the rest of the family; Mum and Dad decided that my prospects would be best served by the Gough family returning to Monk Bretton. They have been there ever since. My lasting memory of the caravan era was going to see a gypsy in Great Yarmouth. She told me I would be successful in professional sport, I would have two kids and be wealthy but never a millionaire.

Most of us tried to find jobs that would allow us plenty of spare time rather than spare cash. I worked in a garage for a month. Then, with all my mates, I did a building course at Barnsley College on Mondays as it was something to do. I enjoyed bricklaying, but I did not want to rush into a job; I had just left school and enjoyed larking around. I was playing lots of cricket, lots of football. Academic life never appealed to me. At school, I had been captain of rugby, soccer, cricket and athletics. That meant lots of missed lessons, time off to play and travel. Sometimes, if I was tired from a hard session or match, I would just stay at home. Mum and Dad knew about my skiving most of the time, and anyway it was really only in my final year that that happened. I was always a good attender at school; I would have missed too much sport if I had stayed away. In my fifth and final year I was supposed to be revising, and everyone was winding down anyway. I used to walk down to school, long after the bell in the morning, and meet up with Chris Lycett. I came away with two 'O' levels – English and metalwork – and five C.S.E.s. Maths was a complete nightmare to me. I hate algebra. In my final year, I can't remember going once to a Maths lesson. My school reports used to say I was quite bright.

Our group used to meet up at seven o'clock most evenings outside the church next to the 'Norman' pub, play pool and have a good laugh. I learned to drive in Mum's car. I used to go and pick my mate up in Mum's car with 'L' plates on. He'd sit beside me, like an instructor. I'd drop him off at eleven o'clock and then I'd drive back on my own; I lived only a mile away. My dad wanted me to find a job, but I've always been able to get round him. Dad's softer than Mum. I've always been able to do what I wanted with my dad – not the case with my mum. Dad knew I was not going to be pushed; I just needed that time. I was lazing around, I suppose. I wasn't drinking vast amounts. Go out, have a laugh, play darts, play pool and walk round the village. We didn't terrorize anyone or generally misbehave. I'm glad I did that; a lot of kids miss out on it. As a result I'm very street-wise. We would go round the shops on Saturday or play the bandits in the amusement arcades; I generally spent the Y.T.S. money before I got it. I wasn't paying my rent at home. When I started working, I handed over a tenner.

We used to go and watch Barnsley every Saturday, home or away. There was a lot of football violence at the time. Our group were on the edge of the trouble-makers. We would sit with all the idiots and sing with them, but would keep out of the scraps if we possibly could. A couple of times we got chased. The Barnsley–Blackburn match was one of them: we were surrounded by Blackburn fans and got away by throwing vegetables at them and legging it before the police arrived. We didn't have to travel far to watch them. Sadly, I was away when Barnsley gained promotion in 1998. I know they came straight back down, but I was as proud as punch; it was a great effort for a small town to reach the Premiership.

I've kept in touch with my mates. Most of my pals I've known since school. As well as Chris Lycett, there is Ian 'Chuck' Uttley; he was my brother's mate. The gang that I used to hang around with when I left school also included Mark Spacey, Neil Blackshaw, Matthew Benson, Stephen Dyson, Matthew Elliott and David Booth. We were the sensible group from Monk Bretton. Chuck has joined us in the last three years. He'd been with the idiots, but has grown up. Chuck's got a heart of gold. While I was in Pakistan, he took Liam to football and played golf with him. He even picked me up at Heathrow when I came back at six in the morning. That's the sort of mates I have.

I'll never lose touch with them, even though I have moved south. In fact I will probably see more of them. I'm still playing for Yorkshire. Moving south won't change me. I'm a Barnsley lad, born and bred, and I love going out in Barnsley; it will always be my local town. When I go there with my mates, I never get bothered. That's where I'm from and that's where I feel most at ease. I'm left alone. If I'm approached, it's usually a 'Well done' or 'Congratulations' – I never get any trouble. By and large, that's how I'm treated around the country.

There is one slight blemish in the Gough peace-loving image. It was Christmas Eve and I was with my mates in Visions in Barnsley. We'd been drinking all day and one of my mates threw a glass at me, so I went over and thumped him. The bouncers thought I was beating him up. I'd just slotted him, like mates do. Before I knew it, the bouncers were kicking the crap out of both of us. One grabbed me and opened the fire-exit door with my head as he held me with my arms behind my back. I wasn't going out without a goodbye. He was wearing a huge sovereign ring and smacked me straight in the mouth. I didn't flinch. Then I was picked up and dumped in one of those huge wheelie-bins. I scrambled out, hurling abuse at them. Then my mate came out in rather less dramatic fashion. We just hugged each other.

Then he screamed, 'What's happened to your lip?' It was hanging off. The bastard. I had my best shirt on that I'd just bought.

I said: 'My dad's going to kill me.'

We scarpered.

The police had seen what had gone on but did nothing and wouldn't take me to hospital, so we ran all the way, two miles. The casualty department was a scene of desolation: guts and blood everywhere, sisters who had stabbed each other. All on Christmas Eve. My lip was pinned. After being pinned, I had to wait for the lip to be stitched. Fortunately I was feeling no pain. I was at the hospital for over an hour. Afterwards, naturally enough, we headed back to the nightclub. There was blood all down my shirt, but they still let me in.

When I woke up the next day at home, I thought, Oh my God. I could hear the rest of the family moving around. I got up to go to the toilet. Then I went into the kitchen. Dad said, 'What's happened to you?' I told him the bouncers had picked on me for no reason. He did not wait to hear the whole story. He was fuming, and I got another clip round the head for getting into trouble.

On Boxing Day I had to go to work at the Headingley Cricket School, with eight stitches, drinking out of a straw. The scar's still visible, and it was painful for quite a while. I never went back to Visions. It closed down shortly afterwards. The bouncers were a group who'd been brought up from Nottingham for the week. It didn't hurt at the time. I couldn't stop laughing.

I've had scraps at school, but very few since. Once I thumped someone in Essex: it was just a kid who was getting on my nerves in a nightclub. I was only 20. All the Yorkshire lads were in there. This one bloke kept coming up to me all night, pestering me. Just a pain in the arse. 'Go away, or I'm going to hit you.' Eventually I did. He went down, I walked out of the club and went home. I wasn't getting involved with bouncers again.

I know I can handle myself. I'm from a place where, if you step out of line, you get a crack. That's the way you're brought up in Barnsley. People used to be wary of me because they knew where I was from: 'He's from Barnsley.' Paul Grayson tried it once when we first met, calling me 'pit pony'. I responded carefully and simply; I picked P.G. up and threatened to throw him down the stairs. There were no hard feelings: P.G. was best man at my wedding.

It's just the way we are in Barnsley. I'm still aggressive. If someone gets on my nerves, I still let them know it – as one or two Sri Lankans found out early in 2001. I can take a joke and wind-up, but they know that, if it goes over the mark, watch out. It's like my hair, it's off-limits. No one's allowed to touch it. Except Athers. If I hadn't fought back at school, I would have been bullied, especially as I was good at sport.

3. Keep It in Your Britches!

My greatest love while growing up was football. I loved playing the game. I thought if I was to have a professional sporting career, that would be it. Then slowly the dream began to fade away. That was hard. I came to realize that I wasn't going to be good enough. Mum and Dad always believed I would become a professional cricketer. If you ask people who knew me as a youngster, they would all have opted for football. In summer 2000, before our one-day international at Chester-le-Street, I watched Newcastle train on the next pitch. I know Gary Speed, formerly of Leeds, who is a big cricket fan. One of the blokes training them was Mick Wadsworth, who used to be in charge of Barnsley's youth system. 'Is that Goughie? Well, I never thought you'd make a cricketer. I'd have put money on your being a footballer.'

I have often reflected on my football demise. I think I was good enough. I had been captain of Barnsley Schools from 11 years old. I think the bottom line is that I lacked motivation. I don't why, maybe it all came too easy. I was very skilful; I won all the Superkids coaching badges. During one Butlin's holiday at Minehead I won a special soccer competition that got us all a free family holiday at Skegness for the finals. I've probably got more soccer medals than cricket ones, certainly as a youngster. The trouble is, at the very age when I should have been making a real start and working hard at the game, I just wanted to be with my mates. I used to take corners, goal-kicks, throw-ins and penalties all through my football career. One rather important commodity that I lacked – strange, considering what I do now – was speed. My brother Adrian had more pace.

My 'professional' soccer career started and ended with Rotherham United on the Y.T.S. I was paid £27.50 a week. I was there for only a few months, and it was not very fruitful. I used to catch three buses to get there for 8.30 a.m., put the kit out, clean the toilets and boots. I did not enjoy cleaning boots. I didn't get on with the coach, either. As youth-team manager Phil Chambers said: 'Gough was a midfield player whose aggression and enthusiasm were far and away his biggest assets – but he only showed these qualities when playing.' He was right. The simple fact was that I lacked the desire or commitment necessary to be a professional footballer. So one day I left and never went back.

If I was to have a professional sporting career only one avenue was now left. I had already met the two most important influences on my cricket career. The local hero in Monk Bretton was Martyn Moxon. I wanted to be like him because he had played for England. And I made the same move that Martyn did on his way to the top, and joined Barnsley. That brought me into contact with Steve Oldham, who took me under his wing, and I've been there ever since. Without him, I would not have achieved half of what I have done, I might not even have played for England. That is how important 'Esso' has been to me. I have always had a rather tempestuous relationship with coaches. I am very loud and can be a real nuisance at times. That's the way I am, always taking the mick. 'Esso' would give me just enough rope to hang myself. And when I did, he'd be down on me like a ton of bricks. There was a limit to his patience and even I knew not to go beyond that. The best way of describing him is to say that 'Esso' is like a football manager. That's his mentality. He has all the referees' and coaches' badges.

My experiences with Yorkshire Schools had left me in two minds about my cricketing ability. I knew I was a good footballer. Cricket was more difficult to judge. After struggling to get a game for Yorkshire Schools, I was suddenly opening the bowling for the county's Under-19 side. I don't believe that there had been that massive a jump in my cricketing ability. Then I took 8–25 against North Yorkshire at Bedale and found myself in Yorkshire's second team, along with my mate, P.G. My first game was at Studley against Warwickshire, where one of the umpires was John Holder. We have remained good friends ever since.

I was able to measure my progress in 1988 when Yorkshire came to play Barnsley as part of Arnie Sidebottom's benefit year. 'Esso' played for Yorkshire to give me the opportunity. I know that professional cricketers treat these games as a bit of a show, but I can't believe they were that keen on a 17-year-old making mugs of them. That is not the Yorkshire way. I took 4–11, as well as a couple of good catches. My bag of wickets was impressive – Moxon, Phil Carrick, Phil Robinson and David Bairstow. It was a big day for me. My mum says I've always been lucky, and you need breaks like that – and it was a big break.

By this time I was on a new Y.T.S. scheme, working at Yorkshire's Indoor School at Headingley. The Indoor School was run by Ralph Middlebrook, who is on my Benefit Committee; he must be a glutton for punishment! If he was honest about what we were like in those days, he would have to say 'a pain in the arse'. As well as me, there was P.G., Stephen Bethel, Antonio Richardson (he's a bouncer in Leeds now; his brother, Bill, won a Mr Universe competition) and Richard Damms from Barnsley. Richard and I shared a flat. At first we lived in Cockeridge Lane, Cockeridge, in an old couple's house. It was hell. They were Hungarian and were always arguing, and the food (we called it rations) was always cold, and we soon got out of there. What made it worse was that the other lads, P.G. and Stephen Bethel, were at Mrs Bert's. She's famous now and has been looking after young Yorkshire cricketers for years. Her house is right next to the ground and we were two or three miles away.

In the end, we moved into a house just down from the Indoor School. Some girls from Carnegie College were there. Richard and I shared a room and we had a really good laugh. That's when my weight started to go up and I became known as 'Guzzler'. Football had kept me fairly slim and fit. When I joined the Y.T.S., we would eat rubbish all day and then go out of an evening because there was nothing else to do. We couldn't afford to go to the pub. Instead, half a dozen of us used to go to the shops and get 50p worth of mixed biscuits. Some guys put on weight easier than others. P.G. never put on a pound; he's the same weight now, and P.G. used to eat just as much rubbish as me.

Yorkshire must have seen something in me; I was put on the

staff in 1989 and my wages went up from £27.50 to £35 in the second year of Y.T.S., then to £75 when I joined the Academy. My first Yorkshire contract was for £4,500. The Yorkshire Cricket Academy was being set up in Bradford. It was a grand title for a bit of a tip. We used to practise hitting the ball over the fence. All we seemed to do there was tidy up. I felt it was like the football Y.T.S. all over again, trying to rebuild and clean up a stadium with cheap labour. We ended up with a paint brush in our hands as often as a bat and ball. When it was officially opened, I was on the bowling inactive list because of a back problem, so I was chosen to receive the first ceremonial ball, bowled by Yorkshire legend Bob Appleyard. Well, I know he's a legend now. At the time I had never heard of him and thought my job was to try and hit the ball as high and as far as I could. That was not too difficult, considering Appleyard was 66. I charged down the wicket with no humility or sense of occasion and swatted it miles over his head for six. The press were there, cameras, dignitaries, the lot.

I got a right rollocking. I am afraid that was the type of bloke I was. I simply saw it as a chance to show off my skills, and I could not resist. Poor old Bob. The pensioner could just about turn his arm over and was expecting a gentle ceremonial blocking at the other end. No such luck.

Us Academy lads used to have to go around the local schools and do a bit of coaching. Part of the scheme included a leisure course at Wharfedale College on a Friday, but I would often bunk that and head home to see my mates in Barnsley.

Within a month of the start of the 1989 season I had made my first-team debut. Admittedly, it took the 'worst injury situation I have ever known', according to skipper Phil Carrick. There was a one-day friendly against Leicestershire two days before the team headed to London to face Middlesex. Paul Anderson and Mark Bowen were two others with a chance of playing. Afterwards 'Fergie' (Carrick) told me I was in the squad for the Middlesex game. I found out afterwards that 'Esso' had been asked to come back and play. He turned them down, saying there was no point. He added, 'Play Darren Gough.'

I always remember my dad driving me to Leeds station. He was as excited as I was. I had never been to London. Dad felt he should offer some fatherly advice to his 18-year-old making his way to the big city for the first time. 'Keep it in your britches!' was his parting shot.

I was in seventh heaven on the train, sitting among the likes of 'Bluey' Bairstow, Paul Jarvis and Arnie Sidebottom. I am not quite sure why I attracted the attention of the quieter element in the side. Not having been to London before, everything was new to me. Lord's, the home of cricket, for my first-class debut. Everything, going through the Grace gates, into the pavilion, into the visitors' dressing-room, through the Long Room, on to the hallowed turf, was so special and exciting. I remember just before going out (it was the same on my England debut) I wasn't going to cry, but I felt as if I was going to. I might have done if someone had said something at that precise moment. I always remember that. But I had no problems once I was out there.

I had one thing on my mind. Take a wicket. Until you do, you never know. Once taken, whatever happens, it can't be taken away. I would have to wait. There was rain about, and Arnie and 'Jarvo' opened the bowling. Finally I got my chance, and eight deliveries later I had my first first-class wicket. Not a bad scalp, either: Paul Downton, Middlesex and England, caught by Arnie at first slip. I have always been lucky. I was to repeat the dream start in my Test and one-day careers. The rain kept us in the field until midday on the third day. My final figures were 3–44 off 16 overs.

I was far more nervous about going out to bat. You could understand why, the way I tried to push forward to an Angus Fraser bouncer. Whatever happened, I had decided I wasn't getting out first ball. The ball went straight over my head. I did the same next ball. This time it hit the bat and went down to fine leg. I was off the mark. Seeing my predicament, Arnie had a slog and quickly got out. 'I want to see you stay alive,' he told me as we came off. Yorkshire had been bowled out for 130, our last eight wickets falling for 38 runs. That was a scenario I was to get used to.

The highlight of my trip came when Middlesex batted for the

second time. I thought my luck had changed when 'Jarvo' dropped Mike Gatting in the slips off me. What a wicket to claim in your first match. Gatt nicked the next ball through the slips for four. The next ball was nothing special. Gatt tried to pull it. The first sound of trouble was when I heard the former England skipper exclaim, 'Shit!' just before the ball landed in the safe hands of Richard Blakey at mid-wicket. 'Bluey' had been fairly physical when I removed Downton; now our wicket-keeper was in full bear-hugging mode as I struggling to breathe. I finished with 2–46.

Five wickets on my debut and mentions in all the big national newspapers. In the *Daily Telegraph* I was billed as the 'son of a Barnsley rat-catcher'; it was my first experience of the media taking liberties and getting their facts wrong. My dad was angry, mainly because he thought the soft South was having a pop at the cloth-capped North. Bluey went looking for the guilty journalist, threatening to put one on him.

This was also my first experience of the social side of county cricket life. What I saw there was every bit as eye-opening as on the pitch. I remember going into the Tavern every night after the day's play. Bluey, Fergie, Arnie and Jarvo were all supping as though it was going out of fashion, and I was trying to keep up. I couldn't believe how much they were drinking. I can remember thinking: 'What a life!' I had been getting £27.50 on the Y.T.S. Now I was receiving £250 match fees, plus match and travelling expenses and loads of free grub. I'd never seen so much money. I had such a wad that I felt like a millionaire. On top of that, there was Nancy's cooking at Lord's, and we were staying in a nice hotel. This was when I finally decided I wanted to play this game. I went home proud. I had played for the White Rose, the first guy from the Y.T.S. to do so. I've always been proud of being the first. I had played first-class cricket and had taken wickets. That couldn't be taken away. I paid £4 for a Lord's print, after Bluey told me to get one signed. I got both teams and umpires, and it is on my wall. You only make one debut.

A couple of months later, Gatt presented me with a tankard just before the first Ashes Test at Headingley to commemorate my rise

from the Y.T.S. to Yorkshire first team. Ironically, that was the
Test match that started Australia's retention of the Ashes, which
remains to this day. I was working on the ground for the Test and
certainly needed a lift.

I had experienced most of English county cricket's problems in
my debut at Lord's – the poor weather, poor attendances, the heavy
socializing and, finally, the overbowling of young and inexperienced cricketers . . . in this case, me. I bowled 13 overs on the trot
before leaving the field with a back problem that was to keep me
sidelined for most of the rest of the season. I was bowling well with
the new ball and was happy to carry out the captain's wishes.
Suddenly I felt my back lock, and that was it. It was crazy for a
youngster to bowl that number of overs on the trot, sheer madness.

The bowling lay-off did help my batting. 'Esso' encouraged me
to play as a batsman for Barnsley. I hit 50 in my first match,
including three sixes off Scarborough's David Byas, who called me
a 'slogger'. I took that as compliment. My absence as a bowler gave
an opportunity to a 14-year-old schoolboy called Mark Broadhurst,
another Barnsley lad. I was a big fan of his and thought he had a
great future; he was lightning quick, but he lacked confidence,
wasn't street-wise. I remember him ringing home after one game
and he was asked by his dad, 'How many wickets did you get?'
After the reply, 'None,' Mark was told, 'Well, speak to your mum,
then.' Increasingly, I could see he felt the pressure. During our
1991 pre-season tour, Byas was nominating his Yorkshire line-up
for the coming season, not knowing I was sitting behind him.
Broadhurst was in. Gough was out. I'll show you, I thought. You
know even less about cricket than I thought you did.

Mark struggled to cope with dressing-room banter. I was totally
different. Once, early on, Fergie – the captain of Yorkshire – asked
me to go up the road to Headingley and do his laundry. I told him:
'Bugger off. I may be twelfth man, but I'm not doing your laundry.'
Fergie just turned to Jeremy Batty and this time he found a willing
helper. I remember Ashley Metcalfe asking me to go and get a bat
signed when I was twelfth man. The lads had come off for rain and
Ashley was out anyway, sitting around doing nothing. He got the

same response as Fergie. I was a young lad who was not going to take any shit. I remember the lads a few years above me – not the senior guys, who probably just thought I had a chip on my shoulder, but those who had never stood up to that kind of pressure or answered back – thinking I was a cocky little bastard. I am sure they were a bit jealous of me because this young kid was jeopardizing their career and threatening their place in the squad. They thought I didn't listen. But I did listen. I still do. But what I will not stand at any price is being bullied. I won't be bullied.

I managed to make one other championship appearance before the end of the season: my first-team debut at Headingley. Warwickshire's Neil Smith got 161 on a flat wicket. It was then that I witnessed one of my first slanging matches on a professional cricket field. Our captain, Fergie, and Jarvo had a real ding-dong in the middle. Jarvo was far from happy at having to bowl on such an unresponsive track. So he started bowling off five yards. Fergie saw him, stopped him and sent him back to the end of his long run, then returned to the slips. Jarvo walked back to the five-yard mark and ran in. I thought the pair were going to come to blows. I batted at No. 8 after playing in the second team as a batsman. I had been doing well in my new role, scoring 88 against Somerset before being run out by Peter Hartley, as well as managing a couple of fifties. My batting came on by leaps and bounds that year and I certainly lost that 'genuine No. 11' tag.

I had been batting twice a day at the Academy. At one stage it looked as if I would need a back operation. Our physio, Wayne Morton, hoped it would be a final resort, although I had to accept that there might be no other option in the end. Eventually the specialist gave me the green light to bowl again. 'You may feel some discomfort, but just keep bowling. If the back goes totally, then we will have to operate.' He was right about the discomfort but, after about a week, the pain disappeared.

Most of the season had been spent on the sidelines, but my return to full fitness earned me selection for England Under-19 against a New Zealand Young Cricketers side that included Chris Cairns, Adam Parore, Matthew Hart and Chris Harris. I played in the final 'Test' at Old Trafford after England had gone down to an embarrassing innings and 16-run defeat in the first at Scarborough. Mark Ramprakash was skipper, but a broken toe kept him out of my game. Future England colleagues included Nick Knight, Chris Adams, Ian Salisbury and Dominic Cork, as well as P.G. Knightie hit 160 and we forced the Kiwis to follow on. They hung on to clinch the series. A wicket in each innings was hardly earth-shattering, but I was just glad to be playing cricket again. There was more good news at the end of the season: a trip to Australia with England Under-19 at the start of the new year and my first time on an aeroplane. And a Yorkshire contract, after two games in the first team. My cricket had really developed in 1989. I had made the right sporting choice. I was going places . . . or so I thought.

4. M1 to M62

I'm not sure who to blame for the fact that I spent most of the next four summers scratching myself, swaying between wondering whether I had a cricket future or not, or even whether I wanted cricket in my future. I gave serious thought to quitting cricket, as well as moving counties. I would take one step forward, only to mark time for weeks and months. Yorkshire was not a happy place. As usual, we were the last county to opt for an overseas player. There seemed little forward planning. I was only a junior member of the dressing-room, but there was little Team Yorkshire bonding; it was generally every man for himself. We needed success but did not have the talent or structure to achieve it. It might have helped if we had been left to our own devices. But Yorkshire has always been full of former players who live in the past and who are only too keen to remind the world of our failure to recapture the former glory days. For them the world has not moved on.

I started the 1990 summer in great heart. The Under-19 tour of Australia in January and February had gone well. I took five wickets in the first 'Test' at the North Sydney Oval. I did not feel intimidated, playing with or against my peers. This was where I belonged. I knew I had the temperament to cope with the big time. Did I have the ability? My first summer as a contracted player brought me 24 championship wickets at an average of 41 and earned this less than glowing report from *Wisden*, the cricketers' bible: 'Darren Gough did little to justify the high hopes held for him.' The Yorkshire bowling attack at the time was anything but settled. No one reached 50 wickets that summer. Arnie Sidebottom played in only two matches, the same as the number of operations needed on his knee, Jarvo took 37 wickets but was dropped and suffered from a shin stress fracture. Pete Hartley claimed 48 wickets, Stuart Fletcher 27 and Chris Pickles 25.

Help was needed urgently. The previous year, Fergie, now replaced as captain by Martyn, had written an open letter to the committee. He begged them to consider looking beyond the boundaries of Yorkshire – even, dare he mention it, abroad. Fergie had the full backing of the dressing-room. Not that an upstart like me had much of a say. We could not understand why Yorkshire continued to play cricket with one hand tied behind our backs. The players thought we were living in the dark ages, though we appreciated that this was where some of the old-timers still wanted to live. The net result of this handicap was that the White Rose was falling further and further behind. A strong Yorkshire side means a strong England. Sure, but that was back in the 1960s, when we last won the championship. 'Used to be' counts for nothing in sport. Yorkshire had stood still for more than a generation. The world and cricket had moved on. I have no doubt that the influence and the public moaning of old Yorkshire players had a seriously negative effect on the team. When we have meetings with our psychologist now, he tells us: 'They are history. You have got to make your own history. You have got to forget these old players.' It's always been a problem at Headingley. Sometimes it's as if the likes of Illingworth, Close and Trueman have never left the place. It does affect the lads. The passion at the club is huge, so is the level of expectation. I have always made it a point never to have much to do with committee men. I did not feel the need to know what was happening in the corridors of power when I started – and my attitude has never changed.

The outside players issue was finally resolved in November. The loss of over 1,000 members probably had more to do with the issue being debated again than did our poor cricket. And, lo and behold, after years of sticking their fingers in the dike and their heads in the sand, the committee voted by an astonishing 18–1 to relax the 'Yorkshire-born' policy. Those who had grown up in the county could now make their way to Headingley. I cannot imagine what powerful arguments were voiced to inspire such a dramatic turn-around in policy, but this revolution stopped short of allowing the White Rose to field someone from foreign fields.

I took three wickets in five balls against the touring Zimbabweans at Headingley in Leeds. In the next home match I picked up the international wickets of Chris Smith, David Gower and Malcolm Marshall in Hampshire's second innings. Towards the end of the summer, after taking a career best 4–68 against Middlesex, I appeared for England in the youth internationals against Pakistan. In the second 'Test' at Headingley, Moin Khan, skipper when England won in Karachi in 2000, hit 114, while I took 5–106 and Dominic Cork 4–73. In those days I batted above Corkie, scoring 36 in a ninth-wicket partnership of 59 with Jeremy Hallett. Corkie, not wishing to be outdone, hit 45 in a tenth-wicket stand of 79 with him. We had been 187–8, chasing Pakistan's 277, but ended up with a lead of 48. Hallett took five, Corkie another four and I took the other one as we bowled them out for 78 to win by nine wickets. The first and third (saved when nightwatchman Corkie scored a century) matches were drawn, so England took the series. I still treasure the letter I received from Derek Shackleton, the old England bowler, who was in charge. 'The batting and bowling at Headingley will always remain in the memory. I seem to remember saying to Sav [coach Graham Saville] – "This chap might produce something special on his home ground" – you did! Thank you for your good company and hard work.'

I needed a lift, more from the general Yorkshire situation than my own apparent lack of progress. Away from the county confines, I was producing the goods and enjoying the best of company. I was determined not to be dragged down by Yorkshire's problems as others had been. The life of a professional sportsman suited me down to the ground.

The winter offered a new challenge, with a contract to play club cricket in New Zealand. I ended up sharing a house with Corkie in Christchurch, and we had a ball. This was our first Christmas away from home and it was strange, spending the day sitting on the beach. Corkie was the housewife of the 'odd couple' arrangement. I was amazed how domesticated he was: Corkie did all the ironing, washing and cooking. When it was my turn to make dinner, I would head off to the local Kentucky Fried Chicken. He got the pick of the bedrooms. I ended up swapping a couple of my bats for a water bed to replace the tiny single one that was there. Corkie, of course, had the big room with a double bed but we broke that, larking about. It would have been lonely on my own, and we got on well. We played for East Shirley. Part of our coaching duties included going down to the local high-security prison. We came across some scary guys there. They kept telling us they would see us later for a meal.

I was enjoying the cricket lifestyle and was determined to cement a place in the Yorkshire front-line attack in 1991. I was a year older and wiser, with a summer of championship experience under my belt. In the event, I failed, taking a grand total of 16 wickets at over 55. Our bowling attack was going nowhere, yet I struggled to get a game early in the season and I came in only when Jarvo was injured. Pete Hartley was our top fast-bowling wicket-taker again, reaching the half-century this time. Mark Robinson was next with 23, then Stuart Fletcher 20, me 16 and Jarvo 12. Yorkshire's tally of 37 bonus bowling points was the lowest in the championship. Our four victories came when the opposition were chasing targets.

Pete Hartley was one person who kept me going in those early days. We first met in a Yorkshire second-team game. I was on 88 when he came in, and looking for my first century. Pete ran me out first ball. That's how special relationships start. Not that I said much. He was already an established member of the Yorkshire side and was coming back from injury. Pete was easy-going, unlike most of the others in the Yorkshire dressing-room, who always seemed to be feeling the strain. We travelled, roomed and played golf together. It was a sad and stupid day when Yorkshire released him at the end of 1997. Pete had been our best bowler ever since I had come into the side. I wonder whether the club thought they would save money by hiring a cheaper youngster. Certainly that would have proved a false economy. I have always liked his attitude; he was always making out that he didn't want to play: 'Keep batting, lad. That means less time for bowling.' Don't kid yourself. Pete Hartley is as competitive as they come.

I enjoyed a few high spots in 1991. One came in my first

appearance of the season against Leicester in the Sunday League
match at Grace Road. Yorkshire were in trouble at 67–6, chasing
204. I hit 72 not out off 73 balls, including sixes off Chris Lewis
and Peter Willey. Byas and I put on a record 129 for the seventh
wicket in 18 overs, although we fell short of their total by seven
runs. Another highlight was the B&H semi-final at Old Trafford
in front of over 18,000. We lost, but it was a great occasion and an
early taste of what cricket grounds are like when full. My best
performances came at the end of the summer, with a maiden
first-class fifty at Northampton and then an incredible Roses match
at Scarborough. My contribution in our 501–6 was an undefeated
60, the innings that prompted Lancashire's Mike Watkinson to call
me the first white West Indian to play for Yorkshire. The fun and
games came when Lancashire chased the 343 runs for victory. My
figures before lunch were 3–5 off six overs. Lancashire were 129–8
when Ian Austin came to the wicket and belted the fastest century
of the season in 61 balls. This astonishing knock contained six sixes
and he was particularly severe on Fergie, who was our leading
wicket-taker in 1991. The crowd were quick to turn on our bowler
as the ball started disappearing. His efforts had been warmly received
in the closing weeks of the season. Now he was a 'useless fat lump'.
Austin ran out of partners, so my first-ever five-wicket haul helped
Yorkshire to a 48-run win.

I could not work out whether I was going anywhere. After days
like Scarborough, I was sure this was what I wanted. A lot of the
summer had been wasted, though. I had no objection to being
twelfth man occasionally. We all have to serve some sort of apprenticeship. Most of my opportunities seemed to be on flat decks. If
the wicket looked juicy and responsive, I was the man left out.
That made me the odd-job man, making tea, running errands and
reading road maps. A lot of lazing around and, after a day of
boredom, just try and stop me heading for the bar for a much-
needed drink. I was enjoying all the privileges of first-team cricket
without being given the opportunity to run the excesses off. After
the fielding practice and a little bowl in the nets, my physical
exertions were finished before 11 a.m. So when that extra pint was

shoved under my nose, late at night, there was no excuse to push it away. There was plenty to eat, too, when you're in the dressing-room all day. Nobody seemed to monitor your behaviour or habits. Anyway, when you're young, the hangovers never seem that bad; your body recovers quickly. You're a young lad, you're living on adrenalin, playing cricket, and nothing seems to stop you doing that.

The following summer, 1992, was about as bad. I started, but I did not finish and hardly played after early July. My 11 championship games brought me 25 wickets at 36.40. Was it time for a change of scenery? I am not sure whether Yorkshire or I had that thought first. I was astonished when 'Esso' first hinted that Yorkshire might release me; I thought he was joking. He was not.

Another ground-breaking announcement in July 1991 had given me real hope in a miserable summer. Yorkshire were going to sign an overseas player at last. What gave me a boost was the news, a week later, that this player would be the Australian fast bowler, Craig McDermott. Our bowling attack had been a shambles. It was not that we lacked talent and ability, but there were always injuries and inconsistent selection; few of us knew where we stood. McDermott's imminent arrival was a sign that our bowling situation was being treated seriously at last. I could not wait to rub shoulders with one of the world's top bowlers and learn a few things, although it meant one place less to compete for. Sadly, McDermott never appeared, pulling out because of injury. One of the world's great young batsmen, Sachin Tendulkar came instead. That was not much use to me.

Tendulkar's appearance did little for Yorkshire in terms of results. We fell two places in the table to 16th, ended up 15th in the Sunday League after seven successive defeats, failed to make it out of the qualifying group of the B&H and went out in round two of the NatWest. My *Wisden* end-of-season report was not getting any better: 'Darren Gough, on the other hand, could not exert the necessary control. His ability to produce superb deliveries hardly compensated for expensive inaccuracies and he surrendered his rating as one of the brightest prospects, at least for the time being.'

Fortunately, help was at hand – not in the shape of an Aussie fast bowler, but in the more attractive form of Anna Kratovil, who was to become Mrs Anna Gough. After winters away with England Under-19 and in New Zealand, my services were now required by the Sheffield Cricket Lovers Society for a short trip to Fuengirola, near Torremolinos in Spain. I was spending the off-season working on the M62. A friend from Shepley C.C. used to be the boss at Tarmac and I was getting £50 a day. It was tough work. That was when it began to dawn on me that I *had* to make it at cricket. Occasionally I would be let loose with the pneumatic drill, but mostly I had to get the cones and the gear out for the roadworks. It keeps you on your toes, dodging the traffic with signs under your arms – no scope for a slip or fall. The scariest place was at the point where three lanes become two; some drivers leave moving over to the last second. All I had to defend myself with was the cone I was holding. Facing Allan Donald at 90 m.p.h. was a piece of cake after that.

A November break in Spain playing cricket was just what I needed. Jeremy Batty came with me and one night we walked into the London Bar, which is a popular haunt in the summer. This was wintertime, and only about eight people were in. One girl there was gorgeous. I said to Jeremy, 'I'm going to marry her.' Not on the evidence of that night. Anna was not impressed at all; the Gough charm totally failed to work. When I asked her what she thought I did for a living, her answer was a dismissive 'Builder.' Anna was two years older than me and was in no mood for a pushy, chubby toyboy. Jeremy and I did take Anna and her friend Katrina out for a meal. Embarrassingly, the girls had to pay for themselves as we had run out of money.

However, I refused to give up. On my last day Anna relented a little and gave me her home phone number in Dunstable. She had returned to England, after five years working in California, and had taken a six-month contract as an air stewardess. Anna flew home a couple of days after me. I rang her up and arranged to go down to see her the following weekend. I was so nervous, driving down in my Golf convertible. We met up and headed into London, and we really hit it off. Eight weeks later, I asked Anna to marry me. People say you know when it's the right one. I knew. I had never chased after anyone.

'Esso' tells a story in my benefit brochure about this blonde girl turning up when I was playing for Barnsley when I was 16. I had been bowling badly, but suddenly I turned it on to impress her. The story is not quite true: she was my girlfriend. 'Esso' was always strict with me. When I bowled badly, there was no soft soap from him. It was: 'Bugger off to the boundary. That was rubbish. Get down there and think about it.' Then he would move me from fine leg to fine leg at the end of every over. It was his way of getting the best out of me, and it worked. He put me back on. After 0–20 after two overs, I ended up with 5–25. 'Esso' put it down to the girl. She had nothing to do with it; he had got me fired up already.

I was sure Anna was the one for me. Anna's so sensible she still jokes that she doesn't know what possessed her to fancy me. I proposed on the phone. Wrong again. I was told to jump straight in my car and make a personal appearance. I duly arrived, armed with a jelly ring. I bought a proper one the next day.

Anna's dad is American. Her mum is English. None of your traditional Yorkshire reserve there. It has taken me a few years to come to terms with all the hugs and kisses. I come from a Yorkshire family that loves each other but doesn't show its emotions. My mum tends to be more emotional when she's had a drink. That's when she tells me she loves me. Mum and Dad are as proud as punch for what I've achieved. Dad's still so young-looking, everyone thinks he's my brother. He loves that. He's got a heart of gold. If I rang up in Pakistan and told my dad, 'I need you here, now,' he would be on the next plane straight away. If Anna and I got a late invite, Dad would be round to babysit, even though he had something planned. Dad's the softer of the two. He used to give me a belt when I was younger, but my mum was the one who had to tell him to do it. My mum tried to hit us, and we would laugh at her. Dad hated having to do it. Dad doesn't drink much. He likes to be in control. When I have a party at home, Dad spends most of his time watching what people are up to, making sure they don't make a mess. If you put down a half-empty beer can, it's gone and in the bin before you can turn around.

It's hard for people who don't come from Yorkshire to know exactly what that means. I can walk into my folks' house and sit down and watch TV without saying a word. We are not ones for the big greetings. Anna could not believe it. She was used to the full works: hugs, kisses, the lot. And my folks couldn't believe it when that's what they got from Anna's family. We Yorkies don't show our feelings. In a way, that's sad. Anna wants our boys to be outgoing and able to display their emotions. I find it hard, whatever you may see on the cricket field. Sporting highs and lows are something else. I'm hard. It would have to be something serious to upset me. It's not that we don't care. I have never felt unloved. I think the world of my brother and sister, but I've found it hard to be close to them. I don't think I've ever kissed my sister or hugged my brother and told him I love him. Anna's family have shown me the other side. Sometimes I feel caught in the middle. Occasionally it's awkward.

Fortunately for me, Anna said 'Yes' and came up to live with me in a flat in Barnsley. There was no hurry for us to get married; I was always going to live with someone before I got married. It was quite a change for the Gough lifestyle; before, there was no one but me to worry about. Perhaps that was part of the trouble. I enjoyed the change. Anna started working at Barclays and set about sorting my lifestyle. There was plenty of room for improvement, as Anna and the Yorkshire C.C. Club were too well aware.

5. Change of Scene

What made the summer of 1993 such a special one of transformation for Darren Gough? I am still not sure. I had spent the winter training hard, being the housewife while Anna worked. I was as fit as I had ever been at the start of a new season. It was make or break time. Our new overseas player, Richie Richardson, soon gave me the confidence to bowl flat out, not to compromise with my cricket. That was in May at Southampton. A few weeks earlier, Anna and I had moved into our first house at 17 Dimple Gardens in Ossett. By July, Yorkshire and I were in the same old familiar mess. Chairman of cricket Brian Close and chief executive Chris Hassell held an emergency meeting with the players over the state of the county game in Yorkshire. Around the same time, I was out of the first team and found myself being sent to play for the second team at Wellingborough College to take on Northants. I had had enough. I wanted away from Yorkshire. Another injury to Jarvo earned me a recall, but I travelled to Somerset with my mind pretty well made up about leaving and joining Northamptonshire.

That trip changed my life. August was only two days old, but returning home I was a cricketer with a Yorkshire − and, very shortly, an international − future. A month later, I was picked for the England 'A' tour to South Africa after finishing the season in style. Less than a year later, I was playing for England. Everyone reacted as though this sudden promotion had been inevitable. Personally, I certainly did not feel that way. If all that mucking around had been part of a grand plan, I wish someone had let me know. I was on the staff from 1989 and played for the first team very quickly. Some say that is lucky. But the downside of hanging around the first team all the time, especially when not playing, is that I never had a chance to learn my trade. When a first-team opportunity came along, I had to grab it. That can work for or against you. I've seen players in the second team get stale and lazy. Most of my appearances had been in the first team. In five seasons on the staff I had played a grand total of ten second-team championship matches.

Don't get me wrong; I loved being part of the main set-up. Unfortunately, hanging around for half a season year after year can be counter-productive for young and aspiring cricketers. Looking back now that I am successful, I can pretend it was all part of the great scheme of things. I am not so sure. At the time I was tearing my hair out. Had Anna and Richie not come to my rescue, I am not convinced I would have been ready to take my chance when it came.

I'll never be able to thank Richie enough for what he did for me. I must admit my heart sank when I heard Yorkshire were going for another overseas batsman. Eight years down the line, I am still waiting to open the Yorkshire bowling with a foreign star. I've been rather envious of the county attacks that have included the likes of Allan Donald, Glenn McGrath, even Shane Warne. Gough and Warne – now there's a double act. The West Indians have a reputation for being laid back. In Richie's case, it was more like comatose. I can recall numbers of occasions when Richie fell asleep in our dressing-room, even when kitted up and next in. I knew that was down to more than just the traditional Caribbean way. Richie was worn out by the demands of international cricket. His career was nearing its end and I am sure Yorkshire rewarded him handsomely for coming to us. I have got no problems with that, although our committee never seem to have the same trouble finding the extra money for overseas stars that is not available for our youngsters.

Yorkshire being Yorkshire, Richie was informed that the club would prefer him not to wear the sun-hat the West Indies skipper had made famous the cricket world over. I am not sure that the hat was actually banned, but Richie, being Richie, is such a nice guy that he would not rock the boat. The man was pure style. I still don't know how he could manage to drive his car at 10 o'clock at night in sunglasses. Halfway through his first summer, Richie admitted that the only visitors to his house in Adel had been a couple of Jehovah's Witnesses. Richie had personal problems too. His mum died, back in Antigua, that first year, and his son Ari was seriously injured in a car accident back home the following year. Richie quit, midway through that second summer. I was not surprised. My abiding memory is of him asleep in the Edgbaston dressing-room, being woken up and told he was in, him rubbing his eyes and then blasting a century, including hitting Allan Donald to all parts.

Richie was able to contribute more than Sachin in the dressing-room. The Indian batsman was extra special. I only had to bowl to him in one net session to realize that. He was probably too young. He made an instant impact when he turned up to meet us at the Oval. Yorkshire has always had a strict dress-code: blazer and tie, and make sure you shave. Sachin pitched up in jeans and rugby shirt and trainers. Nobody said a word. Our dress-code has never been the same since.

Aussie Mike Bevan replaced Richie. He did wake our dressing-room up. Michael was very big on players watching and supporting their team-mates. Our dressing-room used to clear if he got out to a bad shot or a bad decision. A good delivery was not a problem but everything would go if he wasn't happy, and he holds the world record for f★★★s, making Ramps and Nasser seem like choirboys. Darren Lehmann came when Michael was unavailable the next year and at the end of the summer was the preferred choice. Michael was not happy, expecting to return. I don't blame him. Both are great players and powerful influences in the dressing-room; Darren is just that bit more relaxed. Darren's South Australia team-mate, Greg Blewett, came for a year but never found his best form. He should not have opened; it was one of those summers when the ball was jagging all over the place at Headingley. Yorkshire might have needed an overseas fast bowler in the early days; not now, with the strength in depth we have. A spinner might be nice, but Darren has played a key part in Yorkshire's improvement in recent years.

No one has been as laid back as Richie, but his cricket was geared to aggression and attack. I had performed well on the pre-season tour to South Africa, but nothing startling. We beat Essex before Richie arrived. I took a career best 4–25 in our Sunday League win at Southampton, our first for 11 months. Richie hit 81. The next day, Hampshire went for quick runs to set us a target in the championship game. I took four wickets, but was tiring. My mate Shaun Udal came in and started smacking me. Richie wasn't captain (Martyn was) but he came over from gully to have a word with me. He saw in a second what I was up to. It was hurting because I wasn't fit and I was trying to protect what I had, rather than tearing in for the kill. That's what I had got away with previously. 'What are you doing, man? Get your finger out. Bowl fast. Nobody likes it.' Richie knew what pace could do. I was much fitter than in previous summers, but I was going through the motions again. He was not having it. Fair enough. And what young fast bowler is not going to respond to a kick up the backside from such a world-class cricketer?

I finished with 5–50, my second five-wicket haul for Yorkshire. Richie wasn't satisfied. Our target was 222 runs in 42 overs. At tea, we were 10–0 after eight overs. Yorkshire won by six wickets with over seven overs to spare. County dressing-rooms are full of prophets of doom, worried about who is in the opposition. In this case it was one of Richie's team-mates, a certain Malcolm Marshall, sadly no longer with us, one of the great fast bowlers of all time. Richie's message was simple. 'Nobody in the West Indies worries about who is bowling. Put willow to leather and adopt a positive attitude.' As simple as that. At long last, someone at Yorkshire had told me what was expected of me. My fitness had been a factor, but I had never been sure what was expected of me. Should I be taking wickets or saving runs? Taking wickets was more fun and far better suited to my ability and character. If it was good enough for Richie, that was fine by me.

We had a week's break. I took 7–18 for Shepley in the Drakes Huddersfield League. A week later, I received another West Indian boost when Glamorgan came to Middlesbrough. 'Darren is very quick and, although he is still learning, should have a great future' was Sir Viv Richards's verdict. I had rattled the great man's stumps, but his off-breaks got me out in both the championship and Sunday League games.

Despite such famous support, the *Yorkshire Evening Post* was running out of patience. 'Gough remains the most frustrating member of the attack. He proved against Kent on the last day at Headingley that he has the ability to bowl hostile spells in which he threatens to take a wicket every ball. But he is also prone to erratic bursts and with only 2–107 from 35 overs at Birmingham, needs to harness his skills on a more consistent basis in the second half of the season.' You just cannot please some people. On the same day, I played for an England XI against Holland. We won the first game by 128 runs, then came under fire for losing by seven wickets the next afternoon. I was on my way. Not really. I returned, to find myself back in the second team for a trip to play against Northants at Wellingborough School. My mood that game was one of the reasons why discussions followed about me moving there for the 1994 season. Halfway through my fifth season as a professional, my tally for 1993 was a miserable 16 wickets at 35.50.

I went straight from the Yorkshire second team into the England dressing-room at Headingley, with Australia the opposition. England, 2–0 down in the series, needed to win to keep the Ashes alive. The result was never in doubt, and Goochie resigned after the innings-and-148-run defeat. I was there as twelfth man, a familiar role. This was special, though. I remember being handed an England shirt and looking round the dressing-room. There were the legends like Goochie and Robin Smith. The bowling attack was Andy Caddick, Martin McCague, Martin Bicknell and Mark Ilott. I thought: 'I'm as good as you lot. I could be in there.' I never told anyone, but that experience was another spur to me. I was in charge of the dressing-room so I did not have a chance of fielding as substitute, although I ran on a couple of times with gear.

When Jarvo pulled out of the Somerset trip, I decided that I had nothing to lose. Richie had given me a clear view of what I wanted to be: no steady, miserly seamer, but an out-and-out pace-bowler. I had been going through the motions for long enough. I wanted success in my cricketing life – and excitement. I had been confused about how I should be bowling. I did not realize that it was also about fitness and lifestyle. When your girlfriend tells you to get fit, you want to get fit for her. If the trainer or physio at the club tells you, there's not the same incentive to do it. Yorkshire never gave me the kick up the arse that I needed. Anna did that.

Yorkshire set Somerset a target of 219 runs to win. I had taken three wickets in the first innings, then destroyed Somerset's top order with three wickets for no runs in 13 deliveries. I finished them off the next morning with three wickets in an over. My tally was 7–42, and 10–96 in the match. It had been achieved by bowling wicket-taking balls, by being myself. It may sound like something from a religious meeting when I say that 'I felt the power' – but I did with the ball in my hand that match. By and large, I have felt it ever since. I was off and running. The second half of the summer produced 39 more wickets at 21.74, culminating in my 'A' tour selection. I had gone from 'Guzzler' to 'Dazzler', thanks to 'Esso's' daughters. Apparently I dazzled a lot. Of those 39 wickets, 15 were bowled and six were l.b.w. Four of the catches went to the wicket-keeper. I kept attacking.

I was still leaving Headingley, especially after typical Yorkshire nonsense over my 'cap'. 'Esso' came up to me at Scarborough in mid-August and told me Craig White was to receive his county cap. What about me? I was told this was his home ground, that the committee did not want to cap us both together and that I would get mine in a few weeks. I was absolutely distraught. How could they be so insensitive? I realized then that maybe I had not made the big breakthrough as far as the Yorkshire committee was concerned. When Jarvo was fit again, someone else would have to drop out. As a capped player, it would not be Craig. This had nothing to do with Craig. I was pleased for him, but I was being treated badly. I had spoken to Phil Neale, Northants director of cricket, and to Allan Lamb, the captain, and was still set on leaving. The move would have allowed Anna to be nearer her folks.

It was a close call. Yorkshire did cap me a month later, and the next day I signed a new four-year deal. I was just a few days away from sitting down with Northants and discussing terms. It was that close and very tempting. The money on offer was twice what I was getting at Yorkshire. In the end, I could not make the break. I decided to back my ability against Jarvo's and the other Yorkshire bowlers'. Leaving might have been taken as a sign of surrender, of quitting, of running away from the fight. Mind you, I know of several players who have stayed at Headingley when they should have gone. After another three or four seasons in the second team, they are sacked. I have not regretted my decision to stay.

After I had signed Jarvo was released with two years of his contract left to run. I have no way of knowing how much my form and decision to stay influenced his departure. I think Yorkshire had got fed up with him, not solely with his injury problems. Jarvo could be quite cocky when he came back from playing for England. It certainly affected him. Our skipper, Martyn Moxon, for all his calm exterior, is quite an emotional chap. I remember Jarvo shouting his mouth off and being stunned when Martyn went over and lifted him up against the wall. Jarvo realized he had gone too far.

The 'A' tour was an unexpected boost. I panicked a bit when I saw my name in the squad for the trip to South Africa. I was due to get married in October and had no idea when the tour was. There was no stag night. I have seen the mad things cricketers get up to, tied to lamp-posts, super-glue and no clothes on. I was not having any of that. The wedding day went well, apart from my effort to force Anna's ring onto the wrong finger. Anna and I went on honeymoon to Florida. I had always wanted to go there. The year after I left home, Mum and Dad took Andrea there and I was livid. I fell in love with Disney, being the big kid I am. It's my favourite holiday spot. Now I am invited to the opening of all the new big rides.

The 'A' squad left for South Africa in late November under the captaincy of Glamorgan's Hugh Morris. He was a brilliant captain, so understanding. Before each session, Hugh would explain what we were trying to do; no one had ever done that with me before. He is now walking the corridors of power at Lord's and this may seem like brown-nosing. We started with eight successive victories.

I took seven wickets in the last one, against Western Province, which earned us an extra day on the beach. I have always been something of a sun-worshipper. I like nothing better than a couple of hours by the pool or on the beach.

I was the only bowler on the tour who had not played representative cricket. Our two-month tour finished with an unofficial 'Test'. That was the spot we were all after. The other bowlers felt that Martin McCague was getting preferential treatment. We soon discovered why: McCague was the official standby for the senior tour in the Caribbean, and the management there wanted him fit and ready. Our management played along for a while but then decided to pick the best attack for the Test at Port Elizabeth. How right they were. Mark Ilott took nine wickets and I got seven on a fairly lifeless pitch as we batted out a draw. I managed to bat two hours for 13. I did make the Caribbean that winter, but only with Yorkshire – although we met up with the England boys in Antigua. So near, and yet so far. But for the first time in my cricket career I felt I had a future beyond Yorkshire.

6. Gough the Scoff

After years of frustration, I was a cricketer with a future. Not only did I have my Yorkshire cap and a new county contract, but I had serious England aspirations. I felt tantalizingly close to my goal as the 1994 season got under way. A vital piece of the jigsaw had slipped into place during England's tour of the Caribbean: the new England chairman of selectors was a Yorkie. The expected choice, tour manager M.J.K. Smith, was displaced by Raymond Illingworth, former England captain and proud member of the People's Republic of Yorkshire. Illy promised a wind of change. From reading his comments, that breeze was going to carry a smell of the White Rose. It was not just paper talk. Illy took me aside at Headingley at the start of the season and told me: 'You're doing it well. Keep it going - and try to concentrate on your batting.'

I started well in the 'friendly' Roses clash at Old Trafford, 5-75 in Lancashire's first innings and 43. Wickets continued to come my way. By the time I headed for Cardiff for the championship and Sunday League games against Glamorgan, the media was touting me for a Texaco squad place. I belted a quick fifty, then took a couple of wickets, including my 'A' tour captain, Hugh Morris. I knew that Illy's selectors were sitting down the next day to pick a one-day squad. This might not be a first-class match, but that didn't matter. I've always seen any game as an opportunity for putting my name in the headlines and grabbing attention. I've been lucky. I've never been labelled a 'limited-overs specialist' or a 'Test' player and found myself stuck in one of those boxes. As the likes of Neil Fairbrother have found out, once typecast, it's difficult to escape.

The newspapers announced their own preferred squads on the Saturday morning ahead of the selectors. I was in all of them. I know now that those squads are based on a certain amount of inside information. But, as I was young and naïve at the time, I thought

their lists were all their own work and opinion. Players and supporters kept telling me not to worry. My name would be there
tomorrow. That was the point at which I began to wonder. What
if, after all this build-up, I was not included? How would I cope
with disappointment? Only one thing for it. Go out on Saturday
night and have a shedful. Mission accomplished. I was able to sleep
it off on the Sunday morning as matches didn't start until 2 p.m. I
wasn't getting ready to cope with bad news, just trying not to think
about it. Afterwards, I told the lads I'd merely been celebrating a
day early.

My lie-in meant I didn't hear the glad news until I got to Sophia
Gardens. When BBC Radio's Jonathan Agnew offered me his
congratulations, I realized that my mobile phone must have been
switched off. Then Lord's rang, and I rang Anna and my folks.
Congratulations all round. I celebrated with a Sunday League-best
4–20, as Yorkshire won by nine wickets. My strange feelings had
nothing to do with my Saturday night excesses. I had dreamt of
this happening for years, yet it had been only a matters of weeks
since it had become a realistic prospect. That demonstrates one of
the remarkable turnarounds in my life. Eventually I took an interest
in who my new team-mates were. I was one of three new boys –
along with Yorkshire's Steven Rhodes, now at Worcestershire, and
Hampshire's Shaun Udal. Graham Gooch was brought back after
missing the West Indies tour, and so was Phillip DeFreitas. Only
six of the West Indies tour party survived. As for D. Gough's
inclusion, Illy said: 'Darren Gough is in because he has improved
beyond all recognition. He's quick, he's fit and he's more controlled
in line and length.'

I was about to get my first taste of the media feeding frenzy. Just
as well I'm not a sensitive soul. My fitness – or, rather, fatness –
dominated the press interviews when the England squad gathered
at Edgbaston. 'GOUGH THE SCOFF – I WAS A YORK-
SHIRE PUDDING' was one headline . . . 'BURGER
KING'S SLIMLINE TONIC' was another. The copy beneath
was more of the same. 'Goughie admitted he was a fat and lazy
cricketer going nowhere – until his wife Anna cut him down to

size.' If you can't beat them, join them, I thought, so I went along with the flow. 'I was overweight and into junk food, but she helped me to sort myself out. I was a guzzler rather than a porker,' I confessed. 'I wasn't in Gazza's class for eating burgers, but I used to have more than my fair share.' Maybe I was laying it on a bit thick, but I enjoyed being in the limelight. I gave Anna the credit she was due, so the *Yorkshire Post* came to interview her about my transformation. She did not mince her words. 'It is an exaggeration to say he was sitting drinking and stuffing himself with chips all day, but he knew he wasn't going to get very far unless he pushed himself.'

The press loved the 'Guzzler to Dazzler' transformation. There was only the occasional question about my bowling. I didn't mind. After all, I'd been cut down to size in my quest for an England place and now I'd made it. This was my first real experience of the media scrum. My previous dealings had been with the local Yorkshire lads. I'd had plenty of run-ins with them in the early years when my career was drifting. Strangely, I felt more comfortable and at home with the hacks from the nationals. It wasn't only the absence of the usual Yorkshire politics. I didn't put on a special act for them. I was my usual confident, show-off self, and they seemed to like it. It's been that way ever since. I've always been open with them and, generally, I've had a great press. With me, what you see is what you get.

My Sunday League form and my ability to bowl at the death convinced me I'd get a game in this two-match Texaco series. I must admit I didn't see it as a trial for the Test team. Most of my cricket for Yorkshire had been in limited-overs matches; that was my natural game. It was only at the end of the previous summer that I had become a regular member of the championship side. I would not have expected to be picked if, as nowadays, the Test matches had come first. I had already earned a certain reputation as a bowler in one-day cricket, producing yorkers and in-swingers and an ability to bowl those final difficult overs. That last trait has proved a huge advantage in my career. Bowling at the death is second nature to me; I've done it since I was a youngster. I may still get smacked from time to time, but it doesn't affect me. I'm not sure you can teach someone to bowl those last overs. Either you can do it, or you can't; you've got the temperament or you haven't. It doesn't matter whether you're a quick bowler or a slow bowler. What does matter is that you want to be out there in that situation . . . and I still do.

My only worry concerned the venue for my debut, Edgbaston. I'd played a few games there and had never bowled well. This wasn't a serious problem, it just niggled away at the back of my mind. Athers tried to keep the pressure on by telling the press the day before that I was 'England's second-quickest bowler after Devon Malcolm'. I wasn't nervous and was rather disappointed when England batted first. Athers, who was playing his first one-day international at home for three years, scored 81 and was the mainstay of our 224–8. I had my pads on but wasn't required. It was a decent enough score, provided we bowled well.

I was determined to make an impact, but I wasn't prepared for the noise of the crowd. Edgbaston was packed – 18,000-odd – and what a buzz! Footballers play in front of big crowds, week in, week out, so when they step up to international level the crowd is not a factor. Our county efforts are watched by the low hundreds, if you're lucky, on championship days and by a few thousands in limited-over matches. My only real experience of any sort of crowd had been that full house at Old Trafford in the Benson & Hedges semi-final against Lancashire at Old Trafford back in 1991. This was different. I took a long look around the ground, kissed the single lion on my sweater and charged in for all I was worth.

There's one advantage to being the new kid on the block: you've not been around. You have the wonderful element of surprise or, in my case, shock. You've got to get that first wicket, otherwise the question remains: are you good enough? It was my second delivery to Martin Crowe. My plan, my strategy: I was just trying to bowl quick. I was pumped up and hoped all the adrenalin might add an extra yard. The first ball I'd dug into his ribs. The next ball, the sixth of the over, was easily the worst, short and wide. Crowe tried to play a typical one-day shot down to third man and guided it into Alec Stewart's hands at slip at great speed. Stewie moaned that his hands hurt for the rest of the season. I could not believe it: a wicket in my first England over, and one of the best batsmen in the world, too. No wonder my celebrations went over the top. Can you blame me? Me being hugged and slapped by cricket legends like Goochie, Judgey (Robin Smith) and Athers. Afterwards, I discovered that it was only Crowe's third duck in 132 one-day internationals and his first for a decade. Later on, one of my in-swinging yorkers removed opener Bryan Young, who had provided the main Kiwi resistance with 65. My final figures were 2–36. They could have been 3–24. Unfortunately, Chris Lewis dropped a sitter in the deep. Shaun Udal claimed a couple of wickets, too, and Lewis took three. England triumphed by 42 runs. I felt I was in seventh heaven. This was why I'd played cricket all these years. This was where I belonged. I hadn't expected how easily I took to the buzz, the roar. I loved it, and that stuck. People say I'm a showman and that I play to the crowd, but it's not something I do on purpose; it comes naturally. The crowd understood, that afternoon, and they responded. That's happened to me all over the world. Maybe because it's apparent that I'm trying hard, giving one hundred per cent, and that I want to win for England. It was also quite clear that I loved what I was doing. It had been a long time since an England cricketer smiled as much.

I might have been green, but I was becoming the apple of Illy's eye. The new chairman gave the team only seven out of ten for overall performance, but he went over the top when Gough's debut was mentioned, comparing me to Wasim Akram and Waqar Younis. 'Darren Gough is my sort of player. There aren't many who are more positive, and he enjoys his cricket so much, there doesn't seem to be the slightest fear of failure. Aggression, penetration – call it what you like, some bowlers have it and some don't. That's why I pushed for Gough.' As excited as I'd been that morning in the England dressing-room, the aftermath was twice as special. England had taken a 1–0 lead in the series, and I'd played a part. I was intent on not missing out on a single moment. I went into the Texaco hospitality room where everyone smiled, shook my hand and patted me on the back. No false modesty from me. My joy was obvious to all – I was just beaming. And surely they couldn't leave me out of the Lord's decider now. A day earlier, I would have settled for this one chance. Until you play, you don't know if you're good enough, good enough to take that one wicket. Then you play and you find out that the answer is Yes. I felt at home and I wanted to become part of the England cricket furniture.

Take nothing for granted. That was the lesson I learnt a few hours later. A certainty for Lord's? Not if you're not fit! I woke up next morning, still with a smile on my face and looking forward to reading the papers. I was still excited, but that wasn't the reason I was gasping for breath when I tried to get up. What was that shooting pain in my side? It eased a little as I tried to work out what had happened. I remembered a slight pain there in my second spell, but I had felt it more in my last couple of overs. I had put the soreness down to trying to bowl as quick as I could, to try to get the ball to reverse on what turned out be a cold evening. Don't panic. See how it feels after the drive to London. But by the time I went to see our physio, Dave 'Rooster' Roberts, I was prepared for the worst. I was ruled unfit and out of consideration for Lord's.

Actually, I missed nothing. It rained and the series was ours. I spoke to the national press again in the Lord's pavilion, making positive noises about the Test series ahead. The Edgbaston experience had encouraged me to be positive about going all the way.

The injury didn't dampen my spirits as I headed back home. I had played for my country and got my England cap – and that's what it's all about. As usual, the biggest problem for Wayne Morton, our physio, was finding a way to stop me rushing back. He'd tell (not advise) me to rest. I'd go home, and a day later I'd start gently practising my bowling action, trying to improve on the best medical opinion's predicted recovery rate. It's been a major weakness of mine throughout my career. Instead of accepting injuries and lay-offs as part and parcel of a professional sporting career, I've tried to defy the laws of nature. Physios have found it almost impossible to stop me making the problem worse. Only in the later stages of my career have I become more sensible and grown up. I've almost come to accept that it's an occupational hazard and take advantage of the break. Wayne said I'd be out for four to six weeks after Lord's. 'Rubbish, I'll be bowling in three!' I replied hotly.

I presented myself at the end of the three weeks, ready for duty, telling Wayne I wasn't feeling any discomfort in my side.

'Is that so?' A few prods from him, and he knew I was feeling it. 'Look, you're not right. You're not playing.'

My urgency had nothing to do with any worry about being forced to go to the tail-end of the pecking order again and someone else pinching my place. At this stage I didn't have an England Test place. After my performance and after what Illy had said, I had the feeling that the selectors would give me another chance as soon as I was fit. The press were on my side, too. They'd seen me bowl, and they'd liked what they saw. The simple truth was that I just wanted to play. I'd made a start and I wanted to keep the momentum going; I wanted to cement my place in the England team. There's nothing worse than being a one-cap wonder. You get that first wicket. Now you want your second game.

Despite my inactivity, I enjoyed my new status as Yorkshire's latest international. I flaunted it a bit, especially to those who a year earlier had doubted I would even make a county cricketer.

I missed Yorkshire's innings victory over the Kiwis, and I was still on the sick list when England won the Trent Bridge Test, thanks to a Gooch double-hundred, and then hung on at Lord's thanks to a defiant knock from Bumpy (Steven Rhodes). I needed to prove my fitness on the field if I was to have any chance of making the final Test at Old Trafford. A couple of one-day run-outs were followed by 50 overs against Hampshire at Headingley. This put the ball back in the court of the England selectors. I made it ahead of Devon Malcolm. Athers declared: 'We accept that Gough is not as quick as Malcolm, but he is certainly more accurate.' To be picked ahead of Devon, whom I've always admired, was a big call. As a young player, you've got to believe the selectors know what they are doing.

The build-up was even better and bigger than Edgbaston had been. More press interviews – I didn't realize I'd led such an interesting life – and pictures of me with the Union Jack. Then we were presented with a set of golf clubs by Howson. The cricket was the thing, naturally, but I'm not suggesting for a second that the perks were an unwelcome bonus. This was the life: playing cricket for your country, getting expenses and being paid for turning up and, on top of it all, golf clubs!

I may have been the new boy, but I didn't feel intimidated entering the England dressing-room with all those famous names. That's never been my style. Those who didn't realize that quickly got the message when I pinned a 'Yorkshire Only' notice on the door of the small room next to the Old Trafford home dressing-room. (I think it's the captain's room.) It was time for the White Rose to make its presence felt in this Red Rose heartland, so Chalky (Craig White) and I declared independence. The password to enter was 'Brian Close'. Perhaps it all seems a bit childish, but I've always believed that a bit of life and humour in the dressing-room is essential in order to lift team spirit and improve performance. It also made the statement that, first Test or not, Darren Gough was here to stay and was going to treat his final promotion just like any other game.

My first day as an England Test player was rather uneventful. I made little impression, stuck in the dressing-room all day. Athers won the toss for the first time in ten attempts and did what all opening batsmen do on their home ground, he batted and scored a century. My first tentative steps on to the Test arena came on Friday, after our overnight 199–4 had become a rather fragile 235–7. Put the ball in my hand and I've got no problems. But I hadn't batted in the one-dayer and was as nervous as hell as I walked out to join Daffy (Phillip DeFreitas).

I'll never forget my first delivery in Test cricket. Dion Nash was the bowler and the ball hit me straight in the rib-cage. I'd hardly moved. Then, as now, I'm a slow starter. Get past the first ten minutes and I've got a chance. Otherwise I tend to lose confidence over a period of time and just swing from the arse. My only concern was not to mark my debut with a duck; get off the mark and then play some shots. That's exactly what Daffy and I did. An unlikely eighth-wicket stand of 130 ensued, with the pair of us trying to outdo the other in boundaries. I belted Michael Owens straight down the ground to the boundary, then pushed a single for my fifty. I had dreamt of taking wickets in my first Test, but not scoring runs. I kissed the badge on my helmet and raised my bat to the cheers. This was only my fourth half-century in first-class cricket, and I felt exhausted. I wasn't used to batting for so long – two and half hours – in such a competitive environment. I should have been stumped on 65, but then I chipped the ball to cover without adding to that score. The crowd gave me a great ovation as I came off with a lot more confidence in my step than when I walked on. Not too many had seen me bat like that, even in the England team. Athers had; I'd scored 60 in about 40 balls against Lancashire at Scarborough, when Winker (Lancashire's Mike Watkinson) called me the first white West Indian to play for Yorkshire.

I may have been knackered, but I went out to bowl on a high. This time, at the end of my run-up my England sweater had the full set of three lions. The ultimate prize. What else could I possibly want? That's right, a wicket, and soon, to match my Edgbaston debut. Hope springs eternal. Up at the other end was Kiwi Mark Greatbatch, who'd been off the field with a broken thumb for most of the Test. I felt I had a chance. Greatbatch was the type of cricketer who thought he was harder than he actually was, but the lads told me to stick it up him. How right they were. With my fifth legitimate delivery (the third had been a no-ball) Greatbatch tried to duck out of the way. No escape. The ball gloved to Hickie at second slip. Who writes your scripts, Goughie? More theatrical celebrations. If I'm totally honest, this success was not so much of a shock, and not just because it was Greatbatch rather than Crowe at the other end. That 65 had made me feel a part of the team and I went out to bowl feeling that failure was not an option. It was all totally weird and wonderful.

Athers took me off after three overs. Shrewd captaincy. Daffy came on and got a wicket with his first ball. I came back and had Stephen Fleming caught behind. England 382 (D. Gough 65), New Zealand 84–4 (D. Gough 2–21). As the *Sun* proclaimed on its cricket spread the next day, 'Gough to a Flier'. The *Daily Telegraph*'s Christopher Martin-Jenkins came up with an instant assessment that he was probably to regret in the second half of the 1990s: 'What is more, he can bat.' My folks were there, and there was more backslapping in the Cornhill tent. My only worry was, nobody was talking about my bowling. Illy continued to spout White Rose propaganda: 'Whenever England do well, there are always two or three Yorkshiremen in the side.'

The Kiwis were bowled out by Saturday lunchtime, 231 runs short of our total, and were asked to bat again. My figures were 4–47. I hadn't even taken my sweater off when Matthew Hart hit a loosener straight to Athers in the covers off my first ball of the day. Another Gough loosener, this time down the leg-side, did for New Zealand skipper Ken Rutherford. At tea, the tourists were dead and buried at 75–4. Martin Crowe had other ideas. The Kiwis closed that Saturday night at 205–5. Crowe's 70 had saved them from complete collapse in the first innings. He was a man with a mission. England had refused to allow a substitute fielder for Crowe, who was feeling unwell. He had come into the game on medication, so his side had to suffer the consequences when that gamble failed. Then Chalky knocked the badge off his helmet. Ultimately we were the ones to suffer as Crowe, with some help from the weather (less than 20 overs were bowled on the fourth day), steered the Kiwis to safety. I could sympathize with Crowe's confusion when Daffy was named Man of the Match. Crowe is still one of the best three batters I've bowled at – he was elegant, had timing, brilliant. A nice guy, too. He'd congratulated me after my Texaco wicket. After the series, he kindly gave me his shirt. 'I thought you might like this.' Not half as much as I did his wicket.

7. 'Donald Dies'

Illy rang the changes for Lord's. The papers were full of the Robin Smith axing. John 'Creepy' Crawley came in for his debut, ahead of Graham Thorpe. Being a veteran of one Test, the only name of interest to Darren Gough in the England line-up was that of Darren Gough. It takes a few years in the dressing-room before the politics and in-fighting of selection grabs you and you start to voice an opinion. My sole concern was my own game and position. Would I get picked for the Ashes tour? Actually, that's not quite true. I felt sorry for Judgey. He had been short of runs, but even this relatively inexperienced performer recognized a class act. If ever a challenge would motivate him, it was England's first Test for 29 years against the country of his birth at the home of cricket. Mine was not to wonder why, although even now I believe it was a huge mistake.

My erratic bowling performance at Old Trafford had attracted the attention of a former Yorkshire and England fast bowler. Fred Trueman, it was reported, had met me on Shipley golf course and asked, in that tactful way Yorkies have, 'Who told you to bowl that rubbish at New Zealand in the second innings?'

'I was trying to blast them out.'

'Blast them out, blast them out? Your job is to bowl them out. In future, don't listen to them, I'll tell you what to do.'

That was Fred's version anyway. I was learning that these old-timers have selective memories. Whether that's simply old age or just a long-standing, one-eyed view of life, it's hard to say. It's probably the first time Fred thought he could save my career; unfortunately, it wasn't the last.

I'll never forget my first Lord's Test. The occasion was littered with mistakes and gaffes, most of them from Englishmen. What's generally forgotten in all the controversy is that England got absolutely stuffed. Our skipper cleverly managed to divert attention away from our humiliation by an act of the grossest stupidity. His 'dirt-in-the-pocket' antics were front-page news for a week, apparently threatening the Empire, and they almost cost him the England captaincy. An unbiased view from an England bowler is that Athers wasn't cheating, just keeping one side of the ball dry for me and Ian Salisbury. I'm not excusing him totally. Using dirt to keep his hands dry is probably the daftest thing anyone has ever done on a cricket field, other than U.A.E. captain Zarawani emerging in a floppy hat to face Allan Donald in the 1996 World Cup. The biggest question regarding the 'dirt-in-the-pocket' incident is still unanswered: how could the best-educated man in the side have behaved like a village idiot?

The Test did not go well for Athers from the moment Kepler Wessels called correctly and decided to bat. Goochie took a great running catch to dismiss Hudson early on off my bowling, but the rest of the first day was hard work. My slower ball did for Peter Kirsten. Eventually at the end of the day I removed Wessels after he had scored his century. I finished with another four-wicket haul, the first of many at Lord's. That's one wicket short of getting my name on the famous Lord's bowling honours board. Now we are well into the next millennium, and my name has still not appeared. The South African tail wagged, but the wicket looked good. The tourists' 357 looked a few too many. Soon it was many too many as we were bowled out for 180, with Donald wasting no time in getting his name on that board with 5–74. Our batting was dismal. Hickie top-scored with 38, and nobody else got past 20. When we weren't struggling with Donald's pace, it was Fanie de Villiers's swing that had us floundering. Only some brave hitting from Daffy prevented the follow-on that Saturday morning.

England's cricketers weren't the only ones under pressure from the new South Africa. The Lord's doormen and officials enjoyed some initial success, at least briefly. The Archbishop of Cape Town, Desmond Tutu, has one of the most famous and recognizable faces in the world. Unfortunately, there was no jacket underneath it, which made the Lord's pavilion as accessible to him as the 'whites-only' beaches and hotels had been in the old South Africa. The free world may have rejoiced at the end of the apartheid system, but the unveiling of the new South African flag, hailing the Rainbow Nation, on the tourists' balcony was contrary to M.C.C. regulations. The South Africans were requested to remove it after the first day, but I couldn't blame them when it reappeared during South Africa's victory celebrations on Sunday night.

Back to the events of the Saturday. There was no hiding the fact that we were in the mire that third afternoon. The tourists were piling on the runs. Salisbury and I were bowling, trying to keep one side of the ball dry and the other as shiny as possible; Sals wanted it dry and I was looking for reverse swing. The first hint of trouble came when coach Keith Fletcher sent out a message to Athers, telling him to come straight to the dressing-room at tea because there was a ball-tampering fuss. I remember Goochie giving us the wisdom of his years: 'It must be them. This ball's doing absolutely ★★★★ all.' I looked up at the South African balcony where coach Mike Procter was waving his arms, obviously upset about something. After tea, I kept bowling and South Africa kept scoring runs. By the close, the tourists had an overall lead of 372, with six wickets and two days left. On top of that, it was now clear that it was Athers who was in trouble because of TV pictures, and he had to face the match referee, Australian Peter Burge. I still didn't know exactly what the fuss was about, but I have to confess that I laughed out loud when I saw the pictures. They had to have more on him than that. Here was a batsman who knew nothing about reverse swing trying to dry one side of the ball with dirt. We all thought it was a bit of a joke. Athers met Burge, explained what he'd been doing and the word on Saturday night was that the matter was closed. The umpires were satisfied that the condition of the ball had not been altered. And if Athers had tried anything, he had certainly failed. The ball wasn't swinging round corners or the opposition's bats.

Next morning our skipper led us out down the pavilion steps with his hands in his pockets. Typical Atherton. Unfortunately for him, the fun and games was just beginning. The joking soon stopped. The incident was developing into a supposed major sporting scandal, like match-fixing or drug-taking. All the while, England were going down the pan. It emerged that, although Athers told Illy he kept dirt in his trouser-pocket, our skipper had been more economical with the truth when questioned by the match referee. Burge was furious when he found out and wanted to throw the book at him. The rest of that Sunday degenerated into the usual behind-the-scenes discussions, cobbled-together statements and kangaroo-court justice. Fair enough, the matter had to be sorted out. But not then, when England were fighting to stay in the Test and Athers was key to any rearguard batting action.

Athers was on the field until lunch-time, when Wessels declared, setting us an impossible 456 to win. Athers returned to the dressing-room to find that Illy and others had been deciding his future for him. Not for the first – or last – time, our chairman should have been shown the dressing-room door. This was a serious distraction. My figures at lunch were 4–46, including hitting the stumps three times, and I was ready for a final burst that would take me on to that honours board. I didn't make it. Wessels declared. At the same time, even my inexperienced eye could see that something serious was going on with the men in suits and blazers; you would have to have been blind to have missed it. This was not the preparation or atmosphere conducive to an England fight-back. So it proved. All the South African quicks chipped in and England were dismissed for 99 and defeated by 356 runs.

The drama was far from over. Athers was presented to the media on a plate as Illy revealed that the England captain had been fined two lots of £1,000, one for not telling the whole truth to the match referee and the other for having dirt in his pocket. Our captain read out a prepared statement; it was not his work and he was far from happy. I couldn't blame Athers. The huge Test defeat was bad enough. His bosses showed little sensitivity to his or England's position all through the day as Illy tried to resolve the matter quickly. Fat chance of that. I'm afraid that's the English way of doing things. Priorities are all wrong. Why disturb everyone during the game instead of waiting? The 'dirt-in-the-pocket' affair was a matter that needed to be examined in the cool light of day, with lashings of common sense, rather than in the emotionally charged atmosphere of a Lord's Test going belly-up. The English always get these incidents arse-about-face. The scandal rumbled on all week. You'd have thought Athers had been caught short-changing the Queen Mum, such was the trumpeting of the pompous editorials, and an apparent threat to the very fabric of the nation.

I didn't know Athers that well then, but I thought he handled the whole nonsense really well. After spending a few days in the Lake District, Athers decided to continue as captain, although it took a long time for some of the scars to heal. When I'm asked, 'Was he guilty?' I reply, 'Guilty of what?' Athers was certainly guilty of being daft, but that's all. If he'd been up to anything dodgy, I hope he would taken slightly more care to be discreet and have kept out of sight of the prying TV cameras. Bowlers are taught the tricks of the trade on first entering club cricket. Lip-salve, Vaseline, gel, chewing-gum, sugar sweets – all are used to keep the shine on the ball. It's a closed book to batsmen, as Athers so perfectly demonstrated that afternoon. You would have thought the England captain had taken a bottle-top out of his pocket and scarred one side of ball, such was the scale of public indignation. It wasn't my call. I hoped Athers would carry on because it was an innocent act, and naïve and stupid, which is what Mark Waugh and Shane Warne said in 1998 about taking money in 1994 from a bookie for information. It did bring home to me what being in the sporting spotlight means . . . and the status of the England captain.

Athers may have been hit badly in the pocket that Sunday night. I didn't escape, either. In my case it was in the arm and it was a lot more painful. At the moment of defeat, I was in the casualty department of St Mary's Hospital after a short delivery from Donald smashed into my right forearm. I was sure it was broken. 'Rooster' almost had to drag me off. I knew I wouldn't be coming back. I was fuming and didn't say a word as I made my way back to the dressing-room. Once there, I got hold of a piece of paper, scribbled a couple of words down and put it in my coffin. The doctor was astonished when the X-ray revealed no break. I was just relieved that my season was not ended.

I proved my fitness in the televised Sunday League game at Durham University. Our physio Wayne had written 'no pain, no gain' on protective plaster. That was for public consumption. What had not been was that note in my cricket coffin. Yet there it was in the *News of the World* for all to see. How it got there, I still don't know. 'Donald Dies' had been my way of marking the event. It was a private memo. I'd done it before, ever since I was hit by a cricket ball as a youngster. It wasn't to be taken literally – it was my way of saying that I owed Donald one; his name was in the book and would remain there until revenge had been exacted. It's still there.

One that's been ticked off is that of Pakistan opener Wajahatullah Wasti. England went to Lahore as part of our 1999 World Cup preparation. Wasti took part in one of our practice matches and he got right up my nose. He behaved as if we were there for his benefit, not the other way round, strutting around as if he was Viv Richards. My response was: 'You're in the book. I'll have you one day.' My chance came on our winter tour to Pakistan in 2000. Wasti was opening the batting for the Governor's XI in Peshawar. I broke his hand in the third over of the match and he wasn't seen again on the cricket field.

I always remember. It's not a hatred thing. I have the highest respect for Allan Donald. He's a brilliant bowler and good bloke. Maybe it's a Yorkie thing. When I started at Yorkshire, I was told a story about Imran Khan, playing for Sussex, giving 16-year-old Jarvo a torrid time, bouncing him and hitting him a few times. Four years later, Jarvo paid him back. That's the way we Yorkies are. It's just another part of the battle.

Surely that Lord's weekend couldn't get any worse. It did. Richie Richardson had decided to go home midway through his second summer with Yorkshire. Nobody was surprised. He'd been struggling all summer to focus on the cricket. The demands of the international schedule had wiped him out. Richie began to think he was losing it and even started wearing a helmet. Several times that summer we had to wake him up to go out to bat, that's how exhausted he was. I was sorry to see him go, but it was the right thing for him to do. Yorkshire were the last county to go for an overseas player, but we struck gold with Richie. I benefited more than most. I doubt I would have been anywhere near the England team at this stage without his influence and advice. My farewells included a promise to give him a hard time when he came back next summer with the West Indies.

Lord's was my first defeat in an England shirt. All the England players were hacked off at having to turn up at St John's Wood on the Monday morning for a combined photograph with the South Africans to mark this historic Test. My pride, as well as my arm, was hurt and I wasn't too keen on smiling for the camera alongside the beaming South Africans. Fortunately, my car was an automatic. As I headed up the M1, I took a more rational view of the events of the past four days. We'd got thumped. There was no escaping that. But I'd done my job, taken eight wickets and twice been one wicket away from appearing on that Lord's honours board. There was plenty of time ahead. Provided my arm recovered, the next Test would be my first on home soil at Headingley, where a year earlier I'd first entered an England dressing-room as the home-based twelfth man.

A second X-ray cleared me to play. The weekend before the Test I could move my fingers but still could not clench my fist. I was as keen to play as the Yorkshire public were to have me play. Amazingly, the last current White Rose players to have appeared in a Headingley Test were Geoff Boycott and Chris Old, during Ian Botham's Ashes game of 1981. My picture and story were everywhere. Even Botham had a message for the England selectors about me. 'Don't destroy Gough, as you did Devon Malcolm.' The great man went on to write that he liked my attitude. The feeling was mutual. For a whole generation of youngsters, Botham was the sporting hero. Match referee Burge also had a public message for Athers. It sounded more like a warning: 'The whole world is watching you.' Our skipper had the full support of the team. Former cricketers were more divided on the matter. The BBC's cricket correspondent, Jonathan Agnew, called on Athers to go. This stubborn Lancastrian responded in the only way he knows. Athers won the toss, decided to bat, came back to a standing ovation after a gutsy 99 and then got himself in more hot water by claiming that that was the best response to the 'gutter press'.

Athers was not the only England batter with a point to prove. Thorpey was given his chance at last after a summer on the sidelines. Stewie was not happy at being shunted down the order to accommodate Goochie as Athers's partner. The Surrey pair made 72 and 89 respectively, so England were in good shape at 394–7 when I made my way out on the second afternoon to join fellow Yorkshireman 'Bumpy' Rhodes. First home Test, first current Yorkshireman for 13 years and a fantastic welcome from the Yorkshire crowd. I was on cloud nine as I reached the wicket. Unfortunately, the one person who was looking for me was the one with the ball in his hand at the other end of the ground. It's called Sod's Law, I think. As luck would have it, Allan Donald – of 'Donald Dies' fame – happened to be the South African bowler who had knocked Daffy's poles over. Deep breath, Dazzler. Smile and look aggressive. The first delivery would be short, I was sure. Be brave, don't duck. It *was* short, but not as short as I had expected. I knew that retribution would be swift when my pull shot sped to the boundary in front of square. Yet I was not prepared for what happened next. One of the advantages of receiving the quickest ball you've ever faced, or are ever likely to face, is that there's no time to engage the brain. Fortunately the moment was captured for posterity, in one of my favourite cricket pictures. I claim now that I'm still bravely behind the ball. The truth is, I had no time to get out of the way. It kept rising on me like some heat-seeking missile. By the time it had gone past, I was a couple of feet off the ground, my head contorted back as I tried to avoid the ball, which kept going, over the wicket-keeper's head and one bounce into the Headingley boards. 'Donald dies.' Not this time. It was the picture of the day and my discomfort was all over the next day's morning papers. The Yorkies had the last laugh, though. Donald could not keep up the barrage because of an infected toe. Bumpy and I had great fun adding over 50 runs for the eighth wicket before he ran me out.

South Africa recovered from 105–5 to get within 30 runs of

England. I bowled quickly, but was expensive and rather wayward. The complaints that first surfaced at Old Trafford reappeared. Was Darren Gough getting carried away by all the razzmatazz of the international scene? Did the influence of his Headingley home crowd make it worse? South Africa, down and out, recovered. It must be bad bowling, not good batting. I charged in that second evening, had Hudson caught in the slips and could have had another wicket. One of the problems is the public perception of Headingley as bowler-friendly because of the conditions and the pitch. I can assure you it's not. For a start it slopes. Bowling uphill, you go round the park if your length is not right. Bowling downhill, you can bowl short and a lot of no-balls. Even now, with all my experience and knowledge, there are days when I don't get it right. That 1994 South African Test was one of them. My final figures were 2–153 in 37 overs – Donald's were 1–135 in 29. I must admit I was beginning to run out of steam. After four summers trying to establish myself in the Yorkshire side, my sporting world had been turned around in the last ten weeks. Adrenalin can fuel you for only so long. I had bowled a lot of pressure overs in a short space of time. Remember, I had never played a full county season for Yorkshire. I'm not making excuses. My job is to take wickets. Wickets or no wickets, I go for runs. When I start to go for runs, I don't try to drag it back by bowling within myself. Appearing on my home ground was also a factor. Charging in a little too fast and losing rhythm is a problem of mine. I did bowl quick. I hit Peter Kirsten, who went on to make his maiden Test century at 39, on the head. He dropped like a stone. I thought I'd killed him, but he dusted himself down and carried on, with more than a little help from the South African tail.

I was wicketless in South Africa's second innings as the match drifted towards a draw. It was then Athers told me to give Cronje a real working-over. The South African skipper did not like the rough stuff and kept backing away. It was a useful exercise and was to pay dividends when Devon was brought back at the Oval. I was disappointed by events at Headingley, but was not down. Inevitably I was going to come down to earth at some time. I took two wickets, both front-line batsmen, and scored some runs. It just wasn't as spectacular as my other two appearances. England cricket has a habit of getting ahead of itself. The series with South Africa wasn't over, but all the talk was of the Ashes tour to Australia. I knew I'd be going. Even if I wasn't part of the starting XI, I'd go as the up-and-coming bowler.

The final Test at the Oval has gone into the history books as Malcolm's Match. His 9–57 is one of the most sustained pieces of fast bowling I've seen. Yet that was only one of many incidents in a remarkable encounter that saw England crush South Africa and level the series. Jonty Rhodes was taken to hospital after Devon hit him on the helmet. Devon was also hit, Athers got in trouble with the match referee and was fined for dissent, and so was Fanie de Villiers; both teams were fined for the slow over-rate in a Test where runs came at four an over and a wicket fell every 48 deliveries, and Goochie had an amazing Saturday. Me? I took only one wicket in the match, but it was enough to deny Devon's chance of taking all ten.

On Friday evening, Daffy and I played a major role in turning the Test England's way. South Africa must have thought the series was saved when I went out to join Daffy, half an hour before the close. Wessels had decided to bat and England were struggling at 222–7 in reply to the tourists' 332. Don't ask me why, but Daffy and I decided to have a slog and a laugh. 'Let's have a bit of Old Trafford. See who can hit the most boundaries.' I can't quite explain what caused our mood. The sun was out and Donald was unable to bowl because of his toe problem. Those final 30 minutes brought 59 runs, and South Africa's advantage was reduced to 51 runs. We blasted the ball everywhere. Wessels didn't appear too happy with Donald, and the tourists were rattled. Rhodes had been taken to the neurosurgery department of the Maudsley Hospital; his epilepsy condition makes any blow to the head potentially fatal. Rhodes was given the all-clear but was kept in on Thursday night and did not return to the fray until South Africa were seven wickets down on Saturday. Donald's foot problems eventually required an operation, but Wessels felt that A.D. was not digging deep enough. Not for the first time, the South Africans were in danger of letting another series slip from their grasp.

Daffy and I came off to a great ovation. Illy felt that it turned the match: 'That Friday night was the most aggressive display I've ever seen. Gough and DeFreitas started our revival. They do not like blocking and I was happy for them not to try.' Our dressing-room was really buzzing, but the mood changed when Athers was hauled in front of Burge again, this time for dissent. Umpire Ken Palmer had adjudged him l.b.w. to his first ball. Athers's body-language suggested that he thought the ball had hit his bat first. Palmer did not complain, but Athers had been in Burge's sights since Lord's. Another fine, this time £1,250, half his match fee. When we were all docked another 30 per cent for the slow over-rate, Athers declared: 'It's been an expensive series. I'm playing for the love and honour of the game at the moment.' I was glad he was able to joke about it, but on Saturday morning we had serious worries about our skipper. Illy had made no secret of the fact that Mike Gatting was his ready-made replacement if Athers chose to quit. Gatt had been in the Oval dressing-room as cover for Goochie. At a time when Athers was out of the dressing-room on the Saturday morning it was Goochie who brought us together. He reminded us of the pressure Athers had been under all through the series. This was the time for us to go out and show him what he meant to us.

We got to within 28 runs of South Africa. I finished with 42 not out, but the key moment came when Devon was smacked on the helmet by de Villiers. The popular myth is that Devon announced, 'You guys are history', as he picked himself up. Far be it from me to dent the legend, but I don't remember him saying anything. I was up at the other end. I'm not denying that Devon wasn't fired up when he got knocked over, but he didn't need any words; that look was more than enough. A few balls later, I reminded him I was after a 50. Could he just block the final delivery of the over? No worries. No traditional block, however. He tried to hit Craig Matthews for six and was caught. I could only smile. Devon has stranded batsmen far more talented and important than me. Devon was not enjoying his Test recall up to that point. Athers had given him a right rollocking for not following orders in the first innings. The skipper wanted it fast and short as South Africa struggled at 136–5 (effectively six, with Rhodes in hospital), with Brian McMillan and Dave Richardson at the wicket. The pair almost doubled the tourists' total. Athers was fuming. 'When I tell you to do something, do it.' But that was always the problem with Devon. Goochie reckoned the secret with Devon was to tell him to do the opposite of what you actually wanted. Part of the problem was that Devon's such a nice guy, so getting him fired up was one of the toughest jobs in cricket. Luckily for England and for Athers, the South Africans, and de Villiers in particular, hit the right buttons that Saturday.

Athers gave the first over to Daffy, so the fireworks didn't start until the second! Devon was on fire. I'm someone who likes to be in the middle of things, but I was an enthralled spectator for most of that day. South Africa lost three wickets for one run. Devon caught and bowled Gary Kirsten, had his half-brother Peter caught at fine leg and rattled Cronje's stumps. The tourists recovered to 73–3, then 137–4. We were back in the game but were by no means favourites by this stage, as South Africa led by 165 runs. Another four-wicket spurt by Devon evened things up at 143–7 with Cullinan and Rhodes at the wicket. Although his pace was lightning and the South Africans did not fancy the fight, Athers was aware that a few wayward overs from Devon could cost us the game. The final three wickets fell on 175. First to go was Cullinan, who had held the innings together with a spirited 94. It was my first success of the match, the edge being taken by Thorpey at second slip. A cheer went round the Oval, then I sensed the crowd's disappointment at the realization that Devon's chance of all ten had gone. He still mentions it every time I see him. I felt no sense of guilt or dismay. It was a Test wicket, a vital one. England needed the breakthrough. South Africa were over 200 ahead, always a difficult target in the final innings. Anyway, as Cullinan wandered off, I fancied taking two more, but Devon was not to be denied. Rhodes and Donald were sent packing and our fast bowler left the field to a standing ovation and the sixth-best Test bowling analysis of all time.

With about an hour left, I expected us to see out time carefully with no mishaps. I reckoned without Goochie. After his double century in the first Test against the Kiwis, our veteran batsman had struggled to put together a big score. He was unhappy batting at No. 5 in the Lord's Test, then he failed to build on two starts at Headingley. Another low score at the Oval, and he was beginning to wonder about the likelihood of another Ashes tour. The final straw came when he put down a catch on the boundary that Saturday.

Goochie went out to bat with all guns blazing. When he was bowled by Matthews for 33 after five overs, our score was 56. The South Africans had been demoralized. Athers and Hickie caught the mood. By the close, we were more than half way there and the contest was over. Victory was clinched before lunch on Sunday. Devon was Man of the Match – who else? – and, despite only one appearance, was chosen as Man of the Series. On the Saturday he was unrecognizable as the bowler who had merely trundled in on the Thursday. I could understand his captain's frustration. Saturday showed Devon at his very best: quick, short and bowling at the speed of light. That's all his skipper ever wanted him to do. I certainly was looking forward to forming a partnership with him. With Devon bowling that quick, batsmen were going to be happier facing me and playing a few shots. Easy pickings. It didn't happen.

South Africa's disappointment was evident in the Texaco series, which we won with two relatively easy victories, batting second at Edgbaston and Old Trafford. The Ashes squad was announced during our county game with Derbyshire at Sheffield. A year earlier, I had been astonished to given an 'A' tour chance. Now I expected an Ashes tour. My abiding memory of that morning was arriving at the ground, walking out to the middle where Corkie was lying on a wicket. 'You're going to Australia. I've got to go to India and Bangladesh, you lucky so-and-so.' Corkie was distraught. I finished the season in some style, taking 6–66 against Surrey, including a 5–5 spell in 29 deliveries, in the championship game at Scarborough. Revenge was sweet for them in the Sunday League match, when they hit a record 375–4 in 40 overs and won by 205

runs. The final word was mine in the last Sunday game, against
Sussex at Hove. I took my first one-day five-wicket haul – 5–13 –
on my 24th birthday. I had plenty to celebrate.

8. Fasten Your Seatbelts

An Ashes tour. It had been my dream since Ian Botham's heroics in 1981 and now it was a dream come true. Australia are the enemy, *the* team to play against. It's also a fabulous country to visit. I'm sure England commands the same spot in an Aussie youngster's ambitions. Sport is about timing. Quite right; it was just the luck of the draw that the Ashes tour was the carrot at the end of my first international summer. Australia had been on my agenda since coming back from the 'A' tour. The downside was that I also knew all summer that my selection would cost me the chance of being present at the birth of our first child. Anna had slight complications before I left. There was a chance I might have to delay my departure. There was never any discussion about not going. The last thing Anna would have wanted for the final weeks of her pregnancy was me prowling round the house, trying to come to terms with missing an Ashes tour.

I was determined to enjoy Australia. And I did. The Ashes battle was everything I thought it would be. I was heartbroken at having to fly home before it finished, but my foot injury gave me no option. The tour marked the start of several long-standing relationships. Before the trip I was approached by the *News of the World* to write a weekly diary. I've been with them ever since. 'Darren's Diary' became a big favourite back home that winter, at least in Monk Bretton. Just before my injury, the paper's cricket correspondent, David Norrie, fixed up a lunch with Shane Warne, and we've been good mates ever since. Norrie also arranged for me to interview Harold Larwood of 'Bodyline' fame in his Sydney home, and that was an afternoon I'll never forget.

My Ashes dream started on the flight, when I found myself sandwiched in between two cricket legends, Goochie and Gatting. I think I was due the aisle seat, but I showed respect and wasn't going to argue. One drank white wine and the other red. I was looking forward to a bit of a chat but, after a few glasses, they both nodded off and I was left, stuck in the middle. I managed to squeeze out and chat to the others. The lads had a good laugh at my expense when I took a sleeping tablet on the second leg of the flight. I assumed those pills sent you to sleep. I was waiting to pass out, rather than trying to go to sleep.

I wasn't ready for the welcome at Perth Airport. The flashing lights and TV cameras were something I hadn't experienced before. This Ashes stuff was serious business out there. I don't think it was because the Australian media had gained advance information of my award as Yorkshire's Sporting Personality of the Year. Well, not quite.

The Lilac Hill opener gave me a chance to face some Aussie legends – Dennis Lillee, Jeff Thomson and Greg Chappell. My 5–32 included Chappell, as well as Ricky Ponting and Tom Moody, but the highlight was watching D.K. (Lillee) bowl. His run-up was shorter now and the deliveries slower, but his action was still awesome. I ran in hard, as much to impress those former Aussie stars as our management. I was a new name in the England team and the home spectators wanted to see what I was made of. I went out to show them that Darren Gough was a competitive cricketer who was going to cause them problems.

The big incident of our stay in Perth passed me by. Phil Tufnell's personal problems had been well publicized during the summer, and there must have been doubts in the selectors' minds about bringing him. When Tuffers was admitted to a psychiatric ward in Perth, it looked all over, but he discharged himself. I roomed with him a couple of weeks later. He was still tense. I remember him coming in one night and thumping and kicking the telly. I was still a junior player while Tuffers was on his fifth tour. He was obviously struggling and I felt for him, but there was little I could offer in the way of help or advice.

We had four games before the first Test in Brisbane. I might have been confident about my tour place, but I was less certain of a Test spot. My form had dipped at the end of the summer and I wasn't too happy to miss the Western Australia game on the famous WACA wicket. My first opportunity came on the famously batsman-friendly Adelaide strip. I needed to perform. South Australia were bowled out for 102 after collapsing to 21–6. I missed out. No wickets. I wasn't used to waiting so long to get off the mark. My first wicket came at the start of S.A.'s second dig, when I had Greg Blewett caught behind. I collected five wickets in all as we won with two overs to spare. We travelled to Newcastle, up the coast from Sydney, for the N.S.W. clash. Again the Gough name was missing. My situation was now clear. Either I was definitely in and was being looked after . . . or I wasn't going to play. I wasn't completely sure at this stage which scenario was more likely.

The Ashes series was not uppermost in my mind when I found myself struggling in the Newcastle surf. Afterwards, the rest of the lads joked that this was my way of grabbing attention because I wasn't playing. Sky and Tetley, our sponsors, wanted some beach shots. Being a show-off, I grabbed a surfboard and paddled out. The fact that I couldn't surf seemed only a minor drawback to me. I'd been warned about the 'rip' – a swirl that you can't move out of – but I've always been a good swimmer, which was just as well. I never expected to get into trouble. What probably saved me when I did was that I didn't panic – I didn't even lose my Tetley's Bitter cap. Fancy being worried about the team sponsors when your life's in danger! My lack of surfing expertise was obvious as I kept falling off. What I didn't realize was that I was drifting further and further out. I tried to get back but got stuck in the rip. I should have abandoned the surfboard. It was only when I reached the shore once more that I realized how exhausted I was. One of the lifeguards had come out and asked if I was okay. Being a stubborn bugger and not wishing to give the Aussies an inch, I replied that I was okay; no problem. So he moved on to the next silly sod having problems. Then Richard Moore, the Tetley representative, arrived. The time had come to be more honest. 'How the hell do I get out of this, Richard?' He took the board and told me to swim sideways out of it. When I'd done that, I had to swim back to the beach. I could hardly stand, let alone speak, and all these cameras were shoved in my face. It caused quite a stir, and my dad heard about it on the radio. I had been in danger and found the experience frightening, but I wasn't about to drown. I'm not sure what would have happened if Richard hadn't appeared. I can't believe now that I was too macho to refuse help from the Aussie lifeguard. The sea holds little attraction for me now, and I'm still rather wary.

Newcastle was an interesting stop. While there I also met an English bloke from Birmingham who'd been under police protection as he was a key witness in the Australian 'Backpackers' trial. Ivan, the man accused, had pulled a gun on him, but he escaped. Ivan was eventually convicted of several murders. Australia's a great place for bumping into interesting people, famous or otherwise. One night in Sydney, we shared a taxi with a grey-haired Aussie who was making for a restaurant near ours. He talked to us about his house in Hertfordshire. He didn't introduce himself, but the cabbie told us that he was Alan Bond, the successful businessman who won the America's Cup for Australia, bought Van Gogh's 'Irises' for almost £30 million, went bankrupt and, since we saw him, served time.

Goochie and I drove down to Sydney for the flight to Hobart and stopped off at Harold Larwood's. David Norrie had rung the great man up from Newcastle to arrange the meeting. His daughter Enid came to the door, warned us that Harold was a little frail – hardly surprising for someone who had just celebrated his 90th birthday – and that he didn't like talking about the infamous 1932/3 'Bodyline' series. He didn't like the word 'bodyline', that was for sure. I got a real telling-off. 'Leg theory' was the politically correct phrase in the Larwood household. But the 1932/3 series off-limits? No way! You couldn't stop him talking about it. It was fascinating. Harold showed me his cuttings book. The Aussies gave him countless nicknames – 'Larwood the Wrecker', 'Larwood the Killer', 'The Silent Killer' and, my favourite, 'Murder on Tip Toe'. There was a letter addressed to 'The Hangman's name is Larwood'. I couldn't get over how tiny he was, or how proud he was, even now. He pointed to his favourite series of pictures. 'I only hit Bradman the once. Do you know where it was? Ribs? No. There it is. On his arse, as he turns away.' Harold took 33 wickets in that series at 19.52 – 16 clean-bowled – and a wicket every 40 deliveries. He never played for England after that tour. Dragged into Lord's and told to apologize, Larwood refused and retired from international cricket. There was time for just one more daft question before I left, when I asked if he ever pitched it up with four short legs and two men back on the leg side. 'Did I what? Pitch it up with a leg-theory field? Never.' I took my leave, and Harold Larwood's last words are still with me: 'Darren, never give the Aussies an inch.' His daughter sent me a video of our visit, and I was to hear from Harold again during the Sydney Test.

We looked anything like Ashes contenders at Hobart, being forced to follow on against Australia's second string. I've always found that a misleading description. The batting line-up was Hayden, Blewett, Langer, Martyn, Ponting and Law – four of them appeared against the West Indies in the winter 2000 series. I bowled too short and too wide, going for four an over, McCague almost five. Fletcher called our batting 'pathetic' as Merv Hughes took 4–51. Merv and I had been engaged by the series sponsors, Benson & Hedges, to appear, wearing all the new gear, in promotional pictures and at the launch. I told the audience that I was looking forward to bouncing Merv and was happy for him to bounce me. Merv told me, 'I have to get in the team first.' He'd been out of the Aussie team for a while and he felt this was his last chance. He bowled well at Hobart but pulled up, injured, and never played for Australia again. It was great to take him on, even socially.

Our Ashes preparation soon went the same way as Merv's. Devon went down with chicken-pox three days before the Test, and from London Illy started a war of words with the captain. You could put both events down to acts of God, but the Illy outburst was totally unnecessary. All the papers reported Illy's comments at a sports writers' lunch in London. The general gist was that Illy had saved Athers's job after the 'dirt-in-the-pocket' incident and our skipper had not even had the decency to call the chairman and thank him. Athers decided he had enough on his plate without responding to this. Our physio also found himself busy. 'Rooster' rushed round the squad to find out who'd already had chicken-pox. I had to ring home to find out that I had. That night, a group of us went to see singer/songwriter Billy Joel. The lads were only trying to educate me, pointing out he hadn't written 'A Hard Day's Night'. Really. Who did? The England squad spent the next evening with the Aussies at Pier Nine to launch the Ashes series. Only two days to go.

McCague was Devon's replacement. I wasn't sure about this. Ever since my experience in South Africa the previous winter, it seemed obvious that someone with influence thought he could bowl. I couldn't see why he was selected for this tour ahead of Gussie, who was left at home. Joey Benjamin, who had made his debut at the Oval and had taken four South African wickets in the first innings, would have been my choice for Brisbane. Gussie had been called up from Sydney as cover for Devon; but Athers was instructed by Illy that he could not pick him ahead of an original selection. I couldn't argue with that. McCague had been nowhere and wasn't bowling well on the trip. No one liked his attitude, and our fears were proved correct during that Brisbane Test. No one could work him out. He liked a beer and wasn't keen on working on his fitness. During the Test, one morning McCague turned up, complaining of food poisoning, and couldn't bowl. We knew he'd been out late the night before and weren't too impressed. McCague didn't bowl at all in Australia's second dig. He lost a lot of respect that day, and the lads weren't too sorry when he went home with a stress fracture of the shin. Our physio 'Rooster' joked that there was no stress fracture; he'd drawn it on the X-ray himself. The Aussies knew all about him and they laid into him. They were trying to expose a weakness. They were right. McCague couldn't take it.

I must confess I was slightly distracted when I made my Ashes debut. Anna had told me the night before that she was going into the hospital the next day for a check-up. Actually, she was already in there getting ready for the delivery. At half past seven the next morning Daffy passed me the phone.

'Hello.'

'Hello.'

'I've had it.'

'What?'

'Is that all you can say?'

'Well, I didn't even know you were in hospital.'

I already knew it was a boy; the doctor had let me know after the scan because I was going to be away. Liam had arrived at 4 a.m. Aussie time, but Anna had waited. He weighed in at 7 lb. 11 oz. with light-brown hair. My mum, who's a midwife, was there, along with Anna's mum Margaret and sister Lyn. I spent that first day convinced his birthday was 25 November, until someone pointed out that we were 11 hours ahead of England, so Liam had actually arrived on 24 November! Another story going the rounds that day was that Liam's middle names were going to be the Christian names of the Aussie batsmen I dismissed on the opening day of the Ashes series. Had that been the case, it was just as well that Warnie, who edged one to our keeper, didn't join David Boon and Michael Bevan as my first-day victims. I've never celebrated a wicket as much as when I bowled Boon. My first Ashes wicket. A great feeling, especially as it was Boon, whom I came to respect. There was no tougher competitor, but a nice bloke. No sledging from him at short-square, just the stare – and that could be just as intimidating.

I got my first sight of Liam on the third night of the Test when it came through on a computer belonging to Graham Morris, one of the English photographers. This proud dad toasted the new arrival that night. I just wish England had enjoyed a better first day of the series. We were always coming second after the first four overs from Daffy and McCague went for 26 runs. Australia finished well past 300 for the loss of four wickets, with Michael Slater scoring 176. We were in dire straits the second evening, with six wickets down for 133. Craig McDermott and Shane Warne finished the job on the third morning. I remained undefeated after clubbing a couple of sixes off McDermott. England were 259 runs adrift. Athers was sure Taylor would enforce the follow-on and was waiting, padded up. He didn't. Taylor set our victory target at 508. Just as daunting was our survival time of 11 hours. Hick and Thorpe gave us hope with a day to go. I livened up Channel 9's pitch report by doing a handstand behind Tony Greig. I didn't think they'd use it. They did. Warnie's 8–71 finished the job with plenty to spare. Not the first Ashes Test finish I'd imagined. For the fourth Ashes series in a row, England had lost the opening Test. In the other three, it had been the first two Tests.

We had little chance of regrouping because of the crazy itinerary which twice scheduled one-day matches in the middle of the Test series, after the first and third Tests. Who agrees to this nonsense? What was more insulting was the inclusion of Aussie 'A', as well as Aussie and Zimbabwe, in the one-day tournament. The final served them right: the home fans had to make do with watching the Aussies playing against themselves. Not that we were covering ourselves in glory. After losing our opener against Australia, we went down twice in a single weekend to the Australian Cricket Academy – fortunately I had a slight hamstring strain – and then to Zimbabwe in Sydney. I got 5–44 that night and wrote my name on the board in our dressing-room to make up for my Lord's blank. I didn't play at Toowoomba, where Gatt hit a double-hundred before being hit in the mouth while fielding. Our physio ordered him not to eat that night, but we spotted a couple of empty pizza boxes outside his room. Gatt claimed he'd been framed. That was rich. I remember asking him directions in Sydney. 'Easy. It's right at the Italian, left at the Curry House and just beyond the Chinese.'

All that was outside Fletcher's door was a huge pile of faxes. The *Sun* had kindly printed our hotel number after those two defeats by the Cricket Academy and asked readers to let Fletcher know what they thought of us. We knew what the paper thought. Fletcher was on the back page with a huge pair of rabbit's ears, although they looked more like a kangaroo's. I'm sure Fletcher's wife Sue wasn't too impressed with some of the abusive language. I liked Fletcher. He rated me and encouraged me to play my natural game. Go out and swat it, he said. Fletch was never a big one for actually coaching. He encouraged you and then let you get on with it. I played golf a lot with him that trip. Him and Dave Roberts. Fletcher batted and bowled every ball in the dressing-room, while drinking umpteen cups of tea. He was the eventual scapegoat for this Ashes failure – which was rather unfair, considering the selectors sowed most of the seeds of our destruction and we did the rest. Fletcher was only half way through a five-year contract but was dispensed with after another Lord's crisis summit, a month after we returned. He wasn't able to offer much defence as he was on a ski-ing holiday at the time and was unaware that his future was being decided.

Melbourne's Boxing Day and Sydney's New Year's Tests are two great sporting traditions. The M.C.G. match actually started on Christmas Eve, with a break the next day. The lads were rucking about the disrupted festivities. I wasn't bothered. Most had their families with them, but Anna wasn't due to fly out with Liam until the middle of January. I paid due homage to Anna's American background by wearing an Uncle Sam costume at the traditional Christmas Day fancy-dress party. Actually, I was supposed to be 'Robin' to Daffy's 'Batman', but the costume only came down to my knees. The media entertained us with a topical reworking of 'Amazing Grace' entitled 'Amazing Ray' poking fun at our chairman of selectors, who had flown out for these crunch Tests. The entertainment committee paired me with Stewie for the karaoke, choosing Carly Simon's 'You're So Vain'. Were we being told something? I was in bed by half three in the afternoon. Woke up at seven, ordered a club sandwich and went back to sleep again. I'm always amazed by the celebrities who pop in to see us whenever the England cricket team are in Melbourne, Sydney, Cape Town, Barbados or Antigua. Over the Christmas period I enjoyed a drink with Gary Lineker, not a bad cricketer; I'd played against him when he scored 50 in a charity match in Huddersfield a few years earlier. He wondered if he could get one against me now. No chance, I told him. Stephen Tompkinson, of 'Drop the Dead Donkey' and, later, 'Ballykissangel' fame, is another who loves his cricket and was out in Oz with us.

We'd pegged the Aussies back after Athers put them in on the first day. Devon was back, but a shadow of his Oval self. The contest was still evenly balanced after Boxing Day, although Athers, Thorpey and Hickie all received dodgy decisions. There was a recent statistic that revealed the Aussies get more favourable l.b.w. decisions on home soil than any other country. I can well believe it. Our hopes went belly-up when Goochie hit the first ball of the third morning straight back to McDermott. Warne finished with 6–64, and we were 67 runs short. The luck was certainly going Australia's way. I had David Boon plumb l.b.w., absolutely dead, on nought after dismissing Taylor. I couldn't believe it when Steve Randell's finger didn't go up. Daffy eventually got rid of him the same way. Unfortunately, by that time Boon had 131 runs to his name.

This time England had a small matter of 120 overs to survive in order to hang on for a draw. Unlike Brisbane, there was no hope at the end of the fourth day. We were 79–4 and Stewie was coming in at No. 7 because of a broken finger. The fifth day's play lasted 12.3 overs and produced just 13 runs, as well as a little piece of cricket history. Warnie, wicketless up to that point in our second innings, took the first Ashes hat-trick for over 90 years. Daffy was the first, l.b.w. playing back. Off I set. At 91–7, I'm not sure what my game-plan was. It didn't matter. Warnie got one to turn and bounce. I tried to leave it, but Healy took a great catch as it flew off my glove. As I turned to leave, I suddenly realized what a big ground the M.C.G. is and what a long way back it was. The stupid duck was quacking on the big screen and the crowd were roaring 'Warnie, Warnie,' at the prospect of their favourite son taking a Test hat-trick on his home ground. I suppose there is no better sight for a bowler on a hat-trick than seeing Devon walk out. In golfing terms, it's the nearest thing you can get to a 'gimme'. As Devon passed me, 'Good luck' was all I could think of. He was still fiddling with his thigh pad and gloves. We all knew what was coming – the googly. It had to be. The expected Devon wind-up never came. He pushed forward, the ball hit his glove and Boon took a magnificent catch at short square. The M.C.G. went wild.

'Why didn't you have a go at him, Dev?'

His reply was pure Devon. 'I was going to, but then I thought I'd try and play properly.'

Properly! Can you believe it?

Shane Warne on a hat-trick and Devon Malcolm thinks he can bat!

Australian joy was complete the next over when McDermott had Tuffers caught behind. Defeat by 295 runs, and two down in the Ashes series. Only a win in Sydney could keep us in the hunt for the little urn. This was not how I planned my first senior trip to Australia.

We basked in the reflected glory of some English success in Sydney by going to see *Cats* at Her Majesty's Theatre and then we went on to a special celebrity party. The Aussie team had to leave before midnight, but we waved them goodnight and saw the New Year in. My resolutions were simple: not to lose a Test match to Australia in 1995 or to get out in the middle of a Shane Warne hat-trick. The first resolution looked rather shaky the next morning when we were 20–3. The Lancie lads – Athers and Creepy (John Crawley) – added 174 runs before another collapse: four wickets for four runs. Overnight I was not out, with no runs to my name, blissfully unaware that my cricket life was about to change for ever. Don't ask me why, but I woke up next morning determined to go down fighting. I was padded up and waiting for the start when Mark Nicholas, then of Sky and now of Channel 4 fame, came by. 'Fasten your seatbelts!' was my prediction. I still don't know why I said it. Maybe it was an excuse made in advance for the slogging approach I was about to take.

The next hour was heaven. I swung from the arse . . . and connected. The Aussies got rattled and started moaning at Craig McDermott. 'Bounce him.' He did and that's when I hooked him for six. Then I hit him back over his head. Finally, I pushed a single for my 50 and then gave the crowd that famous lasso salute, swirling the bat around my head. Of course I was carried away. The S.C.G. was full, I'd never heard a noise like it and I'd belted the cream of Australia's bowling to all parts. I was out soon afterwards, caught hooking, but the whole mood of the game had changed. Gussie, now part of the official squad, and even Devon – not playing properly – carried on the fight to take England past 300. Devon even hit Warnie for two sixes. *Wisden* described my efforts as a

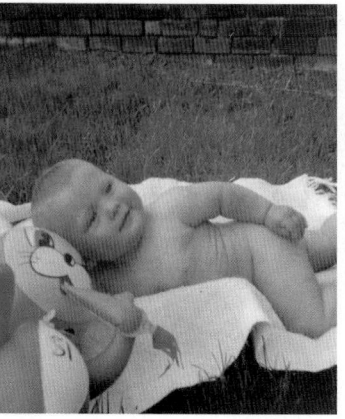

Happy to pose naked for the camera at six months with my first inflatable doll, Bugs Bunny.

The laughing cavalier with sword in hand. Taking a break, lying in my pram in our back garden, aged ten months.

I'm two years old and looking like Jimmy Osmond here, especially in those flares, as I try to hold three puppies.

In a replica No. 10 Spurs shirt and hoping to emulate my hero, Glenn Hoddle.

An early example of my love of rock 'n' roll, dancing with my mum in 1981.

The Barnsley Schools Under-11 cricket side, with my long hair covering my Spock ears.

An Old Master with the Young Pretender. Me with Boycs (Geoff Boycott) at a Monk Bretton awards dinner.

At the helm, aged fifteen, with a new hairstyle and my young-looking dad.

Trying to look the business at the age of eighteen. Where did I get that hat!

My first Christmas away from home. With Corkie in New Zealand in 1990, celebrating with turkey and tomato ketchup.

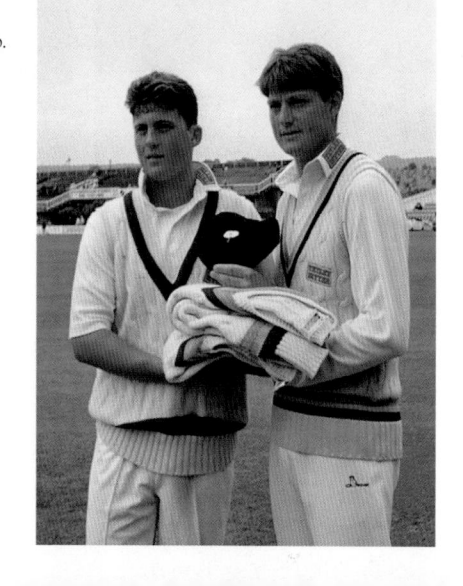

After a long and frustrating apprenticeship, Martyn Moxon presents me with my Yorkshire cap in 1993.

The perfect start to my England career. The world-class Martin Crowe is on his way in my first over.

Celebrating my first Test wicket with the lads at Old Trafford after Mark Greatbatch fended the ball to Graeme Hick.

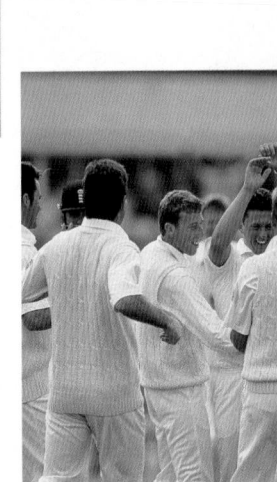

My first Test knock, and still my highest Test score – 65 against the Kiwis at Old Trafford.

Proud to be Yorkshire, proud to be English – showing my colours before my Test début in 1994.

This is what happens to you when you dare to pull Allan Donald to the mid-wicket boundary. A.D. had me hopping at Headingley in 1994.

Merv Hughes and I model the one-day kit at the start of the 1994–5 season. A great lad and a great bowler, fitness ruled Merv out of the series.

The famous surfboard incident at Newcastle, N.S.W. – here I am definitely drowning, not waving.

A special day, a special man: with England's 'Bodyline' hero, Harold Larwood, just after his ninetieth birthday.

The two Fat Boys, but pretty with it. Shane Warne and I hit it off immediately during the 1994–5 Ashes trip and have been mates ever since.

Athers may be holding a full house, but with Illy looking over his shoulder in South Africa on the 1995–6 tour, our skipper was never sure what cards the manager had up his sleeve.

'Fasten your seatbelts.' On my way to 50 at the Sydney Cricket Ground by smashing Craig McDermott for six.

If you want a job done properly, do it yourself. I collect my first five-wicket haul in Tests at the S.C.G. with this caught-and-bowled off the Aussie captain, Mark Taylor.

My Ashes tour ends in tears after collapsing in Melbourne and I'm carried off by physio Dave 'Rooster' Roberts and Shaun Udal.

A week earlier I had been the centre of attention at the S.C.G. Now I'm a sad, solitary figure at Sydney airport, waiting to leave Australia.

Undone by Curtly in spectacular fashion. But the mighty Ambie was the scourge of far better English batsmen than me over the years until his retirement at the end of our 2000 series against the West Indies.

The Keith Arthurton catch in 1995 which put the name of Angus Fraser on the honours board at Lord's.

Victory on the final day at Lord's in 1995 became much more probable when Stewie took a magnificent one-handed catch to remove Brian Lara off me.

The famous Gough 'airplane' after removing my England captain, Mike Atherton, in the NatWest quarter-final at Headingley.

'jaunty innings of village-green innocence and charm'. I think that's the Establishment's way of saying I had a slog and got away with it. The only disappointment was that Australia's reply was cut short by rain after less than four overs. Devon, Gussie and I were all pumped up and had been ready to create more havoc, this time with the ball. Goochie claimed that my presence was 'just like having Ian Botham around', without adding whether that was a good or a bad thing. Illy insisted, 'Don't let us compare him to Beefy, Fred Trueman or anyone else. Let us just be happy we've got Goughie.'

Fat chance of that after the next day's events. My swashbuckling efforts with the bat were outshone by my best-ever bowling display for England. As the wickets fell, I realized that this was my Test. Everything I tried – yorkers, slower balls, off-cutters, leg-spin – worked. It's a great feeling when anything seems possible. You must grab the moment, because it doesn't happen that often in your career, however gifted you may be. I reached four wickets for the sixth time in my short career, before Mark Taylor and Craig McDermott fought a rearguard action. I wasn't going to be denied this time, surely. McDermott should have been my fifth victim, but Devon at mid-on left the catch to Goochie, who was much further away at mid-off. Anyway, removing the Australian skipper was a more fitting scalp to mark the occasion. Taylor had saved his side from complete collapse, taking an hour to get off the mark and three before he hit a boundary. But he was undone by the Gough leg-spinner which had accounted for Warnie in Melbourne, one short of his 50. I took the return catch and McDermott was the first to shake my hand. Australia had saved the follow-on by then. We had them at 65-8, only a few wayward overs from Devon saw them escape that indignity; but we would cheerfully have settled for 116 all out when we started. I finished the job by bowling Fleming and came off to another standing ovation for my 6–49.

My head was spinning. But the fawning and fanfare had only just begun. 'Harold Larwood on the phone for you, Dazzler.' I tried to move nonchalantly to the phone by the dressing-room door, as though famous fast bowlers from the past are always calling.

He'd been listening on the radio. Larwood, too, had enjoyed a standing ovation for his batting at Sydney after scoring 98 as nightwatchman. Later I opened a note from the great Aussie fast bowler Ray Lindwall. 'Well batted. Well bowled. A great effort – you will remember this match for ever. Keep up the good work and best wishes for the future.' It's framed on my study wall. I couldn't stop smiling.

I waited until early evening before ringing Anna. She'd missed my bowling heroics. The night before, she'd stayed up to watch me bat. She blamed Liam. Looking after and feeding a six-week-old baby was tiring enough, without sitting up all night to watch cricket. Anna did explain that my picture was in all the papers and on TV, and all sorts of folk from my past were applauding my success. One was Phil Chambers, who'd been the manager at Rotherham United and who'd told me seven years earlier: 'You're too lazy, too fat and too slow – you haven't got the desire or stamina to make it.' I love it, the way these football types soft-soap you. Now Chambers was rather more complimentary. I think. 'Gough was a midfield player whose aggression and enthusiasm were far and away his biggest assets – but he only showed these qualities when playing. When there was work to be done on the training ground, he was lazy, had no desire or appetite. I knew then he just didn't have what it takes to be a top footballer.' Apparently, all sorts of agents were going to come knocking on my door and make me a multi-millionaire. Gary Lineker, who visited us in the S.C.G. dressing-room, told the journalists the best piece of advice he could give was 'Don't be a Gazza'.

England had extended their lead to 283 runs by the third evening for the loss of only Goochie, who got another dodgy l.b.w. As I packed up that evening, I couldn't believe the transformation. A couple of days earlier, we were one of the worst Ashes teams ever to visit Australia. Now this squad had pride and a future. Midway through the next afternoon, that recovery was destroyed at a stroke, not by the Aussies, but by a clap of our skipper's hands. Our lead was approaching 450, but the wicket had flattened out. Athers wanted to get at the Australian batsmen as soon as possible. We could all see he was fuming as our captain moved around the dressing-room. He'd sent a message out to Hickie that he'd got half an hour to get his 100. As he got close, Hickie started blocking. I don't know if Hick had two overs left, but when he blocked the last three balls of the first one, Athers said '★★★★ it. I've given him his chance,' and clapped them in. The silence in the dressing-room was deafening. Nobody could believe what he'd done. The spirit that had been built up over three and half hard-fought and inspired days evaporated in that split second. Hickie never said a word, just took his pads off. He had obviously got nervous. Athers felt any delay was going to reduce our chances of winning. I felt sorry for both of them. It was a no-win situation for Athers. He went to Hickie's room that night to explain his decision, but Hickie wouldn't accept his explanation and didn't speak to him for weeks. He has yet to hit a century against Australia.

The drama continued. At lunch on the final day, Australia were 206 without loss. Then the rain came. Not that many overs were lost, but Taylor knew that any sort of run-chase was out of the question. The juiced-up pitch, though, had Gussie rubbing his hands in glee. Taylor and Slater hit centuries before our old war-horse took four wickets in 14 deliveries, and Australia were in trouble at 292–7. We ran out of time or, rather, light. Gussie and I could only bowl three of the final 15 overs, and Warnie and Tim May held out. We actually came off, then Athers noticed there was time for another over. More in frustration than anything else, England returned for four more deliveries from Tuffers. It was a bizarre end to an amazing Test match. No one could deny that we had fought back bravely, but the draw meant that Australia retained the Ashes. I couldn't be down after that performance. I dedicated my Man of the Match award to my dad in typical fashion as we spoke on a live TV link-up. 'You can have the medal, Dad. I'll keep the cheque!'

My phone never stopped ringing: one woman from New Zealand rang, asking me to coach her son. Not that a call home from me went down too well when we reached Brisbane. I'd rung Anna at three in the morning, her time. My new-found fame earned me a lunch with Warnie in Brisbane the next day, courtesy of the *News of the World*. Their cricket correspondent fancies himself as something of a wine buff and he took us to a high-class fish restaurant. That was the moment when I realized that Warnie and I were soul-mates. All he wanted was a toasted cheese sandwich and a beer, same as me. We left Norrie to drink a bottle of chilled Chardonnay on his own, not for the first time. Warnie's been the biggest influence on cricket in my time. Spin bowling was dying until he burst on the scene. Look around now: leg-spinners everywhere. That's down to Warnie. Not just his ability, but his looks, his personality – the whole package. He's given cricket a new dimension. He has to be admired and congratulated for what he's done for the game. I know that not everyone holds Warnie in such high esteem, but he'll do for me.

Two days after Sydney, England were back on the one-day treadmill. Several of us could have done with a longer break, and Thorpey ended up in the Mater Hospital on an intravenous drip after suffering dehydration and heat exhaustion. But we won, and that gave us a chance of making the finals. Little did I realize that I'd bowled my last ball of that tour. The day before, I'd been to see a foot specialist in Brisbane with 'Rooster'. My left foot had begun to get sore during the Sydney Test. A scan in Brisbane revealed nothing, although another was planned for when we got back to Sydney. It was only a minor irritation as Hickie and I revived our innings. I was still in S.C.G. mood, thumping 45, including my own version of the reverse pull. Another standing ovation. My foot had felt sore while I was batting and I took some painkillers in the interval. I never thought of pulling out as I'd bowled in the nets in the morning and had had no adverse reaction. The next time I left the M.C.G. I was being carried off by 'Rooster' and Shaun Udal, my tour over. I heard my foot crack as I charged in to deliver the first ball. I hobbled through the crease, then collapsed. After the euphoria of Sydney, my world had crumbled. I couldn't put on a brave face. I knew it was bad. All sorts of thoughts flashed through my mind. Had Anna left England? What about my mum and dad's trip to Adelaide? If I can't play, should I stay? Am I going to become the forgotten man of the tour? All sorts of nonsense like that. The full extent of the injury hit me in the dressing-room. The press wanted to see me, but I couldn't face them. I was in tears as the boys carried me on to the bus. So much frustration, and I could do nothing about it. There was no point in staying. I couldn't have coped with that. I flew back to Sydney with the team, a squad I no longer felt part of. Nothing for it but to wish the lads well and fly home on the day Anna was due to fly out with Liam to see me.

9. Playfair Jinx

Home the hero. Not for long. By July, English cricket had a new superstar and Darren Gough had been dropped from the Test team for the first time. The heroics of Sydney were consigned to history and I was worried that I might be heading in the same direction. My old chum, Dominic Cork, had made an even more dramatic entry into Test cricket. Everyone has a team and the West Indies seem to be his. I was delighted for him. I couldn't believe how quick some were to write me off. More names for the little black book. I put it down to *Playfair*, the pocket-book cricket annual. At first, I had been honoured to be chosen for its front cover, then some of the senior players started shaking their heads. It had proved the temporary kiss of death for several careers. Gussie, Daffy, Stewie and Ramps are among those who've suffered. Add my name to the list.

I wanted to slip home quietly. There was no chance of that with my bosses at England and Yorkshire. Our performance in Australia had been slammed, other than Sydney, so the opportunity to present a successful aspect of the tour was too good to miss, however keen I might be to get home and see Liam. First, it was suggested I do a press conference at Heathrow. No thanks. Then the Yorkshire chief executive picked me up at Manchester airport and wanted to head straight for Headingley. Sorry. When I got home, my house was surrounded by TV cameras. The police were there. Anna wasn't at home, then she came through the back door and I saw my son for the first time. A special moment.

I couldn't believe the media attention. Anna had already found out the hard way. The front of the *Mirror* carried a story with the headline 'I'LL RIP OFF HIS BAILS' – 'Love hungry missus is gunning for Gough.' I've never known Anna so upset. Eventually she got an apology and flowers, but that wasn't the point. The next morning, we set off for Headingley for a press conference. The rationale was that it would stop the press bothering us. What it did do was make me determined to take charge of my own life. Nobody, not Yorkshire, not Lord's, was going to order me around like this again.

My foot was put in a pot for six weeks. The doctor told me that my original X-rays did show the crack, but that it had not been spotted in Australia. That made me hopping mad, but there was nothing I could do about it now. The specialist was confident I would be ready for the new season. I also had a scan on my calf to check there were no blood-clots from the flight. I'd probably injured my calf at the same time as my foot. The least I could do was compensate the family for missing their trips to Australia, so I flew off to Barbados with Anna, Mum, Dad, sister Andrea, Anna's mum and, of course, Liam. I sent two faxes to Australia, one to the England team, telling them I was sure they'd win in Adelaide, and another to Shane Warne, saying the same, but adding that I had enjoyed the series, nice to meet you and I hope our paths cross again.

The England casualty list continued to mount up in Australia, even after I'd gone home. No one was safe. Even the England physio, 'Rooster', broke a finger. Crazy. Yet Atherton's Barmy Army – or, rather, Walking Wounded – won in Adelaide with a patched-up side. Great news. I didn't feel jealous of that success, just a little envious of the lads who had beaten Australia in a Test.

There was plenty to adjust to at home. One was being a father. Fortunately, Liam was now sleeping through the night. Anna had had to cope with interrupted nights on her own. And our easy-going lifestyle had gone; no more going out on a whim, although my mum and dad were more than happy to babysit. I had responsibilities. Another adjustment was my newly acquired celebrity status. My Aussie exploits had made me a wanted man. At first it was fun, sitting on the bed with Paula Yates on the 'Big Breakfast'. Soon it became clear that I needed some help, an organization or an agent to allow me to concentrate on my cricket. I'm normally impulsive, but I took my time over this one. I didn't go with people who said they could make me a millionaire and whose whole pitch

was about money. I had a meeting with most of them and narrowed
the possibles down to two – Jon Holmes, who had Will Carling,
Gary Lineker, David Gower and Athers on his books, and Advantage International (now Octagon) who looked after Steffi Graf. It
was a difficult choice. What finally swung it Advantage's way was
the impression Clifford Bloxham made, not only on me, but on
Anna and Anna's dad, John. I'm still with them. I've never had
cause to regret my choice. I've always felt that they do what's best
for me, not just sell me to the highest bidder.

My calf had almost wasted completely away after six weeks in
plaster, and already I was struggling to get fit for the 1995 season.
Inactivity and Darren Gough do not make a good combination.
I'd already shown a tendency to put on the pounds, and this
enforced break was no different. The cricket schedule doesn't help.
There's always a date or a match you feel you must or want to be
fit by – instead of letting nature take its course. I was rushing to get
fit for the start of the season. I never made it. For the next year or
so, my career was disrupted by niggles and problems that left me
frustrated and out of sorts with the game.

Yorkshire's pre-season tour to Cape Town gave me a chance to
test my foot. Martyn Moxon told me to take it easy, but I charged
in. There was no point being tentative. The good news continued
with ten wickets in the 'friendly' Roses match, including a career-
best 7–28. Yorkshire and I were on a roll, and I emerged unscathed
from our clash with Derbyshire at Chesterfield in early May – one
of the lucky ones. Only three batsmen reached 30. At the end of
the first day, Illy, now England's cricket supremo, had seen us
bowled out for 177 and Derbyshire left struggling at 122–7 in
freezing conditions. Martyn Moxon broke his thumb and I cracked
Daryll Cullinan's right index finger. Two days later, Derbyshire
looked on course to win at 76–2, needing another 66 runs. Then
Pete Hartley took five wickets in nine deliveries, including a
hat-trick, and, despite some lusty blows from Devon, including a
six off me, we scraped home by seven runs.

England took the Texaco series against the West Indies 2–1.
Most people remember it for Athers's magnificent century in the

deciding match at Lord's. Athers took 27 balls to get off the mark, but then amazed us with all sorts of improvised shots that we never knew existed, certainly not with him at the wicket. I remember the series for getting Richie Richardson out at Trent Bridge and Lord's. His was the wicket I wanted in the summer of 1995 – not Brian Lara's. It might appear ungrateful, but I wanted to show him how much I owed him. Richie's the man who got me fired up and gave me confidence when I most needed it. I always target a batsman. The previous winter, that man had been David Boon. It has nothing to do with their technique or if I think I've found a weakness. It's because I respect them, both for who they are and for what they've achieved in cricket. Actually I got Lara as well as Richie at Trent Bridge, this time with the famous Gough leg-break.

But it was Gough and England who got a hiding in the opening Test at Headingley. Suddenly the Gough up-and-at-'em style, that breath of fresh air, was going stale in some people's eyes. I was no longer the flavour of the month. I'd been told it would happen. The very qualities that had taken me to the top were now my weakness. I had to conform, to curb my attacking instincts. I had never made any secret of the fact that I was going to have bad days. I'm not a safety-first cricketer. I like a challenge and I like to gamble – in the competitive sense. You can't have the benefits of a wicket-taking bowler without the downside. Some days – hopefully, not too many – I'm going to go for runs, a lot of runs. My batting is more hit and miss, but I was never one for keeping up an end. No fun in that. The message was that I should become a serious cricketer. I've always taken my cricket seriously, but I don't find it a chore walking out to represent my country. I love it and I'm going to show the fans I love it. I'll smile, I'll take the mick and take risks. There's method in my madness. I am a more effective cricketer if I play that way.

The trouble was, England were in trouble when I went out to bat on the second morning. Dilemma! The West Indies bowlers were going to bounce me. Do you accept that challenge or wimp out? The Headingley crowd gave me a fantastic reception. I couldn't let them down. Goughie, cowering and getting out of the way? No chance. All I was thinking of was Ian Botham's strategy. 'You've got to get on top early against the West Indies.' There was a man back against the boundary rail. Must be a bouncer. Right, here we go. Ian Bishop was bowling. I made good contact, but was snapped up on the boundary by Curtly Ambrose. Home ground and a first-ball duck. Most of my mates hadn't even got in the ground. Walking off, I felt a bit of a mug. I'd fallen for the sucker-punch. But I couldn't play any other way. I couldn't believe how it became an issue. 'Gough's getting too big for his boots!', 'Can England afford such recklessness?', as though I was becoming a liability. Obviously, my Man of the Match performance at Sydney, the last Test I'd played in, belonged to a different era.

Worse was to follow. The very strategy I wanted to employ when batting was used on me when bowling. Ian Bishop told Dev that their orders that day when they came out to bat were to knock me and Dev out of the attack from the first ball. And they did. Even though Dev dismissed Carl Hooper without a run on the board, the West Indies batsmen laid into us. Devon went at seven an over. I lasted only four overs before my back went. I came back at the end of the innings for a single over to try it out. I picked up the wicket of Courtney Walsh slogging, but I was struggling. Those five overs were all I bowled in the match, as we lost by nine wickets inside four days. Maybe I was trying too hard. Maybe I wasn't back to full fitness. It felt as if my back had locked. I couldn't go through my action. I was lucky not to get a pair. I nicked the first ball, but I was so square on, the ball also flicked my shirt, which stopped it carrying through to the wicket-keeper. I finished up England's second-top scorer with 29. That didn't stop the press laying into England or me.

Lord's was going to be a big match. My foot was still throbbing, but that was only to be expected. My back was better. Between Tests, I took four Kent wickets in five balls, including my first hat-trick. Martyn Moxon enjoyed that game at Headingley, too, scoring 203 and 65 without being dismissed. I didn't feel I was on trial, going into Lord's, but I knew I needed a good performance. But something special was always on the cards when the England selectors decided to bring the Sunshine Boys together for the first time in a Test. Corkie had been champing at the bit for ages. I remember how distraught he'd been the morning the Ashes tour squad was announced. We went back a long way and had always got on. I knew Corkie got on a lot of people's nerves, but it never bothered me.

There was a fair bit of coming and going on the first morning of the match. Corkie got the nod over his Derbyshire team-mate Daffy, while the selectors changed their minds about including a specialist wicket-keeper. Bumpy went home and Stewie put on the gloves again. Still a junior member of the side, I was just happy to be playing; voicing opinions on selection wasn't my job. Our batting held up better than at Headingley, but we still trailed by 41 runs on the first innings. I'd taken a couple of wickets when I managed to hang on to a spectacular catch at long leg. The lads thought I'd made a bit of a meal of it, but it knocked me silly for about ten minutes, and I had to lie down when I got back to the dressing-room, I felt so dizzy. Although it was a different sort of catch from the one I took off Sherwin Campbell five years later, it was on almost the same spot and just as important. Keith Arthurton was a left-hander. I was there for the hook but I had come in from the boundary rope quite a way. I remember it going up and up, and I caught sight of Gus Fraser out the corner of my eye willing me on. He had claimed four wickets already. If I hung on, our Middlesex fast bowler would take his place on that Lord's honours board. It wasn't that I misjudged it, but it went high and it's a long boundary. At the last moment I had to dive backwards. Fortunately it stuck, even after I crashed my head on the ground. Gus and I weren't the only relieved ones. The West Indies were ahead of our first-innings 283 and Arthurton was leading the way. There were the usual comments from the lads about the Yorkshire show-off making an easy catch look difficult and giving me low marks for style. I was pleased for Gus. I knew only too well that you need catches like that as a bowler. I also knew how keen Gus was to get on the board at his home ground. To be fair, he's always been grateful. I'm never short of a drink when Gus is around.

But it was Corkie who was buying the champagne on the final

day after his record 7–43 on his debut won us the Test by 72 runs. It was an incredible afternoon. Hickie, Thorpey – who had to go to hospital after ducking into Courtney's slower ball, a delivery which came back to haunt him in the summer of 2000 – and a fighting 90 from Judgey gave the Windies a 296 target. It was close and tense. I had a little spat with Ian Bishop while I was batting. There was one name on everyone's lips overnight: Brian Lara. He was the threat, still there, and the target had shrunk to 228. The sole aim on that Monday morning was to remove Lara quickly. One session of the left-handed genius and we were history. He came out blazing. I was the man who got him out, but even I was reluctant to claim the credit. True, I found the edge of Lara's bat, but it took a brilliant one-handed left-hand catch by Stewie in front of Athers at first slip. Wickets kept falling. The West Indies were 177–6 – three each to me and Corkie. Now I had my eyes on that Lord's board again. Just like the series in the summer of 2000, another bowler slipped into gear and, before I could react, the Windies were all out. In 2000 that man was Caddie. In 1995 it was Corkie. Seven wickets – SEVEN WICKETS – and the best figures ever on an England debut. Thanks to the England domestic schedule, there was time for only a quick dressing-room celebration before we headed off to all parts of the country for the first round of the NatWest the next day. I went back to Leeds to face the might of Ireland.

There was plenty to reflect on as I headed up the M1. I was no longer the new kid on the block; Corkie was the man now. It makes me laugh that we always used to be called rivals. We're totally different cricketers. I am an attacking strike bowler and he's a swing bowler. We're similar in attitude, though Corkie's more Mr Angry than I am. I wasn't unhappy that the limelight had moved away. I didn't feel any pressure in Australia. You don't when you're doing well. It's when the form and the appeal fade, that's when the mind starts playing tricks. What do people want from you? Why is what was acceptable last year not finding favour this summer? You have to find your own answers and follow your own instincts.

I've never seen a dressing-room transformed like England's was at Edgbaston after a few seconds of the third Test. Traumatized might be a better word. The first ball from Curtly Ambrose took off, flew passed Athers and went over the keeper's head to the boundary. I don't know what was more frightening, that or the huge grin that spread across Curtly's face. There was silence in the dressing-room as we watched on TV. Tuffers was first to speak. 'Bloody hell. I ain't going to bat on that. Was that a quick ball – or was it the pitch?' Yes was the answer to both questions. Curtly limped off early, but Ian Bishop bowled about as quickly as I'd ever faced, nearly as fast as Donald the previous year. England were completely snookered. Rolled over for 147! Jason Gallian had his finger broken on his debut. Yet the Windies got 300. If the pitch was such a bitch, why didn't we cause carnage? I was skidding on to the bat and I was wondering: 'Where's this dodgy wicket?' It was there for the taller West Indian bowlers and the length they bowled, but not for us. I didn't get a wicket and I came off knowing that was my worst bowling display for England on a helpful wicket by quite a distance.

The one England performance that sticks in my mind from that Test was Robin Smith's. Judgey was hit by ball after ball after ball. For sheer guts, it's the bravest knock I've ever seen. Judgey scored 46 in the first innings and 41 out of 89 in the second. He just wouldn't given in and his body was black and blue by the finish. Such courage did not impress everybody. Judgey was on the receiving end as one angry fan followed him into the toilets when we went out for a drink on Friday night. 'You're a disgrace – all of you.' Normally Judgey would have come out fighting in the face of such taunting. After exchanging blows with the likes of Bishop, Walsh and Benjamin for most of the day, Judgey decided he'd seen enough violence. It was a blunt reminder of one of the hazards of playing team sports for your country. Many who watch are just as passionate as those who play. A few drinks can give them the courage to have a pot. Most are good-natured. A few are not. I have to confess that I've taken stick in public places as an England cricketer that I would not have stood for as a youngster. But the blazer and badge bring responsibility. But if someone abuses me, I won't say 'Fair enough' and walk away; I will confront that person, no matter what. I've managed not to be involved in any scuffles since I became an England cricketer. However, I will always stick up for myself. I won't let anyone talk to me as though I'm a piece of dirt. Generally, cricketers don't seem to get involved in the brawls and bust-ups that are part of the soccer scene. Maybe cricketers are thought to be more mature and able to cope with developing situations. Also the public is aware that we're not getting paid £50,000 a week. Anyway, playing almost every day means there are few opportunities to go out and get shedded.

There are always those who complain that you shouldn't be out enjoying yourselves after a bad day at the cricket. Catch 22. Bad days at the office are part of the job. You can either sit in your room, sulk and not be sociable, or you can go to a bar. It's not my style to hide myself away and fret. If people approach you and you don't respond, you're labelled standoffish. If you're too nice, you get landed with someone you can't get rid of. That's why you're better off in a group. Don't forget, I had to go out and bat on that Edgbaston pitch again the next day. Sure, I needed a drink.

We started the day at 59–3. Seventy-eight minutes later, we were all out for 89. For the first time in my career I was part of a team that was booed by the crowd. You could sense the hostility. Corkie and I were the only other guys to reach double figures. Stewie didn't bat because of a broken finger, and Richard Illingworth also suffered a hand break. I could understand the crowd's frustration. Lord's had given them high hopes of an England revival. Now what? We'd not played well. In fact, we played crap cricket. I'd never been in a dressing-room so down. We should never have played the West Indies on a pitch like that; it was cricketing suicide. Nowhere else in the world would a home side suffer a handicap like that. Yet the fact remains, we should just have got on with the job. We were too negative about the pitch from that first ball, and it showed.

No time to celebrate at Lord's. No time to recover at Edgbaston. As soon as we returned to the dressing-room, the phones started ringing. Sunday League, here we come. It's all rush, rush, rush. I was keen to keep playing. I felt I had lost time to make up through missing the end of the Ashes series. I played against Judgey the next day and hit him first ball. 'Thanks, China' was the look I got. Actually, it woke him up and he laid into us, although I bowled as quickly as I had done all summer. I was getting stronger, but something wasn't right. I didn't feel one hundred per cent, but I couldn't put my finger on it.

Obviously the selectors must have felt the same, and I was sent packing before the start of the Old Trafford Test. The reason given out for public consumption was that I was not fit. Not true. For the first time in my career, England dropped me. It was a farce. The Old Trafford pitch looked like it would take spin. John Emburey was brought back and Mike Watkinson was brought in. We'd beaten Essex in the NatWest, but my foot was still bothering me. As soon as I met up with the squad, the atmosphere told me something wasn't right. I don't know whether it was a polite way of letting me down gently, but they asked me to bowl two spells in the nets on the Tuesday to prove my fitness. I bowled on Wednesday and was sent to the specialist for an X-ray. There were no fractures, just bruising, and I was advised to rest. I was keen to play and I asked 'Rooster', the physio, what he thought. I couldn't believe his reply. 'It's not up to me.' I told him, 'Of course it's up to you. You're the physio.' I wasn't happy: the doctor had cleared me and I'd bowled my spells in the nets. Because we would be playing two spinners, 'Rooster' didn't want to put his head on the block, and I thought that was wrong. So I told him, 'Yes, I'm fit.' I was left out. My fitness obviously wasn't up to me; the selectors weren't prepared to take a risk, so I was released.

Small wonder that I was fired up when I ran in to bowl at Athers in the NatWest quarter-final, less than a week later. England had levelled the series, thanks to more Cork magic (including a hat-trick), but I was still very angry about the way the whole affair, so far as it affected D. Gough, had been handled. I soon sent Athers on his way and, in front of the sell-out Headingley crowd and TV cameras, covered most of the square with an over-the-top aeroplane celebration. Athers did not look impressed. A little while later, Gus told Athers in front of me that the perfect riposte would have been: 'That's the only bloody plane you'll be on this winter!' A good line, but Athers wasn't sharp enough that day. To be fair, Athers did have a long chat with me in the NatWest tent after the match. My departure at Old Trafford had led to a lot of speculation in the papers about bust-ups. Athers tried to argue the England case with me, but I wasn't having any of it. I told him I wasn't happy with the physio. It wasn't an argument. We agreed to disagree.

Actually I was relieved not to be part of England's plans. I couldn't believe I was feeling like this, but I'd been through a lot in my first international year and I was looking forward to playing just county cricket. It was the same the following year, and it wasn't until June 1997 that I appeared for England in a home Test match again. Yorkshire's home semi-final against Northants in the NatWest was a big disappointment as we lost by 87 runs. There was brawling on the Western Terrace, 15 were arrested and six were charged the next day. Chasing 287, we got bogged down. Byas managed 19 runs from 71 deliveries.

I played for the county against the West Indies at the end of the season, as well as the final two county games. In my heart I didn't feel that my England days were over. Illy had already told me I would be going to South Africa in the winter. But another problem was emerging that was to trouble me through a disappointing winter.

10. Dark Destroyer Destroyed

South Africa should have been Devon Malcolm's tour. His 9–57 at the Oval and his West Indian background made him the main attraction. England were venturing to the Rainbow Nation for the first time since South Africa had been readmitted to international sport after their apartheid sporting isolation. It wasn't just the media who identified Malcolm in that way, even Nelson Mandela singled him out. Illy, our manager, and his coaching team had other ideas. They tried to change his bowling action. Then they tried to change Devon. All they succeeded in doing was demoralizing him and, at the same time, they destroyed the one man the South Africans feared. Illy's insensitive approach was not reserved for Devon alone, but he had to bear the brunt of it. He was written off by the management as a 'nobody' even before the Test series started and then, to cap it all, Illy poked him in the chest on the final day of the series and told the whole England dressing-room: 'And you, you, you f★★★★★★ lost us the Test match!'

Devon wasn't the only fast bowler under fire. For some reason my action was also under intense scrutiny. I'm sure it was all done with the best of intentions – as with Devon – but it turned into a nightmare. I worked with Peter Lever to change my action because of my foot going over. The comments had started in summer 1995. Bob Willis and Michael Holding said my run-up was too explosive, short and bustling. The change was intended to protect my front foot. I'd always gone over on it as I landed. By making my action more open, the pressure would not be so intense. That was the plus side. The downside was, I bowled like a drain. I never felt comfortable, but you'll try anything when you're desperate. And desperate is a fair description of my time in South Africa. Fortunately, I wasn't the only person who was unhappy with the changes. I was bowling to Athers at practice early on in Johannesburg, and he wandered down after a couple of deliveries. 'What are you playing at?'

'That's my new action.'

'Don't be silly. Get back to bowling properly.'

Although I'd been working hard with Plank (Peter Lever) for a while, I was relieved at Athers's reaction. I knew I wasn't bowling right, but the damage had been done. I'd wasted a month of work. I went back to my normal action, but the niggles kept disrupting my build-up. I'd not had a clear run since I came back from Australia. And there was another problem on this South African tour: it rained . . . and it rained. I didn't bowl a single ball in the inaugural Test at Centurion Park, when the final three days were washed out. I was given the game off between the Tests, which was a nonsense. And, surprise, surprise, I bowled like a twat in the Johannesburg Test, which Athers saved with that heroic undefeated 185 over 644 minutes. After my hamstring went completely in the next game at Paarl that was about the end of me. I couldn't wait for the Test series to finish and the one-dayers to start, so that England could prepare for the World Cup in India, Pakistan and Sri Lanka. It's funny how you remember little things. My sunglasses came off while I was fielding during that second Test, and the TV commentators had a go at me. A couple of bad games and everybody was on my back. Or that was the way it seemed.

That's when my hamstring problems started. It never rains but it pours. I also got thumped on the arm by Brian McMillan. I thought I'd be making another early tour departure as I headed for the X-ray department once more. Luckily, this time it was only extensive bruising. The wheels really started to come off when we reached Durban. I was already sidelined with a hamstring injury after limping off in Paarl. Illy changed the bowling attack almost completely. Our supremo reckoned it was going to swing and the South Africans had a weakness against spin. It was probably the liveliest wicket we came across all tour – it was green, so it swung, it seamed. I really felt for Devon and Gussie, who were dropped in favour of Mark Ilott and Peter Martin. The discarded duo were furious, especially Devon. I will always remember them doing laps at Kingsmead. I had just started jogging again, but those two kept running lap after lap after lap, trying to run their anger, disappointment and frustration out.

To say that Devon and Illy didn't get on with each other was an understatement. Devon, as I've already indicated, was not always an easy bowler to deal with. Occasionally he had the opposition batsmen hopping about, but more often it would be his own captain who was tearing his hair out. Ask him to pitch it up and he'd bowl it short. And vice versa. Goochie wasn't joking when he said you were better off telling him to do the opposite of what you wanted. Yet I always found Devon to be great fun. There was no side to him, no hidden agenda. This South African tour should have been the crowning glory of his career, especially after his exploits at the Oval the previous year. Instead, it was a disaster, far worse than any disappointment I had to contend with. I know Devon was difficult, and sometimes you had to tell him twice, but I have to lay the blame at the feet of the management. After Devon's meeting with Nelson Mandela at Soweto at the start of the tour when, not unnaturally, he was singled out by the President, who called him the Dark Destroyer, Illy and his subordinates decided Devon had got too big for his boots. Maybe it did go to his head a little. Who can blame him? We were in a country that had experienced political racism and Devon felt, as the black player in the England side, that he had a responsibility on the trip in addition to just bowling. And they looked upon him as a hero in South Africa.

I first noticed there was a problem when I was bowling in the middle net at Port Elizabeth. Devon was next to bowl. A little black kid asked Dev something, and he was trying to help coach the youngster. Illy then just bellowed: 'Devon, f★★★ off out of the way until it's your turn to bowl.' The fact of the matter was that Illy was more concerned about how many balls we were losing in the nets than any social niceties. John Edrich also gave Dev a hard time. My view is that Dev was treated unfairly on the trip. I'm not saying that it was a deliberate policy, but that's how it looked. The man-management of him was poor, especially when they ridiculed him in that press conference, calling him a 'nobody' without his pace, and swearing at him. Devon's a proud bloke, and it was totally insensitive in many ways to have a white cricket manager in the new South Africa telling our West Indies fast bowler to 'f★★★★★★ do this' and 'f★★★★★★ do that'. It was totally unnecessary.

The final showdown was both spectacular and frightening. The venue was our dressing-room at Newlands. In the red corner was Illy, so wound up I thought he was going to have a heart attack. In the blue corner was Devon, strong, silent and ready to punch Illy's lights out. By this stage the tour had gone pear-shaped. A few minutes earlier the entire England squad had been standing on the field at the end-of-series presentation. After four draws, England had lost this deciding Test by ten wickets within three days. Our mood was one of despondency, as you might imagine. Then came the bombshell over the loudspeaker. It was announced that England would be playing a hastily arranged one-dayer against a Western Province side on Saturday – the scheduled final day of the Test. This came as news to the crowd. It came as news to us. I thought Athers was going to explode; we were all fuming. It was the final straw. Illy had been moaning about the wives and families being a distraction and a nuisance over Christmas and the New Year. Now he wanted to give us another day's cricket, when England's prime need was to regroup after this heavy defeat.

I should have played in that final Test. I'd bowled well in the nets. Steve Oldham was over in South Africa with Yorkshire and thought I was in the groove. I'd proved I was fit and I bowled quickly, yet Illy left me out. That told me he was losing the plot. His argument was that I'd not played a game. A few days earlier I'd proved I was fit for the one-day squad, surviving a special fitness workout at Port Elizabeth. I passed, but was ignored. Sitting it out in Cape Town in the New Year was in sharp contrast to my heroics at Sydney a year earlier. All the frustrations and tensions came racing to the surface as the tour fell apart in three days.

Illy's selection had grown stranger and stranger: England's five specialist batsmen against South Africa's seven. Our five-man bowling attack included three men – Devon, Gussie and Winker (Mike Watkinson) – who had played little part in the series. In addition, the South Africans brought in the best sports psychologist in the business. President Mandela met Hansie Cronje's team and was photographed with his arm round Paul Adams, the young spinner with the amazing action. Adams has his head turned away from the batsman as he delivers the ball. We'd faced him at Kimberley in only his second first-class appearance. Now he was making his Test debut.

Athers decided to bat. Our 153 all out put England under pressure, but our bowlers put us right back in the game, with South Africa tottering on 171–9. The new ball had just been taken and new boy Adams was making his way to the wicket to join wicket-keeper David Richardson. Runs had been hard to come by all day. Just one more wicket and England would have a chance. Unfortunately, Devon lost the plot. Four wayward overs went for 26; his direction was all over the place, and South Africa took full advantage.

His despair spread through the team. You could see and feel it from the dressing-room. Heads went down as South Africa ended up with a lead of 91 runs. Disaster. Illy was steaming. Athers was boiling. Our dressing-room was like a morgue. Hardly anyone spoke . . . probably frightened about what they'd say if they did open their mouths. It wasn't all Devon's fault. He didn't need telling that his last spell had probably cost us the Test and the series. Athers and Devon had an uneasy relationship; most captains who had Devon in their attack did. This was another occasion when Athers kept telling him to bowl it short, but Devon wouldn't or couldn't comply. You could see how upset Athers was as he padded up to go out again for the few remaining overs. Athers, especially after Johannesburg, was our main hope for a recovery. On this occasion he was in no fit state to bat. Illy admitted afterwards that he should have dissuaded Athers from going out. Illy had not been slow to act for most of the tour. It's a shame he didn't react this time. The inevitable happened: Athers was out, just before the close. The final disappointment in a depressing day at Newlands. There was no escape. England lost by ten wickets after being bowled out for 157.

We had not enjoyed the rub of the green. Umpire Dave Orchard gave Thorpey not out when the South Africans claimed a run out. Somehow Cronje persuaded Orchard to go to the third umpire, which Orchard should have done in the first place. The TV replays sent Thorpey on the way. Judgey was given out caught behind when the replays showed he was nowhere near the ball. Hickie received a dodgy l.b.w. I'm not making excuses. There was no doubt we were the architects of our own downfall.

We must have looked a pretty bedraggled bunch at the presentation ceremony as Mandela handed Cronje the spoils. That was the background to us hearing that one-day bombshell. I had the feeling the action for the day wasn't over after all. Both Illy and Athers were itching for a fight. Athers made a general inquiry about who had arranged a 'f★★★★★★ one-day game'. It was a rhetorical question. Illy's not one to go on the back foot, and he laid into us big-time, ranting and raving. And then he moved towards Devon: 'And you, you've lost us the f★★★★★★ Test match.' Illy's finger was poking towards Devon's chest. I was just waiting for a big right hand to come over. I was sure Devon was going to hit him and I wouldn't have blamed him. Illy had been on his case all tour. Suddenly, Illy went red in the face and started choking. Devon didn't need to thump him after all; our manager was going to have a heart attack in the dressing-room. He rushed across to the sink for a glass of water. This defused the situation, but the whole episode demonstrated how Illy had lost touch with his players. He even moaned about the music we used to play in the dressing-room and the volume. Illy went out and bought a Johnny Mathis CD.

Robin Smith never played Test cricket after the South African tour. That was a crying shame. Judgey likes a good time, everyone on the cricket circuit knows that. He's also just about the nicest bloke you'll ever come across. No side to him. He's a magnificent man, a great competitor, and I enjoy our scraps out in the middle even now. Judgey's the bravest cricketer I've come across, as he demonstrated at Edgbaston in 1995. Like Devon, Judgey did not find favour with Illy. Illy could not see beyond Judgey the Party Animal who enjoyed himself too much, rather than recognizing a cricketer who never spared himself in England's cause on the international field. Illy was not happy to be woken up by the BBC in London, trying to raise Judgey to talk on Michael Parkinson's radio show. I'm not sure what upset Illy more, being woken up at 11 p.m. or finding out that Judgey was not in his room.

Athers's defiant 185 at the Wanderers sparked off a serious celebration. Athers drank himself to a standstill with Ian Botham in Vertigo in a 'Cane and Coke' challenge with England's famous all-rounder. The rest of us weren't far behind. The England party was looking rather shabby as we flew down to Cape Town. I must confess that another drink was the last thing I wanted that morning. The Judge was made of sterner stuff and was still on treble vodkas at eight in the morning at Johannesburg airport. I think Corkie had been dragged into his drinking circle. At times like that, Judgey had a habit of thumping you in the chest, insisting, 'Be strong.' It's a rites-of-passage sort of thing, but it was a mistake to make himself a target for Illy. During the flight, Judgey stood at the back of the plane, next to the galley and bar, while Illy remained in his seat, sunglasses on and stony-faced. From that point on, Judgey was history, although he continued to battle hard for the cause.

I found the South African tour tough. From the non-stop action and being centre of attention in Australia, I was a bit player here. And the rain. I've never been on such a stop-start trip. I wasn't the only tourist who never found any rhythm. Fixtures were rearranged and we even travelled from Johannesburg to Pretoria for net practice early on. I spent more time on the golf course than on the cricket field. Even there, Illy would be moaning. England players still shared rooms in those days. At Kimberley I had the pleasure of rooming with that legendary snorer, Peter 'Digger' Martin. Not for long. At 2.30 in the morning I was down at reception, demanding another room. It was not a happy stop for me. I became Steve Jack's 200th first-class victim. I was given out caught behind. He was appealing for l.b.w. Most of my best form was shown on the golf course. Thorpey and I won the first prize in the Oppenheimer Pro-Am, though I must admit it was a surprise to receive a wildlife video from such a famous diamond magnate.

Cricketers are used to the rain and having their lives disrupted, but somehow it's worse when you are on tour, sitting in hotel rooms and dressing-rooms watching the rain when you could be with your family at home. That South African trip was the worst for kicking our heels. Some of us like to lark about. Most of it's harmless, like Stewie and Corkie messing about in the background of a live interview at Centurion Park. However, our physio Wayne picked the wrong target when he gave one of our security cops a rub-down with whitener. Later on in the tour, Wayne was 'arrested' in Johannesburg arrivals as a reprisal. He got the works. He was fingerprinted, handcuffed and thrown in the back of a paddy-wagon without windows and given a rough ride to the team hotel. Their excuse was the drugs medication he was legitimately carrying in his capacity as team physio. It was not an experience he enjoyed!

Christmas Day at the Summerstrand in Port Elizabeth was a disaster. We ended up cooking for ourselves after two cooks walked out with most of the staff. The night before had been karaoke time. Vanda Ramprakash and I were paired together for Little Eva's 'Locomotion', while Anna and Judgey gave a hilarious rendition of 'The Lion Sleeps Tonight'. New Year's Eve was spent at the British Consulate, and I was only too happy to see the back of 1995 and raise a glass to the New Year, although a few hours later I was excluded from the squad for the fifth Test.

Throughout the tour, Illy and Athers were often found together, sitting round a table playing bridge. They were a formidable combination, the pair to beat. Sadly for English cricket, that was about the only time they formed anything remotely resembling a winning partnership.

11. Generation Gap

I would have come home from South Africa at the end of the Test series if there had not been a World Cup to follow. After the Ashes, the World Cup's the big one for me. England had been in three finals – 1979, 1987 and 1992 – but had never lifted the trophy. I've played in the last two – that 1996 tournament and the 1999 event held in England. Both have been bitter disappointments, making me determined, body willing, for one last crack in South Africa in the spring of 2003. Our problems in 1999 could be put down to a horrendous build-up because of an unseemly and totally unnecessary squabble over our contracts. England were eliminated from the later stages on run rate, the unlucky side of three with three wins. England actually reached the quarter-final stages of the 1996 World Cup; it would have been almost impossible not to. Our fourth place in Pool A matched us against the winners of Pool B. Yet it gave us the opposition we wanted most. We missed Australia, the West Indies and India. Despite the lack of any game-plan or form, we really fancied our chances against Sri Lanka. What fools! We were only deluding ourselves, although England took some comfort from seeing Sri Lanka go all the way and become World Cup champions.

Our demise and defeat in 1996 was inevitable. Illy had no grasp of what was required to compete and our failure marked the end of his role as England's cricket supremo. That, too, was inevitable. I took no pleasure from a former Yorkshire and England great's failure, but his mission was doomed from the start. Illy's heart was in the right place, make no mistake about that. He was right to be annoyed with some of the things he was forced to witness. Nobody could deny that Illy had been a good captain. His record proves that, as does the ruthless way he came back with the Ashes in 1970/71. But 1970/71 was the trouble; it's a bloody long time ago. For example, I'd only just been born. Illy acted as though we were still in the 1970s. Often, he behaved as though he was still captain. Illy, when captain, would certainly not have put up with some of the things he did as chairman.

The minute Illy became chairman, he hung his jacket up in the dressing-room . . . and his fellow selectors, Brian Bolus and Fred Titmus, also became part of the furniture. For me, any cricket dressing-room is the holiest of holies. Coach, yes. Physio, yes. Twelfth man, yes. They are directly involved with the team on the day. Nobody else. No. No way. Not Ray Illingworth. Not Lord MacLaurin. Not Tim Lamb, the E.C.B.'s chief executive. That's not to say they can't be invited in on special occasions. But nobody should expect to be given the right to walk into an England dressing-room. Maybe it was Athers's fault. These things don't matter to him, and he let it ride. It's a big call, but he should have kicked Illy out. Suddenly the England dressing-room was no longer private. I – and I know most of the other lads felt the same – wasn't able to relax. There was another problem. The media loved Illy. He was great copy and he loved talking. Illy would sound off at the drop off a hat or the switching on of a tape-recorder. And his timing was legendary. England's cricketers arrived back from the Caribbean to read just what the new chairman thought of them. Illy helped Athers prepare for the Ashes campaign in Brisbane by telling a group of assembled sports writers in London that he, Illy, had saved Athers's job in the summer over the dirt-in-the-pocket episode, and the ungrateful captain hadn't rung him up to thank him. At the end of the South African tour Illy told the media that the Test careers of Robin Smith, Alec Stewart, Mark Ramprakash, Angus Fraser, Richard Illingworth and Mike Watkinson were almost certainly over. Considering half that lot were part of our World Cup party, his timing must be called insensitive, to say the least. But sensitivity was not one of Illy's strong points. Often the England team felt the media were kept better informed of the chairman's views and intentions than they were.

The simple fact is that Illy had been out of the game too long. He was too old. Illy's not a stupid man and he has a great cricket brain. I enjoy talking cricket with him even now. These days I can have a decent conversation with him about cricket; I learn things from him on a one-to-one basis. But Illy's a stubborn bugger. His ideas were always the best. He was always right. I remember us having an argument on the way back from that 1996 World Cup. Illy told me, 'Shut up. You should just listen at your age!' I wasn't having that. I can be as stubborn a Yorkie as him, and I gave him a mouthful back. He was on about Yorkshire and the rights of seniority and rubbish like that. I was arguing from a young player's point of view, but Illy only ever sees things from where he's sitting. He didn't argue with me, he just kept telling me to shut up.

The biggest problem was that Illy had the man-management skills of Basil Fawlty. His over-reactions usually made matters worse. Devon was the main case in point, but there were many others. And Illy moaned, about his breakfast, his laundry, his room. Maybe I'm wrong, but it appeared that Illy focused on the rest of us only once *he* was A.O.K.! He whinged non-stop. The trouble with that is that it gives the players a perfect excuse to do the same. As an adviser, Illy would have been excellent because of his huge knowledge of cricket. To be out of the game for so long and then to come back at 60 as manager, coach and chairman of selectors was too much to ask of anyone, even a Yorkshireman. The two guys he brought in, batting coach John Edrich and bowling coach Peter Lever, were both from his vintage. Suddenly, Athers's young team was dragged back a generation. Plank (Peter Lever) was a great laugh and he fitted in brilliantly with the lads. But the attempts to change the action of both Devon and me failed. Just the same as I felt about Illy, I felt Plank and Edrich were out of date. Edrich just said, 'Show them the bat,' and made a forward defensive gesture. The coaches and players were generations apart, far from the ideal preparation for a World Cup. The team we picked showed that.

Sadly, by the time of the World Cup, everyone was fed up with Illy. The lads felt he wasn't the man for the job. Perhaps Illy wasn't appreciated in the way he should have been. I can't understand why he wanted to do everything. Illy shouldn't have been coach.

In my eyes he did have a role to play, but as an adviser. Illy was past his sell-by date for an active role. I was sad to see the lads taking the mick out of him by the end of the trip. They weren't laughing with him, but at him.

My World Cup campaign could have ended at Port Elizabeth during the fourth Test. I was lined up with Neil Smith, Dermot Reeve (who'd just been awarded the OBE – Other Bears' Efforts) and Neil Fairbrother for a full fitness test. That trio had been flown in for the one-day series in South Africa. I came through well and had hoped to get a place in the final Test team. No such luck. Instead, my first game of cricket for nearly a month was that hurriedly arranged fixture that caused such an uproar in our Newlands dressing-room.

The seven-match one-day series against South Africa had seemed to be the perfect preparation for the World Cup. All it did in fact was confuse our strategy and thinking, and when we left for a ten-day break at home before flying out to Pakistan, I for one didn't have a clue what was going on.

We actually lost that one-day game against Western Province. I must confess that I've played in England sides that were more committed than we were that afternoon. Perhaps subconsciously, those who'd been part of the losing Test side wanted to show Illy what they thought of his decision. England lost for a third time in a week at Newlands when we took on South Africa. Athers summed up the mood: 'We did pretty well to lose.' We'd been coasting at 155–3, chasing 211. The ball might have started off white, but it was more of a green hue by the time I went out to bat. I could hardly see it and was last man out. England failed by six runs.

Nobody saw anything of our next game for three-quarters of an hour after a power failure put out the lighting system at Bloemfontein. The usual African conspiracy theory was mentioned in our dressing-room, since Athers and Thorpey were making steady progress towards the victory target of 263 when it happened. The ruse didn't work, although it was after midnight by the time we got back to our hotel. It was too late to celebrate, which was rather unfortunate, as South Africa won the next five one-dayers. Rather, we lost most of them. Chasing 199 at the Wanderers, Daffy and I had South Africa on 114–5. In the next game at Centurion Park our 272–8 wasn't enough. It got worse. We played like novices at Durban, then got bowled out for 115, chasing 129, at Buffalo Park. Strangely, though, I felt good and confident for the first time on the trip. After three months I was charging in and doing my job. I knew it was too good to last.

President Mandela turned up at St George's for the final match of the series, which we lost by 64 runs, so presenting yet another trophy to Cronje. But I didn't meet the great man this time; I was in our dressing-room, absolutely distraught after coming off with a sore hamstring again. I'd bowled well, but I felt discomfort while batting. Wayne tried to give me a rollocking because he could see how upset I was. Not only that, but we were about to fly home and he wanted to spend some time with his family. Another Gough injury was going to require his personal attendance in the short period we were back in Yorkshire. The hamstring didn't feel too bad, but it was beginning to look as if this run of niggles and problems was never going to end. I'd hoped the arrival of 1996 was going to bring a change of fortune. No such luck yet.

Despite this shambolic workout, you always travel in hope. The World Cup squad gathered in London for a special dinner as a part of Judgey's benefit year. We were optimistic about our chances as we flew out the next day. I don't know why; for a start, it wasn't the right squad for the sub-continent. Nobody knew who was opening the batting. Daffy had opened with Athers, Judgey with Stewie. No one knew who was opening the bowling. We didn't know what was our best XI. We tried every option leading up to the World Cup, but there was no set plan. Instead of sticking to one plan, we tried something new every game in South Africa. We never talked about tactics for the World Cup. We weren't good enough in batting, bowling, fielding or tactics. But we travelled in hope.

We were based in Pakistan at the start of the World Cup. Together with India, Sri Lanka was hosting the event. A bomb went off in Colombo, killing 73 people, so the Aussies refused to go near the place and were quite happy to forfeit their match against Sri Lanka. So were the West Indies. And so Sri Lanka had four points before the off. Our build-up was not so dramatic. The key in competitions like this is to get off to a good start and get on a roll. New Zealand were first up against us. The Kiwis aren't one of the very top-notch nations, so it was a golden opportunity to show that our 8–1 odds against winning the World Cup were more than generous. Judgey went into that game minus his moustache and with a short back and sides. Our senior batsman had been dismissed twice in three balls by a Pakistan Under-19 bowler in the nets before our two warm-up matches. 'I don't want anyone to recognize me,' the Judge explained. He nearly went home after straining a groin while taking a catch, and Corkie went off with a damaged knee in the second match. I was still taking it easy because of my hamstring, but I was fit enough to parade around Eden Gardens in Calcutta in front of 100,000 at the opening ceremony. We weren't that happy to be there. Our flight from Lahore had been delayed for five hours and we got to bed at three in the morning. The ceremony itself was a bit of a disaster. The laser show was disrupted by the wind, and the Pakistan team found themselves being introduced as South Africa!

The journey to Ahmedabad was even worse than the one to Calcutta had been. Again, we got to the airport, only to find a delay; for some reason, we couldn't go direct, so we had several hours to kill in Delhi. At least that gave us the chance to head for the British High Commission and tuck into sausages, chips and beans. We finally arrived at our Ahmedabad hotel 17 hours after setting out. Oh, the joys of touring England. It's called the best tour . . . and it's the one England cricketers never go on. Finish a game, sit in a luxury hotel and check into your new hotel the same night. No flight. No delays, no days out of your life.

For once Illy was right. He criticized the organizers for ensuring that we went four days without any serious practice because of the nonsense of having to attend the opening ceremony. Our lack of practice showed as the Kiwis beat us by 11 runs. I couldn't believe it. We were beaten by one of my chums from my New Zealand stay in 1990: Nathan Astle, who hit a century and took the Man of the Match award. He'd been dropped after scoring just one. Our next two matches were bankers – the United Arab Emirates and Holland. Even in our dreadful state, I never imagined the unthinkable happening. Our eight-wicket win over U.A.E. was spoilt by the news that Craig White was out of the World Cup with a side strain. His replacement, Dermot Reeve, had been in South Africa and had complained afterwards that the management had not given him a chance of gaining a World Cup spot. The most memorable moment of that game was the sight of Man of the Match Neil Smith throwing up on a length.

Holland in Peshawar was more of a struggle, especially when a specially sharpened seven-inch, spear-like piece of wood went whizzing past my head. Fielding on the boundary in the sub-continent has always been hazardous. Fruit, ice-cubes, plastic bottles (some empty, some still with their original contents, others full of more natural substances), plastic bags filled with sand and water, and bits of rubbish are standard ammunition. I wasn't in the best frame of mind anyway after being thumped around the park and sent to the boundary as the Dutch chased our 279. I'd had an argument with Athers because I'd bowled only three overs and I needed practice. Thorpey bowled no fewer than six overs. It was a perfect time to get some overs in, but Athers saw it differently. The locals were quite keen to see an upset, anyway. Our attempts to practise on the edge of the square had been interpreted by the local media as England trying to find out how the wicket would play, acting in breach of the World Cup rules. Worse than that: it was suggested that money changed hands. It had. The groundsman had been thanked with a tip of 93p. The headline read: 'Englishmen at it again!'

I've always enjoyed a good banter with the crowd. I like a laugh and a joke, but this was turning nasty. It was the last straw when that spear flew by my head. What if I'd turned round at the wrong moment? I took the weapon to the umpire, who contacted the match referee. The police got involved and I think someone was arrested. Yorkshire get a lot of stick for the laddish behaviour that takes place on the Western Terrace at Headingley, but there aren't many scraps. I prefer crowds that get involved and make a noise; it gives the game a bit of atmosphere. I know there are the traditionalists who like to sit in a blazer, shirt and tie and quietly watch the cricket. But grounds have also got to cater for those who come to make a day of it, down a few beers, have a burger at lunchtime, have a laugh and a singsong . . . so they go home with a sore voice and a sore head. There's nothing wrong with that as far as I'm concerned. I love the atmosphere at Edgbaston, where that happens, and Headingley. Those are the best two places to play for atmosphere. It's more like a football match than cricket. The crowd gets behind you and lifts the team. Old Trafford tends not to be as busy as it used to be, and Trent Bridge is not as lively as Edgbaston or Headingley. I'm not a big fan of the Oval as a ground, it's too big. Lord's has a great atmosphere because it's different and because of the history. The additions and changes made to Lord's in recent years have been imaginative, in keeping with the place, and they have worked. I still smile when I walk through the Long Room, down the pavilion steps and all the ladidah. Yet at the Nursery End there's singing and chanting from the lads. The best of both worlds. That day in Peshawar is the only time I've felt in danger, apart from the time at Melbourne when someone used a five iron to knock golf balls on to the square during a one-dayer. The M.C.G. may have changed, but the spirit of the riotous Bay 13 still lives on. During our last tour, Warnie had to come on and calm the crowd down. The Zimbabwe crowd enjoy a drink and they can come out with such classics as 'Lend us your brain, Mullally, I want to build an idiot.' Some crowds are witty and clever, others just like to abuse you. We're advised not to get involved with spectators, but I made the front page of the *Sun* when I rugby-tackled a fan who came on during a semi-final defeat by Northants.

Two wins out of three almost guaranteed us a quarter-final place, but we needed impressive displays against South Africa and Pakistan. South Africa carried on from where they left off a month earlier. England were soundly beaten by 78 runs. Athers had a miserable day. He departed to the fourth ball of our innings, then got into hot water by calling a local journalist a buffoon. There were calls for his head again as the media made a meal of this incident. Despite apologies, there were threats that the journalist was going to sue Athers when we returned to Pakistan at the end of 2000, claiming that he had suffered ridicule and had lost his fiancée, who did not want to be the bride of a 'buffoon'.

Our state of mind can be gauged by the five-wicket loss to a Karachi XI in a warm-up game before the final group game against Pakistan. Two of our lads were playing for the opposition (Thorpey and Jack Russell) but they made little contribution. Our disposition was not helped by a running commentary from the loudspeaker announcer. I wasn't too pleased, walking down to fine leg, to hear bellowed across the ground, 'Not a good over from Gough.' The man was eventually gagged by the management.

We'd shown ourselves poor chasers so far. Could we set Pakistan a decent target? Yes . . . at 147–0 – courtesy of Judgey and Athers – in 28 overs. No . . . at 249–9 after 50 overs. We'd lost our way again. That was a great shame because the atmosphere in the National Stadium was something the like of which I had never experienced before. When Javed Miandad came out to bat the noise was deafening, and the only man to play in all six World Cups responded by seeing Pakistan home by seven wickets. That made a mockery of the rumours that Pakistan might throw the game so as to benefit from a home quarter-final tie. Later, during the match-fixing crisis of 2000, Illy revealed that he had been contacted by a bookie before the match. I couldn't imagine anyone paying money for England to play badly. We were perfectly capable of doing that by ourselves during this World Cup.

We hadn't played good cricket, but England were through. Not only that, we had the draw we wanted: Sri Lanka in Faisalabad. We thought that, despite our stuttering performances, the gods had smiled on us and given us a route to World Cup glory. That shows how much we were out of touch in this 1996 tournament. Harvey (Neil Fairbrother) and Corkie were both injured, so we turned to Daffy. The day before, Daffy was bowling off-spin in the nets. Illy was watching. 'That's what you've got to bowl,' he announced.

We were practising on a huge bunsen. Daffy was turning it – as anyone would with any idea of bowling. Our strategy had gone to pot. It was our biggest game, the World Cup quarter-final, and England were totally oblivious as to what was about to hit us. Jayasuriya and Gurusinha. We never got enough runs. Only some bold hitting from Daffy, Dermot and me got us past 200. That turned out to be well short of the mark. I could not believe the way the Sri Lankan batsmen came at us. The ball wasn't seaming and they just tee'd off. Desperate situations require desperate remedies. We opened with Richard Illingworth. He took one wicket and might have got another if I'd held on to a hard chance from Gurusinha. But his first two overs cost 27 runs. Jayasuriya's 50 came in 29 balls, a new World Cup record. My ten overs cost only 36 runs, quite an achievement. But it was too little, too late. England were out. At least we had lost to the team that would go on to be World Cup champions, but that couldn't disguise the fact that we had had a poor winter.

England had not won a Test in South Africa and lost the 1995/6 series. In 13 one-day internationals in the first three months of 1996, our record of three victories included Holland and the United Arab Emirates. It was clear to one and all that Illingworth was not the answer; our manager had created more problems than he'd solved. Keith Fletcher had been the scapegoat after our Ashes failure. Illy was too old for the job, and he returned to the role of just being chairman of selectors. Who was going to be the next lucky guy to coach the England cricket team?

12. The Wives' Tale

Step forward, David Lloyd . . . or Bumble, as he's known in the cricketing world. Most of the management returned from the World Cup to lick their wounds. Illy's public row with Devon carried on long into the summer. The publication of Illy's book, aptly titled *One-Man Committee*, got him into hot water with Lord's over his criticism of Devon, who had attacked Illy in the papers on his return, and our supremo was charged with bringing the game into disrepute. That was nonsense. Despite our problems with him, I was glad when Illy was eventually cleared on appeal.

Athers came home to consider his future, too. Illy had got him down and, after such a poor winter, he was wondering whether it was time to step down. That possibility certainly played a part in the selectors' choice of coach as a successor. Bumble was coach at Lancashire and had known Athers since he was a boy. Bumble's the eternal optimist and enthusiast. And as mad as a badger, and the lads loved him. But he had a job on his hands; he entered a dressing-room that was soul-less. Bumble was a good choice. He brought enjoyment back into the dressing-room, put messages around the walls and got the spirit back into the England camp. But there was one problem beyond even his considerable skills.

Again, it all started with Illy. 'Blame the wives and families' was his public verdict after we lost the Test series in South Africa. According to our boss, they were a distraction and we had lost our focus. That's a rather strange diagnosis, because I remember that Illy had his wife, Shirley, there as well. From a personal point of view, my wife Anna has never ever got in the way of my cricket or affected my cricket, nor have any of my family. I just laugh when it's suggested that this can affect your performance because I think it's a load of rubbish. When I'm playing in a Test match at Head-ingley and then go home, does that mean I'm going to perform badly next day? Of course not. Touring is hard work, and so is being stuck in hotel rooms for weeks on end. Having your family around you can be a big boost to a cricketer's wellbeing.

Illy was right. The families *were* a distraction. But that was the Board's fault. Our nearest and dearest were not catered for; there was no organization surrounding their visit. Today, there is. Coaches pick them up at the airport and take them to the ground, so the players don't have to worry about them. At Newlands in 1996, our wives, girlfriends and kids were left to fry, with no shade, during that final Test when the temperature was well into the 90s. Three winters later, in Australia, the transformation was remarkable. The Test match tickets were for boxes, in the shade, and a crèche was provided for the children. In South Africa, no thought was given to our other halves being there, not even as an afterthought. It should have been part of the tour preparation. Today, when a wife comes out with kids, we get an extra room. In South Africa, we were cramped into poor hotels that were not suitable for families in the first place.

Although my place was assured in England's one-day line-up, I had the feeling at the end of the South African tour that my Test match future was not so certain. After taking part in the Texaco series against India, which we won with two wins and one no-result, I took no part in the Test series against India. Instead, all my energies were devoted to Yorkshire, and I couldn't have been happier. An awful lot had happened to me in a couple of years and I was grateful for the chance to take stock. 'I hope they don't pick me this summer,' I told Martyn Moxon in July after some newspapers were talking of the possibility of my recall. It seems strange now, but that was the way I felt. I didn't even miss the Lord's Test. The game had become a chore over the past year and I just wanted to get back to enjoying my cricket again.

I don't know whether performance affects enjoyment or vice versa. The various niggles and injury problems hadn't helped and nor had Illy's period in charge. Test cricket may be tough, intimidating and hostile, but I have always found it enjoyable. Recently, I hadn't been looking forward to matches. My summer away from the Test arena helped me regain my love of cricket, just by being on the county circuit again.

This was reflected in my performances, taking 66 wickets and hitting my maiden first-class century. Yorkshire actually hit the top spot in the county championship for the first time since 1987 when we beat Surrey by 221 runs at Middlesbrough in early June. Ben Hollioake made his first-class debut in that game. Our success was based on centuries from our Michaels, Vaughan and Bevan, and I chipped in with 5–36 in Surrey's second innings. My form was even better in the next game, against Warwickshire. My first county century, 121, included four sixes and 11 fours. I also took six wickets in our ten-wicket win. Yorkshire's ascent came to a shuddering halt when Leicestershire beat us by an innings and 151 runs at Bradford, with Vince Wells and James Whitaker both hitting double-hundreds. Consistency was still a problem. A ten-wicket win over Hampshire was followed by a 197-run defeat by Somerset, both on Yorkshire soil. Sussex beat us by two wickets at Eastbourne, having been 114–7, chasing 226 for victory, when a win would have put us top at the start of August. What annoyed us here was Ed Giddins's career-best 6–47 in our second innings. We believed he shouldn't have been playing, having failed a drug test and been ordered to appear before the T.C.C.B.'s disciplinary committee. There was no question of being innocent until proven guilty here. Giddins had already failed the test, and he was subsequently banned from all cricket for over a year. I find it ridiculous that Giddins was able to produce a career-best performance between being caught and being sentenced. Our title aspirations disappeared when Gloucestershire beat us by ten wickets at Bristol, our third defeat in a row, and Yorkshire eventually finished sixth.

The loss of Test income can seriously affect a cricketer's standard of living. I was lucky, though, with the various deals and endorsements Clifford Bloxham had arranged for me outside cricket, so my Test income was not crucial to my standard of living. The key for me was that I was taking wickets again and feeling wanted once more, knowing I could still bowl and getting my head straight. There had been times when I went home to Anna and asked, 'Have

I lost it?' I remember getting quite upset. In a short space of time I'd gone from being the next Ian Botham to being unable even to get in the side. You can blame the niggles, but the longer you are out of the team, the greater the worry about how you'll do if and when you get back. Having made an immediate impact first time around, how will you cope next time? If you don't make an immediate impact, will the doubts creep in? I never doubted that I'd get another chance for England. I'd done it on the big stage once and I could do it again. All I needed was to get certain things right. Basically, I probably needed to grow up a bit. When you go from being a young county cricketer with limited experience to an international superstar overnight, it's hard to cope. Nobody teaches you how to handle that. You have to learn the hard way in England. I went through it. I'm a better person for it, and I grew up a lot in that period away from the Test team. And that's when I started saying I'd play every game as though it was my last. I've played my cricket that way ever since.

I was told halfway through the summer that I'd be going away on tour. There was a move to bring me back for the final Test against Pakistan with England 1–0 down in the series, but it was decided that it would be best to leave me alone until the winter. Half of me wanted to play, the other half thought the selectors had made the sensible choice. Everything seemed to be going against me at a time when I needed a bit of luck. Ultimately, the time away from the national side meant I was working on my game and having time off. It worked for me. When I did come back in Zimbabwe, I was ready and raring to go. I took part in the Pakistan Texaco series which is often discussed when match-fixing is mentioned. England had taken the series 2-0, with victories at Old Trafford and Edgbaston. The final tie at Trent Bridge was a 'dead' game, and Nick Knight's second successive century gave us a good chance of achieving a whitewash. Pakistan got home with two balls and two wickets to spare, thanks to an unbeaten 31 from Rashid Latif. Even at the time, it seemed strange that his team-mates did not share his joy at dragging his team back from the brink.

They say that things get worse before they get better. That's true so far as our wives and families were concerned. After the problems in South Africa, the authorities decided to ban this travelling circus from our tour to Zimbabwe over Christmas and the New Year. I couldn't believe what I was hearing. It wasn't just Illy's comments, Athers was also in favour of 'no sex, please, we're England cricketers'. At the pre-tour camp in Lanzarote everyone was moaning, and we held a meeting. I told Athers it was easy for him to take a stand; he was a single man. I seriously considered quitting the tour and it was Anna who really talked me out of it. She had seen how hard I had worked to get back, and she thought I would have been the one to be harmed most by such a gesture.

I'm sure Athers only wanted what was best for the team, but it was the attitude of Lord's that got under my skin, and I told chief executive Tim Lamb as much after a very heated phone call. I asked him what other sportsmen go away for such a long period of time and are denied their conjugal rights by their employers. Top businessmen who go away for a tenth of the time we were going to be absent would get their families flown out at the company's expense. We had to pay the air fares for the privilege of being with our loved ones.

Lamb's answer was typical. 'What would you do if you were in the army?'

'I'm not in the f★★★★★★ army, Tim! I'm in the England cricket team. I should be allowed to bring out my wife for ten days in the middle of a three-and-a-half-month tour.' (Anna wasn't going to bring the kids. She just wanted to see me for ten days.) 'I can't see the problem.'

Lamb's only riposte was: 'Isn't your marriage strong enough for you to go away this winter without your family?'

I have to confess that at this point I lost it. I can't recall what my reply was; I can, however, imagine. I was furious. Anna was standing beside me trying to calm me down, but I just told Lamb what I thought of him and then slammed the phone down.

Nothing was achieved by our Lanzarote meeting. The only person who backed me up on the wives-on-tour issue was Ronnie Irani. I thought we had offered a reasonable compromise: no children, no parents, no nannies, just the other halves. But the Board would not move. And it showed in our performance, as our team morale reached a new low on tour. I felt that the Board was being totally unreasonable. How can grown men be treated this way? They knew how I felt about the issue. To this day it still rankles with me that they could ban my wife from seeing me when I was away from home for over three months. I had only two recourses: either to drop out of the tour or to smuggle Anna out and put her in a different hotel. I told the management that I was considering the latter. They responded by telling me that they would have to think seriously about sending me home if I did. In a way I would have loved them to have tried. The publicity would have made them the laughing-stock of the cricketing world. This was my third Christmas in a row away on tour. I understand and accept the demands and traditions of a five-Test Ashes tour. But a two-Test series in Zimbabwe over Christmas? Do me a favour. That's a joke, and it shows a complete lack of consideration for the England players.

It got worse. We spent Christmas sharing small rooms in the unexceptional Holiday Inn in Harare, while Tim Lamb was staying in the top-class Sheraton with his wife – talk about rubbing salt into our wounds! The one good thing that emerged was that Lord MacLaurin, who was about to take over as chairman of the E.C.B., radically changed our living conditions. From that day on, England players have not had to share rooms. Another compromise we suggested was coming home for a week before going on to New Zealand, but that idea was kicked into touch as well.

Hopefully, we've learnt from these acts of mismanagement. In the winter of 2000, the tours were separate, allowing the players to go home from Pakistan in mid-December and leave for Sri Lanka at the end of January. Spending Christmas at home should be the norm rather than the exception. But the two winters of 2001/2 and 2002/3 are scheduled to include Christmas away, the first in India and then back to Australia in 2002/3. We're touring more places and, despite fewer first-class matches, the schedules are getting tighter and longer. Something has got to give.

Zimbabwe was a watershed tour for many reasons. I was happy to be back in the England camp. Unfortunately, we had to struggle to come to terms with conditions off the field, and an air of gloom descended over the tour that did not lift until we landed in New Zealand. We lost to Mashonaland by seven wickets in Harare, but we beat Matabeleland in Bulawayo in a match in which I took 11–139. Even that win failed to lift the mood of the party. We lost the first one-dayer after being bowled out for 152, although Zimbabwe were in trouble at 106–7, before easing home by two wickets. Then it was the 'we flippin' murdered them' Test in Bulawayo. All the drama came on the final day as we chased 205 to win in 37 overs. We needed three runs off Heath Streak's final delivery, but Knight and I managed only two. Knight was run out for 96 and, for the first time in Test history, a match was drawn with the scores level. Knight had hit a magnificent six in that last over, leaving five needed off three deliveries. Heath Streak then bowled a wide; I can't describe it any other way. Zimbabwe official Ian Robertson made no move or signal. That saved Zimbabwe. Streak admitted afterwards he was 'lucky' that the ball was not called. That admission earned him a fine.

We were fuming. Our great effort had just failed. Bumble was beside himself with rage and wanted to get out of there as quickly as possible. His conduct that afternoon led to a reprimand from the soon-to-be-formed England Cricket Board.

I don't think I've spent a more miserable Christmas, and it was no comfort to wake up looking at the face of Robert Croft rather than Anna; Croftie was no substitute. He'd been sent a CD, *Child of Mine*, by Mark Owen of Take That; it was his first solo single. We played it about 25 times on Christmas Day and couldn't stop laughing. At least it was better than crying.

The day was a disaster. Nets in the morning were rained off, so we practised in the afternoon and our Christmas lunch was not a lavish affair. Part of the problem was that there was nothing to do in Zimbabwe, especially in Bulawayo. This was also the tour when relations between the players and the travelling media turned sour, culminating in the squad voting not to attend the press panto. We'd taken a lot of stick from them, and most of the lads didn't want to go. Why should we go and have to pretend to be friends? We went there to win the series.

It turned out to be a harder tour, both on and off the field, than we had expected. Even our trip to Victoria Falls was a shambles. The plan was for us to charter two planes, only one of the pilots went down with malaria, so 16 of us squashed into a 12-seater, with four guys on the floor without seat-belts. Coming back, another plane pitched up: a four-seater. Wayne, Ronnie and I went to the toilet at the wrong time and drew the short straws: the big plane was taking off. We flew back to Harare in a thunderstorm. Our journey took us over two and a half hours as we tried to avoid it.

We were bowled out for 156 in the Harare Test, but the roomies – Gough 4–40 and Croft 3–39 – pegged Zimbabwe back to a lead of 59 runs. Stewie hit a century as we pressed for the win that would have shut up our hosts; however, the rain put paid to that. Instead, the locals had plenty to shout about as we resumed the one-day series. Our performances at this time showed how low we were as a team, and we fully deserved our whitewashing. We couldn't lift ourselves up. I hate to admit it, but we just wanted to get out of the place. The final shame was the 131-run defeat in the last game as England were bowled out for 118, a total that included five ducks. Eddo Brandes, a chicken-farmer, collected a famous hat-trick. His occupation gave the touring journalists a field day. We'd been struggling with the balance of our one-day side for quite a while, since South Africa and the World Cup in fact. England were still experimenting, trying to find the right balance between Test match and one-day cricketers. Zimbabwe demonstrated that we did not have the right blend. The trip affected some players more than others. Caddie was out of sorts and he just wasn't up for it. As soon as we hit New Zealand, we saw a new Andrew Caddick. But in Zimbabwe, both in the nets and out in the middle, he didn't look interested. Not that Athers showed a great deal of understanding. As soon as Caddie's attention faded, his future participation became surplus to requirements. Unless we picked ourselves up, New Zealand was going to see more of the same.

13. Rocket Man

No group of visitors has ever been so grateful to set foot in New Zealand, not even Captain Cook's crew on the *Endeavour*. Several of our party – including Athers, Ronnie Irani, Tuffers and Wayne – dumped their luggage at the hotel and went straight out to the bar next door. They returned to the hotel for a champagne breakfast the next morning and went straight to bed to sleep it off. They came in doing the 'Two Ronnies' and singing 'Walking on Sunshine'. I could not believe how the mood and spirit of the side had changed overnight.

Someone compared landing in New Zealand to going to Heaven; it might even have been me. A few weeks later, England's fast bowlers were sent on another journey. This time we were put in a rocket that was heading into space. That was our punishment for failing to bowl out one of the worst No. 11s in world cricket. Our failure to remove Danny Morrison, holder of a world-record 24 ducks, in nearly two sessions, cost us victory in the Auckland Test. When we mess up abroad, the normal cry is 'Send them home.' That was too good for us. After Zimbabwe, that was what we wanted. Instead, the members of England's frustrated bowling attack – Mullally, Cork, White, Tuffers and me – were pictured peering out of the windows of a cartoon rocket on the back pages of the tabloid press. Fly me to the moon. At least it was an improvement on the bunny rabbits we had been labelled in Australia, two winters earlier, or the various vegetables that have been associated with the England soccer team.

One player who should have been sent home was Dominic Cork. He hadn't even wanted to go to Zimbabwe, and he pulled out of the tour at the last moment. I don't know why he bothered to go to New Zealand, either. His behaviour out there nearly cost him his Test career. He should have been sent off the field in

Auckland. After a furious argument with Athers, he told his England captain to 'f★★★ off'. Lord MacLaurin got to hear of the problems, and the word went out that he wanted Cork put on the next plane. We all knew Corkie was having problems, going through a divorce. But that was no excuse for his behaviour. He clearly wasn't in the right frame of mind. It would have done us all a favour if he had stayed at home. I dread to think what would have happened if he had been in Zimbabwe. For some reason the selectors did not think we could manage without him; they obviously thought him too valuable to leave at home. However, he wasn't mentally right; his cricket was at the stage I'd gone through a year earlier. When you make an immediate impact for England, you think the free ride is going to carry on for ever. It doesn't work that way. You can't keep on acting like a kid; you've got to grow up. And I had not had his personal problems.

Dominic wasn't at his best, and he started alienating his friends. He was struggling. Corkie had never been the most popular of cricketers and he has rubbed plenty of people up the wrong way over the years. This was their chance to put the boot in; there's nothing nicer, some feel, than helping someone on his way when the slide begins. That wasn't his particular problem. Many county cricketers resent the success of others. It's the English mentality, especially cricketers'; they are jealous of others. That's what happened to the Hollioakes: instant success and money. Suddenly the boot goes in. I've toured with them both, and they're good lads. Corkie's problem was that he didn't start out with too many friends.

I am not here to put the boot in. Corkie and I go back a long way and I've probably been closer to him than most. Our two families were close and I'd known his then wife Jane, who's a Yorkshire lass, a long time; my sister used to sit with her at the cricket. Maybe I know him too well. Corkie's got his faults as well as his good points. During the 1996 summer, Anna and I rang up Jane to say we were dropping in to see them after going to Alton Towers. Dominic had actually left home that morning. Jane panicked, rang him and told him we were coming, so he rushed back. We didn't have a clue that this had happened. When we got there, though, it wasn't difficult to work out that something was up. They hardly spoke and, when they did, it was just snapping at each other. Anna and I looked at each other; time to go. Once we had left, Jane rang Anna up, explaining that Dominic was moving out. I hadn't been aware there was a real problem although afterwards you realized there had been signs of them drifting apart.

It hit Corkie hard. No one wants these things to happen, but they do. His exploits on the cricket field had made him a public figure. It's harder when your problems are displayed in public for all to pore over and discuss. That public scrutiny of private matters is part of the price of fame in the UK. It doesn't seem to be so important in other parts of the cricketing world. The Aussies are confused as to why English papers seem as keen to put Shane Warne on the news pages as on the sports pages. I don't accept that sporting prowess should mean that your private life has to be sacrificed. I appreciate that international recognition brings certain responsibilities and we have a duty to behave when in the public eye. It is a fact of life in the UK.

Corkie's split was also tough for me. I was friends with them both, and I still am. Cricket can take a heavy toll on relationships – not surprisingly, with the lengthy separations. Even in the summer, I'm hardly at home. That's one of the reasons I moved nearer London early in 2001. Even coming home after a tour can be hard. You've had weeks in hotels with only yourself to bother about. You are waited on hand and foot. You put your laundry in a bag, and you return the same night to find it, cleaned and pressed, hanging up in your wardrobe. If you don't want to eat in one of the top-class restaurants, just pick up the phone and a man will appear with a trolley of whatever you fancy. The television is all yours: watch what you want, when you want. Fancy a beer, a glass of wine or a packet of cashews, open the mini-bar. If the room gets rather claustrophobic, pick up the sun-tan lotion and make your way to a sun-lounger by the pool. Much as you may have waited for weeks to return to the family home, it doesn't work that way; it takes time to adjust to becoming a normal human being again. You have to start doing things yourself instead of having them done for you. If I don't remember to stop myself dropping my clothes all over the floor, Anna soon reminds me. All cricketers have to learn to share their living space again.

Dominic never discussed the breakdown of his relationship with me. Corkie has always kept things to himself, whereas I am much more open with him. Although we go back a long way, there are periods when we're not very close, not even communicating by phone that much. I used to be the one who rang him up when he had done well. Occasionally I got into him because he never did the same for me. Then one day, quite out of the blue, he rang me up a couple of years ago and we've kept in touch regularly ever since, especially since he got back into the England side in summer 2000. Corkie has his mates. New Zealand is where the clique started: Corkie, Tuffers, Ronnie, Nasser and Thorpey. They've always been close buddies.

Corkie never gave himself a chance in New Zealand. He failed to turn up for a fitness test before leaving England and it was downhill from then on. Our coach was far from happy with Corkie, but Bumble had his own problems; the whole Zimbabwe experience had left him shattered. Ian Botham, as he had done in Bulawayo, decided to lend a hand – not that this aided Bumble's recovery: Botham took Bumble out for a day's fishing. While the others headed for the river, Beefy put his arm round Bumble, locked the cabin door and opened a case of wine. Bumble was not seen for 24 hours. He was certainly feeling the pressure.

After Zimbabwe, we needed a good start. After winning two provincial games easily, Athers made the perfect start to the Test series at Eden Park by winning the toss. The conditions were perfect for bowling; the ball would seam and swing. Our luck had changed at last. The lunchtime score was 63 without loss. Nobody could believe it. We bowled so badly and we couldn't make them play, despite the fact that the ball was swinging everywhere. Corkie, Mullally and I all bowled. We couldn't even hit the cut strip. Athers showed his disgust by bringing Tuffers on in the eleventh over. Stewie was exhausted after a session of goal-keeping, even dislocating a finger after another dive.

We came off at lunch, and Bumble was nowhere to be seen. He wouldn't come into the dressing-room, he wouldn't speak to us, and eventually he was spotted wandering around the practice field, talking to himself. He did not speak to us for the rest of the day. It was Athers who finally went up to him and said 'For Christ's sake, grow up. We had a bad session. You can't treat the lads like that just because they've bowled badly.' We did bowl badly, no one was arguing the toss about that. We just could not believe his behaviour. We had heard about Bumble's famous explosions; Bulawayo was a case in point, but that had seemed justified. Bumble was a great bloke to have on tour. But we were discovering that, every so often, he gets into a flap and loses it big time. Bumble wants to fight the world – and he's not the biggest of blokes. The best way I can explain it is that Bumble so badly wants England to win that the pressure gets to him. You could never question his motives; Bumble had the best of intentions and he always had our interests at heart. He is so proud to be English. That was the heart of the problem. Whenever England got into a tight spot, Bumble would start to lose it. When we lost one-day internationals by not running down the wicket and hitting it over the top, 'Run down the wicket. You don't go down the wicket and miss it,' was Bumble's repeated cry. That always made me laugh. The best players of spin in the world all sweep the ball. You can't run down the wicket and hit it down the ground when it's spinning both ways. It was that sweep shot that worked so well for England in Pakistan in winter 2000/1, especially in the Lahore Test.

I thought Bumble was a good coach. Overall, I found him very helpful; we spoke the same language. He got team spirit and belief back in the side after a bad couple of years. He deserves a lot of credit for that. It had been missing for a long time. Sadly, on occasions he let himself down. We came to accept his behaviour because we knew what lay behind his outbursts. He also backed up his players. I can't remember a single time when he slagged us off in public; after the Illy era, that was a welcome change. Still, he could make the dressing-room a nerve-racking place when he got uptight. That was the downside. Dressing-rooms can be tense places at the best of times A coach with his heart on his sleeve makes it worse. For me, the pluses outweighed the minuses as far as Bumble was concerned. All he wanted was for England to do well, and he tried his hardest to make that happen.

New Zealand made 390 at Eden Park. My dropping of Cairns on the first evening was costly. The next day I claimed three quick wickets, before our batsmen took control of the game. Stewie and Thorpey hit hundreds to give us a first-innings lead of 131. At the close of the fourth day, the Kiwis were 56–3. Victory was a formality when I knocked out Simon Doull's stumps after half an hour of the afternoon session. The Kiwis' lead was 11, with one wicket left. Exactly 266 deliveries later, Morrison was 14 not out and that man Nathan Astle had completed his century. Both men faced the same number of balls in that undefeated last-wicket stand of 106 in almost three hours. Athers tried everything, and so did the bowlers. Nothing worked. The curse of Zimbabwe had followed us to New Zealand, it seemed.

Bumble's relationship with the media deteriorated even further when we lost to N.Z. 'A' by 90 runs in Wanganui; apparently we had upset the locals by not hanging around afterwards to let them gloat. It was clear that nothing less than a Test win was going to get the press off our backs. I was the next person in hot water. That first Test 'failure' had me fired up for the second Test in Wellington. We soon had New Zealand in trouble. Tail-ender Geoff Allott was holding us up, so I tried to unsettle him with a few well-chosen words. Before I knew it, umpire Steve Bucknor had walked over from square-leg to have a word with Athers in the gully. Athers came over and told me to cool it. It was no big deal, and the match referee Peter Burge wasn't involved. I was trying to get him out and was warned for bowling bumpers at a tail-ender. He'd been in for half an hour and I was told I could not bowl short at him. I thought it was ridiculous, so I got into him in another way, via a bit of chat. That was also out of order. It was a lot of nonsense about nothing. I wouldn't apologize, not a chance. I will do anything to get a wicket. When bowlers run in at me, they don't bowl half-volleys. Tail-enders can be just as hard to get out as front-line batsmen. They just defend and try to hang around for as long as they can, especially when they are fast bowlers. They don't want to get out to other fast bowlers. There is not a soul in world cricket who can't protect himself. If he can't, he should not be out there.

I got warned against Gussie one year – and I never bowled a single bumper at him. I was told if I bowled another one, I would be warned off. He'd got 25 not out at the time. I bowled everything at his ribs; not one ball went above his head. I was peppering him and he kept gloving it. It's the worst law in cricket. Bowling at the body means you are not bowling at the stumps.

Somebody had it in for me during that Wellington Test, which we won by an innings and 68 runs on the final day. Only the rain allowed the Kiwis to last that long. I took 9–92 in the match, and Caddie claimed six. Thorpey's century was backed up by fifties from Nasser, Stewie and Creepy. After all the disappointments of Auckland, I was delighted when I was told I was Man of the Match. So how come, you might ask, has G.P. Thorpe that honour according to the *Wisden Almanack*? Let me explain. Some old-timer was making the presentation – I can't remember his name – and it had all been written down for him. The first page contained details of my bowling in both innings, plus the achievement of the other contenders, finishing with Thorpey's valuable knock. At the top of the next page, it read: 'The Bank of New Zealand's Man of the Match is . . . Darren Gough.' Unfortunately, our man never got to page two; I don't know if he even realized there was a page two. Apparently he decided that the last name on the first page had to be the Man of the Match. I must confess, my face must have been a picture when Thorpey's name was announced. The officials came into the dressing-room straight away and apologized. They kindly gave me another award, but they added that it couldn't be changed officially. That's why Thorpey's name is in the record books. Now you know the truth.

The Barmy Army drive some people mad with their non-stop singing and chanting. I've never felt that way about them. Wherever we are, anywhere in the world, they pitch up in varying numbers,

even in Pakistan in winter 2000/1. I've always welcomed their
support and commitment. And Atherton's Barmy Army has never
been as appreciated as in the winter of 1996/7. They held a disco
at the end of the New Zealand innings, and several of us went
along. As we got to the door, we were all picked up off our feet
and carried in on their shoulders. I remember seeing sixty- and
seventy-year-old blokes who go on Yorkshire pre-season tours in
there. The atmosphere was amazing. We got up on stage and did
'Alouette', which was a party piece Croftie originally brought into
the side. Some may find the Barmy Army, who have been part of
all my England tours, too noisy and too crude. But when I am
charging in on the flattest wicket in the world somewhere on the
sub-continent, you wouldn't believe the lift those guys have given
me at various times. It helps tremendously to know that you are
not alone.

The final Kiwi Test in Christchurch belonged to Athers. There
would have been a riot if the Man of the Match had gone to anyone
else. The early exchanges went the home side's way. Despite Athers
carrying his bat for 94, after a series of casual shots we still finished
118 runs short of the Kiwis' first-innings 346. The match was more
evenly poised on the third evening, with New Zealand 95–6. Brian
Young got off with a warning after appearing to ignore Darrell
Hair's raised finger the first time it went up, when Nick Knight
claimed a catch at silly point. What was most damaging to us was
Cairns's eighth-wicket partnership with young left-arm spinner
Daniel Vettori. England needed 305 to win. Only once before
had England reached 300 for victory in the fourth innings. Such
historical statistics and match situations are meat and drink to
Athers; he gladly accepts any excuse for a prolonged stay at the
wicket.

Overnight, we were two wickets down, with another 187 runs
required. Athers reached the century he was denied when he ran
out of partners in the first innings. Athers's departure led to a
wobble, from 226–3 to 231–6. Another 74 needed, with Creepy
and Corkie at the wicket. Vettori took 4–97 in 57 overs in only his
second Test, but our pair kept their nerve. I knew Corkie was

desperate to see us home; the trip had been hard work for him, especially after he had celebrated taking a Test wicket earlier on by pulling his shirt over his head, soccer-style. This was not the sort of behaviour that the new boss of the new England & Wales Cricket Board, which came into existence on New Year's Day, wanted to see.

England cricketers welcomed Lord MacLaurin's appearance and appointment that winter. That wasn't only because of the improvement in our living conditions. I've never been one to get too close to cricket officials – Yorkshire has taught me that – nor for believing everything that they tell me. At a meeting before the 1997 summer, Lord Mac told us about the changes he had in mind, the new ideas, and that the money would get better. Three years later, we were still waiting. He made an instant impression with the lads. As time went on, the squad began to have doubts about his promises. Gradually the changes and the money came through, but it took a lot longer than Lord Mac or we had expected. We were less happy with attempts to make us socially acceptable. After that trip, we were sent to the NatWest offices in the Midlands for a two-day course. The team-bonding adventure games were good fun. Afterwards, we were sent in to a dinner with loads of NatWest top brass, and were told to find the answers to ten questions. The lads got together and decided not to do it; it was degrading. We heard nothing more on the subject.

Athers's endurance effort was the perfect way to sign off the winter. Not so fast. We had another fortnight and five one-day internationals to play before we could go home. Tuffers claimed four wickets in the first game, after being accused of smoking cannabis in an Auckland restaurant. No evidence was ever produced – not that Tuffers took any notice of the story. Our four-wicket win denied the crowd the spectacle of Tuffers walking out to Oasis's 'Cigarettes and Alcohol'. We had each been allowed to choose a piece of music as our individual theme-song. Naturally, mine was Katrina and the Waves' 'Walking on Sunshine'. No prizes for guessing Croftie's – Tom Jones's 'Delilah' – or Jack Russell's – 'How much is that doggy in the window' by Lita Roza.

I took a battering in the second game at Auckland, but we won by six wickets when our target was revised down from 254 in 50 overs to 132 in 26 overs. Don't ask me to explain. The Duckworth/ Lewis is a closed book to me, as it is for most cricketers. I recall one game in England when the side that scored more runs in fewer overs for fewer wickets . . . lost! This Auckland game marked a winning start to Nasser's career as England captain because of Athers's bad back. Nasser would have to wait another two and a half years for the official nod.

I should have sewn the series up in the next game. Needing two off the final ball from Allott, I could scramble only a single bye, for a tie. That was the final result of this five-match series, since we lost the last two matches batting second, as we did throughout the series. We were chasing only 154 at Auckland, failing by nine runs. We ran out of steam at Wellington, the highlight of the day coming when Ian Botham had his head shaved for charity, raising £50,000 for the Child Cancer foundation. The date was 4 March and we had left England before the end of November. It was time to go home.

14. Flatter to Deceive

1997 should have been England's summer. After losing four consecutive series against Australia, we made the perfect start. The Texaco series was already England's before we gave the troubled tourists a real thrashing at Edgbaston. The country caught Ashes fever in a way I'd never experienced before. Yet, by the end of that summer, Australia still had a firm grip on the Ashes and Athers had tried to quit as England captain. If it had not been for the rain at Lord's and a couple of dozen runs at the Oval, England might have lost that series 5–1. This was not England's traditional style of playing. Normally we start badly and never quite catch up. This time, it was something new. Even with everything in our favour, England did not have the character, determination or ability to stay the course. England blew a golden opportunity.

The Aussies had arrived with an inbuilt weakness. This was identified as Mark Taylor, the captain who had helped make them the greatest Test team in the world. Taylor was struggling for runs. The Aussies are a hard bunch. Sentiment plays no part in their camp. The word went out that several senior Aussie players thought he should not be playing, no matter how good a captain he might be. Our media weren't slow to highlight his problem and tried to present him with a nine-inch bat at an early tour match. 'Tubby' Taylor is one of the most popular cricketers of recent times and is perfectly capable of looking after himself. Yet the Aussie management began to get protective, not their style at all. Obviously, they were worried.

The Texaco series belonged to the Holliaokes as England won by six wickets in all three games. Adam hit the winning runs in all three matches – chasing 171 at Leeds, 250 at the Oval and 270 at Lord's – while Ben, 19 years old, made his debut in that final game and smacked Glenn McGrath all over the place. I finally got my five-for at Lord's that Sunday afternoon, but it didn't count. You don't get on the honours board for wickets in a one-day international. At least this time the adjudicator did not make a mistake over the Man of the Match, and I went home with the award. Taylor was still struggling and had dropped himself for that final Lord's match. Even before his loss of form, there had been talk that Australia should have separate captains for the Test and the one-day team. Taylor was not the only Aussie who had not hit his straps, as they say. Edgbaston was our big chance.

How we took it. Taylor decided to bat, and we skittled them out that first morning. Devon came in for his first Test since his Cape Town confrontation with Illy. The latter was no longer chairman of selectors; David Graveney had taken over, with Graham Gooch and Mike Gatting the other selectors. Having won the toss, it can't have been an easy decision for Taylor. Conditions were going to offer the bowlers some assistance. We couldn't afford a first morning like Auckland. It was up to the England bowlers to make the initial impact. I felt good, though. The winter had gone well. My problems were behind me. I was part of the England Test team again, and this was my first home Ashes series.

I was keen to take the first wicket. It wasn't Taylor, but I got through Matthew Elliott's defence and broke a stump. Devon had Taylor caught, and then one of the most amazing incidents in my career occurred. I bowled Greg Blewett, only to hear umpire Peter Willey call, 'No ball.' This is one of the most deflating moments for any bowler. Test wickets are hard enough to come by, and you always feel as though you've thrown one away. The bowler's on a low and his target, the batsman, is on a high because the bowler's carelessness has granted him an extra life. Batsmen often pretend that the 'no ball' call allows them a free hit with no risk. Don't fall for that one. Ninety-nine times out of a hundred, the batsman would have played the same shot anyway, especially to a fast bowler. Against the Aussies, as Harold Larwood would say, 'Don't give them an inch.' I walked back to my mark, smiling. Part of me didn't want to show the Aussies any frustration or disappointment. But mainly I had this strange feeling. 'I've got you out once, Mr

Blewett. I'm going to do it again.' I really believed it and tried to bowl an almost identical delivery. This time Blewett got his bat on it, but only the edge, and it flew to Nasser at third slip. I've rarely celebrated a wicket as wholeheartedly as that one. It was almost as good as taking a hat-trick but not quite. You know it's going to happen only a few times in your career. There's a great photo of me jumping several feet into the air.

After I'd bowled Mark Waugh, Caddie got stuck in, and the best Test team in the world were in tatters at 54–8. Australia reached 118, but only thanks to Warnie blasting 47. Nasser and Thorpey's fourth-wicket stand of nearly 300 destroyed Australia. It was becoming clear that we had caught them cold. It was the chilly start to the summer that helped us. Warnie was not bowling at his best and McGrath had not found his rhythm. We took full advantage because we knew that this situation would not last long. In our innings McGrath took 2–107 and Warnie 1–110. Nasser's knock was the best I've ever seen him play. Not just for the score: 207. Some of his cover drives were inspired. Edgbaston seems to bring out the best in him.

Our first-innings lead was 360. But show an Aussie an impossible task, and he takes it on immediately. Taylor played one of the most remarkable knocks I've ever witnessed from an opponent. All sorts of former cricketing greats were calling for his head, he wasn't in form, and now his team were playing badly. Not too many cricketers have walked to the wicket with the amount of pressure that Taylor was under that Saturday. There was no miraculous return to form; Taylor kept playing and missing. Yet nothing seemed to bother him. He nicked a couple from me over the slips. We had a good contest that afternoon. I was bowling better than he was batting but, by sheer character and determination, Taylor refused to be beaten. Eventually, with help from Elliott and Blewett, the Aussie skipper hauled his team back into the game. At one stage, the Aussies were 327–1 and the pitch was flattening out. Croftie got the top three out, then I got the next trio, but they refused to fold. At 465–6, Australia were 105 in front, and thoughts of a 200-plus run-chase began to loom. It was Mark Ealham who settled

English nerves with three wickets. The victory target was 119. Only the Aussies could have bounced back like that. Theirs had been an almost hopeless cause but they refused to give up, and the England dressing-room was mightily relieved not to be chasing a bigger total.

The Aussie fight-back cut no ice with Athers and Stewie. They wanted the job done . . . and quickly, so as to emphasize our domination. There was to be no crawling to victory in an empty Edgbaston on Monday morning. England won by nine wickets in front of a packed Birmingham crowd on Sunday night, scoring at almost six an over. It's difficult to define, but you know when it's a special Test victory. This was the tops, better than beating South Africa at Headingley or the West Indies at the Oval. This was the big one: the Aussies . . . the Ashes. The best Test team in the world were on the ropes, and now we had the confidence to finish the job. Nasser was named Man of the Match, but this had been a real team effort. Everyone had chipped in.

Edgbaston had been fantastic. It was hard to believe that the last time I had played in a Test here, the England team had been booed and abused by spectators. This time we were acclaimed as national heroes. It was a reaction that was to sweep the country, but when we went out to celebrate that night, entry was barred to us. It turned out that the city of Birmingham was in no mood to celebrate. We tried to get into a nightclub, but a snotty, up-himself bouncer decided that beating the Aussies in the first Ashes Test wasn't reason enough to let us in. We didn't argue, we just laughed and left. Can you imagine the Aussies having the same problem in Brisbane? Fortunately, this was an isolated incident.

I was not prepared for the national reaction to our victory. I had played in winning Tests before, but those achievements were applauded only in the cricket and sporting world. I suppose it's the final step to fame when you are recognized outside your world and become a celebrity, like Ian Botham, Gary Lineker or Frankie Dettori. It's difficult to know why some cross that boundary and others don't. It's a right-place, right-time thing, catching a special mood, maybe giving the country something they hadn't expected.

Whatever it was, I have never known an England win affect the country the way our Edgbaston success did. I can only imagine that it must have been similar to the feeling after Headingley in 1981. A massive buzz. Previously, people would always acknowledge me in the street with a smile or a wave, but now they were patting me on the back. Perhaps for the very first time, I realized what the England cricket team meant to the country. I have to confess, all the razzmatazz was very enjoyable. But it evaporated as quickly as it had appeared after we were rolled over for 77 at Lord's.

We were later accused of taking the Aussies too lightly. Get real: England on top; Australia in disarray. That was the media and the country, not the England cricket team. We knew differently. We had taken a positive first step; that was all. Steve Waugh, Mark Waugh, Shane Warne and Glenn McGrath were all going to go away from Edgbaston and find some form. We knew it would be difficult. What we didn't expect was the reversal of our fortunes to take place as quickly as it did.

Thursday's play at Lord's was rained off and the conditions were overcast. Whoever won the toss was going to have a big advantage. If Glenn McGrath had regained his rhythm and form, we were in trouble. He had. We were. McGrath took 8–38, one of the best returns possible. He gave a masterful display of controlled fast bowling and was basically unplayable. McGrath hit the stumps only once, but he's a caught-behind man; he knows how to find the edge of the bat. McGrath was already a world-class performer, but England had not seen the best of him till now. He was the up-and-coming star and successor to Craig McDermott on my first Ashes tour, but he was wicketless in the Brisbane first Test and did not reappear until the end of the series, in Perth. There we saw more of the real McGrath as he took six wickets, including Atherton twice. He was out of sorts at Edgbaston. Rhythm is the secret to McGrath, and when he tries too hard it can go. We were not daft enough to think McGrath had lost it, just grateful that one of the best fast bowlers in the world was having a bad Test.

I'm not a cricket watcher when I'm at the ground, but there are certain bowlers I really admire: Allan Donald, Courtney Walsh and

McGrath. I've become a big fan of the Aussie. When I first came across him in Australia, I thought he was an arrogant arse. (He probably thinks the same about me.) But as time's gone on, I've watched him bowl and have followed his progress, and I've grown to respect him as much as I do any other cricketer in the world. His performance level is staggering, as the West Indies found out in Brisbane at the end of 2000. McGrath's known for being unfriendly and foul-mouthed on the field, but all he's trying to do is get you out and he will do anything he can and everything it takes. McGrath's a nice enough guy away from the action. Of course, he does have the advantage of having the best spinner in the world at the other end to create additional pressure. It's the one thing that's been missing from England in my time: we've lacked a class spinner. That means England seamers have bowled on wickets and at times when it's not been to their advantage. Australia have had Warne at one end, so the seamers have been rotated and kept fresh at the other end. I've never been a great believer in ridiculing the opposition just because they are Australians or South Africans. They are cricketers, like me. If they perform, I respect them. That doesn't make me fear them or think they are better than me. Credit where credit's due. After all, it makes for more of an achievement if I come out on top.

That didn't happen at Lord's. McGrath came in from the pavilion end and was virtually unplayable. He was on target, and we had no answer to him. I was one of only three players to reach double figures. In the end, the rain did more to stop the Aussies winning than we did. Athers put a brave face on it, highlighting our second-innings recovery. To save the Test match after being skittled out for 77 was going to take some doing without the help of the weather. The truth was, the Aussies were back in the series. England still held that 1–0 lead. We were happy to be heading for Old Trafford and a traditionally flat wicket with that advantage in a six-Test series. England got out of jail at Lord's and the pressure was on the Aussies to get back in the series. They had given us a real fright, but had not gained anything materially. The Aussies pride themselves on being a resilient side under pressure but I'm not so sure. They seem to struggle when going after small totals. We've always said in team talks that if Australia are chasing 150 or so in the last innings, we would back ourselves to win. And we have done so on several occasions. The key to competing with Australia and South Africa is staying with them in the first innings. That's been our weakness in my time; we don't get a good enough score on the board.

There was no doubt the tourists had regrouped, even though the skipper's personal batting showed no such signs. Much as I admired Tubby, he was getting no sympathy from me on the field. I knocked over his poles for a single at Lord's, and we were determined to keep the Taylor captaincy dilemma a major issue in the Aussie camp for as long as possible. Former Aussie stars were even questioning Taylor's mental state. So did we, when he chose to bat first on a damp wicket in Manchester. What Taylor realized, and we didn't until later, was that the bowlers would dig holes in the wicket. As the holes dried out, they got deeper and deeper. By the fourth innings, the wicket was almost unplayable. Taylor knew that batting first on that wicket was the last thing an out-of-form opener wanted – he managed only three runs in the match when debutant Dean Headley had him caught twice – but it gave his team the best chance of winning. Ian Chappell had been one of Taylor's harshest critics, yet his verdict was: 'Batting first was the correct decision, but I don't know if I would have been brave enough to make it.' It could have backfired on the Aussies.

At 42–3, Steve Waugh was absolutely dead to Caddie's first ball. The finger didn't go up. We couldn't believe it. If there's one batsman in the world who'll make the most of a second chance, it's Steve Waugh. And how he did at Old Trafford, with a century in each innings! The first was the killer, as it enabled the Aussies to reach 235. Steve Waugh is so hard to bowl at. You bowl a good over, then throw one up because you fancy getting a nick. Sometimes he uses no feet and slashes at the ball, but he has the art of edging it past fielders, or else it doesn't carry. It's very frustrating. I don't believe it's luck, it's part of his natural batting ability. He never gives his wicket away. You can bowl him maiden after maiden and think you've got him tied down, then he smashes two fours. Some bowlers wear batsmen down. He's a batsman who wears bowlers down.

I got him on this occasion, bowled, as were my other two wickets: Greg Blewett and Paul Reiffel. We weren't unhappy with Australia's total. I couldn't say the same about ours – 162. That was well below par on that wicket, especially after being 94–2. We should have gone past them, but we batted badly again. My old mate Warnie did the damage, 6–48 off 30 overs, on the ground where he had launched his Ashes career four years earlier with that wonder ball to Mike Gatting. I was one of his six victims. We might have been mates for a few years, but the bat–ball contest is always very competitive. He wants me to attack him, come down the wicket and hit him for four or six. I'd like to oblige, but Warnie keeps getting me out.

England were in trouble and we knew it. Batting in the fourth innings was not going to be pleasant. Headley gave us a great start in Australia's second innings. Deano had been brought in to trouble the Aussie left-handers and he did just that. Six of his eight wickets in the match were those of Taylor, Elliott and Michael Bevan, all twice. For Bevan, the most accomplished of limited-overs batters, this was virtually the end of his Test career; he has played only one Test for Australia since. Unfortunately, the pitch flattened out, Steve Waugh would not budge again, and the Aussie lower order of Healy, Warne, Reiffel and Gillespie smacked us all over Old Trafford. We tried everything, but it was one of those days. I remember thinking, 'How the hell do I get this man Waugh out?' I do, every time I play against him. Of all the batsmen round the world, Steve Waugh is the one I'm most glad to see the back of. The Aussies were batting when we should have been, when the pitch was at its easiest. Give the Aussies a sniff of victory and they go on and do it. Once the momentum is there, the Aussies are almost impossible to stop. In the end we were steamrollered. I kept bowling my yorkers to Reiffel, but he kept squeezing them out. You could sense the crowd was growing restless and frustrated, but we felt exactly the same way.

Those Aussie runs also gave the home crowd hope. If England can't get the Aussie tail out, we must have a chance of saving the game. Unfortunately, it never works like that. There's a new ball to contend with, fresh top-class bowlers, and batsmen with a mountain to climb. There's a spring in your step when the opposition need 464 runs for victory. We got to 44 without loss, then it was 55–4 and curtains. Warnie tied us up, and only Creepy's 83 got us to 200. Now the series was level. But the Aussies were ahead on points. They'd had the best of the last two Tests, rolling us over cheaply three times; they had found their form and momentum and were going to be hard to stop now, with McGrath in full flight and Warnie spinning it and getting drift.

The Ashes battle moved on to Headingley, my home patch. Four years earlier, the Ashes had been decided there, when I entered the England dressing-room for the first time. Graham Gooch ended his four-year reign as captain after Allan Border's side won the Test and retained the urn. This was my third Test on home soil, and I still had to make much of an impact. I've never felt any pressure, playing at Headingley. The problem in the early days was trying to stop myself getting too carried away.

As usual, England's failure with the bat meant that the selectors started tinkering with the bowling attack. This time they managed to pick a name out of the hat that surprised even us. Nobody could quite believe it when Gloucestershire's left-armer Mike Smith was named in the squad. What was even more astonishing was the man who was left out on Thursday morning in order to accommodate him: Caddie. Smith is a very good bowler, and things could have gone differently for him if Thorpey had not dropped a simple slip chance from Elliott off his bowling; Elliott went on to make 199. But the team to a man would have gone for Caddie. Athers was overruled. Grav, chairman of selectors, was adamant that Smith should play. That was a strange situation, because I've always reckoned that the captain should have the final say just before the start of play. As soon as we turned up in the nets, Smith looked like the chosen son. All the management were grouped behind Smithie when he was bowling. It was overcast and it was swinging a little bit. I could hear, 'He's swinging it, he's swinging it.' The rest of the bowlers started discussing which one of us was for the chop. Smith had done well and was a good county bowler; nobody was denying that. But this was big-time cricket, against the biggest of the big guns. You can't just pick players on their county championship performances; it's too easy a breeding ground. The selectors have to look at other parts of their game. As it turned out, Smithie didn't swing a single ball, and the media made much of Grav pulling rank over Athers.

After all the discussion about the England bowlers, it was the unchanged batters who had first use of the Headingley strip after Taylor won the toss. The weather disrupted our innings, but not as much as the Aussie bowlers. We reached 154–4, but the last six wickets then went for 18 runs as Jason Gillespie took 7–37. That's another impressive trait of the Aussies: if for any reason the big guns aren't firing, one of the supporting players takes his chance. Mike Kasprowicz claimed 7–36 at the Oval, two Tests later. Taylor was my rabbit again, going for a duck this time. I had Blewett also caught behind, then Deano removed the Waugh twins. It was then that Thorpey dropped Elliott off Smith. Instead of being 50–5, the Aussies passed 300 before the fifth wicket fell. I felt for Smith, knowing how important that first Test wicket is. The Gloucester-shire man is still waiting. But the groan that echoed around Head-ingley told us, if we needed telling, that this might well be a costly mistake. Sometimes you don't worry; you think: we'll get him soon. Not this time. We had Australia where we wanted them, but this setback knocked the stuffing out of us. It was Elliott's day. He kept edging it, he was dropped on the hook off my bowling when he was 40-odd; even at fine leg, this was not Mike Smith's day. Elliott found a perfect partner in Ricky Ponting, who had come in for Bevan. Ponting is a batsman who loves to come forward at you; but if you drop it short he is so quick on to the pull. The Aussies were in full flow when the Headingley wicket was at its best. I felt I was bowling well and ended up with 5–149; that was probably 30 runs too many. The Aussies declared on 501–9 – and that was definitely 200 too many. I won a small battle when I bowled Elliott for 199. I'd gone back to my mark, thinking, 'Come on, Dazzler, he's got 199 – stop him getting 200.' I went for a yorker and he tried to nudge it to mid-wicket, but it swung and knocked his poles. I was delighted; I'd stopped an Aussie getting to a milestone. That might sound petty, but it was important to me. I knew it was important to him, too.

We lost Butcher, Athers, Stewie and Thorpey cheaply, but Nasser and Creepy gave us some hope on that fourth night of saving the game. I went out with Athers for a beer and we bumped into Aussie rugby league legend Mal Meninga and the Canberra Raiders. They were cricket mad. I've never been surrounded by so many big blokes. The Raiders seemed to be operating a self-service free bar, but nobody was brave enough to make a fuss. Back at the hotel, they were passing Ponting and Justin Langer around as though they were a rugby ball. They carried on the celebrations the next day, running on to the field when Australia won.

Our resistance did not last long on the final day. I ended by bagging my first Test pair . . . and on my home ground. I wandered back slowly to the dressing-room and sat down. I looked down and saw that something was lying in one of my shoes. It was a pear – a 'pair'. I could sense the dressing-room waiting for a reaction. I'm not one of those batsman primadonnas. I just laughed. I was distraught at having scored no runs in the Test, but there was nothing I could do about it. I can name some of our batsmen who would have been looking for blood if that trick had been played on them. My wicket had given Australia victory by an innings and 61 runs. Edgbaston was now a distant memory. It got worse. Towards the end of their innings, my calf had started bothering me. The problem didn't seem too serious at the time, but my second Ashes series had ended like my first – prematurely. I didn't play another Test for 11 months. By then England had a new cricket captain.

15. Hamstrung Again

Mike Watkinson may have called me the first white West Indian to play for Yorkshire, yet I fear I am destined never to tour the Caribbean with the senior England side. I made my international debut in 1994, a month after Atherton's team returned from there. I doubt if my body will hold out until 2004, which is our next scheduled visit. I never imagined, as I sat in the Headingley dressing-room at the end of the fourth Ashes Test, that my sore calf would keep me away from the Caribbean in 1998.

I played in Yorkshire's next county match and broke down completely against Northants. The best catch of the match came when Gough hung on to a blow from the dangerous Kevin Curran. That was Gareth Gough, a young lad from the Academy who was on the field for me. Although the problem had started in the Test, I couldn't claim the England insurance because of that Northants appearance. The next problem wasn't so much the injury, rather how long it took to get a correct diagnosis. In the early weeks I was treated for a torn hamstring and, to be honest, that's what it felt like. The next problem was that the pain returned every time I tried to come back, sprint or bowl. I had injection after injection into my knee, then I had an exploratory operation in September. The knee was cleaned out and I went to the BUPA hospital at Roundhay to recuperate and work on building up my strength. There were so many theories about what was wrong with me, it was untrue. Every time my knee got a bit stronger, it would go again. The pain seemed to be coming from both the front and back of my knee, but that was thought to be a secondary condition of my bad hamstring. What I did know was that it was not getting any better, and it was hacking me off.

That's when I went to see Dr Webb in Nottingham, almost as a last resort. I had M.R.I. scans and X-rays, then he injected me, right into the tendon, without an anaesthetic. I can remember that, as clear as a bell. He told me I was getting an injection, got me in a funny position and then, when I wasn't looking, stuck it in. 'Give it three or four days, then try to bowl.' That trial was to be my fitness test for the West Indies, a week before England were due to leave. I bowled four overs indoors at full pelt and never felt a thing. I was just about to declare myself fit after bowling one more over when I felt it go again. Anna was with me, and she started crying when Wayne said: 'We're going to have to pull you out.' England had been to Sharjah in December without me and had won the trophy under Adam Hollioake. Lord's had given me permission to miss the trip because of the arrival of our second child. Missing a birth because of an Ashes tour is one thing, a one-day junket in the Middle East is another. Brennan Kyle arrived on 9 December, and I was present. As it turned out, I wouldn't have been fit to go to Sharjah anyway.

Mr Webb had hoped to get me fit in three weeks, but it took much longer; doesn't it always? Wayne kept ringing from the West Indies and I kept making optimistic noises about being ready for the Test series. Then it was the third Test, and then my final roll of the dice, the one-day series at the end. I never gave up hope and was convinced I was going to get there. The night before my operation in Nottingham, Dr Webb told me there would be a one-inch scar. It was more like six inches, just behind the knee. When I complained, he replied that there had been a bit more of a mess in there than he had expected. When he couldn't find out what was wrong, a bit more was opened up. The cause of all my troubles turned out to be tears in my tendon all the way up. They were repaired, it was all cleaned up and then it was a question of rest. I was in hospital for five days. Lord MacLaurin and Tim Lamb came to see me with a bottle of champagne, but I wasn't ready to celebrate yet. This injury had been the most frustrating of my career, especially with the Caribbean tour disappearing from my itinerary.

More strengthening of the knee was the order of the day, this time at Lilleshall, where they really put you through your paces.

God, it's hard work. After so many disappointments, you begin to wonder whether it may all be a waste of time. But the staff at Lilleshall aren't in the business of letting you feel sorry for yourself. I was making some progress, but I realized that the Caribbean was a pipe-dream. I was desperate to go. As well as being a great place to play cricket, I felt I had something to prove after 1995. I wasn't at my best and dropped out, halfway through the series. Instead of the Caribbean, I went with Yorkshire on a pre-season tour to South Africa, and my first game back was a day/nighter against Western Province. I got a hat-trick. I'd not bowled on the tour and had been told to take it easy. But I couldn't resist charging in when I had the ball in my hand. The injury still felt tight, but I thought, 'This is shit or bust.' For quite a while I felt the problem was going to return. It was the most worrying injury I'd experienced. Above all, it was the uncertainty. Is this going to affect my England career, short term? What about long term? Will I play for my country again? What about Yorkshire? What about my cricket prospects, full stop? It may sound like paranoia, but when you're not sure what the problem is and you have to cope with hours and hours, days and days, and weeks and weeks of inactivity, your mind starts to wander.

England had enjoyed mixed fortunes in my absence. The Hollioakes made their debut against Australia at Trent Bridge. The tourists required only a draw to hang on to the Ashes. That's not the Aussie style. The victory margin turned out to be 264 runs. I watched it on TV and remember laughing at Warnie jigging in celebration on the balcony with a stump on the Sunday night. Two months earlier, we'd been in a similar mood in Edgbaston. Since then, the Aussies had given us a lesson in cricket and had shown us what it takes to be at the top of world cricket. If we are ever to beat them, England are going to have to put in a succession of quality performances – not just one, or even two.

It had been unfair to expect the Hollioakes to rescue this Ashes series and reproduce the form and the atmosphere of the one-day series. That period was long gone. Other countries take calculated gambles; England take risks, big risks. The batting failures had not inspired the selectors to do anything too drastic in that area: last man in, Mark Butcher, was the only man out. Adam replaced him and Ben took Mark Ealham's spot. My replacement was Devon. Taylor may have found runs scarce personally, but the Aussie knew only too well how to call correctly, winning the toss for the fifth time in the series. This time he also top-scored, and England trailed by 114 runs on first innings. Another 450 target was set by the tourists. Having failed by 268 runs at Old Trafford, the margin was four runs fewer at Trent Bridge. The Hollioakes scored runs and took wickets, but there was no miracle.

Four years down the line, both are cricket history as far as England are concerned. The brothers are totally different characters. Adam's a great competitor and does raise that spirit in all the teams he's part of, a real fighter. Ben's laid back. If Ben had half of Adam's fight, he'd be a world-beater. Sadly, everything seems too easy for Ben. I believe Ben has a future at international level. It may require his leaving Surrey, but I'm not sure that will happen. Get away from his brother, get away from all the stars and go and play somewhere where he's going to have to take some responsibility . . . bat at No. 4 or 5, instead of No. 7, and bowl some overs. That would be my advice. Ben's a very talented cricketer who could have a big part to play in England's plans. The clock is ticking, though, and he's got to pull his finger out.

Adam's played his part for England. I can't see him getting another chance. Not that he did badly for England in one-day cricket. He just had a bad 1999 Sharjah and has never had another chance. Craig White and 'Freddie' Flintoff have gone so far ahead of him in the pecking order, it will be very hard for him to get back. But Ben and Adam are both good tourists and are good to have in your team, if for different reasons.

Trent Bridge marked the end of another Ashes dream. It was nearly the end of Athers's reign as captain. Like his Australian counterpart, the pressures on him had been mounting. Also like his Aussie counterpart, Athers was not happy at moves to split the England captaincy and nominate a different one-day leader. Athers had spent three years out of the one-day side when Goochie was captain. Now it was about to happen again. It bugged him, big time. I sympathize with his point of view because Athers has a good record in one-day cricket. It still bothers him. Every so often, you'll hear: 'I ain't good enough to play one-day cricket.' I can understand his feeling because at times we have lacked an opening batsman to hang around when it's seaming. Athers is the obvious candidate. His century at Lord's in 1995 against the West Indies was as good as any you'll see in limited-overs cricket.

Once again, the Oval provided consolation for England. Once again, Tufnell returned, after a summer of county duty, and took 11 wickets. Once again, Australia failed to reach an insignificant target set them. That's the way I describe the 124 runs which would have been enough for them to win the match. There was the usual nonsense about it being a 'dead' Test, the Ashes and series already lost. 'Typical England. Only win when it doesn't matter.' I can assure you, beating Australia is always a big deal. Tuffers bowled beautifully, as well as I've ever seen him, and he brought England back into the game after McGrath destroyed us again with 7–76. The Saturday was one of the best days' cricket I've ever seen on the box. Although the Aussies were firm favourites, the Oval crowd really got behind the team. Once the wickets started to fall to Caddie and Tuffers, even the mighty Australians were unable to stop the rot. Even I was shouting and screaming at the TV, which is very unusual for me. It was a great win and I was only disappointed that I couldn't be in the dressing-room joining in the celebrations.

The Sunday papers were full of pleas from the England players, begging Athers not to quit as skipper. What a difference a baker's dozen of runs make. If the scoreline had been 4–1 to Australia, Athers couldn't have stayed if he wanted to. At 3–2 and following another famous Oval win, the choice was his to make. Actually, the skipper had made his mind up at Trent Bridge when the Ashes were decided. But Lord MacLaurin persuaded him to stay. Perhaps 'persuade' is the wrong word. Lord Mac reminded Athers that he had agreed to be captain for the whole Australian series and he saw no reason for that to change. Athers had taken over from Gooch in the previous home Ashes series, once the Australians had retained the trophy. That allowed Athers two games, including one sensational victory at the Oval, in charge before leading the squad to the Caribbean in 1994. Athers felt that his successor might appreciate the same chance, as it was apparent he did not want to skipper the winter tour. Perhaps the lack of a suitable candidate influenced Lord Mac. He needed time to persuade Athers to stay, to buy some time. If he quit before the Oval, Lord's would have had no option but to look elsewhere and find a hasty replacement.

Athers is mentally one of the toughest blokes I've ever come across, but everyone has his breaking point. The amount of stick heaped on him as England captain, especially in the summer of 1997, was ridiculous. It's bad enough having the likes of Glenn McGrath trying to destroy you out in the middle, but when the mass media are attempting to assassinate you off the field, there is no escape. I'm astonished Athers didn't crack that summer. At Lord's, he led England out for the 42nd time, passing Peter May's record. That fact alone meant that Athers deserved respect. Rightly or wrongly, the England captain is the fall-guy. You take the blame if things go wrong. I've never been in the frame for the job, so I've not given too much thought as to whether I could cope with the pressures, both physical and mental. But I've seen the toll it's taken on Athers, Stewie and Nasser. After the bad start at the Oval, one paper charged Athers with impersonating an England cricket captain. That was way out of order.

It didn't surprise me that Athers allowed himself to be persuaded to carry on for the Caribbean tour. I'm sure Bumble had a big hand in that. What if you step down just before the big breakthrough? You've taken all the stick and got none of the glory. I was less shocked when Athers quit at the end of the West Indies Test series; he had no more to give. I was told that he was pretty choked when he told the lads in the St John's dressing-room before meeting the media. The events of the day had shown Athers that his decision had been correct. England managed to conjure up disaster from an Antigua Test that was meandering to a draw.

Athers had rung me up before he headed for the Caribbean. 'Try and get fit. We need you out there.' He's since told me it would have been a different series if I'd made it and bowled on those pitches. I was badly missed. England lacked somebody to knock the tail over and hit the deck hard. Gussie had a magnificent series. England played back-to-back Tests in Trinidad after the Sabina Park game was abandoned because of the dangerous pitch. Gus took 20 wickets in those two Tests and if there had been any support England would have gone to Guyana 2–0 instead of level. Gus made the West Indies batsmen play and they don't like being tied down. The batting failed in Guyana, and the rain ended England's chances on the final day in Barbados. England were bowled out for 127 in Antigua, but appeared safe at 295–3 on the final afternoon. Cue Athers's resignation as seven wickets went down for 26. Very little changed in his five years of leadership.

Athers as captain had been good to me. Admittedly, I used to get annoyed when I was brought back for one over before lunch; he knew that hacked me off. I have to admit that Athers is not one of the world's great communicators; in that respect he was rather private. But he always backed his players and he hated Illy for knocking the England team, individually or as a unit, and for putting selection arguments and dressing-room discussions that Athers felt should have remained private into the public domain. I was sorry to see him go. He'd given his all for England. I am glad Athers remained in the team. Without him, England would not have won in Pakistan.

The support that Athers and the England camp gave me formed an important part of my rehabilitation. Sadly, I found out that one former legendary Yorkshire fast bowler was not quite so keen to see me back. Fred Trueman stood up at a book launch that autumn and queried my action. He announced that he had rung a 'certain person in authority, saying I was concerned about his action. I said I thought one or two deliveries of his were a bit no-no, and the reply was "Only two".' Talk about muck-spreading! I was furious. I used to turn up in a T-shirt that had Fred's face on the front. Not any more; that went straight in the bin. I could not believe it. I had heard stories about sad old cricketers living in the past, but I never expected someone like Fred to stoop so low. Trueman, the first Test bowler to 300 wickets. Fantastic! But there's a certain sort of player who has to keep reminding everyone just how good he was. We have got a few of them in Yorkshire. Taking cheap shots at today's players is one way of doing that. That was the end of Fred so far as I was concerned. From that day on, I no longer regarded him as a great Yorkshire or England player. In fact, I do not even think of him as a true Yorkshireman any more. Ironically, I had spent the past month working on a training video for the E.C.B. His comments were not what a player fighting his way back to fitness needed. I was not going to get involved in a personal war of words with him, although perhaps that was what he wanted. I had other and more important matters on my mind than the ramblings of a pensioner.

16. Biffing the Boks

Alec Stewart was the man handed the poisoned chalice. The other contenders were Nasser and Adam Hollioake. I have to agree with the selectors; Stewie was my choice. He had been vice-captain under Goochie, but had lost out to Athers in 1993. Adam was the outsider. He would have struggled to hold down a place in the side. I felt Nas wasn't ready yet and was still cementing a place. Nas and Stewie had made their debuts together at Sabina Park when England stunned the West Indies and the rest of the cricket world with that nine-wicket win in 1990. Stewie had been a regular more or less ever since. Nasser had to wait until 1996 before getting any sort of run in the Test team. Nasser also had something of a 'bad boy' tag, while Stewie was cricket's 'Mr Squeaky Clean'.

Image was a big part of that appointment. Lord Mac had made a big play about the 'image' of English cricket when he took over. Stewie's always smart and was a very experienced international cricketer at the time. Knowing Stewie, he would have taken the job only provided there were guarantees about him being captain for both England teams; he would not have settled for being vice-captain to Adam in the one-day team. I don't blame him for that. Within a few months Stewie had given England what we had been striving after for years: England's first victory in a major Test series since 1986. That achievement didn't buy him much time. Ten months later, Alec Stewart was sacked.

When Athers resigned, once again I noticed a distinct lack of bowlers, especially the fast variety, among the candidates for the post. Even attempts to put myself forward as potential captain at Yorkshire have received a disappointing response. But, seriously, why is cricket almost exclusively a batsman's game when the top jobs are handed out? Bob Willis was a rare England bowling captain, and Courtney Walsh got a few games in charge of the West Indies.

Maybe Shaun Pollock is the start of a new trend after taking over from a disgraced Hansie Cronje.

There wasn't a noticeable difference in the England dressing-room when Stewie took over, although it was certainly tidier! The captain's real impact lies on the field of play. Athers generally left you to your own devices, while Stewie was more specific about what he wanted. He was excellent with his fast bowlers and shared the work-load around. Even though he kept for most of the time, there was plenty of communication and I generally got the field placings I wanted. That's not always the case with Nasser, who prefers to back his own judgement rather than yours.

England had a new sponsor as well as a new captain. Vodafone had replaced Tetley's Bitter for the West Indies tour, but their logo had been missing in the Caribbean. That series was sponsored by Cable & Wireless, a rival, so Vodafone first appeared on the shirts in the South African series. More appealing to us was the prospect of a £200,000 bonus if we won. Playing for your country is not about money, but this amount was certainly an extra incentive when the contest was close.

I was just glad to be back in the frame after so long away. I missed not being in the England dressing-room. A couple of days of nets and you're back in the swing. The last time Corkie, Gussie and I had changed together had been at the Wanderers ground in late 1995. It proved to be another short stay for me. I broke my finger on the Friday evening at Edgbaston and did not bowl a single ball in anger in the first test. My mum may have thought I was 'lucky' – I was beginning to wonder. For the fifth successive summer, I was not going to take part in a full Test programme. What made this even more annoying was that England were on top, having posted a big first-innings total after being inserted. That was a new experience for me.

I have to blame the new skipper for my injury. We were offered the light, but the message came out from Stewie to stay on. Soon I was back in the dressing-room, head under a towel to hide more Gough injury tears. I feared the worst when Wayne came out to the middle to look at my finger after a delivery from Donald lifted sharply. What is it with these South Africans using me as target practice? For the third successive series against them, I was off to the X-ray department. Before departing, I tried to carry on. I hit a couple of runs more, but those shooting pains up my finger left me no option. I didn't need that visit to the X-ray department to confirm the break.

There's a consolation in broken bones. At least you know what the problem is, and normally they heal stronger than before. But, just like muscles, tendons, hamstrings, calves and groins, you can't speed the process. Nature will take its own time, no matter how many hot and ice-cold bowls I plunged my bowling finger into. I reckoned this might not speed up repairing the break but it might improve the flexibility. We tend to scoff when others resort to such desperate measures but, when it's your bowling finger, anything is worth a try. I had to get away and decided to take the family to Tenerife. I met Harvey Smith there and he gave me a little metal thing they give racehorses to ease their ailments. Obediently I strapped it on to my finger; I was ready to believe anything by this stage.

I was definitely out of the Lord's Test. The break was right on the knuckle. Take four weeks off, I was told. The teams went to London all square after rain ruined what was going to be an interesting last day at Edgbaston. South Africa found Lord's to their liking just as much as in 1994, and they gave England another fearful hammering after the home side were destroyed by Donald again (5–32) and were dismissed for 110 in reply to the tourists' 360. It might have been different if Athers had held on to a nick from Jonty Rhodes off Deano. The tourists were in trouble at 46–4, but Jonty went on to make a century. There was no escape. Nasser hit 105 and England got to within 28 runs of South Africa's total with seven wickets remaining. Then there was another clatter of wickets, and South Africa needed 15 to win. Goodnight. A crushing defeat by ten wickets. Another big game at Lord's . . . another poor England performance. Apart from the two wins against the West Indies (1995 and 2000) it's not been a happy hunting-ground. There's nothing wrong with the place, except that it seems to have too much of an uplifting effect on the opposition.

My finger wasn't right; I was still getting those shooting pains. However, I figured that if I didn't play at Old Trafford, the series might be all done and dusted before I entered the fray. With a little help from Wayne I made myself available, and the selectors felt it was time to take a chance. Just my luck. Old Trafford was the flattest wicket of the series. The South Africans batted into the third day, compiling over 550 runs. It took us slightly less time to get bowled out for 183, but the South Africans' cautiousness offered us some hope of escape. Gary Kirsten hit a double-hundred and Kallis a century, but we couldn't believe how slowly they batted on the third morning. It was the same at the Wanderers, three years earlier, when Athers had defied them.

It was ridiculous to have been bowled out so cheaply first time on the best wicket of the series. Knight and Nasser went early as we followed on, and it looked like curtains. Athers and Stewie put on over 200, but there was still a long way to go. At 329–8 and nearly two hours to go, I walked out more in hope than expectation. My recent record with the bat did not fill the lads with confidence. The good news was that Croftie was at the other end, determined to make an impact after failing to take a wicket in his 51 overs. We stayed together for nearly an hour and a half and didn't look in any danger until that man Donald produced one of his thunderbolts. It bounced and hit me on the finger again. Even though I had a finger-guard on, I thought I'd broken it again as the ball flew to Kirsten. I'm not sure which hurt more: the loss of my finger or getting out. I passed our last man, an even more ashen-faced Angus Fraser, on his way to join Croftie.

I didn't even take my pads off, I just went on to the balcony to watch. South Africa were one delivery from going dormie two-up in the series. There were a couple of big l.b.w. shouts, but the umpires remained unmoved. I've decided that you're better off out in the middle than watching when it's that tense. I can slog with the worst of them, yet if 'Stonewall Gough' is what is required, I'll do my best to oblige. Just watch the ball and do nothing silly. If

I'm honest, I didn't think we had a chance when I went out to bat. Moreover, I had to contend with South African verbals as well as their bowlers. Most of the chirping came from Paul Adams, but that didn't bother me. I could see the desperation growing in their faces. That gave me an extra buzz and an incentive to hang around. I've never been keen on them. The South Africans thought the Test was won when I came out. It wasn't. Gussie and Croftie did us proud, and we held on. Croftie was chuffed to bits.

South Africa were still 1–0 up, but this battling draw had turned the series our way. Our relief and pleasure were there for all to see as Stewie led the charge on to the field at the end. So, too, was the South Africans' deflation. They came off as though they'd lost. In a way they had; they'd lost the win. Cronje's team had this Test in the bag before the fat lady had even warmed up. England had pulled off the Great Escape, and we sensed that there were more surprises to come. Our dressing-room was buzzing. Another crucial factor was the injury to Lance Klusener, which meant his early departure for home. If South Africa had gone 2–0, that injury would merely have taken a little of the shine off the winning gloss. But 'Zulu' was having a tremendous summer with bat and ball and would be sorely missed – but not by us.

Our two Old Trafford heroes almost missed out on Trent Bridge – thanks to rather ungrateful selectors. Croftie's failure to take a wicket in three Tests meant a recall for Ian Salisbury, the leg-spinner whom the management wanted to take to Australia. Andrew Flintoff made his debut and Graeme Hick made one of his many returns to the England team. Gussie also looked under threat, with Alan Mullally back in the squad for the first time since the New Zealand tour. I've never understood this reluctance to play Gussie if it was reckoned the conditions, the wicket or the ball was not in his favour. The implication is that without help he can't do a job and is going to struggle. I don't know where that idea came from. The theory does not stand examination if you look at his record, but Gussie has had to prove himself time and time again. Without him, England would have disappeared without trace in the Caribbean. But, I heard people say, those pitches were poor. Well, pitches all over the world these days are pretty poor and Gussie has exploited most of them. Gussie was our best bowler in the West Indies. As soon as the wicket might prove to be flat, the selectors started to look elsewhere.

It's not just Gus who suffers from this crazy selection policy. All bowlers seem to be under threat all the time with England. I can remember having a light-hearted argument with Nasser, who maintained that England should pick different bowlers for different wickets. What about batsmen, then? On a seaming wicket, do we choose the best players of seam, and likewise with spin? 'Oh no, it's different,' Nas insisted. Is it, hell. It's exactly the same principle. It's just that the batsmen are the ones who pick the sides. A bowler is exactly the same as a batter. He needs to keep playing for the sake of his confidence. I then wrote down my three batting line-ups for flat, seaming and spinning wickets. There weren't too many who featured in all three sides.

It's a pass-the-buck sort of thing. As soon as we play on a flat wicket and Donald bowls a yorker, a bouncer – as he did in the first innings at Old Trafford – all the batters agree on the miracle solution: let's do the same as Donald. The main drawback is that we don't have Allan Donald in our side. Because South Africa got 552 and England got 183, it was a weakness in the England bowling rather than the batting; we, the bowlers, were the ones who needed shaking up and told to produce something different.

During my time with England, when a bowler has a couple of bad games he's out of the side, and it takes some getting back. So far as the England batters are concerned, you can replace a couple of bad games with a couple of bad series before there are any moves to replace them. This annoys me, as it does most England bowlers. Carrying the can is not something that fits easily into an English batsman's coffin! I suppose it's easier to hide a bad batter than a bad bowler when the team's playing well. One of my great regrets is that Caddie, Gussie and I never played together for England. Can you believe that? My dream England attack over the second half of the 1990s would have been me and Caddie opening, with Gussie and Corkie in support. Those are the best pairings we could have had. Sadly, it is a dream, because the England selectors never thought to put us together. It's too late now for Gussie, and I'd have to replace him with Craig White these days.

Gussie did make the final line-up at Trent Bridge, which was just as well. He just edged me out of a five-for as South Africa made 374 quickly, in contrast to their Old Trafford crawl. It was another sign that we had got to them. We couldn't afford a bad start. Athers and Butch put on 145 and got to within 38 runs of their total. We took three wickets on Saturday night, but next morning South Africa increased their lead to 157 with seven wickets left. Step forward, Fraser and Cork. Their collapse started with a magnificent catch by Ramps at square leg to remove Cullinan. Our victory target was an interesting 247, no 'gimme', but a lot better than it could have been. Another ten wickets for Gus in the match as his amazing 1998 continued. Another five-wicket haul would follow at Headingley, but he was still only three Tests and a few months away from being dropped again.

That Sunday night produced one of the greatest cricket contests I've ever witnessed. Donald came out with all guns blazing, as I knew he would. Athers refused to buckle, as I also knew he would. Entertaining, enthralling, it was X-certificate stuff. Not for the faint-hearted or those of a nervous disposition, but sheer magic and theatre. There wasn't much respite at the other end for Athers, with Pollock charging in just as fiercely. These are the kinds of situation when England needs Athers the most. And he rarely lets us down. Donald had bowled well in the series, but not that quick. He stepped up a couple more gears that Sunday night. It was what Test cricket is all about: one of the best bowlers in the world bowling as quick as he can. Despite getting hit, despite nicking it, despite edging it, Athers refused to budge. Donald could not believe it when Mervyn Kitchen failed to raise his finger for a gloved catch behind, and he suggested that Athers might like to walk. There's more chance of Nasser dipping into his captain's expenses! I thought Donald was going to explode, and the deliveries started coming down even more quickly than before. Athers raised the temperature even higher with an inside edge off the next delivery that shot to the boundary. Eventually Donald got the breakthrough he wanted, but the simple edge off Nasser's bat bounced in and out of Boucher's gloves. Again, Donald could not believe it. Neither could we. The dice were rolling England's way as the pair came in at 108–1. Next day, we squared the series by eight wickets, when Stewie came in and smashed it to all parts, scoring 45 out of the 55-run partnership with Athers. Our anchorman ended up undefeated on 98. Stewie had offered him his hundred. 'No, let's just win the game,' was the reply. Typical Athers, totally unselfish. I can't think of any other England batsman who wouldn't have had an eye on a century when one was only a couple of runs away.

Our celebrations weren't as spontaneous as at Old Trafford. But we had really felt that Manchester was the turning-point. We were full of confidence, and they were down. We had held the upper hand in the last seven days of cricket. England were flying and we couldn't wait to get to Headingley. I was delighted the decider would be on my home ground and not at the Oval. Give us good weather in Leeds for five days and there was sure to be a result.

Stewie's most important job was to win the toss and make sure England weren't batting last. The drawback with that strategy is that it can give the opposition the use of the strip on days two and three, traditionally the best for batting in Leeds. Mark Butcher saved us on that first day, scoring more than half of our 230 runs. We were happy to be trailing by only 22 on the first innings, knowing that South Africa had to bat last. Gussie claimed his third five-for in a row, and I was pleased with 3–58. Athers went to Donald's first ball on the Saturday morning. A.D. didn't need firing up after being fined half his match fee after Trent Bridge for claiming that umpire Kitchen made 'a few shockers'. It could have been worse; the match referee did consider a one-match ban.

Nasser dug in on the Saturday with untypical restraint; Athers could not have done it any better, and I can't pay a higher compliment than that. This wicket was not one for quick runs; it was tough, batting and bowling once the ball went soft. The edges didn't carry and the batsmen couldn't force the pace. At 200–3 we were firm favourites. Nasser fell, six short of his century, after seven hours at the crease. No one deserved a hundred more. That's why the Headingley crowd gave him a standing ovation. I don't think Nasser noticed. He was distraught and in tears because his departure left us at 229–8. Our last seven wickets could muster only 40 runs against the new ball and Pollock and Donald. 'Freddie' bagged a pair and was so upset he lay down on the dressing-room table for the next two hours with a towel over his head. I knew how he felt, after my pair the previous year. This time nobody thought of putting a pear in his shoe. The Lancies are a sensitive bunch, and that would have been too cruel.

Both teams were clear what was required. If South Africa reached 219, the Test and the series were theirs; if they fell short, England would be the victors. With five sessions left, there was no way this match was going to be a draw. The England dressing-room was confident. Always at the back of our minds was the feeling that the South Africans knew they had let this one slip from their grasp. And if they forgot, we were keen to remind them. But the way the South Africans were hugging each other on the field suggested that they felt the match was won. More premature thinking. It's rare for a five-Test series to come down to the final innings in the last match, but even I wasn't prepared for the drama that would unfold.

First blood went to England – or, rather, to me and Gussie. We destroyed the top order, and half the South Africans were out for 27! Kirsten, Liebenberg, Kallis, Cullinan and Cronje all gone. Then the ball went soft, and Jonty and Brian McMillan batted magnificently to give South Africa some hope where previously there had been none. The target had come down from 192 to just 75 runs. Gus and I were struggling. Gussie had a back problem and I was feeling sick, all fluey and weak and bothered with stomach cramps. Athers had had the same problem the day before. Those early wickets had dulled any pain I might otherwise have felt. As the ball went soft, so did I. I had the feeling that the series was slipping away from us.

Someone had to make something happen, and that man was Dominic Cork. He chose his target well: Brian McMillan. Corkie got into him big-time and really wound him up, teasing the South

African to take him on. Our opponents had no reason to take any risks at this stage, yet the Cork magic worked again. McMillan could contain himself no longer and was caught behind, trying to hook a bouncer. McMillan was furious and came looking for Corkie after the match to offer something more than a congratulatory handshake. I wouldn't fancy being on the receiving end of McMillan's temper, but he knew he'd been suckered and had possibly cost his country the series. That's one of the reasons why Corkie's such a valuable player; he has a natural aptitude for getting up people's noses, especially the South Africans'. If you're any good at cricket and you have a bit of balls, the South Africans don't like you. Top of their hit-list were Corkie, Nasser, Stewie and me, because we gave them a bit back off the field.

The target was down to 52 runs when I finally got rid of Jonty, who had played carefully and cleverly for his 85. That was my hundredth Test wicket, one of the targets I'd set myself when I started out for England. When it came, I was just pleased because of the match situation. Jonty had batted well in the series, but we had difficulty understanding how a born-again Christian could reconcile his religious beliefs with sledging and appealing for catches that were clearly not out. 'We are all sinners,' was Jonty's facile explanation. Boucher was my fifth victim, and Donald came out to join Pollock.

South Africa wanted to finish the job. So did we in a way, but Gussie and I were on our knees. As soon as we realized how much they wanted to stay on, Stewie let the umpire know that England had no intention of claiming the extra half-hour. So umpire Peter Willey removed the bails with the Test agonizingly in the balance: 34 runs or two wickets for glory. South Africa could have claimed the half-hour. I don't know if they were too wrapped up in the action to be aware of the rules governing the situation, but Cronje made his move too late. Donald and Pollock didn't seem to know what was happening. As we started coming off, they tried to stay on. Stewie just said, 'Keep walking, we'll come back tomorrow,' making it impossible for the South Africans to stop the exodus. It was the right thing to do. The tourists had the upper hand and I'm convinced we would have lost if we had stayed out there.

What a day it had been. I was physically and emotionally drained. I drove my dad back home with my stomach in agony and had to spend three-quarters of an hour in the toilet as soon as I got through the door. I was bad and needed Lisa, the Yorkshire C.C.C. marketing manager who lives next door, to drive me back to the team hotel in Leeds. She had to stop on the hard shoulder of the MI to let me be sick. I had my England tracksuit on, so I stayed in the car and leaned out of the window. I was sick again, back at the hotel, although I hadn't eaten all day. Wayne and the doctor came to see me during the evening. I began to worry that I might not make it to Headingley the next morning. I didn't know if Gussie was going to recover, either. The doctor gave me pills to knock me out, but I kept waking all through the night.

I felt better, but still not great, in the morning. The skipper knew, but when he saw me sipping a glass of water at breakfast, all he said was: 'So you're not going to be able to bowl this morning.' It wasn't a question, more of a challenge. Wayne gave me some imodium. However bad I felt, I'd decided England were not walking out without me. Gussie, who'd had an injection in his back, felt the same way.

We needed a lift, and we got it from an unexpected source. Woodie (Matthew Wood), in his first full season with Yorkshire, was the twelfth man. We were warming up in an almost deserted Headingley when Stewie asked Woodie to say a few words. I'm not sure what prompted our skipper to ask him, but it was a master-stroke. I don't think he knew it was coming, but Woodie went straight into a speech about all those people listening on radio and watching on TV and how we could all be heroes today. It was brilliant. Nobody could quite believe a little second-team cricketer from Yorkshire giving us the Winston Churchill bit. We went back to the dressing-room and I took some more pills to stop me being sick.

I pulled my sweater on to go out for a quick bowl in the middle, about a quarter of an hour before the start. My head was spinning and I felt weak. But I came alive when I walked out into the daylight and heard a massive roar. I couldn't believe my eyes:

Headingley was almost full. We knew it was free entry, but a half-hour earlier there had been only a few hundred in. I've never experienced a lift like it. I felt strong again. I knew then how big a day this was. Bob Cottam was holding the bowling mitt and had seen how lethargic I'd been. Now I was pumped up. Bob was a bit slow with the mitt, and I hit him straight in the chest with my first warm-up delivery. That was all I needed. I was ready now.

The South African plan was for Donald to keep up one end and Pollock to score the runs. England needed wickets, and that was up to Gussie and me. We were just beginning to get nervous, then breakthrough! In the sixth over of the morning Gussie got Donald to nick one to Stewie. I rushed over and gave the big man a big hug. One to go; but I knew then we would win, with South Africa still 25 runs short. Makhaya Ntini was a reluctant No. 11. Who could blame him? This was his seventh match of the tour, but he had not batted once before coming to Headingley. His four not out in the first innings were the only runs he had scored all summer. While Pollock knew Donald could hold up an end, Ntini was going to need protecting. I already had my five-for, and it would have been fitting if Gussie had finished them off. But the final act of the series fell to me as I had Ntini trapped l.b.w. off the last ball of the next over. I never had any doubt that Javed Akhtar would raise his finger. It started to move and I was hit from all directions, firstly by Woodie. He was on for Athers, who'd gone to hospital for a stomach check-up and heard the finale on the radio in the taxi coming back. Stewie and Corkie as usual had a stump, and I managed to grab one. Then I collected my sweater and cap as the crowd charged on. It was pandemonium. I've heard since all the nonsense about how this final delivery was going down the leg-side. I've watched it a thousand times and Ntini is as plumb today as he was that morning.

It doesn't come much better than taking the final wicket to win a major series on your home ground. I just remember the crowd chanting my name as we celebrated with champagne on the balcony. The champagne was just for show in my case. Ecstatic as I was, I was still too ill to face a drink. I'm glad we had that balcony scene because the dressing-room was ruined. Bumble had allowed the TV cameras in and they were waiting for us when we burst in. None of us knew beforehand, and we were furious that we couldn't let our hair down properly. There were no spontaneous reactions, and we were all annoyed that it spoiled a very special moment. It shouldn't have happened. That's why we celebrated with such gusto on the balcony. Why not? England's first win in a major series since Mike Gatting's side won at Melbourne in 1986. Bring on the Aussies.

17. Bunsen Burner

Warnie was on the phone a few days after our Headingley win. He was recuperating after a serious shoulder operation and was a doubtful starter for the Ashes series. As we chatted, he made two foolish predictions. The first was that he'd be in the line-up for the Brisbane Test. Secondly, after beating South Africa, he forecast that England would be on a huge high when they reached Australia. Warnie was way off the mark on both counts. His shoulder took longer to heal than expected, although he appeared for the Ashes finale. More crucially for England, much of our South African elation was punctured by a unique Sri Lankan spinner and an Oval pitch that was straight out of Colombo. Those five days at the Kennington Oval had serious consequences for our Ashes challenge and sealed the fate of our coach Bumble.

I still can't get my head round the whole business. I had no problems with Sri Lanka coming over to take part in a triangular one-day tournament. As the current World Cup holders, that was only right and proper, especially as they would be defending that trophy in England the following summer, starting out against us, the hosts, at Lord's. But why a Test match? Sri Lanka had come over for one-off Tests in 1984 and 1991 – Caribbean summers – but did not come in 1995 as the series against the West Indies was six matches. I don't believe England should play one-off Tests, at home or abroad.

The new triangular tournament took place after the South African series. As is usual with England, this addition to our schedule was long overdue and, initially, was a rather tentative step with only four matches, a single round-robin and a final. Considering how many split tours we have to England, a triangular one-day event was a long time coming. The inevitable happened. Sri Lanka beat South Africa, we beat Sri Lanka and, finally, South Africa beat us. England topped the group on run-rate, just ahead of Sri Lanka, with South Africa eliminated on 0.43. This experience should have alerted us to the workings and dangers of run-rate, which was to cost us so dear in the World Cup the following year. The side batting second lost all the group games. South Africa never recovered from 32–4 against Sri Lanka, who were struggling against us at 28–3. England got to within 14 runs of South Africa's 244 at Edgbaston and were best placed, needing 84 runs from 16 overs with seven wickets left. Another collapse, although England were already in trouble when Jonty Rhodes took the catch of the summer, an unbelievable two-handed effort diving upwards at full stretch which left our Welsh off-spinner just a little gob-smacked.

England actually qualified for the final when we reached 198 runs at Edgbaston. At last, a Lord's one-day final. I'd long dreamed of getting there with Yorkshire, but playing for England was just as satisfying. We should have won after Athers and Knight gave us a great start, but the latter and others got bogged down to Muralitharan, who took three wickets in five balls, ending up with 5–34, a great effort when the batting side reaches 256–8 in its allotted 50 overs. I'd lasted one ball, but I gave us a great start when I squeezed one between Jayasuriya's pad and bat. Unfortunately, as Sri Lanka had shown in the World Cup, early wickets do not upset their rhythm or purpose. Kaluwitharana and Atapattu added 138 runs in 26 overs and de Silva carried on the attack. Two great catches from Knight gave us some hope, but Atapattu was there at the death, undefeated on 132. I had to make do with a runners-up medal as Ranatunga lifted the Emirates Trophy. I'd bowled pretty well throughout, taking eight wickets, but our batting line-up was still not right. With no Thorpe or Fairbrother, England were short of a nudger, a batsman who could pace a run-chase or work out the target to be set. There was no need to hit the panic button just yet. The World Cup was still nine months away, and we had tournaments in Australia and Sharjah to come. Still, it appeared that Sri Lanka would defend the trophy with some style.

Experimentation was definitely in the air that August. Yorkshire hosted its first-ever floodlit match. With 10,000 turning up at

Headingley, I thought I'd grabbed the headlines with a late hat-trick (Akram, Hegg and Yates), but I was upstaged by Lancashire's Glen Chapple. Yorkshire collapsed to 81 all out and were defeated by 101 runs. Chapple finished with 6–25 as we were rolled over in 25 overs.

The England players were not too happy about this one-off Test. There was little to be gained, other than putting the kings of one-day cricket in their place as regards the traditional form of the game. But English hospitality knows no bounds, certainly not on the cricket field. In bending over backwards to be fair to our guests, we often prepare pitches which not only remind them of home and which suit their bowlers and batsmen, but negate our strengths and expose our weaknesses. Do our lords and masters think for one second that this courtesy is extended to England abroad? Of course, we are looked after well, wined and dined, nothing too much trouble abroad – except when we venture near the cricket ground. Our hosts make sure the conditions and pitch are as unfamiliar as possible and that they suit the talents of the home bowlers and batsmen. I have no complaints with that strategy and philosophy. That's cricket. I just wish someone had mentioned these facts of life to the Oval groundsman. Sri Lanka were – and are – a side with hardly a seam bowler, often playing three or four spinners. That was the format in the 1996 World Cup, when they took us apart. Grav had been down there twice and Stewie was based at the Oval and told them what sort of wicket we wanted. England had just destroyed South Africa with seam and swing, so what did we find in south London? An absolute shirt-fronter which spun – the exact opposite of what was requested and required. It was like playing in Colombo, and the Oval authorities have to take a lot of stick for that. How could you prepare a wicket that suited the Sri Lanka spinners! Small wonder that Saqlain and Salisbury have taken Surrey to the last two championships.

Now that's off my chest, it's also fair to say that we should never have lost this Test after making 445 in the first innings, even allowing for the magic of Muralitharan. Not that every member of our dressing-room felt the same. Our coach felt we were being dealt with unfairly. Athers was the one moaning before the start, after he and Nasser had dropped out through injury. Athers complained that, after facing Pollock and Donald all summer, he was going to miss out filling his boots playing against this lot. Ranatunga surprised us by deciding to bowl, correctly judging that this was his best chance of victory. Creepy hit one of the best hundreds I've ever seen in Test cricket, and Hickie also scored a century. Those two were battling for the last batting spot on the Ashes tour. I was at the other end when Creepy reached his ton, but it was his last-wicket stand of 89 in 16 overs with Gussie (two sixes and three fours) that brightened up the Friday afternoon. It didn't take the Sri Lankans long to show us how easy it was to bat against pace on that pitch and how inadequate our score was. Jayasuriya and de Silva belted us all over the Oval, passing our total with three wickets down on the way to 591. I wasn't too unhappy with figures of 2–102 off 30 overs on that track. Most of my weekend was spent at fine leg and third man, pinching myself to make sure I was still in south London, not somewhere in the South Seas. Our spin attack consisted of Salisbury, Ramprakash and Butcher. The only Sri Lankan wicket that fell to spin was last man out, Muralitharan, slogging. That was the second and last Test wicket claimed by England spin in the summer of 1998.

We were in trouble. Muralitharan had taken 7–155 in the first innings. We had a day and a half to survive and bat Sri Lanka out of the game. The writing was on the wall by Sunday night – 54–2 off 42 overs. I couldn't really understand our tactics. We started, only 146 runs adrift; by scoring so slowly and turning the contest into a war of attrition, England played into Sri Lanka's hands. Our survival was not the only topic of discussion on the Sunday night. The man who stood between England and a draw, Muttiah Muralitharan, was public enemy number one as far as Bumble was concerned. In so many words, he questioned the legitimacy of Muralitharan's action. Our coach was careful not to accuse him directly of having an illegal action, but he made it crystal clear what his thoughts were: 'I have my opinions that I have made known to the authorities.' Not for the first time, Bumble was fired up and couldn't control himself. I think Bumble genuinely believes Muralitharan throws it, and Bumble's never been one to hide his feelings. Bumble, being Bumble, wanted people to know. He also believed that a lot of other people felt the same way, including umpires, but that nobody was doing owt about it. His reckoning was that if this controversy had been about an English bowler, the laws would have thrown him out of first-class cricket and he would never had played Test cricket. I couldn't argue with that. It was hard to escape the idea that he was being treated differently. That is what was annoying Bumble. The Sri Lankan Board weren't too happy either, and Lord's were soon dealing with an official protest. Bumble was brought in shortly afterwards and received a reprimand and another final warning. Not surprisingly, our coach did not head off for the Ashes tour in the best of spirits, and this incident played a big part in his decision to quit after the World Cup.

I'll defend Bumble's right to his opinion, but it was wrong to voice it so clearly during the Test match, which we were striving to save. Again, it was a convenient crutch to lean on for those who didn't relish the fight. I'd never accuse anybody of 'throwing'. It's another cricketer's career. To make that accusation is a hell of a statement. If someone is certain, then those views should go through the right channels. I don't believe you should be made a scapegoat by umpires calling you, out in the middle. It should be reported, then investigated. Darrell Hair had called Muralitharan for throwing in Australia three years earlier, and it's degrading for the bowler. The after effects of umpire Darrell Hair's decision are still felt. Sri Lanka refused to let him officiate in the 1999 World Cup in England or the 2000 I.C.C. Trophy in Nairobi. That's also nonsense. Muralitharan has been cleared to play against any team in the world; Hair should officiate on the same basis. Muralitharan has a strange action because he's unable to straighten his arm. It seems as soon as someone can bowl it quicker than anyone else or turn it more than anyone else, the view is that he must be throwing it. Look at those who've been mentioned in the past year or so; they all do something extraordinary with the ball: Shoaib Akhtar and Brett Lee, who are the two quickest bowlers in the world, and Muralitharan, the biggest spinner in the world.

I could not believe how much he turned the ball at the Oval, even allowing for the assistance of the ground staff. We had two spinners in that game and they didn't turn it off the straight. This bloke turned it both ways . . . unbelievable. We had a day and a half to survive and there was danger from only one end. This was no two-man attack. We couldn't do it. Had Stewie not got run out, Muralitharan might have claimed all ten, instead of 9–65. Ramps and I were together at tea on the final day. We'd prevented an innings defeat, but our slow scoring rate meant that England were only 16 runs ahead. We lasted another hour, but Sri Lanka needed only five overs to score the 37 runs needed for victory. Well as Muralitharan bowled, we had only ourselves to blame. Our second-innings 181 took almost 130 overs, less than one and a half runs per over. I find it hard to compare his bowling that day with Warnie in his pomp, but he was almost genuinely unplayable. All I can say is, if Muralitharan keeps going the way he is, he'll go past Warnie, Kapil Dev and Courtney and become the leading Test wicket-taker of all time. 'Muri' has an amazing record and is getting better and better. He's been cleared totally now, and there's nothing in his way.

The Oval marked the end of my summer because of a damaged hamstring. That was a big disappointment, as Yorkshire were enjoying their best championship for years. Not that I was missed at all. The White Rose won the final five matches to finish third, the best placing since being runners-up in 1975. More significantly, our young players were making an impact, with Paul Hutchinson taking 57 wickets, Gavin Hamilton 56 and Chris Silverwood 46, while Matthew Hoggard collected 31 victims in the last six matches. The two Yorkies who reached 1,000 runs were Matthew Wood, then aged 21, and Michael Vaughan. Out of sight is not out of mind as far as Yorkshire goes when I'm on national service. I played only five Britannic games in 1998, and only two after the middle of May. But I want to pick up the papers or the phone and learn that Yorkshire are doing well. An England player's availablility has drastically reduced since I started in 1994.

That Oval defeat was a disastrous way to end the summer and

I've always felt that the defeat had long-term consequences in Australia. Having beaten one of the best two teams in the world in a major series, we came crashing to earth because of the Oval wicket. Stewie made a point of comparing it to Colombo afterwards; that's how upset he was. It would not have happened anywhere else in the cricket world. I don't remember seeing too many green seamers in Sri Lanka in the winter of 2000/1. I've always felt that the Oval people wanted it to go five days. Money rather than the welfare of the England cricket team about to embark on an Ashes mission appeared to be the greater concern. If that was the case, then there's no doubt those pieces of silver had a seriously damaging effect on our Ashes challenge.

18. Heads We Lose

Another Ashes tour. Was it really four years since this fresh-faced lad from Barnsley took his first England steps abroad? I was still fresh-faced, but I had yet to play throughout a full major series, at home or abroad. I'd played 26 Tests for my country but had missed 23 others since my debut, four years earlier. I was 28 now and I felt the jury was still out as to whether I was up there with the great bowlers of my era. The best bowler in England, probably. But would I get in most people's World XI? No, not until I had an uninterrupted run at Test level. My periods of success, my impact were too spasmodic. Returning down under gave me renewed hope and ambition. I was determined to finish what I'd started on my 1994/5 Ashes trip. The Sri Lanka defeat had taken the gloss off our summer, but we had to forget it. It was blip, a freak result on a freak pitch instigated by a freak bowler, nothing more. That's how we had to treat it. I genuinely felt that the overall strength of our squad – plus that first major series victory – gave us a real chance of competing against the Aussies. I was just as enthusiastic for the tour and up for the challenge as I had been in 1994. Australia's a great place to tour and, in my time, has produced the cricketers who ask the most demanding questions of the opposition.

Alex Tudor was the surprise pick for our Ashes squad. It is always helpful to include someone the opponents don't know too much about. Peter Such and Alan Mullally came back, and Creepy got the nod over Hickie. I don't think I've been away with a stronger England squad or one in which selection has caused less argument. The only points of contention related to leaving Hickie behind (that was settled when he flew out early on because of Athers's back problem, and he stayed when Thorpey came home with a similar problem after the Brisbane Test) and selecting two off-spinners, Such and Croft, instead of Tuffers. Our manager was the recently retired legend, Graham Gooch. Nor has the England team been better prepared. 'Team England' had a full supporting cast: specialist coaches, fitness coach Dean Riddle, sports psychologist Steve Bull, team analyst Nick Slade and media relations manager Brian Murgatroyd, who was to defect and take up a similar post with the Aussies a year later. The ever-helpful Medha Laud was our day-to-day contact at Lord's; she was the person who organized us, made sure we had the right gear and that we turned up when and where we supposed to – no easy task. At the top of this pile was our International Teams Director, former NATO Commander of the Western Mediterranean, Simon Pack. You might wonder how relevant a military background was to running the England cricket team. So did we. My mind flashed back to Tim Lamb's 'What would you do if you were in the army?' remark when our wives were banned from Zimbabwe.

The flashing lights at Perth airport came as no surprise this time, although I was rather peeved to be missing from an Aussie media guide which listed the England tourists. The alphabetical England squad went straight from Giles, A.F. (who would be touring with the one-day squad) to Headley, D.W. The English papers had been full of Warnie before we left, claiming that his recovery was ahead of schedule. I knew differently. Warnie had told me that the Boxing Day Test in Melbourne would be his earliest comeback date. Much as he would have loved to tie us in knots again, that shoulder injury had threatened his career and there was no way he was going to be rushed back. This was his first real break since bursting on to the international scene in 1993, and he admitted to me that the lay-off was doing him good. I hoped it might do England some good as well. Unfortunately, a young leg-spinner called Stuart MacGill had been waiting for his chance, and he was to take the same number of wickets, 27, as Warnie had collected against us in 1994/5.

Our failure in Australia this time has prompted more soul-searching by me than any other losing series. Looking back is not my style, but I have struggled to understand why we failed to build on the South African success. There's no doubt that the Sri Lanka defeat had undermined our confidence, and not just in the team, but in our team selection. What was our best line-up? That shouldn't have been too difficult after recovering to beat South Africa. Yet we seemed racked with self-doubt and, as usual, it was the bowlers who suffered. Gussie arrived in Australia as the second-highest wicket-taker in Tests in 1998 with 54 victims. Yet our Middlesex seamer was dropped twice and played in only two Tests. Alex Tudor came from nowhere to make his debut at the WACA; he made an immediate impact, was dropped for the next Test and was brought back at Sydney when he was not fit. I was the only bowler to play in all five Tests. Cork played in two, Mullally in four. The belief that Croftie and Such would take advantage of Mullally's footmarks proved more flawed thinking. The decisions didn't seem so bad at the time. Looking back, however, there was some seriously muddled thinking.

'Horses for courses' became England's watchword. This was considered the best way of beating the Aussies, instead of trusting the attack that had beaten the South Africans. What that policy did do was to leave most of the bowlers frustrated, confused and short of confidence and momentum. It will not surprise you to learn that four of the batters played the entire series; it would have been six if Hick had not replaced Thorpe and Athers had not been forced to withdraw because of his back on the morning of the Sydney Test. What I can't accept, even now, is that there was no reason for us not to have a settled side. But we didn't. The discussion started before we left England. I believe that, when you walk on to the plane, nine of your Test team should be inked in; that number was probably only seven when we left for Australia. Leaving for Pakistan in the winter of 2000/1, I could have named the entire first Test team. It was that Sri Lanka defeat that created the doubts. Our tour selection panel did the rest. So did our skipper. Stewie refused to budge from his call of 'heads', despite much prompting from the England dressing-room. Losing the toss in all five Tests was a significant factor in our defeat.

Our doubts and discussions continued during our opening stay in Perth. Negative predictions held sway over positive ones. The word was that certain pitches would not suit certain bowlers. Despite Gussie's heroics that year, he was virtually ruled out of the Perth Test after getting hammered in the State game against Western Australia. The Aussie tour now traditionally starts at Lilac Hill. I remember the occasion as having been a great baptism, four years earlier. Now it was the turn of Ben Hollioake to make a name for himself and I, now a seasoned traveller, was due to sit the match out. I trained hard in the morning and looked forward to mingling with the 11,000 crowd during the afternoon's festivities. Unfortunately, Ben slipped, damaged his groin (he didn't play for another five weeks) and one rather shattered Darren Gough was thrust into the fray. Stewie told me, 'Don't worry, you'll only bowl three overs.' Pull the other one. It was the full ten overs, including the last over when the Invitation XI needed six to win. One to tie, two to win off the last ball. My competitive spirit had taken over. No run, and we ran off as though the Ashes had been decided.

England's other big failing on this tour emerged on day one of first-class cricket at the WACA. I was happy with my three-wicket haul, but not the sight of six catches going down – not all off my bowling. Not that I was too worried; the edges fly harder and faster at the WACA. Even the best fielders take time to adjust. So do batsmen. Mark Butcher misjudged the length of the second delivery from Matt Nicholson and ducked into the ball, which got through the grille of his helmet. Butch needed ten stitches above his right eye and took no further part in the proceedings. A training collision with Such and another cut, this time over the left eye, did not prevent Butch from playing in Adelaide. Not that our left-handed opener was seeing the ball too well. He went into the first Test with nine runs in five knocks.

It was Creepy's turn for a smack in Cairns. He and Corkie came out of a bar and were walking back to the hotel when a bloke rushed up, thumped him and ran off. Corkie took him back and told Wayne that Creepy had fallen over. Wayne gave them a look, signifying that he hadn't been born yesterday. The management got that right and just told the media exactly what had happened. We had drawn the games against W.A. and S.A. The

W.A. skipper, Justin Langer, criticized our 'negative' approach in settling for a draw soon after tea on the final day with only four wickets down. The Aussie had got a bit upset with my 'positive' assertion that our bowling attack was better than theirs. My view was that, without Warnie, McGrath was Australia's only proven strike power, whereas Gussie, Corkie and myself had all been in good form.

No one could argue with the magnificent way Ramps and Thorpey dug us out of a real mess at the Adelaide Oval. They came together at 80–4 in our second innings, still 58 behind the home team. The match ended with them still together, Thorpey on 223 and Ramps on 140, in a stand of 377, the third-highest stand by Englishmen abroad and the highest by a touring team in Australia. We needed more batting heroics to beat Queensland, though from the most unlikely of quarters. On a juicy wicket, which I'd enjoyed bowling on (six wickets as well as breaking Matthew Hayden's finger), England were 106–9, still needing 36 runs for victory. The sight of big Al Mullally striding out to join Croftie had us all packing our gear and preparing to cope with our first defeat of the tour. An amazing 78 minutes later, the England camp was saluting our new batting hero: Mullally, 23 not out. The England dressing-room saw a chance to make a killing. Mullally's reputation and record with the bat meant his spread for the series was extremely low. 'Buy Mullally' was the spread-betting talk that ran through our squad. Please remember: this was long before the Warne, Waugh and Cronje revelations. Anyway, if we had followed it up, this venture would have cost us a fortune. At the end of the third Test, in Adelaide, our newest batting star had amassed the grand total of four runs from five innings; the first four efforts saw him walking back to the dressing-room accompanied by the quacking duck on the giant screen!

I was happy with my form, but my Brisbane preparation was again being disturbed by events back home. Had it not been for this opening Ashes Test, I would have flown home to visit my grandad, Fred, who was seriously ill with cancer. Fred died the day before the match started. As a mark of respect, I decided to wear a black armband. I didn't ask anyone's permission; this was going to be a personal gesture. I was quite choked when the rest of the lads decided to follow suit. Stewie said: 'If he wears it, we all wear it. When one of us is hurting, we stick by him.' I know there was some outside bewilderment at an England team reacting in this way to the death of someone who had nothing to do with cricket. That was up to them. I know my grandma appreciated it, as did my dad. I planned to go home after the Test, even though we had back-to-back matches. My dad persuaded me to stay; he knew my grandad would have preferred me to carry on playing for England. Fred held an almost unique position in my life: my grandad was the only person I didn't give any lip to. I was always a cheeky lad, but he belted me early on and that taught me I had to behave in his presence. I've always been close to my dad's side of the family. My mum's folks were dead and it was my nan and grandad who looked after us kids when my mum and dad were working. Grandad was a hard man. He'd worked down the pits and had 'LOVE' and 'HATE' tattooed on his knuckles. Fred wasn't the sort to give you a hug – more likely a clip round the ear if you stepped out of line. I wasn't used to getting thumped, Mum and Dad never did that. But I grew to love and respect him. I knew he was ill, but when I left England the medical opinion was that Fred had around nine months left. I was sure he'd be there when I got back. The phone rang in Brisbane at midnight and I just knew. My dad then rang Croftie, and he came to my room. We chatted for a bit, then went downstairs for a couple of beers. Four years earlier in Brisbane, I had celebrated the birth of Liam. Now it was a death in the family.

Much as I appreciated the lads' support by wearing those arm-bands, I would rather they'd shown Fred respect by hanging on to some of the seven catches they dropped that left me with figures of 1–185 in the Test. At least I got one wicket for Fred – Justin Langer. This butter-fingers approach was to last throughout the series. I pretended to lose count of the number of catches that had gone down. Actually, I kept a careful running total: 17 in all. And I still got 21 Test wickets. That's the problem with a cricket scorecard. It doesn't always tell the whole or the true story. Gough 1–135 and

0–50 at Brisbane in 1998. Why was he kept on for so long? The truth is, I bowled pretty well and could have had more than decent figures. The England first-innings scorecard has D. Gough l.b.w. McGrath 0. That was a shocking decision as well. The two key facts the Brisbane scoreboard doesn't tell you are: (a) we blew a great opportunity of putting Australia on the rack on the first day, and (b) England would have lost heavily if it had not been for the most violent thunderstorm I've ever seen. Day became night as the Gabba was completely flooded.

My abiding memory on the first day of the series was of one of the most bizarre incidents I've ever seen on a cricket field. I'm not just talking about international cricket but any cricket: the village green, beer matches or even in the back garden! Mark Taylor – no longer a batting liability after equalling Sir Don Bradman's 334 in Peshawar a few weeks earlier – had chosen to bat. Wickets fell regularly. If we could just get rid of Steve Waugh, it would be a perfect day. And he looked dead and buried when Stewart hurled the ball towards the non-striker's end for a run-out with Mullally behind the stumps. Even without a direct hit, Waugh was stranded. That's the moment Big Al decided to place his hands in front of the stumps and divert the ball from hitting the target. What was he thinking of? I'd never seen anyone do that. Big Al, who took his first five-wicket haul in this innings, has done many daft things over the years, and normally they have us in stitches. Not this time. It was a horrendous mistake, made worse by the sight of a mightily relieved Steve Waugh. I knew immediately we would regret that lapse.

It went from bad to worse. Gussie dropped Healy at third man off a mis-pull. Then Nasser missed Waugh at second slip with two balls of the day left. Both chances were off me. I tried not to show it, but I was annoyed. Not because it was wickets lost to me, but because our good start was disappearing and the match was drifting away. Waugh and Healy – two cricketers who just love to make you pay – completed their hundreds next day. Another delivery from me rolled on to Healy's stumps, but the bails stayed put. We'd missed the boat. Australia could easily have been bowled out that first day. We batted the same way; we got in a good position, before collapsing to McGrath and ending up 100 runs short. Then Slater belted us around the park as only he can. I always fancy bowling at him with the new ball. At the same time, he can take you apart. Slater's unlike most openers. He doesn't come out to see off the new ball, he wants to get on top of you. He always attacks. If he stays, the scoreboard goes into overdrive. At Brisbane, Adelaide and Sydney in this series, Slater put us out of the game with a quickfire century in the second innings.

England had a day to survive. Our main hopes rested more on the Queensland weather than on our batting prowess. I spent much of the day in the groundsman's room, which was full of computers, video screens and the latest weather technology. We could see the huge storm that was approaching. Would it arrive in time? Wickets were falling quickly, too quickly, including three to Warnie's stand-in, MacGill. I was on successive pairs against Australia. Fortunately, I wasn't put to the test. With six down, the storm clouds came into view, racing to our rescue like the cavalry. To be fair, it was worth the wait. Lightning, thunder, the lot, real end-of-the-world stuff. It was as though someone had turned the lights off. Actually, nobody turned the lights on. The Aussies had requested the use of floodlights if conditions became dark during the series. England said 'No', and that's remained the norm. (We could have done with them in Karachi in December 2000.) Would Australia have won if the rain had stayed away? Officially, we said 'No' – again. You must give the Aussies nothing, not even in the war of words.

Perth was the next stop and the next Test. This was where we really fancied our chances. The WACA wicket took their spinners out of the equation, and we had enough batting in depth to cope with the likes of McGrath. As I've already stated, our thinking was rather confused on this trip. Two days plus one and a half sessions later, Australia were 1–0 up in the series.

After one mediocre Test and figures of 2–128, Gussie was dropped for Tudor, the new boy. It didn't take Tudes long to find out what it's like playing Test cricket for England. By teatime on his first day, Tudes had both batted and bowled for his country; I can't believe that's happened too often before. Tudes did amazingly well in the circumstances, taking 4–89 and then roughing up the Aussie batsmen as they chased 64 to win. We'd done most of the chasing in the game after making only 112 in 39 overs on the opening day. So much for the extra batsman. We had wanted to bat anyway, and it was the only time in 46 Tests that Taylor decided to bowl. Our batsmen can't take all the blame, nor can Stewie, who called 'heads' again. Only 607 runs were scored in a match that claimed 33 wickets. The wicket was damp on that first morning and it was Damien Fleming, not McGrath, who did the damage, with five wickets bowling into the Fremantle Doctor (that's the wind which blows from that direction) and getting it swinging. With the WACA's pace and bounce, the nicks were carrying. Healy caught five, slips Taylor and Mark Waugh two apiece. It was one of those days to get out of the dressing-room and watch from the viewing room. All you are trying to do is keep out of the way. When there's so much to'ing and fro'ing, pads on and off, nothing being said and a Test going down the pan, it's not the time or place for a smart remark or silly prank, even from me. Fleming destroyed our top order in the second dig, then Gillespie finished the job. The Aussies had shown their ruthlessness on the pitch and off it. MacGill, despite his impressive Gabba showing, had not even made the Aussie squad. Instead, the 34-year-old journeyman, Colin 'Funky' Miller, who lived above a pub in Hobart, made the XI and came in to face my hat-trick ball after I'd removed Healy and Fleming. Miller survived, but I was to get another opportunity at him later in the series.

We went out for a drink that night. Teams do after a Test. The winners go to celebrate. The losers drown their sorrows, question the quality of the pitch and speculate how it might all have been different if the captain had won the toss. The toss hadn't been important in Brisbane. We fielded badly and the rain saved us. I'd like to think Australia would have been on the back foot if we had bowled first at the WACA. But England couldn't escape the fact that we hadn't bowled or batted well. What was more worrying was that the confidence and spirit from the South Africa series had vanished. Much of that damage had been self-inflicted. We now didn't have a clue what our best bowling line-up was. I blame the media to some extent: one bad game, and your worth in the side is questioned. The media, with help from the management, created an atmosphere of uncertainty in Australia.

The draw against Victoria, who were missing eight regulars, pushed Deano into the Test line-up. It almost cost me my place. I was resting, but I decided to put a video of my bowling on to watch in the dressing-room. I was balancing on a chair and table, trying to change the TV channel, when I suddenly found myself in a heap on the ground with my leg aching. There was pain coming from the back of my leg; fortunately, it was only from having ripped off some of the skin. Of course there were the usual comments about getting what you deserve for trying to watch yourself in action. The skipper's dad, former England coach Mickey, was in Melbourne, and he spent a couple of hours with the bowling machine, getting Stewie's feet moving properly. It worked. Stewie hit his first hundred of the tour.

With another seven-batter line-up and a spinner, Such, included in our four-man attack, the three fast bowlers prayed that Stewie would call correctly at the Adelaide Oval. Australia would retain the Ashes with a win, and Taylor's side would be halfway there if he won the toss. Although it's 50–50 every time that coin is spun, we reckoned it was our turn after two wrong calls. Wrong again. Our heads went down; the mountain to climb had just become a few hundred feet higher. The heat was unbearable; the temperature was over 100°F, but the side batting knew that a cooler snap was due some time the following afternoon. It's bad enough suffering in that heat, but it's doubly bad if you think your opponents are not going to have to bake as well. That Friday was the hardest day I've ever spent on a cricket field. We were grabbing drinks after each over, using the underground box that stores helmets as our supply depot. I wouldn't have minded the heat so much if the wicket hadn't been so flat. Adelaide has a well-deserved reputation for being a batters' paradise. I prefer to think of it as a bowlers' nightmare. I bust a gut that day, took the second new ball, but my only rewards were the wickets of Steve Waugh with the new ball, just before the close. We simply didn't get a break.

One of the few Aussie failures was Steve's twin, Mark, who was caught and bowled cheaply by Peter Such. That came as no surprise, since one of Australia's most talented batsmen in recent times had been booed to the wicket. It had been revealed a couple of days earlier that he and Warnie had been fined by the A.C.B. for accepting money from a bookmaker in Sri Lanka four years earlier. Warnie made his first appearance of the series in front of the media, along with Waugh. I don't know what surprised me more: the offence itself or the fact that the A.C.B. had kept the fines quiet for so long, especially as this information had not been supplied to a recent Pakistan inquiry into match-fixing. It's one of the few times I've seen Mark Waugh with little stomach for the fight. Alas, the same couldn't be said of Justin Langer, who batted for over eight hours for an undefeated 179.

Our response was hindered by one of the worst third-umpire decisions I've ever seen, when Athers got the red light. In cricket, red means move – and green, stay where you are! Taylor claimed the slip catch off MacGill. Athers, easily batting his best of the tour, watched the ball all the way and was adamant that the ball had not carried. We settled ourselves for several minutes of replays. This was obviously a close call. Obviously not. Athers was not the only Englishman left shocked when Paul Angley hit the 'out' button after a matter of seconds. Right or wrong, it doesn't matter. I couldn't understand how he could have made a judgement that quickly on what he had seen. My verdict after numerous watchings was 'not out'. Athers takes most of what life throws at him in his stride, but not this time. Our former captain was fuming. Nasser and Ramps gave us some hope that second night, but we collapsed next morning. Midway through the series, another England Ashes bid was destined for the dustbin.

The Aussies turned the screw in typical fashion and set us a victory target of 443 in 140 overs. We never got close, not even to saving the game. The only memorable batting moment came when Mullally managed his first runs of the series after four ducks, and it could have been five, when he was nearly run out. McGrath, Fleming, Miller, MacGill – they all took wickets at Adelaide. England's Nos. 6–11 managed a grand total of 42 runs between them in 12 knocks. The Ashes had gone, as early as they possibly could. My third losing series against Australia – but spare a thought for Athers. This was his sixth series on the receiving end. Athers knows that summer 2001 will be his final chance.

Another Ashes opportunity gone. Worse than that. More post mortems into 'what's wrong with English cricket'. The following few days were depressing as we came to terms with the fact that, once again and only midway through a series, the main prize had gone and we were left playing for pride. How many more Ashes chances would I get? I'd taken a trip out to the famous Australian Cricket Academy, run by former Aussie wicket-keeper Rodney Marsh. The élite institution for the best young cricketers has certainly given Australia a lift in the past decade and has stolen a march on others. I've heard plenty of talk of a similar establishment over here, but we are still waiting while the counties and the Establishment quibble over where it should be, how it should be run and who's to be in charge. After our disastrous Ashes tour four years earlier, there was an overwhelming vote for a national academy. A year later, the same people rejected the idea. Self-interest was still the governing factor in English cricket. Interestingly, Marsh pointed out to me that the Australian Academy had taken in players from India, Malaysia, Zimbabwe and Bangladesh, but none from England!

Stewie took stock after Adelaide. By now we had stopped joking about him being a lousy tosser. He sat out our game against an Australian Second XI in Hobart to consider his options for the final two Tests. The Ashes had gone, but the series hadn't. We had fought back well in 1994/5. Stewie was convinced we could do it again. Not that anything in our Hobart performance improved our captain's wellbeing. I was rested, along with the skipper. It was a good one to miss. England were humiliated. Stewie needed all his powers of persuasion to prevent Bumble resigning on the spot. This was the not unexpected consequence of a crazy Atherton declaration and a response from a bunch of touring bowlers who'd had the stuffing and confidence knocked out of them by our selection policy. Athers scored the first double-hundred of his career after deciding to bat. My Yorkshire team-mate, Darren Lehmann, declared while still behind, and then Athers decided to make a game of it. The bowlers were absolutely furious. That doesn't excuse our performance. The bowlers went for about seven an over as 345 runs were scored in less than three and a half hours. Greg Blewett was on the field throughout the entire game, scoring an undefeated 169 and 213. What our bowlers couldn't understand – and I was one of them – was why a touring team, trying to regain some confidence and spirit, would allow some of Australia's finest batting talent a second use of the flattest wicket (flatter than Adelaide) we had seen all tour so they could embarrass us: Elliott, Blewett, who came into the game on the back of two centuries, Lehmann, Stuart Law and Michael Bevan. Adam Gilchrist didn't get a bat. I don't know what Athers was thinking. We finished the game – in which 1,337 runs were scored for the loss of 14 wickets – in tatters and in crisis. Goochie was as furious as Bumble. 'If we'd set them 500, I think they might have got them,' as the home side came home with 22 overs and nine wickets to spare.

As ever, I tried to find some humour in the darkest moment and came into the dressing-room at teatime dressed as Father Christmas. 'Yo, ho, ho, I'm looking for Angus Fraser!' Then I sat Gussie on my knee and said: 'Guess what I've got in my sack for you.' Gussie looked rather perplexed, knowing there was no genuine present in there. 'I've brought you some wickets. How lucky you are. They are in very short supply at the moment. Yo, ho, ho!' Gussie smiled. Well, I think he did. It was a rare but necessary moment of light relief in the dressing-room that afternoon.

We were not laughing by the close. England had been stuffed, after declaring against the second-best players in Australia on a flat deck when we had nothing to gain. Again England's well-known cricketing generosity had backfired. No other team in the world would have been that stupid. Unlike the Hick declaration four years earlier, Athers stubbornly maintains he would still do the same. I'm not so sure.

The Hobart stop saw the arrival of some of the wives, including Anna. However hard and depressing cricket life can be in Australia, there are always compensations and distractions. The hotels are first class, and now we enjoyed the benefits of rooms on our own. The food is also first class; but all that wouldn't matter if the locals weren't so friendly. I know Aussies can be loud, cocky and brash away from home, but that is not the case on home soil. Nothing is too much trouble for England's cricketers. Several leading wine-makers, including Adelaide's Geoff Merrill, are big cricket fans, and their hospitality is never restricted to their own side. Life would be unbearable in any other country if England were 2–0 down in a Test series. South Africans would certainly not let a minute pass without reminding us of our predicament in that subtle way of theirs; they would want you to go home humiliated. Not the Aussies; they want you to fight. Where's the pleasure in beating an obviously inferior team? We enjoyed some festive cheer with the touring media in Hobart as the players were entertained to drinks and nibbles. Relationships were rather frosty again. That had nothing to do with criticism of our recent performances, which were deserved. But the *Daily Telegraph*'s correspondent had suggested that part of the reason for our poor form on the field was our 'philandering' off it. I wasn't quite sure what it meant, but it sounded like something we should not be up to, and it gave a totally wrong impression of our behaviour and attitude in Australia.

19. Hat-Trick Heroics

Stewie had come to a decision after Hobart. Batting at No. 4, keeping wicket, leading the side and calling 'heads' was too much for one man. Something had to give. Unfortunately, it wasn't the 'heads' call. Instead, Stewie passed the gloves to Warren Hegg when Tudor was declared unfit on the morning of the match and moved himself up to open. I was pleased for Heggie. Second-choice keeper is a tough job on tour. Opportunities are extremely limited and, unlike us bowlers or batters, there's only one place up for grabs. When it's the skipper you're up against, it's not much of a fair contest. Stewie's role in the England side is a subject of debate that's been raging for over a decade, longer than my England career. My tuppence worth, for what it's worth, is that Stewie should keep wicket and bat down the order. He's been our only genuine all-rounder since Botham's demise, and he provides the best balance when he's behind the stumps. Our main concern now, however, was our coach.

The rest of the families arrived in Melbourne. The players' traditional fancy-dress party was abandoned because of our tight schedule, although my Liam and Stewie's lad, Andrew, spent most of Christmas Day charging around in Batman and Robin suits. Our entertainment came from Butch on the guitar. This was my fifth Christmas as an England player. I'd been on my own for two (one enforced), had the family with me abroad for two, and I had spent one at home when I was trying to get fit for the 1998 Caribbean trip. There are two big differences when you are touring abroad to Christmas at home. First, the temperature is usually a couple of dozen degrees higher. Secondly, you don't get shedded when there's a Test starting the next day. A glass of champagne, a glass of wine and perhaps a couple of beers: that's your lot. Nobody wants to spend six hours charging around the M.C.G. with a hangover.

Actually, it wouldn't have mattered this time, because rain wiped out the entire day's play on Boxing Day. That was a great disappointment. It's one of sport's special days, particularly when more than 90,000 are packed into the M.C.G.

Boxing Day wasn't a complete non-starter. The rain slackened enough for Stewie to call 'heads' once more. Taylor decide that England could bat, although it was the next day before Athers and Stewie made their way out. Any day stuck in the dressing-room is no fun. I couldn't believe the way almost 60,000 remained at the M.C.G. in the hope of some cricket. Athers, as had happened to him on Boxing Day here eight years earlier, was soon on his way back with no runs to his name. His former partner, Butch, now at No. 3, also failed to disturb the scorers. Stewie showed his fighting spirit with his first century in 23 Tests against Australia.

We should have gained a first-innings lead. Aussie trailed our 270 total by 18 runs with just two wickets left. I'd got five and was really racing in. The speed gun was in attendance and I cleared 140 k.p.h. several times. Yet we still ended up 70 runs adrift as Steve Waugh, with help from a career-best 43 from MacGill, orchestrated a ninth-wicket stand of 88. Our policy of giving Waugh runs in order to try and get at MacGill backfired. That third night Athers bagged his first-ever Test pair. Butch had also gone without us clearing the deficit. It had been a long day; the new regulations added another 30 minutes at the end of each day to make up for the lost play on Boxing Day. That had nothing on the fourth and final day. The historians informed us that that Tuesday in Melbourne was the longest in Test match history: a total of eight hours and three minutes. What the experts didn't need to tell me was that it was one of the very best.

England hailed many heroes that afternoon. The popular choice was Dean Headley, but Alan Mullally deserves a special mention, not so much for his dismissal of Taylor and Langer – the latter was down to a stunning catch by Ramps – but for his batting prowess. As he walked out to join Gussie, England were 221–9 – a mere 151 runs ahead. His Test tour batting stats to that point were innings 6, highest score 4, total runs 4, ducks 5, average 0.66. That last wicket carved out 23 valuable runs, 16 of them off the normally wafer-thin bat of Big Al. A target of 175 wasn't Mount Everest but, as I've already said, this England camp believes Australia have a problem and a weakness chasing small targets. England had beaten Australia thrice in my time, and twice (Adelaide in 1995 and the Oval in 1997), that weakness was exposed.

When Australia reached three figures for the loss of only two wickets, I must confess we'd just about given up. Then came one of those magic moments that make playing sport worth while and which give a losing team renewed heart. Langer looked stunned when a full-blooded pull off Mullally ended up in Ramps's right hand. Ramps provided the spark and it was Deano who caught fire, reducing Australia from 130–3 to 140–7 with a spell of four wickets for four runs in 13 deliveries. There was mayhem in the M.C.G. As well as the thousands of Aussies eager to watch their heroes read us the last rites, hundreds of England supporters had flown out for the two holiday Tests. Now it was Aussie nerves that were jangling, and Steve Waugh's in particular. We had nothing to lose. I just love seeing the best team in the world under pressure, displaying all the frailties normally shown only by us lesser mortals.

After the dramas of Headingley, Stewie and all of us were keen to get off the field and let Australia sweat overnight. Unlike Cronje, Steve Waugh was on the field and was fully aware of his right to demand that extra half-hour. The problem was that, in trying to make up time, the clock was showing 7.22 and this session had already lasted three hours and fifty minutes. On top of that, Deano and I had bowled the last 16 overs together. I kept saying to Stewie: 'I'm knackered.' The only response I got was, 'One more over. We can't bring anyone else on. They might bowl some looseners, and we can't afford the runs. Keep going, keep going. There's no other way.' Deano and I were both running on empty, or, rather, adrenalin.

I felt sure the umpires would use their discretion and lead us off the field. Waugh saw that this was what we wanted to do and insisted on his right to do the opposite. This was Test cricket on the edge, every bit as thrilling as Atherton *v*. Donald, except this time I was in the middle of it.

I'd often wondered in the months since Headingley what would have happened if South Africa had been allowed to claim that extra half-hour. At the time, I felt we would have struggled. The targets then were 34 runs or two wickets. This time, the odds were on the batting side – 14 runs or three wickets. Australia had to be favourites. Gussie and I were injured and ill at Headingley. Deano and I were fit and healthy this time, we were just on our knees through exhaustion. What was clear was that this final exchange was never going to take the extra half-hour. Unless we took wickets, it would all be over in around four overs. Matt Nicholson's departure in the first over to Headley increased the tension, but not necessarily the odds. I ran in to bowl to Steve Waugh with MacGill, batting hero of the first innings, at the non-striker's end. A day earlier, Waugh had taken the singles we offered and trusted in MacGill's ability. This situation was different, surely. Not according to Waugh, who took a run off the first ball of my sixteenth over. 'After a not-outer,' I said, walking past Waugh.

This was no time for faint heart. I went back to my mark with one delivery on my mind: the in-swinging yorker, the most deadly ball to tail-enders. MacGill may have been celebrating a career best, but he was still a No. 10 batsman, the position he'd batted at for Devon that summer when we beat them in the first round of the NatWest. For the record, Ryan Sidebottom had MacGill caught behind for a duck. I knew that, if I got it right, MacGill was dead meat. I saw the whole scenario so clearly. A few seconds later I was running in to bowl, and my vision became a reality. MacGill was beaten all ends up, his stumps shattered, and England were one wicket away from sensation. As I celebrated, I made a determined effort to catch Steve Waugh's eye; his ploy had backfired. The Australian skipper was stuck at the non-striker's end, unable to protect Glenn McGrath, one of the world's best bowlers and worst batsmen. I had a possible four deliveries to win this Test before Waugh could get back into the action. Had taking that single cost Australia the Test?

The trouble with bowling at a rabbit like McGrath is that everyone *expects* you to get him out. I knew he had to go this over. If Steve Waugh got back on strike, we would not be allowed a second sustained assault on McGrath. I had one thought in my mind: 'Bowl at the stumps. Get four on target, and surely McGrath cannot survive.'

It was the second delivery that speared into McGrath's toes.

'Howzat?' Actually it was less a question, more a statement.

Up went the Aussie umpire's finger. You beauty. I have never made such a spectacle of myself as I did at that moment. All the frustration and anger of the previous two months came bubbling to the surface. You may be the best team in the world, you may have the Ashes – but you can't chase small totals. We'd proved it again. I gave it a real King of the Castle pose, very Tarzan, very defiant, stump in hand. I'd lost it for a minute. This was my first Test win in Australia, and I'd taken the last wicket. After all the stick we'd had to take, I was in no mood to be modest. 'Shove that up your arse, you Aussie w★★★★★s,' is what I mouthed to a TV cameraman as I ran past, thinking he was an Aussie. He wasn't, and Sky took great delight in replaying my less than diplomatic mutterings.

What a night we had, back at the hotel: all the families, all the supporters, the Barmy Army. Great. We all took turns, standing on the table, to sing. Wayne was on the guitar. We sang Oasis songs and Goochie led the rendition of the National Anthem. Two months' pain and hardship were wiped out at a stroke. I don't know why, but winning that Test match was probably my greatest moment on a cricket field, better even than beating South Africa at Headingley and the West Indies at the Oval in 2000. Australia are rugby's All Blacks and soccer's Brazil. They set the standards and they have been the outstanding team in my time and in the years before. From Allan Border, through Mark Taylor to Steve Waugh, the Aussies have got better and better and better. No wonder we raise the roof when we beat them. Our celebrations carried on while we watched the fireworks on Sydney Harbour Bridge bringing in the New Year.

Gussie's efforts in 1998 earned him an O.B.E. in the Honours List. His reward from the England management was typical of his tour. He was sent off to Bowral on New Year's Day to strengthen the one-day squad playing against a Bradman XI there!

Sydney was no longer a lap of honour for Taylor's team. We could share the series. Warnie was fit at last; would it be him or MacGill, who had taken 15 wickets in three Tests, who would be selected? A month or so earlier there would have been no discussion. Not now. MacGill, not as accurate as Warnie, bowled a mean googly and had grown in stature as the series progressed. In typical Aussie fashion, the selectors played them both, along with 'Funky' Miller, who doubled up as McGrath's opening partner. Our selection panel stuck to the horses-for-courses tack. The last-wicket pair whose runs had given us hope and, ultimately, victory in Melbourne were both dropped. Tudor returned to the fray and we included a spinner, Peter Such. Crawley came in for Butch, who eventually played when Athers's back flared up on the morning of the match.

Over 43,000 packed in the S.C.G., the best Test crowd there for 23 years, and they were rewarded with a cracking opening day. The pressure was huge for Stewie to change his call, but our captain was not for turning. 'Heads' again, we lose, they bat, and Taylor became the first skipper since 1953 to win all five tosses. In fact, in his last dozen Tests against England, Taylor had lost only once. The highlight of the day, until the penultimate over, was the performance of the Waugh twins, batting in unison and manufacturing an Aussie recovery as only they can. You always know what you're going to get with Steve: a fight with no frills and no concessions. Mark's the unpredictable one, sometimes brilliant, occasionally inspired. Steve never makes the game look easy the way Mark does. Steve wants it hard; that's where his motivation comes from. We saw the best of both the Waughs that afternoon as the runs flowed. Australia looked well placed at 242–3, then 321–6 with a couple of overs left.

Then came the Gough hat-trick with the new ball. As was the case four days earlier in Melbourne, I was wicketless until the last knockings. Unlike Perth, I made no mistake with the hat-trick ball this time. What a moment, an Ashes hat-trick, especially in front of your wife and mum and dad and family. Well, nearly. I discovered later that they had left the ground early to beat the rush and get back to Coogee, where we were staying. They listened to my heroics on the car radio. I've heard from so many people who missed it.

It was after six in the evening when I ran in to bowl at Healy. Unlike Melbourne, Stewie had wondered if I wanted a rest. Whether it was a hangover from Melbourne, I don't know, but I'd felt sluggish and lethargic all day. My fourth delivery found the edge of Healy's bat. Big nick and Healy went to walk, then he stopped and pretended there was something in his eye. As Barry Richards said, the Aussies walk only when the car runs out of petrol. Umpire Steve Dunne sent the Aussie keeper on his way. As the lads gathered round, I saw MacGill coming out. 'He's going the same way as at Melbourne,' I predicted, and out went his middle pole.

Another hat-trick ball. The same batsman as at Perth, though – 'Funky' Miller. I had plenty of hat-trick experience around me. Warnie was not offering any advice from the non striker's end. I couldn't say the same for Corkie, who brought on drinks as each wicket fell. As he came towards me, I shouted, 'Don't even say it.' I knew there would be some nonsense about 'Come on, join the club' or how to bowl 'a successful hat-trick ball'. In analysing my previous failures, I'd tried too hard and had not given myself a chance.

The ball that did for Healy I held for the outswinger. It was just a good effort ball and he nicked it. I did the same for MacGill, but it swung in. I was trying to york him, obviously, but it drifted in. Miller was expecting the in-swinging yorker, but I went for the outswinger again. The most important factor on a hat-trick ball is to give yourself a chance of getting the wicket. The delivery must be on target. It was. At the very last moment the ball swung away in the air and clipped his off-stump. It was the best ball I'd bowled all series. There's always a bit of luck involved, but it all went according to plan.

Bedlam. The lads hit me from all angles. My initial sensation was pain: Tudor had sunk his teeth into the back of my head by accident. Warnie congratulated me. A Test match hat-trick is something that may or may not be part of a great career. You need that little bit of luck. Was it the Sydney factor again? My happiest England memories abroad are on that ground. Later I was astonished to learn that the last English hat-trick in an Ashes Test had been on my home ground, way back in 1899. Afterwards, I was asked if the hat-trick was better than trapping McGrath l.b.w. at the M.C.G. on Tuesday. No contest, and I've already explained why.

Warnie, being Warnie, got a wicket with his fourth ball back. But it was MacGill who ensured that England were left over 100 runs adrift. As Australia batted for a second time, we found ourselves on the wrong end of a TV replay again. This time the Slater green-light consequences were more serious than Athers's red light in Adelaide. Australia were 60–2 and Slater was on 35 when Headley scored a direct hit for a run-out. It was out. We weren't worried when umpire Steve Dunne referred the decision to the third umpire. Athers had been chopped in a few seconds. As we were wondering why there was a delay, the green light came on. No way. It transpired that Slats had been given the benefit of the doubt because the camera angles were not in line with the stumps. Imagine how we felt as Slater saved the Aussies from total collapse with 123 out of 184. That was 66.84 per cent of the Aussie runs, the highest percentage since the first ever Test in 1876. Mark Waugh was the only other Aussie to reach double figures, as Suchie took 5–81 in his last bowl for England. Repeated watching of the incident has not shaken my view that Slats was well short of his ground.

We had to get on with the game. England needed 297 to win and level the series. We lost both openers stumped, but were still in with a chance that third night at 104–2. The Aussie papers were quick to point out that only one side had ever chased more than 200 to win at the S.C.G. MacGill put paid to our resistance the next day as we surrendered tamely to go down by 98 runs. The series was Australia's, 3–1. Once again the difference was a leg-spinner.

Warnie took two wickets on his return; MacGill ended up with 12–107, the second-best figures in a Sydney Test and the best for over a century. Dean and I took 40 wickets between us – the same as McGrath and Fleming – don't forget those 17 missed chances. Such and Croftie took 13; MacGill, Miller and Warnie 38, with 27 going to MacGill in four Tests. Maybe he wasn't in Warnie's class, but he was still too good for us, and he got better as the series progressed. His wicket-taking was the Aussies' most telling statistic. Ours was the 17 players used in the series. After a successful summer back home, that was a nonsense, and I wasn't alone in thinking the 'horse for courses' policy should have been consigned to the knacker's yard!

20. One-Day Punch-up

No sooner had the Test series finished than I jumped on one of those endless one-day rollercoasters. This one careered around Australia, then Pakistan and Sharjah, supposedly to prepare us for the 1999 World Cup in England. It was a brutal, bruising, never-ending, ill-tempered journey that ended in disappointment after we had scrapped with the Sri Lankans and then with our own Board. Nobody's reputation was enhanced. The public squabble over our World Cup contracts was an unseemly affair which did considerable damage to our prospects. After an early show of strength and solidarity, we bottled it as a team. I was ready to turn my back on a World Cup place for what I thought was a fair deal. So were others. Ultimately, this players' protest ended because we did not stick together. Our divided stance was in marked contrast to the Sri Lankans during the one-dayers in Australia. The second one of their own was threatened, even by the I.C.C.'s own Code of Conduct, Sri Lanka moved the battle to the courts. Generally, over the years the cricket authorities have not enjoyed an easy time in legal disputes. As someone who witnessed and experienced their disgraceful behaviour at first hand and close hand at the Adelaide Oval, I was appalled at subsequent events. If Sri Lanka do not want to play by the I.C.C.'s rules, on and off the field, fair enough. The minute all that legal nonsense in Australia started, Sri Lanka should have been threatened with expulsion from the World Cup. Kicking out the holders might seem extreme, but I wouldn't have shed a tear if the 1999 tournament had not included Sri Lanka. Most of the England team felt the same way.

I can't believe we played 12 one-day internationals in Australia at the end of the Ashes series, including seven against our hosts. Small wonder that friends were on the phone, wondering if I was okay. My appearance at the final presentation was the reason. My eyes had 'gone' – and so had the rest of me. I was absolutely shattered. Stewie was in a similar state. Non-stop international cricket for almost three months had taken its toll. In England the previous summer, it had taken three games to produce the two finalists for the Emirates Trophy. Here 15 games were scheduled in order to exclude one team. There must be a happy medium. We started the one-day series well and got into a winning streak. Then tiredness took effect. On my days off in a one-day competition I normally like to play golf, go to the beach or lie by the pool and sunbathe. In the final fortnight, I can hardly remember getting out of bed or leaving my room. That's how bad it got. I was physically and mentally exhausted. Not that there was much understanding to be had from my employers. When I heard that the next winter's tour to South Africa was scheduled to be even longer than this, I thought it was madness and I said so. My reaction was captured by the Sky cameras. The powers-that-be were not happy, although the E.C.B. had asked me to do the interview in the first place. Tour itineraries, I was told, were not the concern of players and in future I should keep my comments to myself. That was my good luck message from International Teams Director Simon Pack, transmitted through manager David Graveney, before our scheduled three-match final with Australia.

Our journey to the final had taken us from Brisbane to Melbourne to Sydney to Melbourne to Adelaide to Perth to Sydney. England won four of the first five ties and then lost four of the next five. I bowled like an idiot in the first game. I wasn't up for it, I hadn't bowled with the white ball for ages, it was too soon after the Tests, I tried too hard and nothing was happening for me. Still, we beat Australia by seven runs, thanks to Mullally's career-best 4–18. I'm often asked why Big Al is such an effective performer in limited overs and yet so limited in the first-class contest. He doesn't like to go for runs, so he tends to bowl wide. He knows that in one-day cricket the batsman will either smash him or the umpires will penalize him, so he bowls straighter. It's his mentality. If he bowls straight, Al's a good bowler and he can swing it both ways. But when he loses it, the ball goes miles wide as he lets the ball go out of the side of his hand.

It was a winning first weekend for England as Neil 'Harvey' Fairbrother led us to a four-wicket victory over Sri Lanka. Harvey was back in the side, so it must be a World Cup year. Harvey had been put out to grass after the previous World Cup, yet I had no qualms about his return. I'd have him in even now. The only thing that lets Harvey down is his fitness; he's injury-prone. Yet I still rate him as one of the best one-day players in the world. While Harvey's at the wicket, you've always got a chance. I know that from bitter experience. When Yorkshire play Lancashire, he's the guy we want out. Athers digs in, Creepy strokes it around and Freddie gives it the lash, but Harvey's the danger man. Thorpey's the nearest we have to him now in the England squad, lacking only Harvey's ability to devastate an attack. I've never understood why Harvey's dumped between World Cups. 'England are building for the future, the next World Cup' is what we are told. The experience of the last two campaigns should tell us that this is flawed thinking. We missed Harvey. No one can judge and pace a run-chase better – or know the right target to put on the board. And, for a little bloke, he hits the ball a long way. We tried to play without him, failed and brought him back for the big one.

Warnie, too, was back in the big time. My pal was skippering Australia because Steve Waugh had a damaged hamstring. Warnie did a brilliant job, full of invention and challenges. True to Warnie, almost everything he tried came off, even when remonstrating with the M.C.G. fans who were belting us fielders with golf and billiard balls. Ever the showman, he borrowed Mark Waugh's helmet before pleading with the culprits. I'm not sure why they felt the need to interfere. Australia coasted home by nine wickets after our poor show of batting.

Revenge was gained in Sydney two nights later when Hickie and Nasser set a 283-run target. The Aussies have always paraded Michael Bevan as the best one-day batsman in the world. I agree there's not much between him and Harvey, but our man was better. Harvey would take the risks that Bevan considered too much of a gamble. Bevan's undefeated 45 that night did not contain a single boundary, and his side fell seven runs short. That would not have happened with Harvey. I bowled a maiden to Bevan at the death before Ashley Giles held his nerve in the final over.

Bevan was not the only Aussie Yorkie on show that night. Darren Lehmann has been a tremendous asset for the White Rose, but he had made a subdued entry in the Ashes series after Ponting was dropped. Lehmann came out of his shell in this tournament and was devastating that night.

I'd shaken off the one-day cobwebs by now. Melbourne was the start of my recovery. I regained my zip in my second spell, got the yorkers working in Sydney and totally destroyed the Sri Lankans with a four-wicket opening spell back at the M.C.G. That earned me the Man of the Match as we strolled home by seven wickets. Our next match against the World Cup holders was much less of a walk in the park. We scored over 300 runs at the Adelaide Oval and lost in the most ill-tempered, controversial one-day international ever played. I lost my cool, and so did Stewie and Adam Hollioake. You couldn't blame us. I genuinely believe Sri Lanka cheated in that game. They did anything and everything they could to win, irrespective of the laws of cricket or the spirit in which the game is played. The big mistake we made was in losing. The turning point came when Jayawardene was run out by a couple of yards. We couldn't believe it when umpire Ross Emerson failed to seek a decision from the third umpire. Mind you, Emerson had been having some sort of day. After this game, he was removed from the officiating panel; apparently he was on sick leave from his job for a 'stress-related' illness.

So much happened that I had better take you through it slowly. Ranatunga won the toss and asked us to bat. I had a hint that this might be an interesting day when Emerson from square leg called Muralitharan for throwing in his second over, just as he'd done a few years earlier. As I've stated before, I don't believe that's the right time or place to question a bowler's action, especially as Muralitharan had recently been cleared by the I.C.C. One of the reasons why Emerson was standing was because Darrell Hair was being kept away from officiating in Sri Lanka's matches. His recent book had described Muralitharan's action as 'diabolical' – hardly likely to reduce the growing tension. There was no excuse for Ranatunga's reaction to Emerson's latest questioning of Muralitharan's action: Sri Lanka's captain led his players to the boundary. The dressing-rooms are next to each other, side-on to the Oval wicket, with the viewing areas next to each. We were interested spectators, waiting for Sri Lanka's next move. Word spread that Ranatunga was speaking to his Board in Colombo on the mobile – so much for new technology in cricket. After a quarter of an hour, the Sri Lankans were ordered back, but Ranatunga decided to make a mockery of cricket for the rest of the day. He switched Muralitharan to Emerson's end, making the Aussie umpire stand almost on top of the stumps. It was humiliating to watch.

At this stage, we were rather bemused and innocent bystanders as Hickie and Harvey took us to 302–3. That was to change when we went out to field. Emerson appeared to have lost the plot. I went for a run-out and Mahanama barged into me. It was a genuine run-out chance. I've been around long enough to know when someone deliberately goes out of their way to impede you. I gave him a mouthful when I got to the other end and told him to watch himself. His reaction was that he'd do it again if he got the chance. Boys from Barnsley don't take crap like that, and I very nearly laid into him. I really had to hold myself back and I just stopped myself in time. Then I made a gesture of head-butting him in order to let off some steam. Then it was Adam Hollioake's turn to have a few words with Ranatunga. Then Stewie was overheard on TV telling Ranatunga: 'Your behaviour today has been appalling for a country captain.' Stewie wasn't much better; he barged into Mahanama. I couldn't blame him: it was the sort of game where you wanted to hit somebody. I've never known such physical tension on a cricket field. What made it worse was Muralitharan hitting the winning run with two balls remaining. I half expected an all-out punch-up when we got back to the dressing-rooms. You could have knocked me down with a feather when Ranatunga and his men appeared at our door, all smiles and wanting to shake hands. With one voice, we told them where to go. Ranatunga couldn't have stayed long anyway as his presence was requested by match referee Peter van der Merwe.

The whole day was sad enough, but what followed was even more depressing for cricket. Ranatunga had been bad-tempered (I don't know why, because he went past Allan Border's record 178 appearances as a one-day captain) and hadn't played the game in the right spirit. His behaviour was out of order. We reckoned he was for the high jump. Not Ranatunga. When the I.C.C. Code of Conduct was waved in his face, he brought in the lawyers and threatened to sue everyone in sight. His action spoiled more than a game of cricket that day. Ranatunga was charged with breaches of the Code of Conduct, and appeared to be guilty. Yet he escaped with a six-match suspension and a small fine, after his lawyers argued that suspension would be a restraint of trade. It was a joke. Once again the I.C.C. showed itself toothless and gutless. Sri Lanka, Ranatunga's employers, had agreed to adhere to the Code of Conduct before the series began. Can you imagine any England player charged with five offences escaping with anything less than a custodial sentence? Match referee van der Merwe was almost in tears after the whole shenanigans.

Ranatunga's let-off was all the incentive we needed to demolish Sri Lanka at the WACA for 99. It was the perfect bouncy pitch for peppering their batsmen, and I wasn't the only England bowler charging in with extra venom that night, looking to send the Sri Lankans on their way any way I could. David Graveney, who'd taken over from Goochie as manager for the one-day leg of the tour, wasn't alone when he voiced the opinion that this one-day victory was the most satisfying in his experience.

The last three group matches were meaningless. Australia and England had already made the final. Despite my tiredness, I turned down the chance of a break in our final group match. You can call that selfish or stupid, but I've missed enough one-day internationals in my career. If the selectors decide to drop or rest me, fair enough; that's out of my hands. If it's left to me, you'll only ever get one answer.

Warnie was back in charge of Australia. Steve Waugh returned briefly, but his hamstring went again. Australia won seven out of ten in the qualifiers. A rare setback came early in the tournament when Ricky Ponting was suspended for three games after being laid out in a Sydney bar-brawl. This talented cricketer took his punishment on the chin, also confessing that he had a drink problem for which he would be seeking help. Our first final game at Sydney probably cost Nasser his place in England's original World Cup squad. Chasing the Aussies' 232, it was in the bag at 198–4 in the 43rd over. There was no need for risks, nudge a few here and a few there, and the job was done. Warnie started to wind Nasser up: don't be scared, come and hit this one, where's your courage? Verbals followed. No problem there. Before we knew it, Nasser had come charging down the wicket and was stumped. It was as sucker a punch as they come. Why react? We were walking the game. Warnie lives for that reaction; it's what he loves. That's why he plays the game. Sometimes you have to accept his challenge, there's no alternative. Not this time. Nasser had shown himself to be naïve and headstrong. Australia had first a sniff, then a strong smell of victory as five wickets went down for six runs. I went, first ball, to McGrath, yorked. I didn't even get my bat down. We lost a contest by ten runs that had been ours for more than 90 of the 100 overs. Michael Bevan was named Man of the Match. Rubbish. Warnie was Australia's match-winner that night.

That was the end of our challenge. It was a three-match final, but England were finished. Our 162-run defeat in the second game came as no surprise. England – especially Stewie and I – were a spent force. I remember standing at the presentation at the M.C.G. shell-shocked, tired, but glad it was all over and desperate to get home to Anna and the kids. My tour had gone well in both types of cricket. I felt I'd improved as a bowler and had shown greater consistency. I'd played a full major series abroad at last. Now I was looking forward to the World Cup, unaware that the seeds of disharmony and distrust had been sown, months earlier, at the start of the Ashes series.

21. Gutless . . . Cupless

England bottled the 1999 World Cup. That is the only honest conclusion. As a team we should have been stronger, on and off the field. We caved in over our contracts fight with Lord's. Our tournament performance reflected that dispute. We started confidently, thought we were in a winning position, then folded at the first sign of trouble. I had been prepared to put my World Cup place on the line for what I believed was right. So had Neil Fairbrother, Graeme Hick, Graham Thorpe, Ian Austin and Alan Mullally. We were ready to be dumped on a point of principle. The others, like us, wanted more money but wouldn't sacrifice a World Cup place for it. If we had all stuck together, the Board would have given in. Lord's would never have got away with selecting the second-best 15 players in England. Had we won that battle, we would have shown the resolve necessary to prevent England being dumped out at the group stage. In our final group match against India, rain forced us into a second day. As we sat in the Edgbaston dressing-room that first afternoon, watching Zimbabwe shock South Africa – a result that meant we had to beat India – I am ashamed to say this England team slowly but surely raised the white flag in the 1999 World Cup.

I never anticipated any problems over our World Cup fee. Stewie had met with Simon Pack in Brisbane before the Ashes series. As far as he and the rest of us were concerned, a deal had been done. The E.C.B. were regularly predicting that this would be the best, biggest and most successful World Cup ever. Figures of £50–60 million were being bandied about in the media as the likely revenue, with the profits about half that. Our fee for the just completed Carlton United one-day series in Australia had been about £17,000. We were gobsmacked to be offered less for what our Board called the Carnival of Cricket. Rightly or wrongly, all the England players thought the basic fee would be in the region of £30–40,000. The offer was around the £12,000 mark. The £30,000 fee was the amount the E.C.B. were paying our counties for each player's release. Our fee did not just include the five pool matches but the training camp and three practice matches, as well as many promotional events and appearances.

What had been offered and agreed in Brisbane did not materialize. Part of the confusion was that Pack never confirmed in writing the terms agreed with Stewie. The intervening four months or so had led to differing opinions about the precise details. Stewie was in no doubt, nor was I. Had he been concerned at the time, there would have been discussions in Australia. The big problem now was time. This was a huge event for all of us, playing in the World Cup as the host country. My failure to be part of a single winning side in a Lord's final often led to dreams that, when I did eventually succeed, it would be the big one. Out there on the Lord's balcony, holding up the World Cup as winner. The Sharjah event was to be our final preparation. Our sole concern by this stage ought to have been cricket. It wasn't.

Pack had been appointed International Teams Director in late October 1997. Pack was new to the sports world. I wasn't the only person who wondered why the E.C.B. had gone for a former NATO commander. I'm afraid he never lost that military bearing – and, consequently, never gained our trust or respect. Pack liked giving orders and he expected us to obey without question. You will have gathered by now that's never been Darren Gough's style. We first came across him at the Lanzarote training camp before the West Indies trip. At the end of one meeting, Pack finished with, 'We will rendezvous in the lobby at 20.00.' If something wasn't working, Pack would suggest a military solution and say, 'In the army, we did it this way.' I had already let Tim Lamb know my feelings as regards military discipline during our disagreement over the ban on wives going to Zimbabwe.

Pack wanted to be trusted by the players and to act as a bridge between us and the Board. Relations had not always been cordial. Lord MacLaurin wanted the E.C.B. run on a more business-like footing and structure. Our two-way relationship with Pack did not last long. At the first hint of conflict, Pack flexed his muscles and made it clear that he was our boss. His lack of any sporting background became only too clear. The improved communication with the Board did not happen. In his three-year stint in the job, the England team had three heavily publicized rows with the E.C.B. over money and contracts. None of them need have happened. Unfortunately, Pack had no affinity with us or any understanding of what life as a professional sportsman is like these days.

When rows started, Pack became difficult to contact. Disputes escalate quickly in modern sport. Contractual issues don't go away by being shoved to the back of a drawer. The warring factions have to be readily available for meetings, even if it's only a conference call. Decisions can't be delayed. Two of our calls to Pack during the World Cup wrangle got the responses 'He's having his dinner' and 'He's cutting the grass'. Our World Cup contracts failed to arrive by the agreed date. When they did appear, Lord's wanted them signed and back by return of post. Two small points: one, most players have legal advisers, who prefer to study the small print; two, this World Cup contract was huge, full of clauses about what we couldn't do, say or wear. The contracts went with us to Pakistan and Sharjah.

The first meeting in Lahore comprised just the players, no management, no coaches. The room was stunned to learn that we were going into the biggest cricket tournament in the world unsure of our fee. The squad was only too aware of the downside if we were to kick up a fuss and start arguing about money at this stage. The media would have a field day and the England national cricket team would be accused of putting money before the honour of playing in the World Cup. Maybe Lord's hoped that would deter us from making any protest. Our mood was too hostile for that, although our request to Lord's for an immediate summit in Lahore was refused. Instead, discussions would take place in Sharjah. I wonder why. That was a whole fortnight away. Clearly, the well-being of the England players going into the World Cup wasn't a top priority. We began to feel the E.C.B. were deliberately dragging their heels. I remember when the West Indies were unhappy about their South African tour fee and wouldn't fly from London to Johannesburg, officials from both the Caribbean and South Africa headed for London straight away to sort it all out. I still believe our Board thought we weren't serious and would go away. A big mistake.

David Graveney, manager of the one-day party, also had a conflict of interests. He was chairman of selectors as well as leading official for the Professional Cricketers' Association. You can't bat for both sides. Grav had two bosses. The E.C.B. and the P.C.A. were both paying his wages. Where did his loyalties lie? Graveney was getting calls from Pack telling him to sort out the dispute on behalf of the E.C.B. while, as a P.C.A. representative, he should have been on our side. Grav was caught in the middle. So, for once, was Tim Lamb. It was our Chief Executive, not the International Teams Director, who flew out to Sharjah, though he was careful not to stay in the same hotel as us. Lamb was accompanied by the E.C.B.'s cricket chairman, David Acfield.

There was no escape for Stewie, either. Even while England were fighting to remain in the Coca-Cola Cup, our skipper was sitting next to Lamb in front of the dressing-room as we battled to get the runs required not to be eliminated. The pair were not discussing the weather or even the dining arrangements for that night. Our masters seem totally insensitive to the demands of modern sport. The original World Cup deal had been negotiated two days before the Ashes series began, when our England captain had more important cricket matters on his mind. Now Stewie was being distracted again in the middle of our last workout before the World Cup. Our elimination from the Sharjah event was of passing interest as we changed and rushed back to our hotel for this long-awaited showdown.

That meeting lasted for over two hours. Nobody minced their words. Acfield came in with Lamb. He tried to make out he was on the players' side. After ten minutes we realized he wasn't. Every player in that room piped up. Each message was the same. 'You want us to market the game and be heroes to kids. What sort of heroes are we? What sort of advert is that for English cricket? Reach the top, play in the World Cup and get £12K – not even the weekly wage of a first division footballer. It's embarrassing.' That was my contribution to the proceedings. Lamb wasn't happy that we taped the meeting. Alan Mullally made his position clear. 'The money's crap and I ain't playing in the World Cup for that pittance.' At that stage I was sure we were going to boycott the World Cup in some way, though not as far as our cricket responsibilities went. Our likely protest would mean not attending promotional events, dinners or the training camp. We were trying not to jeopardize our World Cup chances. We were probably deluding ourselves in that respect, too.

I left that meeting in a hopeful frame of mind. Gussie, Harvey and Stewie were selected as the players' committee to deal with the Board when we got home. The reality was rather different. As soon as we split up as a team, our power base also disintegrated. The Board kept sending out contracts: 'Sign or else, by this date, or a new squad will be announced.' Sharjah was the last time we were all together before the World Cup. I don't know if any pressure was put on Stewie, but he never made that Lord's meeting. Nor did Lamb. It was Pack who was dealing with Gussie and Harvey. We were wrong to make the England captain an important member of our negotiating committee. Stewie had more to lose than any of us.

The dispute ended when Harvey called me. 'Sign, we're turning up for the training camp.' Game, set and match to the Board. It was farcical. I had increasingly felt we were in a no-win situation. Even at the point of capitulation, the England World Cup squad was going to release a statement. That never happened, either. Lord Mac addressed us when we assembled in Canterbury. The damage had been done and it was not going to be repaired by a few words of peace and harmony. Full credit to Thorpey: he made a protest of sorts by not attending a cricket evening at Kent. It was a small gesture, and he was fined for it. I'll admit we went about the contract dispute the wrong way. It was all done too late, and we should have had legal representation. Now we do. The Board tried the same delaying tactics with central contracts. That time we were stronger. We had learnt our lesson.

Back to the cricket. Our first World Cup casualties were Bumble and Athers. Bumble's relationship with the E.C.B. had deteriorated. He was not going to be offered a new contract, so he was quitting at the end of the World Cup. Athers had missed the end of the Australian tour because of his bad back. The plane journey to Pakistan caused that problem to flare up again. The selectors, showing greater urgency than those dealing with our World Cup contracts, and almost indecent haste, replaced our former captain with Nasser, whose charge down the wicket at Warnie had almost cost him a World Cup place. The whole Sharjah experience had a damaging effect on our challenge. We returned to England with even less of our first-choice line-up than when we had gone out. Our sole success was in our final game against Pakistan, by which time our presence was surplus to the requirements of this Coca-Cola Cup Final between India and Pakistan. Those opening three defeats in Sharjah meant that England had lost seven one-day games on the trot. We lost twice to an Indian team lacking Sachin Tendulkar. In the crunch second game, when we had to chase 239 to stay alive, Vince Wells came in at No. 3, Ealham at 4 and Harvey at No. 8. It was madness. England had lost the World Cup plot. All we had left was 'It Will be Alright on the Night'.

The 1999 World Cup opened with the traditional Hosts *v.* Holders clash, at Lord's. After the events of the winter, taking on Sri Lanka was one contest not affected by the contract wrangles. We had a score to settle. The holders were never in the game after the moving ball left them at 65–5, and England eased home by eight wickets. I had the worst analysis of the England attack. Mullally, Austin and Ealham used the conditions to good effect, before Stewie and Hickie knocked off the runs in better batting conditions. That was to be the trend for the tournament. Many sides batting first struggled in overcast conditions. The day's cricket had been preceded by the official opening ceremony. England has never been very good at those sort of extravagances; tradition and natural reserve tend to get in the way. Even by English standards, this heralding of the biggest cricket jamboree ever was ordinary. My memory might be playing tricks, but the show seemed to consist of about five fireworks, with loads of kids running on with flags. Prime Minister Tony Blair's microphone did not work properly. Then there was the smoke, which hung across Lord's so nobody could see what was happening; I'm not sure that was planned. We just stood on the balcony and laughed. This was merely an extension of the contract shambles. The opening of the 2000 Sydney Olympics it was not.

England had made a winning start. This 1999 World Cup had a new format. Instead of eight teams qualifying for a quarter-final knock-out, the top three sides from each group would progress to a SuperSix. Then the competition became even more complicated to find four semi-finalists. That was another complaint about this World Cup. Spectators were left confused and did not understand the format. It was impossible to work out beforehand who was playing where when buying tickets for the SuperSix. This confusion spread to the teams and players. A situation almost arose whereby Zimbabwe qualified for the semi-finals after losing all three games in the SuperSix. I'm afraid England were as guilty as anyone of not studying the rules and regulations carefully enough. Ultimately, this carelessness cost us a top-three spot in Group A. After beating Zimbabwe to record three wins out of four, our dressing-room was convinced we had qualified, whatever happened in the final round of matches.

England's nine-wicket win over Kenya in the second game at Canterbury was a special day for me. My figures of 4–34 were a big improvement on my Sri Lanka form. It was my second wicket which brought an extra-special smile to the Gough chops. Clattering Maurice Odumbe's stumps marked my hundredth one-day wicket for England. I became the third member of that particular club, alongside Ian Botham and Phillip DeFreitas.

Our promising start came to a shuddering halt at the Oval on Cup Final Saturday. That's the FA Cup Final – nothing to do with cricket. The organizers had taken some stick for scheduling

England's key game in the group, against South Africa, in London on the same afternoon as such an important sporting event. In the end, we were grateful that Manchester United's 2–0 victory over Newcastle took some attention away from our dismal display. Another modest target was too much for England. I claimed two wickets in two balls; unfortunately, that prompted Lance Klusener to all-out attack. Fierce clubbing from 'Zulu', which was to be a feature of this World Cup, got the South Africans to 225–7. This was by no means an intimidating total on the wide open spaces of the Oval against a side whose attack is strong but one-dimensional. During the break we felt we had a real chance. Our openers, Stewie and Nasser (the latter displacing Knight for the Sri Lanka game) did not enjoy much luck with umpiring decisions. That was no excuse for the way the middle order folded, faded and fell to Donald. All out for 103 with nine overs left. Jonty took another magnificent catch to dismiss Croftie. Failure to bat your overs is a serious one-day crime. What's the point, when you know you're going to lose, you may ask. Well, this was not a one-off game. Every total, every run, counted towards overall run-rate, not just in the group, but also in the SuperSix. Defeat by 122 runs was bad enough, but a total of 103 – which would be judged as a 50-over score – had a more damaging effect on our World Cup survival.

I can't explain the reason for it, but it was as though we were complacent. It was even more noticeable in the next game, against Zimbabwe at Trent Bridge. The Zimbabweans, like the Sri Lankans, are no favourites of mine or of England. The scars from that 1996/7 tour may have healed, but they are still visible. We tore into them. Paul Strang's pinch-hitting role consisted of a 17-ball duck, and three of us picked up a couple of wickets as Zimbabwe closed at 167–8. Our chat between innings was 'Win this and we are through.' No one queried our assumption or maths, or even mentioned run-rate. 'Team England' was supposed to be a thoroughly professional outfit. There should have been information to tell us how quickly we had to win in order to ensure a last-six place, which would have taken the final group game, against India, out of the equation. There wasn't. We won and won well, and we

came off convinced we were safe with three wins out of four. But
our chase had taken 38.3 overs, and we had slowed as we neared
the target. When the media mentioned run-rate the next day and
the possible consequences if Zimbabwe beat the so-far-unstoppable
South Africa, we accused them of scaremongering. Why couldn't
they just be gracious about an England World Cup challenge that
they had predicted would end in failure? Zimbabwe to beat South
Africa. There was as much chance of that happening as Bangladesh
denting Pakistan's hundred per cent record.

Stewie, unlike his performance in the Ashes, won all five tosses
in the World Cup. India batted first at Edgbaston against us and
scored 232–8. Zimbabwe scored one more run for six wickets
against South Africa at Chelmsford. India's score was well within
reach – except that chasing that sort of total had been beyond us
against good attacks. India probably scored 20–25 runs too many.
I wasn't happy, going for 51 in my 10 overs, after conceding 91
runs in the previous three matches. Unlike the Sri Lanka and
Zimbabwe games, the weather did not brighten up when England
batted. Stewie and Hickie went early but Nasser and Thorpey got
us to 72, before Nasser was bowled in fading light. One run later,
we came off for the day after a heavy downpour. Bad things come
in threes; at least they did that night. Nasser, the rain and finally
the TV pictures from Chelmsford. South Africa never recovered
from 40–6, and Zimbabwe now had three wins, same as us. South
Africa were definitely through with four, India would join Zim
and us if they won at Edgbaston. Our World Cup dreams were
disappearing before our eyes. The England dressing-room was
shell-shocked. One minute you're thinking you've definitely got a
World Cup future, then suddenly you realize it's hanging by a
thread. Not qualifying hadn't occupied a single second of our
thoughts until that horrible moment. I must confess I was ashamed
by the England dressing-room's reaction to our predicament. As
Judgey would have said, it was a time to 'be strong'. Instead, a wave
of defeatism and inevitability swept over the place. Typical of the
English mentality: we're knackered, we've had it – instead of 'So
what'. I stood up. 'Bloody hell, if that's the way you feel, we might

as well not turn up tomorrow. Zim's ended all those run-rate arguments. It's simple now. If we want to stay in this World Cup, we've got to knock off 230.' But we never shook off those negative thoughts.

England needed 160 runs on Sunday with seven wickets left. One thing in our favour: England's two best one-day run-chasers were at the wicket, Harvey and Thorpey. It had been a big week for Harvey, who had got permission from the management to fly out on Eddie Jordan's plane to watch Manchester United beat Bayern Munich in the Champions' League final, the day after our Zimbabwe win. He shouldn't have gone, but we hoped that United's miraculous victory would prove an omen. If that pair got the target down to under three figures, we stood a chance. Unfortunately, Thorpey got a shocking l.b.w. (courtesy of Javed Akhtar of Headingley 1998 fame), and Harvey ran out of partners. The tail hadn't been required in the World Cup, other than when we were blown away by Allan Donald at the Oval. Gussie and I offered some brief resistance, before the dream was over. *The Times* summed up the nation's view the next day: 'There are honourable defeats, unfortunate defeats and then ignominious defeats. The manner by which England's interests in the World Cup ended yesterday rests, unfortunately, in the final category.' England were never going to win the 1999 World Cup. Not because of all the pre-tournament hassle and mistrust. The simple fact is that we played two good teams, and couldn't chase 220 and 230 . . . and failed by 122 and 63 runs.

Our dressing-room was like a morgue that Sunday afternoon. England had failed to reach the later stages of the World Cup for the first time ever. It got worse. The hosts were not only out with three weeks of the competition left, but the official World Cup anthem, 'Life Is a Carnival', sung by Dave Stewart, had not been released. It hit the shops the day after our exit – another brilliant piece of marketing strategy. I gather it's since become something of a collectors' item. Interestingly, the song contained no reference to cricket. Even the speed gun did not appear until the SuperSix, so if you see a list of the fastest deliveries in the 1999 World Cup and see no D. Gough in the line-up, it's not because I was taking it easy or was a few miles behind Shoaib Akhtar and Allan Donald. I never got the chance to compete. Being hosts made it worse. Lose abroad, and you fly home to lick your wounds. Out of sight and out of mind. Not us; we had to attend the World Cup garden party at Buckingham Palace. How embarrassing. Her loyal failures had to line up and meet H.M. the Queen. Warnie and the Aussies were there. We felt like spare parts. We were.

England's early exit was not what the organizers had wanted. The confusing SuperSix left most people waiting for the semi-finals. Cup competitions are about do-or-die on the day, but that applied to only the final three ties of the 42-match tournament. The event was saved by two colossal Australia–South Africa matches. The Aussies started badly and were in danger of going out after two defeats in the first three games. The Aussies showed a lot more awareness of the regulations. Steve Waugh's side took 40 overs to pass the West Indies' 110 at Old Trafford, just enough to ensure a SuperSix place on run-rate. The Aussie crawl improved the Windies' chances of joining them rather than New Zealand, who would carry points from beating Australia, all of which went to show there was more method in Waugh's tactics than just the normal Aussie–Kiwi animosity. Australia went into the SuperSix with no points and had to win all three matches to make the semis. The last obstacle was South Africa on my home track, where I was watching. Chasing 272, the Aussies struggled to 48–3. The defining moment came when Herschelle Gibbs caught Steve Waugh on 56 but, in his haste to hurl the ball into the air, let it slip from his grasp. Waugh wasn't walking off for that. Amazingly, Gibbs's tendency to do this had been mentioned earlier in the Aussie dressing-room by Warnie. Waugh then came out with the quote of the World Cup: 'Hersch, what's it feel like to have dropped the World Cup?'

That was the moment when I realized that Australia's name was on the World Cup. Waugh's century saw Australia home with two balls to spare. In the best Don King traditions, a rematch was scheduled, four days later at Edgbaston. The World Cup semi-final. It turned out to be even more spectacular. Pakistan were already through to Lord's, having overcome New Zealand at Old Trafford. The Aussie–South Africa semi-final was tied at 213 apiece after Donald was run out off the fourth ball of the final over, after Klusener's big hitting looked to have taken South Africa to a World Cup final at last. Australia's higher position in the SuperSix, courtesy of overall run-rate, was the deciding factor. Steve Waugh was right. Gibbs's error had denied his country a place in the World Cup final.

Four days later, Steve Waugh lifted the World Cup after the most one-sided final in seven tournaments. With a delayed start and overcast conditions, I couldn't understand Wasim Akram's decision to bat. Warnie had been in dazzling form in the later stages, bowling Gibbs with a repeat of the Gatting ball in the semi-final. A similar delivery did for Ijaz Ahmed in the final. Warnie finished with 4–33, which earned him the Man of the Match. God, I was jealous as he pranced around the Lord's balcony with the World Cup.

Australia had no need to worry about run-rate as they set off after Pakistan's 132. Yet they marked the occasion with a sparkling show, taking just 20.1 overs to claim the World Cup. No one could deny that Australia were worthy winners, winning all their final seven matches, when a single defeat would have meant elimination. All I could do was watch enviously. Unlike England, Australia were 'strong' when it was backs-to-the-wall time. The tougher the challenge, the harder they fought, and they refused to give in. That was never better demonstrated than by Gibbs's lapse at Headingley or by that final run-out at Edgbaston, when a single slip from any one of three different pairs of Aussie hands – those of Mark Waugh, Fleming and Gilchrist – would have cost them the World Cup.

22. Brave New World

Several old favourites departed after our dismal World Cup show-ing. Bumble was the first to go; that had been planned. Stewie was next; that had not. Someone had to carry the can for our failure and Lord's chose the England cricket captain. Nothing new there. Finally, the BBC, dear old Auntie, lost out in the battle for the contract to televise cricket to Channel 4. The newcomer signed up half a dozen of us to promote its coverage. England's new dream team – coach Duncan Fletcher and captain Nasser Hussain – was unveiled at Lord's before the New Zealand series, but that partner-ship was put on hold. Fletcher was under contract to Glamorgan and would not make an appearance until our winter tour to South Africa. Neither would I. The rest of my summer was spent on the sidelines with yet another leg injury which proved difficult to diagnose.

Bumble had decided to quit when it became clear that the Board would not give him a new contract. The Muralitharan outburst had landed him in hot water at Lord's; our coach had been warned about his future behaviour after the 'We murdered them' problems in Bulawayo. Bumble, whose current contract ran until the end of summer 1998, did not want an extension simply to keep the job warm for someone else, so he signed up for Sky TV instead. It was time for him to go, anyway. England had lost the Ashes and had failed in the World Cup; those were the harsh facts.

The Board seemed to have about as much idea as we did. During the search for a new coach we learned from the papers why Simon Pack had been missing from the Sharjah showdown. Pack had been on a secret mission to South Africa, apparently interviewing Bob Woolmer for Bumble's job. Woolmer was in the frame, along with Jack Birkenshaw of Leicestershire, Dav Whatmore of Lancashire and Sri Lanka, and Duncan Fletcher, a former captain of Zimbabwe, now coach of Western Province and Glamorgan. In my own tried and true style, I knew very little about any of them. All I was sure of was that it shouldn't be Woolmer. True, he was a former England Test batsman and had been a successful coach of Warwickshire, but he was still coaching South Africa and I've made no secret about my distaste for that lot. There was no way he could return to South Africa that winter as England coach. Nor could England afford to wait a year, however good he was. What if the stop-gap was successful? I regard coaching England as one of the top jobs in sport; it's not a makeshift appointment. Whether deliberately or not, the E.C.B. scheduled Woolmer's interview for the day before South Africa's World Cup semi-final. He decided to withdraw his application and return to Warwickshire and the county scene. The final choice was Duncan Fletcher. I knew absolutely nothing about him.

Finding Stewie's successor was a rather easier process. Nasser had lost out to Stewie a year earlier, when Athers resigned. I felt sorry for Stewie. After all the furore about the contracts and the behind-the-scenes nonsense, Lord's were after a scapegoat. The Establishment view was that Stewie had been found wanting in keeping the England players under control. That wasn't his job. But that's one reason why Stewie was replaced. I felt it was harsh. Ten months earlier, he had led us to that historic victory over South Africa. We had come back well in the Ashes series, where Stewie's greatest crime had been not winning the toss. Our one-day form was the problem, culminating in disappointment in the World Cup. Yet Stewart was sacked as our Test captain. Stewie had wanted to be captain of both forms of cricket, so when he lost one job he lost them both. Nasser, as he did in 1998, made no secret of wanting the job. I always remember chatting to Gussie about the possibility of Nasser getting the England captaincy. 'If he does, you and I won't be in the team,' I predicted. Nasser is an aggressive person and can be hard to fathom out. The best way of describing it is that Nasser the captain would not tolerate Nasser the player. His style is 'Do as I say, not as I did'! I had to wait until South Africa to find out what he was really like as a captain.

Channel 4 are part of the reason I missed the New Zealand series. My leg had started bothering me during the World Cup. I was taking painkillers between each game, although I wasn't quite sure whether the problem lay in my shin, ankle or calf. Part of a promotion day at Channel 4 involved my bowling at a journalist for a magazine article. I wasn't keen on the idea because I hadn't played. The journalist came in without a helmet, so I bumped him from five yards and hit him on the finger, and he had to retire. I wasn't much better, I could hardly walk. Looking back, I'm convinced my problem had begun during our preparation in Kent. Bumble wanted to keep the run-ups dry, so rubber mats were put down. As I thumped the mat in my bowling stride, it moved forward slightly. A few days later, my leg started hurting, and that pain remained throughout the World Cup. After the Channel 4 shoot, I decided to go off for scans.

A fortnight after England's exit, I rang Martyn at Yorkshire to tell him I was fit for the Sussex game and would be at nets the day before. The message came back through a third party that the Yorkshire skipper David Byas wanted me to play for the second team against Durham; he didn't think I was fit enough. Typical Byas: he got someone else to do his dirty work. I told Martyn as plainly as I could where Byas could stick his second-team suggestion. That was not an option. Believe me, I wasn't playing Gough the primadonna, the England superstar. How could I be fit enough for the seconds but not for the firsts? I would turn up at nets, then Byas could judge whether I was fit or not. Turned up, was fine, turned up next day and played. I wasn't going to let it rest there, though. When I confronted Byas, he totally denied that it was ever intended I should play at Chester-le-Street. I bowled well enough and took three wickets, but the pain had returned. I kept going. I wasn't going to give Byas the satisfaction; I'd never hear the end of it. On the last day, I bowled 20 overs. The next morning, I could hardly put any weight on the foot. The view at the time was that I had torn some fibres on my skin. The next day, Graveney announced that I would not be fit for the first Test against New Zealand.

The pain kept moving, which didn't help the diagnosis. My ankle, calf, shin and knee all came into the equation. I had X-rays and scans on them all. I was getting plenty of attention, but the treatment depended on who I could see. Wayne knew me best, but he was full time with England. Caryl Becker was now the physio at Yorkshire, but she went away with the county team. So when Wayne and Caryl were away, I had to travel to see another physio at the David Lloyd centre in Morley. That didn't help, either. You want one opinion, one pair of hands, working on the problem. The three liaised, but I felt I was stuck in the middle.

I had a huge incentive to get back. Not for England, but for Yorkshire. The White Rose, after so many semi-final misses, had at last made a Lord's final after beating Warwickshire in the Benson & Hedges Super Cup at Edgbaston. That was where I made my comeback, three days later, and we won our first championship match there for 17 years. More importantly, I bowled 30 overs, took seven wickets and initially felt that the Lord's final, a fortnight away, was a possibility. I wasn't pain-free but the injury was easier. I rang the England selectors, and we agreed that I was too great a risk for the Lord's Test in five days' time. That was a sensible move. As I drove down to Cheltenham on Saturday night for Yorkshire's National League game, the pain got worse. When I woke up on Sunday morning, I could hardly stand. My season was over. I did go to Lord's for the final, but I spent the day in the Sky commentary box as Yorkshire failed to become the first winners of the Benson & Hedges Super Cup.

I often felt that I would be better off breaking my leg or arm; at least then the injury is obvious to everyone. All I would have to do afterwards was wait for the bones to mend. My injury problems have always dragged on. This latest setback was turning into a re-run of my 1997 hamstring problem. Get fit, start training again and, as soon as I tried to do anything at speed, 'ping' – back to square one. Most of my injuries have been stress-related. I tend not to pull a hamstring or my groin straight off. My problems are related to banging my foot down when bowling. That's because of the way I do things – at 100 m.p.h. When the trouble was finally diagnosed as a stress reaction, the specialists decided to put my left leg in a pot, but that idea was later abandoned. My recovery had been delayed because I was trying to bowl again too soon instead of taking my time and strengthening the leg. I was learning the hard way that certain injuries can't be rushed, Nature has to take its course. But the older you get, the harder it becomes to miss a Test or, in this case, a series. Anyway, I felt England needed me back: Nasser's team were making a pig's ear of the Kiwi series.

England's cricketers were under the temporary charge of chairman of selectors Graveney as manager, with Goochie assisting as coach. The series started well enough with a nine-wicket win at Edgbaston. Nightwatchman Alex Tudor saw England home with an undefeated 99 on the Saturday. That made Nasser the first England captain to make a winning start since Bob Willis in 1982. Like most honeymoons, Nasser's lasted two weeks. His brave new world came to a shuddering halt at Lord's inside four days. The Kiwis' nine-wicket success was bad enough, but Nasser had broken a finger fielding in the gully. That kept him out of the Old Trafford Test. Lord's almost saw Gussie return to the fray. The old warhorse was summoned in haste from Taunton as cover. He had to wait for the county ground to open in order to get his kit that Thursday morning, then he raced up the M5 and M4. I would love to have been a fly on his car window when Gussie received the call from Grav. He had reached the Chiswick roundabout before learning his presence was not required and that he could turn round and go back. This drama had started when Tudor dropped out with a bad knee. Then it transpired that Surrey had sent him for a scan the day before the Test without telling England. More country–county aggro.

This was nothing to the bother that greeted the announcement of the selection of the Old Trafford squad. Hick and Such were recalled. Butch was made captain. Last in, first out; Aftab Habib was dropped after two Tests. Even with Nasser missing, England's top six were the Old Guard. I wasn't against that, they were our best players. Unfortunately, they didn't perform. Butch made a mistake in batting first. By the time the Kiwis had amassed 496–9 in reply to our 199, the knives were out. This humiliation, on top of the poor World Cup performance and abysmal Lord's display, had the public baying for blood. The papers presented Lord MacLaurin's dinner with Fletcher, Nasser and Grav on the Sunday night in Manchester as being as significant as the Last Supper. It was for Goochie and Gatt, the two legends I'd squeezed in between on my first Ashes flight. These two former England captains, now selectors, were the sacrificial lambs. There was no denying that England had gone for safety and experience. As far as I understand it, it was Nasser's decision. He even wanted to give Stewie back the gloves. That wish was refused, until the next game at the Oval. That was one of several switches. Debuts for Darren Maddy and Ed Giddins, recalls for Ronnie Irani and Alan Mullally. The skipper was fit again, which meant the axe for England's Old Trafford captain, Butch – as well as Hick.

Graeme Hick has been the easiest of targets ever since I have been involved in the England set-up. He has stopped talking to the media. I don't blame him, after all the muck that's been flung at him. His biggest problem has always been expectation. His brilliant county record, plus his seven-year residential wait to qualify for England, meant miracles were expected when Hickie made his debut against the 1991 West Indies. He was dropped by the end of that series, and he's been dropped many times since. The 1999 recall was typical: a fuss when he was brought back and another fuss when he was dumped, one game later, after one knock and a dodgy l.b.w. decision. Duncan Fletcher had been his captain when he played for Zimbabwe as a 17-year-old in 1983, and I was not surprised when Hickie was named in England's initial dozen contracted players in the summer of 2000. He had been labelled a 'flat-track bully', and his presence in the England side seems to cause more discussion and argument than any other player. His record abroad has generally been better than at home. Winter 2000/1 was the first time Hickie had not been successful, although his innings on that final day in Karachi was crucial to our success. He played several poor shots in that Pakistan series, and he is the first to admit that. Of course he feels the pressure. If you've taken the battering Hickie has, both on and off the field, it must affect your confidence. But nobody in the England team denies his right to be part of our best line-up. He's still one of the first names down on our one-day line-up, and he was still the person we wanted to see walking out in Karachi in that run-chase. The crazy thing is that when he's not around, you hear 'This would suit Hickie' or 'We could do with Hickie now.' I believe Graeme Hick is a player who will finally get his due credit only when he's no longer around. Then England will miss him. The management have tried to replace him on numerous occasions and have always failed. That must tell you something.

More exits followed at the Oval. Cornhill announced that the 2000 series against the West Indies would be its last after 22 years of Test match sponsorship. England's capitulation at the Oval went a long way to explaining why. The Oval crowd chanted, 'What a load of rubbish,' as the Kiwis took the series 2–1. I had experienced that sort of abuse personally at Edgbaston in 1995 against the West Indies. Just watching from a distance, this seemed worse. Chasing 246 to win, England got halfway for the loss of two wickets, before eight wickets tumbled for 39 runs. A disastrous end to a disastrous summer.

The only glimmer of hope was Fletcher's arrival. Nasser's selection had not been consistent, but England's new leader had shown an inventive and imaginative spirit on the field. That Manchester dinner had entrusted the future of English cricket to the captain and coach. That was just paper talk; it didn't last long. The Oval failure resulted in Lord's laying down certain rules for the selection of the South African tour party. I was astonished to find out later that Fletcher had so little input. He was honest enough to admit to not knowing about the players. As for Nasser, the other selectors had given him the teams he wanted. Now Goochie and Gatting had gone. Grav remained chairman. Despite Nasser's pre-Test assurance that nearly all the Oval squad would go to South Africa, Irani, Giddins and Ramps were dumped for the tour. Thorpey announced during the Oval Test that he would not be available for the South African trip. I respect him for that decision. Taking time out is always a risk; there's no automatic way back, but it was the right thing for him. He came back fitter and refreshed.

The New Zealand series had not been a complete waste of time. The Kiwis demonstrated decisively what a team of mainly non-stars can accomplish when they all play for one another. That was the Kiwis' strength. After going behind at Edgbaston, they embarrassed England at Lord's and the Oval. The spoils on that final Sunday at the Oval went to the side that held their nerve, had more conviction and self-belief. And that wasn't England. The tourist who impressed me most was Chris Cairns; he looked a world-class player on that tour. In the past his commitment and performance have ebbed and flowed. Not in 1999. He was top-class and inspired his side to a well-deserved victory. That was the way forward for Nasser and Duncan: find some genuine team-spirit. 'Team England' needed to be a real team in more than name.

23. Fat Boy Slim

Changing England's cricket captain had made little difference. The arrival of Duncan Fletcher would need to be the more significant appointment. If it wasn't, England were going nowhere. Nasser could do a job on the field. More importantly, England's cricketers needed guidance and inspiration off it. Not that our new coach gave too much away on the tour. Fletcher refused to show his hand too early. All through South Africa, I felt our new coach was examining the whole set-up, watching and waiting, finding out who was up to the job, who was not. Wisely, neither Nasser nor Fletch made any bold predictions about our chances; they have a nasty habit of boomeranging back and making you look a clown. Both men maintained that our sole objective in South Africa was to compete. After the summer England had had, even that was a big task. South Africa, the second-best team in the world, had just whitewashed the West Indies and we'd lost to New Zealand.

I was desperate to get on that plane. Several times during the summer I had wondered and worried about whether I would make it. My long lay-off certainly showed when I arrived in South Africa. Not only was my bowling a long way short of its best but, more amusingly for the media, 'Gough the Scoff' was back. I had piled on a few pounds and most of them seemed to have lodged around my middle. That wasn't surprising after a three-month lay-off. I hadn't been able to do any training; complete rest, no running, no walking, to avoid putting weight on my calf.

I needed some matches under my expanding belt. Our opening game against the Nicky Oppenheimer XI was not the workout I wanted; my back went again. So did Dean Headley's. And we lost the match, much to Nasser's disgust. Ten days later, I was back playing. Deano did not bowl another ball in anger on the tour, and he missed the whole of summer and winter 2000 after a back operation and was eventually forced to retire from cricket. My problem was purely due to lack of bowling. That Oppenheimer day is one I won't forget. My last England game had been at Edgbaston under Bumble and Stewie. This was my debut for Nasser and Fletch. Nasser, for one, was not impressed. The whole side felt the full force of his tongue. The skipper thought our attitude, as well as our play, was crap and he gave us a right rollocking.

Nasser and I had spoken a fair bit during the summer. He's never been one for social niceties. Nasser wanted my views as to which untried players might go to South Africa. One name I put forward was Chris Adams. He's a very dangerous player. I still think so now, especially in one-day cricket. Grizzly had a disastrous Test series. The South African pace attack found him out, especially outside his off stump. Rather unfairly, it appears that failure has scuppered his one-day England chances as well. Halfway through the tour, Nasser asked me if my opinion had changed. It hadn't, and it still hasn't. I'll say one thing about Grizzly on that tour: he worked as hard as anyone on his game and his fitness. Having waited so long for his chance, it must have been heart-breaking to have everything go so horribly wrong. However, he never let it show. Grizzly came home early during the one-day series, after the death of his father. I understand he offered to come back for the Zimbabwe leg, but this was not taken up. That's a shame. Grizzly's a fiery character, a fighter with a big heart who likes to win and doesn't give in. Even if it was a football kickabout the day before the Test, Grizzly would still cut you off at the knees. I respect that commitment.

There's a special feeling about the first day of a Test series – or there should be. There wasn't this Thursday at the Wanderers in Johannesburg. The opening exchanges were farcical. The match should not have started on time. The pitch was damp and juicy. I'm used to that. It happens a lot, even in England. Groundsmen are petrified of the pitch not lasting five days. I don't know why. Test matches rarely do these days, especially if you start with the wicket in that state. The real problem at the Wanderers was that the conditions were overcast and the light was poor. Other than blindfolding the batsmen and handing them a one-inch-wide bat,

conditions could not have been more perfect for bowling. The
umpires should have used their discretion and waited for better
light.

Unfortunately, Nasser proved himself as lousy a tosser abroad as
Stewie had been. There were several, almost immediate consequences of Cronje's inevitable decision to put us in: (a) the match
was decided after a quarter of an hour; (b) Michael Vaughan spoke
to four fellow batsmen on the field before facing his first ball in
Test cricket; (c) Grizzly, having waited a decade to play Test cricket
for England, walked out with the score 2–4; (d) after 15 minutes,
Duncan Fletcher knew life as the England cricket coach could only
get better; (e) England's three senior batsmen – Nasser, Athers and
Stewie – all collected ducks. Actually, it was a miracle we got to
122, helped by my last-wicket stand of 19 with Alan Mullally. Big
Al brought a much-needed consolatory laugh to our dressing-room
when one of his wild swings went for six. If England had been
skittled out for 50, we might have been better off. We could have
tested South Africa's batsmen in similar conditions. As I ran in the
next day with the sun on my back, I realized that the man upstairs
was making life as tough as possible for us tourists. The overcast
conditions returned on the third morning, when I wrapped up the
South African tail. Unfortunately, by that stage the South Africans
led by almost 300 runs. We had less excuse for batting badly in
the second innings, going down by an innings and 21 runs. My
five-wicket haul wasn't much consolation. That match registered
the beginning and end of Gavin Hamilton's Test career. My Yorkshire team-mate bagged a pair and 0–63. His performances for
Scotland in the World Cup showed that he was a competent
one-day performer at international level. But this was big-league
quick bowling that exposed all but the best of batting techniques.

That Wanderers wicket must have been bad. Even the travelling
media refrained from putting the boot in; Nasser's style and forth-
right approach had impressed them in the summer. As for Fletch,
they were still trying to work him out, as was everyone else. The
press definitely granted us a stay of execution. After the Test
formalities were concluded that Sunday morning, journalist and

England cricketer alike retired to the Sandton Sun bar in drowning-sorrows mood. We were badly beaten in that contest, too. Midnight was about as far as I got. I gather some of our scribes made it through to breakfast-time. The noise levels were such that the E.C.B.'s media relations manager, Andrew Walpole, was carpeted by the hotel manager and told to keep 'his' media under control in future. The media had been fairly insulting about my white three-quarter-length trousers when I wandered into the bar. If David Beckham can wear them, what's wrong with me? The trouble is, the cricket crowd are not used to real style. The next day, after a dawn departure to Sun City, my golf was anything but stylish. At least I was able to show the lads the lake where Wayne had deposited one of his hired clubs in a rage on the previous tour.

We had quite a few drinks that week. We said goodbye to Deano and hello to Dean Conway's third child, a celebration that went on nearly as long as the birth. I'm not trying to give the impression that Fletcher was supervising one big junket. Fletcher's policy is clear: train hard, play hard. After each game, we enjoyed two days off to relax and let the body recover. Then we would work hard for two days before the next game. The players who aren't involved in the match train twice a day and turn up for nets, but don't have to spend all day at the ground. When there's a team event, we all go. One of Fletch's first social occasions almost got out of hand in the 'Butchers Shop' in Sandton Square. It was a night of boisterous fun. The most astonishing moment of the night came when the quietest bloke on tour, Chris Read, got up and sang a rugby song that contained three swear-words in every sentence.

Touring South Africa is tough work these days. Four years earlier, we had been able to wander around Sandton and walk down to the Sports Café and other restaurants. Not any more. The security advice from the British High Commission was, 'Don't walk anywhere in Johannesburg.' Plush as the Sandton Sun is, after a week I started feeling claustrophobic. You can only meander through a shopping mall so many times. Some of the lads reckoned that was what life must be like in an open prison. The problems aren't limited to Johannesburg. One of our S.A. security men had a knife pulled on him, a few yards from our hotel in East London, and was robbed. I'm not sure what would have happened if he hadn't forgotten his gun, which was back in the Holiday Inn hotel. I've always regarded South Africa as a one-city place: Cape Town. Sadly, even that's no longer a safe haven, after recent bombings and fatalities at the Waterfront and at Camps Bay. I know that bombs go off in London and there's crime everywhere. Somehow, though, it's easier to cope with at home. When you are in unfamiliar surroundings, far from home, it's frustrating not to be able to switch off and relax for a second. The cricket is just as hard in Australia, probably harder than in South Africa. Away from the action, it's not far off paradise: great locations, great food, great wine.

As well as getting used to a new captain and coach, I had to familiarize myself with a new England physio, Dean Conway. Wayne Morton, having given up Yorkshire to go full time with England, had been shown the door when Bumble quit. Dean was the third England physio who's looked after me. I didn't have much to do with 'Rooster' (Dave Roberts) in my first year and a half with England. I was injured quite a bit, but even then I tended to go to Wayne. Being England physio is a big job. It's also an important one. The physio is the person who is entrusted with your worries and doubts, as well as your body and its niggles. He has to be something of a faith-healer, treating you both mentally and physically. The most important thing is, you must have complete faith and trust in him. The last two England physios have been excellent. I had my problems with 'Rooster'. Maybe because I was so used to Wayne. He would never have ducked the issue the way 'Rooster' did before the Old Trafford Test in the 1995 West Indies series.

Wayne has been an important part of my cricket life for as long as I can remember. He's top of my list because of our long relationship. Even when I was being treated by someone else, I'd often ring him up to get a second opinion. One of the troubles with Wayne – but I've liked him for it – is that he likes to get involved beyond his physio's duties. He used to join in our fielding practice and hit catches for the lads. Wayne has actually improved as a cricketer more than anyone in my time with the England squad. In his last couple of years with England, he started playing league cricket and was soon picking up five wickets regularly. Wayne wanted to do it all. He's a strong character and won't be shifted by anyone. He goes into a job with heart, soul and body, and that's why I love him. I can easily understand why some people high up at Lord's thought he was getting above himself. Wayne was very popular with the team. I'll never forget the help he gave me. Any time I felt down, Wayne was the first to notice it. On the 'A' tour to South Africa, when Martin McCague was being picked on orders coming from the senior tour members when I knew I should have had that place, Wayne calmed me down, told me to bide my time, not to do anything stupid or wallow in self-pity. I owe him a lot for that. A few months later, I was playing for England. Although he's not involved with Yorkshire or England any more, we're still friends and I see a lot of him. Now he's working at Castleford Rugby League Club and has his own practice. I've always confided in Wayne. He's a fellow Yorkshireman and I've known him since I was a young lad. Wayne probably knows more about me than anyone else, even my own family. Unfortunately, even his influence hasn't been powerful enough to stop me rushing back too early on numerous occasions for Yorkshire and England.

Dean Conway's totally different. For a start, he's Welsh, a former prop forward who played first-class rugby, and his sporting ambition is to go on a Lions tour, either as a player or as physio. Like Wayne, he's become our social secretary and he organizes events for the lads. But that's all. Dean is happy just being the physio and has no interest in getting involved in the politics of the England cricket team. Some might say that's the way it should be.

Just how far do you trust the physio with your injury worries, or the specialist coach when you have problems with your bowling run-up? How much do they tell the coach and captain? It's hard, sometimes, separating the sensible from the rubbish. I get plenty of advice and suggestions. Who to listen to? Since 1995 I've been told regularly that my bowling action is wrong, that I must change it to ensure a long career. A succession of former fast-bowling greats have jumped on that bandwagon. I don't trust many people. I talk to Martyn Moxon – he's known me since I was a young lad – and Steve Oldham. Now I listen to Fletch. He's very sparing with his comments, a little bit here and a little bit there, advice to help me improve rather than telling me to change this or that. During the Faisalabad Test in winter 2000/1, Fletch told me to move my hands lower down the bat-handle against the spinners. I've always held my hands high on the bat, like Stewie, although that style seems to have brought him over six thousand more Test runs than me. Fletch's suggestion worked; I felt more in control. That's his style. All he wants is to make you and your cricket better.

I've got to trust the person before I can trust his advice. That's been the case since 1995, when Bob Willis and Mike Holding among others went public about my bowling action. Fred Trueman's the same. I'd have much more respect for them if they'd bothered to have a word in my ear. That's not their way; it's plastered all over the media. Fred's been the worst for doing that. It seems to be a favourite occupation for old-timers, making public statements about how they've saved So-and-so's England career. I suppose I have to question their motives. They get no public praise or acknowledgement if they just have a quiet word in my ear. If they discussed it with me first, they might get a public pat on the back from me.

The selectors gave me a pat on the back I didn't really need after the Johannesburg Test. I was rested for the next tour match. My form was good but I needed to bowl for fitness, and South Africa had batted only once at the Wanderers. As we warmed up for the Port Elizabeth Test, I caught an early glimpse of what Nasser the captain was like. He came out for a net and asked where Tuffers was. Our left-arm spinner had done ten minutes and then disappeared. 'Get him here immediately,' our skipper insisted. When Tuffers appeared, Nasser, in front of everybody, laid into him. 'Tuffers, I put my job on the line to get you on this tour. You're a great bowler and I want you here, but you don't take the p*** out of me. Now get your bowling boots back on and get back in the nets.' Nasser wasn't afraid to lay down the law, although I'm not sure how he would have reacted if he'd been on the receiving end of such a dressing-down. If it had been Athers or Stewie in Nasser's position, they would have ducked the confrontation: 'Oh, it's Tuffers, we know what he's like.' Nasser went up in my estimation that day.

Not that I was the apple of Nasser's eye after South Africa's 450 in the first innings; I bowled like an absolute drain. My lack of match fitness became apparent both to the South African batsmen and to my skipper, who started using me in short spells. I bowled half-volley after half-volley and just couldn't get a rhythm. I couldn't recall bowling worse for my country. As I've said before, if I'm not taking wickets, I go for runs. P.E. was one of those occasions. To be fair, I did remove the threat of Klusener; unfortunately, 'Zulu' had smashed 174 runs by that stage. He tucked into me nicely; it was as though I was lobbing throwdowns at him. Nasser bowled me in three-over spells, and my figures of 1–107 off 21.1 overs tell the story clearly enough. What was frustrating for me was that I would have backed myself to get wickets on that track if I'd been at my best. The wicket was skiddy and quick. Batsmen are usually trapped l.b.w. or bowled in those circumstances, and this is how I collect most of my wickets. It was a painful reminder of how much work I still had to do.

Despite batting at No. 7, Klusener was regarded by us as South Africa's key player with the bat. We weren't worried about the top order. Gary Kirsten was someone we liked to remove early, before he got set. The South Africans like to bat around him. Jacques Kallis was vulnerable to the new ball, Cronje has never been regarded as a serious threat, Cullinan would always give you a chance and Rhodes could be hit or miss. The two who concerned us most were Klusener and wicket-keeper Mark Boucher. Several times South Africa lost early wickets, but we struggled and often failed to finish them off. That pair were not only difficult to get out, but they could be dangerous. They both batted positively, came at you and were hard to bowl at. When Klusener's in the groove, as he certainly was in 1999, the bowler's margin of error is tiny. I tried to bowl dead straight in order to restrict his options, but he'd give himself room by taking a step to leg and smashing it through the off side.

Athers and Nasser batted well, but South Africa led by 77 runs when they came out to bat again. Amazingly, they never pushed on. Kallis played a long, slow innings, which included a disputed catch by Grizzly. Cronje was heavily and publicly criticized for his lack of adventurousness. I believed it was those attacks that prompted Cronje's bold suggestions at Centurion Park, a month later; now, I'm not so sure. The South Africans' ponderous batting denied them a realistic chance of victory. Although we lost six wickets, the home side ran out of time and we were never in danger of losing.

Our next journey was a coach trip to East London, including a stop-off at Port Alfred. A few of us took to the water for a shark-fishing trip. Freddie, Grizzly and I boarded with the usual bravado: bottles of wine, ghetto-blaster and food supplies. About ten minutes later we were hanging over the side, wondering what had happened to our sea-legs. We never did find them and, a couple of hours later, we staggered off, shark-less but definitely not leg-less. We hadn't touched a drop.

My Port Elizabeth form convinced the management that I needed more bowling with back-to-back Tests over Christmas and the New Year. East London was another flat wicket, but it was better than hanging around. East London, as the man from the *Telegraph* told his readers, once his third-floor-room telephone had been retrieved from the side of the swimming pool, is a place where it's better to have plenty to occupy you.

Durban was the venue for the Christmas Test. Most of the families arrived there. Anna and Liam had joined me during the Port Elizabeth Test because of family commitments at home over Christmas. The Crown Plaza at North Beach was certainly a lot better organized than the Summerstrand had been four years earlier, as were the Board's arrangements for the families. The players were able to concentrate on their cricket commitments without having to worry about whether the wives were being picked up from the airport or the problems of sleeping four to a hotel room.

We dominated the Durban Test, before another Gary Kirsten double-hundred kept us at bay after the South Africans had followed on. England had improved slowly but surely, and we were now competing. Nasser's 146 was the cornerstone of our first-innings 366 total. Caddie was our destroyer as South Africa slumped to 84–8, eventually failing to save the follow-on by 11 runs. His figures of 7–46 were outstanding on a good pitch; I'd never seen him bowl better. Nasser enforced the follow-on. It was to prove a huge mistake as we were made to bowl for another three days. To be fair to Nasser, the follow-on was the only option, but we knew it would be a grind. Kirsten was unbelievable. The left-hander just batted and batted and batted and never got bored. The man who broke his resistance on 275 was Butch. Perhaps we should have used his off-spin earlier. That really hacked off Tuffers. Butch had picked up two wickets by the end, which compared favourably to Tuffers's match figures of 1–141. Tuffers wasn't a happy bunny, anyway, going for so many runs. He felt Nasser was bowling him because he didn't want to bowl the seamers and there was no one else. I'm afraid Tuffers didn't show a great attitude that day.

My frustration with the Kingsmead pitch led to a public squabble with Sky commentator Bob Willis. The stump microphone picked up my comment, 'What's the point of bowling on a wicket like this?' Willis said on air that if that was my attitude, I shouldn't be out there bowling for England. That made me angry. My remarks had come out of frustration; they were not an indication that I wasn't trying my hardest. I waited until Newlands, then leaned over and said into the stump mike: 'Where would you bowl on this, then, Willis?' It was a bit childish, but I was disappointed that an ex-England bowler should make such a comment. I was coming back after a long lay-off, it wasn't easy on a flat track, and I felt that he had taken a cheap shot.

Every time I've been out through injury, I'm always surprised how long it takes to get back to full fitness and top form. Out for two or three weeks, and the break doesn't matter. Anything more than a month, I find I have a lot of catching up to do. It's not a straight graph. After three months, it's almost impossible to work

out how long it will take. Little things go wrong. In South Africa,
Bob Cottam got the tape-measure out to sort out my run-up. It
was meant to help. It didn't. I started bowling no-balls. That didn't
help my rhythm. Things I didn't normally think about when it's
all working smoothly became big issues. Batsmen are the same.
During a bad trot, they wonder about moving their feet, the
back-lift, keeping the head still . . . all those things you do naturally
when your game's working.

The general view was that England had turned the corner in
Durban. I agreed. We arrived in Cape Town full of hope. Anna
was waiting for me at the Villa Via Hotel, which was a great
surprise. I had found it a bit lonely at Christmas with all the other
families there. Mind you, I wasn't that overcome with her sudden
appearance that I forgot my Yorkshire origins. 'I hope you came
out economy.' She hadn't. The trouble is, once you've travelled in
club class, especially if you've worked as a stewardess, you're never
satisfied with the back of the plane again. The millennium New
Year's Eve was spent on a boat trip round the harbour, then dinner
in the Waterfront, courtesy of Vodafone. Our stay was in marked
contrast to four years earlier. More suitable hotels were found and
the arrival of the families organized, leaving us to concentrate on
the cricket.

This time, England could not point to these distractions as the
excuse for another dismal performance, in every way as bad a show
as four years earlier at Newlands. Cape Town was full of England
cricket fans, and we were determined to give them something to
cheer. We couldn't have asked for a better start as Butch and Athers
put on a century stand. Then we got careless and, instead of ignoring
Donald's challenge to take him on, our senior batsmen got carried
away and we lost the initiative. A total of 258, after being 213–3,
allowed South Africa back into the game. It was a totally unprofessional batting performance and Fletch said as much. Butch was
caught at third man, Athers and Stewie were out hooking. After
Durban, we blew a golden opportunity to keep South Africa on
the back foot. The home batsmen were much more circumspect.
Centuries from Kallis and Cullinan gave them a 163-run lead. We

were chasing the game with a man short; we'd lost Freddie Flintoff with a broken foot from wearing odd boots. That was a great shame. Freddie had bowled well in Durban and was beginning to feel comfortable after a difficult start to his Test career against the 1998 South Africans. Chris Silverwood, who finally ended his one-cap-wonder tag in Port Elizabeth after nearly three years, claimed his first five-wicket haul. I took 2–88 in 37 overs, not a bad return on that pitch. We didn't bowl badly as a unit, but South Africa had all the time in the world to bat us out of the game and resist the rash shots that had cost us so dear. The damage had been done. England never even managed to make South Africa bat again, Athers top-scoring with 35 in our rather pathetic total of 126. The Test series was gone. I felt sorry for all our supporters who had travelled so far for so little. Unlike Johannesburg, we had no excuses for this innings defeat. Most of all I felt sorry for Fletch. I could see he was bemused as to why we could take two or three tentative steps forward, then such a huge one backwards. There was no public condemnation from our coach, though. Fletch had stressed all along that there was no quick fix for English cricket. We had simply proved the validity and accuracy of that statement.

24. Centurion Confessions

Our Centurion Park Test with South Africa in the early days of the new millennium is now something of a *cause célèbre*, the match that was heading for a certain draw. South Africa reached 155–6 at the end of the first day and the scoreboard had not changed when we turned up for the fifth and final day. That's when Hansie Cronje suggested and set up the first contrived finish in a Test, in return for a leather jacket and around £5,000. Cronje's action that day formed part of a dossier of shame that led to the South African skipper receiving a life ban from cricket. Unfortunately, Cronje was not the only person with guilty secrets stemming from the final day of that Centurion Park Test. I'm afraid Darren Gough also let himself down that day, in a way I'm still ashamed of. They say confessing is good for the soul, so here goes. I have never walked on to a cricket field in such a disgraceful, self-induced state of disrepair as I was that last morning in Pretoria. I had already been throwing up in the dressing-room. I felt so bad, I wasn't sure whether I was still drunk or was just beginning to suffer from a hangover. It was all my own fault, although I wasn't the only person who was convinced we would not see a single ball bowled on that final day. This self-delusion was the reason I allowed myself to be led astray by Ian Woosnam and others in celebrating the end of the Test series a day too early.

We were all very low after the events of Cape Town. Against Australia, it's the realization that the Ashes are not coming to England. Everywhere else, the lowest point is when the series is lost. Thoughts were already beginning to drift towards the triangular series. The England one-day specialists turned up in Port Elizabeth, and several played in the first-class game against a S.A. Invitation XI at St George's Park, including Graeme Hick, who captained the side, to give us a rest. There was talk that he might in Karachi. I rate Vaughanie's contribution that day as the reason we won; it was a shame he got out before the end. Another Yorkshireman, Chris Silverwood, joined me with the match back in the balance and all four results possible, including the tie. Nine runs needed from nine deliveries. I didn't subscribe to the view that England had nothing to lose. Not true. Two more wickets meant a series wipe-out, 3–0. We didn't deserve that. Nanti Hayward's first delivery had hit me on the arm-guard. That had nothing to do with the night before; the ball was coming through more quickly than had appeared from the dressing-room. Out in the middle, it was the normal friendly Test match atmosphere when the game is there to be won or lost. All the South Africans were into all the batters. England's hopes rested in the hands of three tail-enders, including me. I don't think I've ever concentrated so hard. The shot that took the pressure off came from Silvers, who crashed Pollock through the covers to the boundary. Our target had been six off seven deliveries before that. Hayward bowled the final over. I was facing. One shot would do it. I decided that I had to be positive. Anything short or wide was going to get the treatment. The first ball was pitched short. I pulled it for four, as sweetly as I'd hit Donald in the same way at Headingley, six years earlier. My celebrations had more to do with relief than anything else. All day I'd really thought that I was going to let England down. Nasser got it right: I did hit the winning runs, but it was an experience I never want to go through again. I'd been totally unprofessional. Fortunately, my lapse did not have serious consequences for me or for England.

I wasn't the only relieved tourist. As all the hugging and jumping around on our balcony showed, this was a big win for the team and the management. It was a first win abroad for Nasser, a first anywhere for Fletch and a first for that new partnership. Even though the big prize had gone, it was a crucial moment, just as it had been in Melbourne the previous winter. Subsequent events, on and off the field, have made that Centurion Park Test an important landmark for cricket and England. At the time Athers thought nothing of the new leather jacket Hansie was wearing when he saw him going out for dinner that night. And me? Well, I had another drink or two. Now I felt fine again, and there was plenty to celebrate.

After the Test, it was off with the whites and on with coloured clothing. As in 1995/6, I was looking forward to making the switch. I'd got better and fitter as the tour progressed. Still, I hadn't made the impact I would have liked, with only 14 wickets to my credit. After that disappointing earlier tour, I had been determined to show the South Africans what I could do. The reality was, there was too much catching up for me to do after such a long lay-off. My spirit was willing, but the flesh was weak. I never seem to have faced those same struggles on the limited-overs stage; that's the style of cricket more suited to my personality and ability. I feel comfortable in that environment. I've generally been consistent ever since I stepped into the international arena in 1994. I like the variety of deliveries – yorkers, slower balls – and I've got the fielders on the boundary to cover the mistakes. There's more buzz in the one-day game. The sad fact is that Test cricket can be boring. Our series against Pakistan during the winter of 2000/1 was as boring as you can get, although I would not have swapped the finish for anything. I rang home from Pakistan and discovered that nobody was watching. It's boring with spinners bowling all day on dead pitches. Cricket fans want fast bowlers and result matches.

Our ludicrous tour schedule became apparent, as England joined South Africa and Zimbabwe for a triangular series which was to be followed by another four-match one-day series in . . . Zimbabwe. Guess who headed for England, a couple of months later, for another triangular event? You've got it. Zimbabwe. I was more nervous going into the Bloemfontein clash with South Africa than I could remember. I'd decided to abandon Bob Cottam's tape-measure and go back to my old run-up, yard and a half and fourteen strides. The new run-up had been devised to protect my body, like most of the other alterations. I didn't feel comfortable, and feeling comfortable is so important. I felt there was little point in making myself a less effective bowler just to extend my career by a couple of years. However long I had left, it had to be on my

South Africa was not the happiest of tours for this England bowling pair. Devon and I spent much of the trip watching from the sidelines.

Drinks are not a great feature of cricket in England, but abroad the drinks trolley is often essential in the sweltering heat. Here I'm at the wheel in Bloemfontein on my first South African tour.

The missile that flew past my head at Peshawar in the 1996 World Cup. The crowd need not have bothered: we threatened nobody.

My cricket hero, Ian Botham, offering advice in his capacity as bowling consultant during the troubled tour of Zimbabwe in 1996–7.

Croftie and I pose near the model elephant at the Bulawayo ground. More than one member of the side observed the animal's passing resemblance to Andy Caddick!

Bumble at the helm. Our wholehearted and emotional coach, David Lloyd, taking England in a new direction in New Zealand in 1997.

Action replay at Edgbaston in 1997 against Australia. I'm celebrating getting Greg Blewett caught at slip after hitting his stumps the delivery before with a 'no-ball'.

England's only emphatic victory over Australia in my time – so far! Look at the delight on the face of Nasser, me, Athers and Croftie at Edgbaston in 1997.

Not again. Wayne (Morton) and I know it's serious. This broken finger kept me out of the rest of this Edgbaston Test against South Africa and the Lord's match that followed.

England victory celebrations in a major series at last. Headingley, 1998, and we have come from behind to beat the South Africans – don't I looked pleased on my home balcony!

Another great victory in 1998, this time in Melbourne, and this time my victim is Glenn McGrath.

The Sydney hat-trick. Ian Healy is the first to go, although I had to wait for the umpire's raised finger. No such problems with Stuart MacGill, who is beaten all ends up, or Colin Miller, as I send down the delivery I wanted. The lads mob me and I end up with Alex Tudor's teeth in the back of my head.

Our clash with the Sri Lankans in Australia in 1999. Here Mahanama and I enjoy a frank exchange of views in an ill-tempered contest.

We managed to beat Sri Lanka in the 1999 World Cup opener at Lord's – but the event was not a happy experience for England, for its cricket fans or for this particular fast bowler.

I was not at my best at Port Elizabeth and nowhere near good enough to trouble the powerful Lance Klusener, who belted me all over St George's Park.

The moment Lord's went mad in 2000 as Corkie hits the winning run against the West Indies. I'm still looking for that single, Courtney Walsh has given everything – and it shows – and umpire John Hampshire watches the ball head towards the boundary.

An amazing Friday at Leeds. Vaughanie hugs me after I've trapped Wavell Hinds l.b.w. and the Windies are heading for a two-day defeat.

The final hope for a West Indies miracle at the Oval goes. Brian Lara is l.b.w. to me, and Corkie and Marcus Trescothick join in the celebrations.

I may be down, but I'm certainly not out. I fall over as I run off with a stump after we have beaten the West Indies to clinch the 2000 series on a very special day at the Oval.

It is getting dark, but there is no gloom in the England dressing-room as Thorpey and Nas scamper the final two runs. Some England spectators go wild.

An award-winning picture of me all zinced up in England one-day gear. It was taken by Clive Mason.

The most important thing in my life – my family. Me with Anna and our two boys, Liam (in my arms) and Brennan.

terms. Along with the rest of the bowlers, I saw the ankle specialist who had treated Allan Donald during the Centurion Test. He was worried about the amount of movement around the ankle and felt that an operation would be required at some stage. That's been put on hold because it may take two years to recover. His only other suggested option was to keep going until the ankle packs up. Dean Conway suggested I start wearing the 'rocket sock', an ankle brace. That has been a big help. During the summer of 2000 I felt pain up the outside of my leg because of the adjustment. Now it has settled down and my ankle is rarely swollen. Every young bowler at Yorkshire, except Oggie, wears one to stop going over on your ankle in the delivery stride.

My four wickets at Bloemfontein earned me another Man of the Match, as we won comfortably. That convinced me that it was no use trying to bowl within myself. All or nothing, that's me. Craig White was called up from Central Districts in New Zealand. Other names were mentioned at the management meeting, but I felt that another chance for Craig was overdue. Illy had selected him too early. That wasn't his fault; but his prospects weren't helped when it became clear that Athers did not rate him. If a captain doesn't rate you, he doesn't bowl you. Craig didn't feel part of the team and lost confidence. That, coupled with injury problems, combined to limit his Test appearances to eight as England entered the new millennium. Many had written him off, but I hadn't. I knew, from playing with him at Yorkshire, that in the right environment Craig not only had an England future but that he could make a significant contribution. He arrived from New Zealand, was given a warm welcome from Fletch and Nasser and hasn't looked back since. One senior member surplus to our one-day requirements in South Africa was Stewie. With claims that England were looking ahead to the next World Cup, Chris Read stayed on instead. Stewie was not happy, either at going home or at being retired prematurely. We're over a year further on and Stewie's still a key member of both England teams. Strangely, Read performed much better than expected, but he has not had a look-in since.

I have to confess that the one-day matches tend to merge into

each other, as do the series. The highlights of this series that have
stayed with me are: failing by two to score the four needed off the
last ball to beat South Africa at Newlands; being demolished by
Henry Olonga on the same ground; Mark Ealham's world-record
five l.b.w.s and the best-ever figures by an England bowler in
limited overs (5–15) at Kimberley against Zimbabwe; and losing
off the last over in East London, when Pollock hit Ealie for two
fours. We won the right to face South Africa in the final on run-rate
after our final game with Zimbabwe was washed out. Even the
Wanderers final was delayed a day because of more rain. Another
final, another loss. It was a bowler-friendly wicket, and Caddie and
I had them in trouble with the new white ball. Once again we
couldn't finish them off, as the home side recovered to 149 from
21–5. Between us, Caddie and I took 7–37 off 18 overs. Our
batting was not as resilient, and Pollock destroyed us with a five-
wicket haul. He was named Man of the Mach and of the Series. I
thought I might have had a sniff, after taking the same number of
wickets as him in one fewer match. After three months of cricket,
I was almost back to my best.

   That would have been the perfect moment to board the plane
home. Unfortunately, the England squad only got as far as Harare,
where we got off for another one-day series. The lads felt that the
visit was a cross between a goodwill trip and a punishment, just like
our Lahore trip before the World Cup in early 1999. 'Oh well, we
balls'd it up last time when we were there, we didn't treat them
very well, we created a bad impression.' Zimbabwe had wanted a
Test match as well, but that could not be scheduled in as our Test
players had been home nearly a month. During the World Cup,
Grav had mentioned the possibility of a few senior players ducking
out of this final leg after the demands of the previous 15 months so
that we could rest up before the summer. When the crunch came,
the subject was never brought up again. A lot of dangled carrots
seem to vanish like that. Many of the lads were survivors of the
1996/7 campaign. All our team talks revolved around giving them
a hiding. The ill-feeling was still there. Comments by Zimbabwe
that they would come out on top also fired us up. Don't get me

wrong: I'm not deriding Zimbabwe. They are a good one-day side, very under-rated. But when someone has got the better of you, getting your own back is all that matters. Our sole aim in that series was to show them who the professionals were. That was our motivation before the 1999 World Cup game – and it didn't help our suffering that Zimbabwe qualified and we didn't after we had thrashed them. The whole of our team were hacked off when rain cancelled the final one-dayer and denied us a 4–0 whitewash to avenge our 3–0 drubbing three years earlier. Hickie was the batting hero in the first and third games, and it was Mullally who edged us to victory in the other match, with me a worried spectator up at the non-striker's end. We had evened things up a bit; the one-day score between England and Zimbabwe was now six apiece.

25. Hedging Our Bets

Cronje's generosity and our goodwill visit to Zimbabwe allowed us to come home winners in both our last Test and one-day international. Whichever way you looked at it, the summer of 2000 was crunch time for cricket in England and for all its top cricketers. Central contracts, two divisions in the first-class and one-day game, a new international schedule with seven Tests and a ten-match triangular series. Yet, before a ball was bowled, the whole of world cricket was put in the dock and under suspension as some of the biggest names in the sport were implicated in match-fixing. England did not escape scot-free; several of our matches and players were thrown into the melting pot. I've never felt so uncomfortable being an international cricketer. The pats on the back and full-frontal abuse had been replaced by sideways glances and whispers. Even a year on, I still can't come to terms with the idea of Hansie Cronje as a cricket cheat.

I dismissed the original story emerging from India of Cronje's involvement as some sub-continental scare-mongering. Stories of match-fixing and bookies and betting were nothing new. That's why Warnie and Mark Waugh had been fined, back in 1994, for receiving money for giving information at the same time as the allegations that Pakistan captain Salim Malik had approached some of the Aussies to play badly. There had been surreptitious phone calls to Adam Hollioake during the 1997 Sharjah tournament. Some of them were reported. A lot more instances came to light in the wake of 'Cronjegate'. I wasn't alone in believing Cronje was an innocent victim. At least my thoughts weren't made public, so they didn't come back to haunt me. Former coach Bob Woolmer, who might now have been with England, claimed the reports were 'absolute rubbish', and South African supremo Dr Ali Bacher declared, 'Cronje is a man of unimpeachable integrity and honesty.'

My first doubts came when I saw Cronje's press conference; he chose his words of denial so carefully. A few days later, the South African cricket captain 'coughed'.

I was staggered. So were all the England team. Cronje not only came from a religious background, he had the squeakiest-clean image in cricket. He was the last person in the cricket world I would have suspected. Once Cronje was implicated, then no other name would have surprised me. Cronje, like the victorious rugby captain François Pienaar, was a role-model for the Rainbow Nation. I must admit, Cronje was a changed man on that last tour. In 1995/6 I found him friendly, willing to chat and happy to mix with the opposition. Not in 1999/2000. He was distant, and we hardly saw him off the field. Four years down the line, I expected Cronje to be more relaxed; his position was secure and his reputation, seemingly, untouchable. Yet he was tense, off-hand and a rather solitary figure. During the first tour, he'd inquired whether I would like to return the following winter and play for Free State. Looking back, on that last tour Cronje gave the impression of a man with something on his mind.

England were slowly but surely dragged into this mess. Our Centurion victory soon became part of the Cronje charge-sheet, and there was talk of Nasser being interviewed by the South African Commission which was being set up to investigate the whole matter. Centurion had nothing to do with us. Whatever Cronje's motive for declaring and making a match of a 'dying' Test, we had won fair and square. I was less happy when our victory over South Africa at Headingley in 1998 was questioned, this time the umpiring coming under suspicion, along with our 1999 World Cup defeat by India.

The mess really hit the England fan when Chris Lewis made an allegation that three England cricketers had been involved in match-fixing. That was actually an old story, but 'Cronjegate' gave it new legs. Ignoring the legal implications, I wanted the three names made public; as it stood, all England players were being tarnished by the match-fixing brush. I did not know whether my name was on the list. I did know that I was totally innocent, and I resented the general suspicion now hovering over the England squad. Lewis was not flavour of the day with his former England team-mates, least of all with me, after apparently selling his story and three of us down the river. An immense cricket talent, Lewis's international career had been a stop-start affair, including many moments of farce, for example his pathetic 'puncture' excuse when late for an England one-day game at the Oval, and suffering sun-stroke after shaving his head. I was looking forward to confronting him on and off the field in our Benson & Hedges game against Leicestershire at Headingley in mid-April, a day after he had been to the E.C.B. offices at Lord's. I wasn't at all surprised when Lewis ducked out, after it was decided the all-rounder was not in a fit state to play. A few days later, he was booed off Old Trafford after making a duck.

I began to feel sorry for Lewis when it became clear he was not the opportunist we had first thought. Lewis had been to the E.C.B. the previous August over these approaches. Lewis had not accused three England players of match-fixing, he had just passed on what he had been told by those who had attempted to interfere with the New Zealand series. The Kiwi skipper, Stephen Fleming, confirmed that he too had been approached. Lord MacLaurin, who had invited the world's cricket chiefs to a summit in London, made it clear that the E.C.B. had acted properly and had not dragged its feet. There was a lot going on behind the scenes that I was oblivious to. I had missed that New Zealand series, when all the England players had been seen by the police. The MacLaurin summit opened with all those present being asked to sign a pledge that they had been involved in nothing illegal. Pakistan was ordered to produce its report into match-fixing that had been completed for over a year. Throughout the 1999 World Cup, we kept hearing that several of the Pakistan squad had been named, but nothing had appeared, even after they lost the final in such a humiliating way.

The match-fixing witch-hunt rumbled on all year. All sorts of names were thrown into the melting pot, some officially, others from not so reliable sources. The World Cup captains of 1999 seem to have been picked out for particular attention. By the end of

2000, Wasim Akram had been fined in the Pakistan report, India's Mohammad Azharuddin and South Africa's Hansie Cronje had been banned for life, while our Alec Stewart, the West Indies' Brian Lara and Sri Lanka's Arjuna Ranatunga had been named in the Indian Criminal Bureau of Investigation report. All international cricketers had signed an I.C.C. pledge regarding their past behaviour.

Hopefully, cricket is cleaner after having all its dirty linen washed in public. Is it cleansed? I do not know. I can only speak for myself. I have never been involved. I have honestly been astonished by the revelations of the past year. But cricket cannot keep digging up its past; excessive muck-raking becomes counter-productive. I believe the cricket authorities have confused the issue by combining two offences, one minor, one serious, into the match-fixing/betting Code of Conduct. It boils down to the Shane Warne/Mark Waugh offence back in 1994: receiving money, probably unsolicited, for information. I would not be surprised if a lot of that had been going on then – players supplying information already in the public domain or which was a matter of opinion, and being offered gifts and money in return. Information seems to be more valuable if you pay for it. Before anyone asks, I have no evidence to support this view, but cricketers chat about the wicket, the weather, the make-up of the side and the toss has been as much a part of cricket as the bat and ball. Wasn't part of the game's original attraction the wagers that took place on the outcome? Could I have changed next to someone who's taken cash for information? Probably. Have I been or would I want to be in the same dressing-room as someone who's deliberately not played to the best of his ability? Certainly not.

Nowadays, if it was found that you had given that sort of information, even without receiving any reward, you would be called a match-fixer. That's nonsense. You're equating fare-evasion with train robbery. That's the scary thing for those people who played a few years ago: if details of a little trinket or hospitality received for some harmless information were exposed today, that player's reputation would be in tatters. Cricket has to have a sense of proportion. If a player is found to have tried to interfere with a match, whenever it was, kick him out and let him face the wrath of an indignant sporting public. That's always been the real sporting crime in my book: not trying your best. Cricket now has to concentrate on its future, not be concerned with finding sacrifices because the game's administrators and officials failed to appreciate what was going on under their very noses. If anyone has brought cricket into disrepute over this scandal, it has been cricket's administrators.

The *Wisden Cricketers' Almanack* dipped into the past with rather more purpose when the first cricket bible of the new millennium was published, in early April 2000. Each annual contains the Five Cricketers of the Year; I was honoured to be chosen in 1999 after my efforts in helping England beat South Africa the previous summer. It was a double honour because the editor himself, Matthew Engel, wrote the eulogy that accompanied my selection. In this new edition, Engel announced he was taking a sabbatical from the editor's chair because of England's poor performance. I presume our revival in 2000 has made him keen to return.

The 2000 edition of *Wisden* also included Five Cricketers of the Century, voted for by 100 ex-cricketers, journalists and other 'experts'. Cricketers, like all other sportsmen, love lists and especially one as definitive as this. Not one of the 100 experts asked came up with all five of the final selection. Only one man polled 100 votes: Sir Donald Bradman. Sir Garry Sobers was next with 90. Only three other cricketers exceeded 20 votes: Sir Jack Hobbs (30), Shane Warne (27) and Sir Vivian Richards (25). As Warnie was quick to point out, he was the only one not to have received a knighthood. There's still time. Yorkshire's best was Sir Len Hutton (11 votes), and I was astonished that Ian Botham received endorsements from only nine 'experts'. There was not a single vote for Darren Gough, but I was in good company. Nor did Brian Lara or Steve Waugh.

One plus from 'Cronjegate' was that it diverted media attention away from another England squabble over contracts. Our negotiations over central contracts threatened a repeat of our dispute over our World Cup fee. The Board did not appear to have learnt any lessons from that mess. We had; this time the England squad had legal representation. As with the World Cup, the English counties were sorted out first, long before our bosses got round to the players. Counties would get £51,000 in compensation for each player contracted to the centre. That was more than even the most experienced England players would be getting. I thought the counties were in business to provide players for England.

Although our central contracts were not ready until April, the players who were getting central contracts were chosen a week after the Zimbabwe tour. I never got a satisfactory answer as to why this élite squad had to be picked in February for an international season starting in May. Fletcher and Nasser did not fill the 16 places available, instead choosing a dozen players. The list did not surprise me. The names had been bandied about during the final weeks of the tour. What did perplex me was the make-up of our squad. All the original arguments about central contracts and tug-of-war problems in the past focused almost exclusively on fast bowlers, especially the need to protect youngsters. Developing England fast bowlers have a dreadful record for breaking down. Yet this first England Super-12 consisted of six batsmen, two all-rounders, a leg-spinner and three quick bowlers. Actually, I should not have been surprised. Batsmen have called the shots throughout my career.

Hickie and Ramps, two absentees from the South African Test series, were included, as was Dean Headley and uncapped Chris Schofield from Lancashire. Someone joked that it was the first time England had picked a Test squad more than 11 weeks before the match. The surprise omission, for me, was Graham Thorpe, while the nomination of Ramps as Athers's opening partner for the summer was a bold decision. The pair had batted together there for England Under-17 and Under-19. Thorpe, who made himself unavailable for the winter tours to Pakistan and Sri Lanka, had obviously not been forgiven for spending the winter at home. Thorpey had actually been available for the two one-day series at the end of our trip, and we could have done with him. There was no place, either, for Alan Mullally, who had made a big-money move to Hampshire. Five of the dozen had not played Test cricket in South Africa. The squad having been chosen, we focused on what these new contracts would say. It became obvious that they were a long way from ready, let alone signing. Our contract negotiations carried on through March and into April, even after our pre-season camp in Cheshire. There was one difference from the World Cup situation: the players had legal representation this time, as well as Dean Headley, who was our spokesman. As Ramps stated publicly at the time: 'We will be acting together and not as individuals.' Much had to be clarified, not least our intellectual rights *vis-à-vis* the enormous growth of information technology, especially internet sites. Some thought we were grasping and greedy. Our motivation was just protection. Athers raised the temperature and the blood-pressure of one or two county tradition-alists by claiming that county cricket 'serves no purpose'. Once again, our most highly educated team-mate had rather put his foot in it.

After all that had gone on, I was just glad to escape on to the cricket field, weather permitting. The rain disrupted much of April and May, so much so that Fletcher cancelled a planned camp before the Tests started, so we could spend more time in the middle. Yorkshire made the knock-out stages of the Benson & Hedges Cup, which had returned in its previous state after one season as the Super Cup. The White Rose started with a bad defeat at Durham, but then beat Lancashire, Leicestershire (minus Lewis) and Notts, with the Derbyshire game being abandoned. My best return was 4–17 against Notts, but I drew a blank in our dis-appointing seven-run home defeat to Surrey in the quarter-final. Matthew Hoggard took 4–39, all four victims England batsmen, and we came back into the game from 15–3 to 124–3 when Darren Lehmann was unfortunate to be given out caught down the leg side. I prepared for the earliest home Test in England's history by helping Yorkshire beat Derbyshire by an innings and 79 runs inside three days. That game cost England Michael Vaughan, who broke a finger after scoring an undefeated 155. He was not the only contracted player out of the Lord's Test. Dean Headley had broken down again and would need spinal surgery, and he was out for the season. It transpired that his medical examination to prove his fitness had not required him being asked to bowl. Sadly, while we were in Sri Lanka, the news came through that Deano had been forced to retire.

Any problems England might have had paled into insignificance compared to those of our Zimbabwe guests. Not much love has been lost between us in recent years, but the troubles back in Zimbabwe were serious. I cannot imagine what it would be like to leave family and friends at home in those circumstances in order simply to go on a cricket tour. The tour to England was given the go-ahead in early April while Zimbabwe were in the West Indies. Television pictures provided vivid images of the internal strife in the country, with elections coming up. The efforts of the war veterans to move on the white farmers resulted in horrible tragedies. The likes of Heath Streak came from farming families, as did Hickie's mum and dad. On the morning of the Trent Bridge Test, the father of Jason Oates, a first-class cricketer, was murdered on his farm. Those political troubles and 'Cronjegate' were relegated to sub-plots when the Zimbabweans' fast-bowling coach started spouting off. This was none other than Dennis Lillee's great sparring partner, Jeff Thomson, who would never have got a job in the diplomatic service. 'The game's biggest crisis,' Thommo blasted, 'is that no one can beat the Aussies!'

For once Lord's did not inspire the tourists. In fact, our victory over Zimbabwe took place in the most one-sided Test match I have ever played in. Had the weather not been so poor, we would have won by Saturday lunchtime. The conditions and the early scheduling meant that the crowds did not flock to Lord's. Only about 10,000 saw us bowl out Zimbabwe for 83 on Thursday, with Ed Giddins returning in style with 5–15, lucky bloke. I felt certain to join him on the Lord's honours board when we came off at the end of play on Saturday. Stewie and Hickie hit centuries in our total of 415. For Hickie it was a first hundred against the country of his birth. You could see how much it meant to him, as he spent over 20 minutes on 99. There was never any danger of the captain

calling him in this time. Stewie's knock required special powers of
concentration, too. His beloved Chelsea were playing in the F.A.
Cup Final and umpire Peter Willey kept him informed of events
at Wembley, including Di Matteo's winning goal against Aston
Villa. Our batsmen rather dragged their feet that afternoon, but I
wasted no time in ripping into Zim's top order. I came off with
figures of 4–22, including three wickets in my first four overs,
in the tourists' total of 39–5. Only one more wicket for Lord's
immortality. Sadly, this turned out to be another lost opportunity
as the final six wickets fell to Caddie and Giddins, who was named
Man of the Match. I couldn't believe it. All the lads were aware
how desperate I am to collect that five-wicket haul. Maybe that's
why Nasser had some special words for me at the after-match press
conference. 'A lot was said and written about Darren in South
Africa, and most of it was correct. But his opening second-innings
spell against Zimbabwe was outstanding, very high on the list of
those I have seen from one of our bowlers. He has been training
hard and the results are showing. He will always be first down on
the team sheet while I am captain because he gives so much.'
Thanks, Nas. I might hold you to that.

I did feel good and was bowling in a good rhythm. Much of the
media coverage commented on the poor public response to such
an early-season Lord's Test match and the poor performance of
Zimbabwe in a first Test at cricket's headquarters. That wasn't our
fault; you can only take on what's put in front of you. It was a
winning start for the new central contracts system and a first home
success for Nasser and especially for Duncan, who had never got
to play at Lord's. The media certainly had much more to complain
about after the next Test, at Trent Bridge. The only change to our
Lord's squad was the absence of Craig White, who had collapsed
in a Scarborough street and was kept in hospital for brain scans. He
made a full recovery, although there was no conclusive evidence
about what happened. The weather again played its part in dampen-
ing down the atmosphere in Nottingham and helped Athers to
spend over 41 hours in the nervous nineties, after Friday was a
complete washout with our opener on 96. He duly completed his

fifth hundred at Trent Bridge. The other notable batting feat was fifty from Schofield who, like me, made a half-century before bowling for his country. What was different was that this was his second Test. Our new leg-spinner had not had a chance to bowl at Lord's in such friendly pace-bowling conditions.

Full credit to Zimbabwe for their attitude at Trent Bridge. At the end of the fourth evening, Zim were 285–4 – three wickets to me – still a long way behind our 374. An hour before the start on Monday, Nasser was told of the declaration, and we responded with another of those wayward batting displays that have cost us so dear. At 110–7 we were less than 200 ahead. Once again Athers came to our rescue. He was batting at No. 7 after being off the field on Sunday with a stomach complaint, and he eventually made sure that the tourists ran out of time. The series was ours, but the England dressing-room was extremely subdued: Nasser had got a duck as his bad trot continued; Ramps, after fifty in the first dig, failed again; Schofield had failed to take a wicket in his 18 overs; Giddins had not recaptured the form of Lord's; Caddie looked out of sorts and took stick for resting between Tests; generally, it was a scrappy and indecisive display. It gave the anti-central contracts brigade a stick to beat us with. I am always staggered by the way English cricket has to be dragged into the present, let alone the future. Other countries see the need to improve, and changes are made. Not England. The four-day game, two divisions and central contracts came about only after hours, weeks, months and years of discussions in committee rooms around the country. Yet this never-ending process is in sharp contrast to the speed with which damning verdicts are produced. After two Tests, central contracts were deemed to be a waste of time and, more importantly, of money. I wonder what the view is now, after a year of some success. 'Has anything actually changed?' was the theme of most discussions on England's form in this series. What neither the media nor we doubted was that this topsy-turvy form would not go unpunished against the West Indies.

26. Last Chance Saloon

The darkest hour is just before dawn. I've always regarded that cliché as a load of rubbish. Well, I did until a year ago. Now I know that it's true. The days before our recovery against the West Indies were the most depressing, despondent and devastating of my cricket career. Time had almost run out for my generation of England cricketers. We were failures who promised much and delivered little. Despite chance after chance after chance, our inability to string two decent performances together meant that England cricket fans had suffered agony after agony after agony during the 1990s. Our three-day defeat to the West Indies at Edgbaston was the final straw. I voiced as much in my newspaper column: 'Will I ever play in a great England team?' I had begun to doubt it. England's position as we were walking out to bowl at the West Indies for a second time at Lord's, five days later, appeared to have sealed the fate of this set of players. Our time was up.

The West Indies series had occupied my thoughts since the end of the winter. Plenty of unfinished business, including injury problems and that 1998 missed tour. Most of the pre-tour discussion revolved around Brian Lara. While Ambrose and Walsh seemed indestructible, Lara was made of more brittle stuff. He had quit as captain after a disastrous tour of New Zealand; both Tests and five one-dayers were lost. More significantly, Lara had threatened to give up the game and was missing for the home series against Zimbabwe and Pakistan. Lara-less, Jimmy Adams's side beat Zimbabwe by 35 runs when the visitors needed only 99 for victory. A few days later, at Sabina Park, Courtney Walsh went ahead of Kapil Dev and took his 435th Test wicket. Early in May, the papers were reporting that Lara had withdrawn from the England trip. The next day, his presence was confirmed in the squad. No Lara? That was too good to be true. He might have been seeing a shrink, and maybe the little left-hander wasn't the consistent force of a few years earlier, but Lara is still one hell of a player, able to torment and torture the best of attacks. Just before leaving for England, the West Indies took the Pakistan series with a single-wicket win in the final Test in Antigua.

How good was Jimmy Adams's side? Take your pick. The West Indies had just won two home series. Away from home, they had not won a single first-class game on the last three tours – Pakistan, South Africa and New Zealand – and had lost the last ten consecutive Tests. I felt confident. My own form was good, picking up 6–63 in our six-wicket win over Durham. The England selectors left the batting line-up alone, ignoring Vaughanie's 94 on his return from injury. He was called up as standby when Ramps woke up with a stiff neck on Wednesday morning, but was not required. The most significant change was replacing Schofield with Croft. Schofield's introduction had not been a success. The critics of central contracts had another field-day. Lancashire got their man back for the greater part of the season and made a nice profit on the deal, having been compensated over £50K for his original selection. Now Lord's was having to pay extra to bring in replacements.

The atrocious weather continued and Edgbaston was under water the day before the start. I am not sure we were right to have committed ourselves to a spinner. Our preparations had gone well, but there was a sense of apprehension, as though we were not quite in control of our own destiny. Edgbaston, the West Indies, brought back memories of 1995. The West Indies side had a familiar look about it: Lara, Adams, Campbell, Walsh and Ambrose. So did our score after the first day: 179 all out, although this time we had not decided to bat. Walsh took five wickets for the twentieth time in his Test career. Things would have been worse if Caddie and I had not put on 39 for the ninth wicket. My knock of 23 was ended when wicket-keeper Ridley Jacobs hit the stumps at the non-striker's end. My score might not appear that large in the Lara scale of things, but it was a major landmark for me. Believe it or not, this was the first time Darren Gough had reached 20 in a Test innings since the

West Indies encounter at Lord's, more than five years earlier. Important as the runs were, we had to get stuck into the tourists that first night. I removed Gayle immediately, and Caddie got Hinds, to leave the Windies 50–2 overnight.

Friday started well. I sent Campbell – my 150th Test wicket – and Lara on their way. Lara was especially pleasing. I put him on his arse and then, later in the same over, delivered the perfect away-swinger, which he nudged through to Stewie. But there was no support. Caddie had one of those days when he wasn't firing. The press had been on his back ever since Trent Bridge. He's the only bowler we've got who is the same height as Walsh and Ambrose. When Caddie doesn't create as much havoc as those two, everyone wants to know why. The Windies recovered from 136–4 to reach 336–7. We were in trouble. So was I when a beamer from me slipped and thumped Curtly on the hand. The delivery was timed at 88 m.p.h. and the big man did not look too happy while receiving treatment. I apologized immediately; it was an accident. Clattering Curtly Ambrose with a cricket ball is not in my 'How to Succeed and Survive in Text Cricket' manual.

One person fighting for his cricket life at the time was Hansie Cronje. The Edgbaston Test coincided with his appearance in the witness box in Cape Town. I couldn't believe what I was seeing when I read his testimony. He had been promised immunity from prosecution and even possible prison if he told the whole truth. Lara was dragged into the scandal that weekend, when a South African businessman claimed in a signed affidavit that the West Indian had taken money for under-performing in a triangular tournament, way back in 1993.

English cricket was in a different sort of crisis that Saturday as we lost by an innings and 93 runs. The tourists were eventually bowled out for 397. Last man out was skipper Adams for 98, giving me my seventh five-wicket haul in Test matches. England needed to fight, but we caved in and any chance was gone at 24–4. Ramps went for a duck, and so did Hickie – his first pair in 390 matches. Nasser made 8 and was dropped twice. The Edgbaston dressing-room was like a morgue. We couldn't even blame the pitch this time.

England's cricketers had come a poor third in national team displays. The rugby team had been robbed of victory in South Africa by the video referee, while Keegan's soccer stars beat Germany with an Alan Shearer goal in Euro 2000. We watched the football, but it was hard to get excited and ignore our own predicament. There was no running for home with our tails between our legs, either. The entire England party – players, selectors and coaches – stayed in Birmingham for a debriefing after Sunday breakfast. We were at the point of no return and we could kid ourselves no longer.

My article in that Sunday's *News of the World* contained some prophetic words:

It is obvious that English cricket has some serious problems. I believe we have started to address them, but we're trying to make changes within the old system and that's got everybody confused. The problems are simple – too many teams, too many players, too many people involved in the decision-making process, too much mediocrity – and a confused structure. We know what has to be done. The game needs streamlining, but nobody wants to give way. Too many people would rather see the game go down the pan than see blood on the carpet. The biggest problem is that survival is the name of the game. Hang onto your county place. Hang onto your England place. And the rewards for success or failure are not much different. The contract system is under attack, but it's only been in place a couple of months. You just can't win – if you miss a county game and then play badly for England, that's wrong. Play in between tests for your county, and do badly, that's wrong as well. If we're all honest about the first Test at Edgbaston, we all got it wrong, as Nasser quite rightly pointed out. We should have scored 220 in our first innings and should have bowled the Windies out for 300 – a lead of 80 – and we should still have been in the game. But at 24–4 in the second innings, we were finished. Saturday night and it's all over. It's embarrassing. I know friends and family wonder what's going on after the promising start at Lord's against Zimbabwe. But that's the England set-up at present. It promises a lot more than it delivers. We can't hide from the truth. I don't want to end my career in a losing set-up, to never even get near regaining the Ashes or winning a test series abroad. I was all very well reaching my

150th Test wicket and collecting my first five-for against the West Indies. But that didn't mean a thing – I was a loser again.

The media got stuck in. I couldn't blame them. Our squad for the triangular one-day series that was to take place after the Lord's Test was named. Paul Franks was brought in and Thorpey returned, as did Stewie. I began to get the feeling that the Test series was being written off. Any repeat of Edgbaston and we were history. My form wasn't a problem. I was even back in the runs. I might not be part of the problem, but would I be part of the solution? I took 5–30 as Yorkshire beat our own Cricket Board XI at Harrogate in the second round of the NatWest.

All week I was waiting to find out what the selectors would do. 'Very little' was the answer. The batsmen survived, but Dominic Cork was added to the squad of 14, as was Yorkshire's young bowler, Matthew Hoggard. Our highest individual score in the last three innings had been 34, yet the batsmen were retained *en bloc*. They might have been our best players, but now was the time for more drastic action. There was still no place for Michael Vaughan. But fate took a hand – or, in this case, Nasser's left thumb, which had been injured just before the selection meeting. Originally the captain had been included, but X-rays revealed a stress fracture and he was ruled out for a month. Vaughanie was in and Stewie, sacked a year earlier, was back as captain. Craig White also returned when Flintoff's back gave out again. The only injury which gave us some hope was the arm trouble which was to keep Chanderpaul out of the rest of the series after Lord's.

We talked a good game before Lord's. We always did. By teatime on Friday England were all but finished. Our apprehension showed during those early exchanges at Lord's. The Windies went in at lunch on the first day with all wickets intact. That was our fault; we tried too hard and didn't use the conditions properly. Fielders were anxious. Three catches went down. We have been notoriously slow starters over the years; it's part of the English disease. We need an excuse. We have to be knocked down before we can start fighting. Playing catch-up Test cricket is a tough and unrewarding business, I can tell you. The Aussies are full-on the moment they step on to the field, from the first minute to the last. The English prefer to dip their toes in the water tentatively, waiting for the other side to make the first move. That's been our big failing.

What really got under our skin that day was not the West Indies' opening partnership, but the reggae din from the Nursery End as part of Channel 4's 'Caribbean Summer' coverage. We could hardly hear ourselves think as we sat in the dressing-room. 'What's this nonsense? Do you think our hosts would put on English music if we were in the Caribbean?' I went out on the balcony and looked along to the opposition's end of the pavilion. The West Indies were jigging and bopping around to the music. It was as if they were celebrating the series: 1–0 up and in a strong position at Lord's, with us in some disarray. The Windies carried that party mood on to the field, giving us our first wicket two deliveries later, when Adrian Griffith set off for a crazy second run and was stranded by Caddick's throw. As we gathered for the celebrations, the general view was 'that's what you get for listening to reggae music'.

The first afternoon at Lord's. Already the Test and the series were slipping from our grasp with the Windies 162–1. We needed inspiration. Step forward Corkie. My mate had been itching for a return to the big time after his disappointing Ashes tour. His return was the key moment of the summer for me. He entered Lord's, along with the bats he wanted autographed for his benefit season, with that familiar swagger. I was glad to see him. Corkie and I go back a long way, living together at 19, making our England debuts close together, both making an immediate impact before struggling with fitness and form for a time. We're both competitive characters – but not with each other, despite the media trying to establish a rivalry between us.

England needed Corkie. Not that he's such an influential player in terms of performance. It's the package you get. Corkie's the sort who loves a challenge, and you need players who respond to desperate situations by sticking their chins out and turning the game around. It's about being a top-class player with attitude. Corkie's not frightened of getting up the opposition's nose. Actually, he enjoys it, and he's not afraid to be called names or be hated by the opposition. Some players needed to be respected by opponents, and being unpopular affects them. Not Corkie. He wants to be unpopular, otherwise he's failing in his game-plan. I've always thought that animosity helps to motivate Corkie to play better. That's what brought us back into the game that Thursday. Sherwin Campbell is a batsman who always gives the bowler a chance, yet he was resisting all short-ball offers with a fielder waiting at long leg. Then Corkie bowled an innocuous delivery and, instead of ducking, Campbell hit it down long leg's throat. Corkie had been getting stuck into him and Campbell wanted to shut him up. Corkie was back, and we were back in the game.

Corkie was cock-a-hoop. He finished the day with four wickets, the same as me, as the Windies closed at 267–9. That was some recovery. The next morning, Caddie finished the Windies off and I had missed out again in my attempt to get on the Lord's bowling board of honour. Fletch just chuckled. He knows how desperate I am to get a five-wicket haul at the home of cricket. I've taken four wickets there six times now. After that four against Zimbabwe, Fletch said: 'You'll have to get them in the second innings.' When I got another four here, he smiled: 'You'll have to carry on for another year!' I think the coach feels that I won't call it a day until Darren Gough's name is on that Lord's board. He's right.

I believe that a quick game is a good game, but I'd never experienced anything like that Friday at Lord's. Almost a year on, I still can't come to terms with the events of that day, when 21 wickets fell. We did well to peg the tourists back to 267, but at 50–5 the problems of Edgbaston remained. Even a majestic hooked six from me off Walsh counted for little. England trailed by 133 runs. Another three-day defeat was looming. It was, but not for the side we expected.

Looking back, my catch off Campbell in their second innings may have been the turning point, but there was still a lot of work to do. When I took a tumbling catch there, five years earlier, to remove the left-handed West Indian, Keith Arthurton, it put Angus Fraser on that Lord's honours board. I was pleased for him. This time was just as important for the bowler. Caddie had been down in the dumps and I saw his eyes light up. He's a bowler whose whole performance can hinge on a single moment, a little bit of luck that sparks his confidence to produce the outstanding form he is capable of. As with Craig White, the Fletcher/Hussain set-up has given him a sense of belonging that was absent in his earlier England career.

The Campbell catch gave me as much of a lift as it did Caddie. We tore into the Windies and left them in shreds at 24–5. Caddie got the key wicket of Lara, while I removed Chanderpaul. The sensible thing was to give one of us a rest. That was me. Caddie had taken so long to get going, there was no point stopping him now. Even with half the West Indies wickets gone, I never thought I wouldn't get another bowl or a chance to bid for that blasted board. Corkie, as ever, was keen to grab a piece of the action. When the Windies collapsed again from 39–5 to 41–9, two apiece to Caddie and Corkie, I realized there was no chance of either of them coming off. It would have been nice to have skittled them out for less than the 46 England managed in Trinidad in 1994. It wasn't to be, however. Corkie finished the job, Caddie had 5–16 and the Friday Lord's crowd went berserk. The crescendo of noise as wicket after wicket fell was something I had never experienced before. It was almost scary.

For all the celebrations as we returned to the dressing-room, no one was fooling himself that the job was anything more than half done. Now all we had to do was turn up on the Saturday and do it all over again. Which, as Chapter One of this book has shown, is exactly what we did.

27. You'll Have to Drop Me

The excitement and cricket hysteria created at Lord's swept the country. Keegan's side were long gone in Euro 2000. We were the heroes of English sport again. We were raring to go and put pressure on the West Indies while they were down. They had to be down after losing like that. Skipper Jimmy Adams put on a brave face and showed a lot of style when he took his players to the Nursery End to thank the West Indies supporters who had travelled from the Caribbean, but the tourists must have been gutted. If another Test had followed, England would have waltzed it. Unfortunately, this final Cornhill series came to shuddering halt. A ten-match triangular series – sponsored by NatWest – with the West Indies and Zimbabwe was scheduled after the second Test.

A week after the Lord's heroics, England were on the other side of London, making a real mess of our opening encounter with Zimbabwe. Fletch was tearing his hair out and had to bite his tongue to stop himself letting us know what he thought of us. It had not been a good one-day week. Yorkshire had travelled to Northampton for a NatWest tie and got soundly beaten. That was to be the last I'd see of my county colleagues for a while. Just before they headed for home and I drove to the Oval, I had a few words for Byas about why we'd lost. From time to time I have my say in the Yorkshire dressing-room. 'We lost because we had the wrong batting order – and it's been wrong all year. And we've done nothing about it.'

'Okay, big mouth, what's your batting order?'

That's generally the tone for any discussions I have with Byas. We often lock horns. Byas probably thinks I'm a big-headed, arrogant show-off. I know he's an above-average county cricketer who can't understand why he hasn't represented England. He would have reckoned that I said what I did on the spur of the moment, for effect. Byas was wrong; it had been concerning me for a while. You don't have to be part of the team to work out what was wrong. I felt that Anthony McGrath should be up the order instead of Richard Blakey, as should Gavin Hamilton. Blakey's great to have in near the end; he's experienced at knocking the ball around and is quick between the wickets. Instead, coming in first wicket down in the first 15 overs, nothing was happening.

Before Byas had time to respond, our overseas star, Darren Lehmann, piped up: 'Dave, I'm sorry to say this, but I totally agree with him.' One of the reasons I said my piece was that I was going to be away. Yorkshire were slipping down the league and were out of the B&H and NatWest. For a county like Yorkshire, that's nonsense. It was hacking me and a lot of other players off. As a senior player, it's my duty to say what everyone else is thinking. I know most haven't got the balls to speak out, they're frightened of the consequences and any possible recriminations that might follow. The batting order changed from that day, and the one-day performances improved. The best way to describe it is that Byas and I have a good working relationship. We look at the game in different ways but there is a mutual respect. He's been the Yorkshire captain for a number of years and I've been the Yorkshire 'star' on the bigger stage for most of that time. Byas wants Yorkshire to be successful, always going for the win rather than a draw. Mind you, I would, too, with our bowling attack of Gough, White, Silverwood, Hutchinson, Hoggard, Sidebottom and Hamilton.

The England dressing-room had changed dramatically in the few days since Lord's. Giles, Thorpe, Solanki, Maynard, Croft, Trescothick and Ealham were part of the one-day squad. It was weird. They had merely been excited onlookers at events at Lord's. When I came into Lord's eight days later for the West Indies one-day clash, I found Matthew Maynard changing in my spot. There was no fuss, and we shared. No one was trying to pull rank or claim one team or one player was more important or more established than another. Players do get funny about their favourite spot. Maybe that's where they went on their debut and when they did well. Maybe it's a spot they don't want because of a bad performance. That's the way cricketers are. I've changed in the same place at Headingley for seven years. Players change there when I'm not playing but, as soon as I'm back, it's mine again and is left vacant by the others.

The batting discipline of Lord's was missing at the Oval. Marcus Trescothick came in and helped us to a great start with Hickie. England were 136–1. A final total of 207 was ridiculous after that. The problems of the 1999 World Cup reappeared as we struggled to set a target . . . or to know what a reasonable target was. We lost wickets in spurts and lost our way completely. Trescothick's introduction was a big bonus, especially for Fletch. The Somerset left-hander was not a member of the original squad, but he was promoted when Knight got injured. Marcus had been in Fletch's thoughts for a while. He'd been asking us about him and had brought him to our training camps. Fletch rarely praises players, but here was someone he obviously rated, and Tresco's taken to international cricket like a duck to water – if that's not the wrong analogy for a batsman. This was Trescothick's first chance.

For Matthew Maynard, this NatWest series was probably his last. The Glamorgan captain had made his England debut 12 years earlier at the Oval and had a deserved reputation as a devastating one-day batsman, but his England career in both types of the game has been stop-start. Mattie had impressed Fletch when the pair took Glamorgan to the 1997 county championship, and our coach felt it was not too late for Maynard to make a contribution at the highest level. Driving to London with Chalky, we both said how pleased we were that Maynard had been picked. He's such a consistent run-scorer for Glamorgan, but once again he failed to do himself justice. His shot at the Oval showed his turmoil and, after another poor knock at Lord's, he never got another chance after that. Mattie had worked hard to get back but failed to take his chance.

After our five-wicket defeat, Fletch told me he wasn't going to show his frustration. I knew what he meant. Starting with the World Cup, through the winter one-day series and now this England trip, I was determined not to lose to Zimbabwe. After our poor batting, a couple of catches went down off me. I was ready to blow off steam but held myself in check. After the euphoria of Lord's had gone, the hunt was on for a scapegoat. Such a big cock-up required an equally big sacrifice, and the media homed in on Freddie Flintoff, who had drilled his second ball straight down long-off's throat. He came into the dressing-room shaking his head. He'd meant to drive the ball down the ground, but he's such a powerful hitter that the ball flew off the bat. In a couple of days, Freddie was reeling.

The media got stuck in, big time. The next (latest) Ian Botham had been transformed into a Fat Slogger who couldn't play. Freddie was in shock and wasn't happy with the support he got from certain people as details of his weight movements were provided for general consumption. He was well hacked off. That was obvious as he smacked the Zimbabwe bowlers all over Old Trafford, then declared: 'Not bad for a fat lad.' After South Africa, I knew only too well what he was going through. Freddie's not fat; he's a big bloke who's ultra-talented. He can be lazy and needs a kick up the backside at times. But he's a great bloke and England don't have so many good cricketers that we can afford to lose him. He was affected by all the fuss; suddenly, people you've never met are telling you how to run your life. I felt for him and chatted to him about it.

His agent Chubby Chandler, England and Lancashire all want the best for the lad, but often their advice is different. Who does he believe? Now he's probably got to decide whether to quit as a bowler and concentrate fully on his batting because of his back problems. Freddie's been confused about what people want from him. In Pakistan he was beginning to realize that it's what he wants for himself that's important. His inclination there was to hang up his bowling boots because he was in agony with his back. The advice to take a month's rest and have a couple of injections wasn't working. Take a year off. I'd have him as a batter. As well as that Old Trafford knock, Freddie played two great innings last year, smashing Saqlain Mushtaq on both occasions. Once for Lancashire, as Surrey were dumped out of the NatWest at the Oval, and then for England in Karachi as we chased over 300 runs. That Lancashire effort was televised and was probably what got him on the winter tour.

Freddie's Old Trafford onslaught gave us our first win of the triangular after a bad weekend in London. Only rain saved us from another defeat at Lord's the day after the Oval game, when the

West Indies bowlers took advantage of the overcast conditions. All during the triangular, the worry was that we would let the Windies back into the Test series. At Lord's, we were rolled over on a juicy wicket. Fletch's response was a hard workout and middle practice in Manchester. It worked. After the Zimbabwe win, England defeated the West Indies by ten wickets at Durham as Trescothick's remarkable run continued. That was England's first victory by that margin in 314 one-day matches. I remember the weekend for another reason: the seven-hour drive from Manchester to Durham after an accident closed the A1. I would have missed it if I hadn't stopped off to see Wayne (Morton). I nearly blew up my engine, leaving the car's automatic gear-box in drive, with my foot on the brake, for over an hour; all these lights started flashing. Just as well we weren't moving, because I had to turn the engine off for it to cool down. Most of the England team were stuck somewhere in the huge jam. When I dropped my kit off at Chester-le-Street, I saw that Newcastle United were training and went to watch. I knew Gary Speed from his Leeds United days, and Mick Wadsworth, who was one of my first football coaches, was assistant there. My day was made when Bobby Robson came over and said, 'Is that Goughie?' I was wearing a floppy hat and was astonished he recognized me.

Bobby was there next day for the match, and so were Peter Beardsley and Sunderland's Peter Reid, and full credit to Durham for the way they organized their first-ever international encounter. Even my dad wrote and thanked them for the way they looked after the families. It was also Liam's first England international. I hope to play Test cricket there before I retire. Just as importantly, it was a belting wicket. I've been before and they've been shocking. I removed Wavell Hinds second ball, and the Windies never got going. It was clear to me that Lord's had had a devastating effect on them. Increasingly throughout the triangular, I felt England getting stronger, while the Windies were struggling for some sort of stability.

After the Durham weekend, even with two matches remaining, Jimmy Adams's side could not qualify. I had been torn between pressing home our domination over the West Indies in the final and giving Zimbabwe another cricket lesson. I was asked at the management meeting if I wanted to take a rest before Lord's to give

Paul Franks a game. 'No way,' was my two-word response. 'If you think Franks deserves a chance and you want to drop me, go ahead. That's out of my hands. I ain't resting.' I was feeling tired and a bit jaded, but I will never, ever, miss an England game out of choice. I said, 'Nas, why do you rest?' Our skipper had been sidelined for the first half of the triangular with his finger injury. 'It's an international game. If you weren't that bothered about it, you'd have gone back to Essex and got in some four-day cricket before the Test.' I wasn't going to draw him pictures, but Nasser had been woefully short of runs all season. 'But you hung around because you didn't want to miss any games if you could. I'm the same. If you ask me, I'm playing.' So they asked Caddie. He said, 'Okay, give Franks a game.' I think that's wrong. The player shouldn't be asked.

I remember when we took on Sri Lanka in the Emirates final, two years earlier. That was when the Lancie lads started. 'You Yorkies won't know this, but this is what it's like to play in a final.' And afterwards, when we beat Zimbabwe, the knowledgeable Red Rose told us all to shut our coffins. 'Well, you won't have been through this before, but champagne can make a real mess of your kit. That comes from playing for Lancashire.' We took no chances with Zimbabwe.

I'd played in a South African final, a Carlton United final in Australia and that Emirates final. A three-time loser. And there have been no Yorkshire finals. For a player whose natural game is the one-day bash, that's a big disappointment. Zimbabwe never recovered from the opening Gough over, when I sent Guy Whittall and Murray Goodwin packing. A total of 169–7 was way short of making the final a contest. That didn't bother me as Stewie capped an amazing week with a match-winning 97. That was actually something of a failure because, after his undefeated 74 at Durham, our wicket-keeping all-rounder had hit centuries at Edgbaston and Trent Bridge. Having skippered England in the first matches and taken a world-record-equalling six catches at Old Trafford, Stewie fully deserved his Man of the Series accolade. I was a Lord's one-day-final winner at last. What a relief. I had been beginning to wonder if my career might have a few unwelcome gaps. That was one plugged at least. Now back to the Test series.

28. Only Bowls for England

Stewie's sense of occasion was never better demonstrated than at Old Trafford. The break in the West Indies series worked to our advantage. We continued to dominate and won the triangular. Including the Zimbabwe series, we'd played four Tests on the trot. The summer of 2001 was better scheduled, with the shorter Test series, the triangular and then the main event, the Ashes. A month away from first-class cricket was probably a week too long, but I've learnt to take my breaks when I can. I'm always amused by the cricket fans who think one-day cricket is the easier form. 'Well, Goughie, you only have to bowl ten overs and probably not bat!' It rarely works out like that. Few days on the Test field are as draining physically and mentally as the limited-overs contest. Try playing three one-dayers on the bounce and you'll find out. Ten overs of that can be tougher than 20 overs of the Test variety. Batsmen are looking to slog you from the start; you're trying yorkers, slower balls, the full repertoire, and you can't bowl bouncers and float one up on a good length. You've got to hit the deck every time. On top of that, you're throwing yourself around in the field and concentrating one hundred per cent the whole time. No wandering down to third man and switching off.

Thorpey came back for Ramps after his winter off. I was staggered by the fuss his decision caused. Professional sportsman puts his family first, shock-horror. He made himself available for the one-dayers at the end of the South Africa tour, but he had to serve his punishment. We could have done with him. I backed Thorpey totally: he had had enough and wanted to spend time with his family. I was envious of him being at home. Yet he got slaughtered. I felt it was a sound, long-term career move, so did Thorpey. Anyone who watched him in Pakistan in the winter of 2000/1 would have to agree. I didn't notice too many complaints when he edged those winning runs in Karachi. Not that Old Trafford was a memorable Test return for him, other than inspiring Courtney to deliver one of the finest slower balls I've ever seen.

We stayed at the Marriott at Wormsley Park for the Old Trafford Test. It's in the middle of nowhere. We tend to hang out at the wine bar down the road. I had a couple of games of golf, which I enjoy before a Test, and I always use a buggy the day before the match. Stewie didn't play golf, so it was banned when he was captain. Over the years my lifestyle has certainly changed during Tests; I'm getting older and, maybe, wiser and more mature. I'm reasonably happy spending a night in now. In my younger days I was usually out. I definitely could not have spent a night in or gone down to the hotel restaurant for a meal and a pint in the bar. Anything less than three or four pints in those days was socially unacceptable. That's no longer the case. The reasons for that are twofold. First, as I've said, I'm older. Secondly, I approach my cricket, as most do these days, in a much more professional manner. There's probably a third reason: it gets harder. I lived on the adrenalin rush when I first appeared for England. That carried me along. However, it tends to lessen as opponents become familiar with my bowling. I suppose it's a bit like a marriage. There's a honeymoon period, then you get down to the reality of the situation and get the stars out of your eyes.

Now I'm one of the senior citizens and old pros. Every new generation thinks they are the wild ones. We all go through the same process. At the start, living it up means McDonald's one night, KFC the next and pizza the one after. A couple of years ago at Yorkshire, the only way I could have a decent meal was to eat on my own because the youngsters would rather have fast food so they could get back to the bar for a few pints or save on expenses. These days, Yorkshire are a more professional outfit. Anna used to watch me a fair bit but, with two kids at school, it's difficult. My mum and dad helped out a lot, but they both work. Hopefully, our move south earlier in 2001 to be near her family will make life easier for her.

No one in the England camp was deluding himself: we had been lucky at Lord's. England showed guts and determination, but the

Windies had sown the seeds of their own destruction. We could so easily have been 2–0 down. This was going to be a result series. The tourists had two of the most prolific Test wicket-takers in the history of the game. We'd seen already that the West Indies' batting was fragile, especially if Lara was not making runs. The spinners normally appear at Old Trafford; it's the nearest we get to Asia in this country. The square has got rather tired in recent years, but I'm a great fan of the groundsman, Peter Marron; he's the first to hold his hand up when he gets it wrong. Usually, Peter gets it right. Bat well, you score well. Bowl well, and you'll get wickets. But you have to put in the effort. I may be the enemy, but I've always felt welcome at Old Trafford in an England shirt. It's only with Yorkshire that my friend in the crowd pipes up as I go out to bat, 'Leave gate open, he won't be long.' I think I found it mildly amusing the first time.

Stewie and Athers were both making their hundredth Test appearance. Both must have wondered over the years whether they'd get that far. Lord MacLaurin made a special presentation before the delayed start. Despite the overcast conditions, Jimmy Adams decided to bat. It was a mistake. The tourists were all out for 157. I took two of the first three wickets to fall, but Corkie, as he did in his debut season, showed a liking for Old Trafford and finished with 4–23. At 17–3, we were in some trouble, especially as the ground was in stitches as Courtney's slower ball – all of 64 m.p.h. – left Thorpey ducking, groping and bewildered as the ball landed on his toes. It was his first ball in Test cricket after almost a year. He had an ice-pack on his foot for the rest of the day. We all tried to keep a straight face, but couldn't. It was hilarious to watch, and Thorpey eventually saw the funny side too, even though it was his third duck in a row at Old Trafford.

The rest of the day belonged to Stewie, who carved out a wonderful century, and all on the Queen Mum's birthday. Typical Stewie. I don't think I've seen him bat better, especially in a tight situation. I've never heard or seen a finer standing ovation. If the Manchester faithful couldn't celebrate an Athers hundred, his fellow centurion was the next best thing. Stewie's a tough competitor, but I suspect – only suspect, mind you – that's his most emotional moment on a cricket field. The Oval crowd were only too happy to reciprocate when Athers manufactured a different sort of century in the final Test, but it didn't match that Manchester moment. Stewie has the knack of getting the big knock on the Saturday, or on the big occasion, or when the Queen or Prime Minister is there, or when the ground is full. He needs an audience and rarely lets them down. Just as admirable was Trescothick's debut knock which kept Stewie company for much of Friday.

The Saturday was dull. England built up a lead of 146, and then the Windies dug in. Sunday was Lara's day. Just when we were beginning to wonder if the little master had lost it, England experienced a genius at work first hand. The lads had a go at him when we thought he'd nicked one to Stewie. The next ball he came down the wicket and smashed a straight six. And he was away. The Test might have taken a different direction if Lara hadn't gone for a crazy run and been brilliantly run out by Nasser. Our skipper had already taken a magnificent catch to dispatch Curtly on Friday. The runs might not be flowing, but Nasser in the field was still an awesome influence. I don't mind a captain who rollocks us for mistakes in the field when he sets such high standards himself.

The Windies batted on, a sign that they were still trying to regroup after Lord's. Actually, I felt they had the upper hand and should have been more positive. I was getting pretty bored as the Windies ploughed on, so, as I ran in to bowl to Ridley Jacobs, I just stared straight ahead and stuck my tongue out, Maori-style. It's something Warnie had done to me. Jacobs played and missed, obviously wondering what I was up to. Just messing about. Boring as the later stages were, we could have done without the countless streakers at Old Trafford. I don't know why we don't employ the tactics used by the S.C.G. If my memory serves me right, there's a guaranteed A$5,000 fine for coming on to the playing surface. That's stopped the practice.

The bookies made the Windies ever so slight favourites for the series, yet the media were on our side. I wasn't so sure: Lara had fired once and was still capable of destroying us. I always feel the

Windies fancy their chances at the Oval. I was convinced that Headingley was the key to England's hopes. Traditionally, the conditions and the pitch suit us. It's a result wicket but, whatever happened in Leeds, this final Cornhill series would now go to the wire.

Headingley was just . . . incredible. After the first day's play, both teams would rather have been in the other one's shoes. The Windies had been bowled out for 172. England were 105–5. The upper hand would go to the team that had the better of Friday's first session. The England dressing-room was tense that morning. The general feeling was that this Test, and probably the series, could be won or lost by a single, simple mistake. A few hours later, that same dressing-room saw the scenes of jubilation that were denied by the TV cameras after the South Africa victory, two years earlier. England's cricket team were making history: the first time anyone had won a Test in two days for 54 years. Now Jimmy Adams's side had to win at the Oval to deny us a first series victory over the West Indies for 31 years.

Hickie was back for Headingley, but found himself at No. 7. I can't imagine that many batsmen with a hundred hundreds have batted that low. With Trescothick taking over from Ramps at Old Trafford, Hickie had been the man who made way for Thorpey. With our four-man attack firing well and spin playing little part, and Nasser still struggling, England could afford and felt better protected with seven batsmen. The word was that Hickie, none too happy to get a late 'Sorry, you're not playing' at Manchester, was not exactly overjoyed to find his way back was so far down the order. I'm sorry, I don't know why batsmen get so precious about these matters. It's a simple question: 'Do you want to play or not?' I felt Ramps got too upset and obsessed when he was put at No. 6. It doesn't help when people get in your ear, saying you're too good to be batting that low, you're better than him. It's about getting on with the job and making a place your own. Instead, Ramps tried to find a way back, opening with Athers. Now he has a hard job to get back into the England team. As it happened, the extra batsmen strategy was a key factor in winning at Headingley.

Not that it really mattered where you batted at Headingley in this match. Jimmy Adams won the toss and batted, I'm sure not with any great conviction. We felt he didn't want to bat last. Well, he got that wrong as well. The first day belonged to two bowlers, one from Yorkshire and the other from Antigua. The Windies had reached 50–1 and Adams's decision was beginning to worry us, when Craig White took three wickets in 16 deliveries, including trapping Lara l.b.w. with one that nipped back with the left-hander's arms aloft in surrender. I took my second when Griffith had a huge swing. The tourists were 60–5. Sarwan and Jacobs more than doubled the score in 15 overs, although I thought Sarwan had been caught behind off me on eight.

The Windies never went on the defensive. Sarwan ran out of partners, while Craig took his first five-for in Test cricket. As Craig admitted afterwards, only a few weeks earlier, he'd been wondering whether his cricket career was over after his collapse. How good was the Windies' 172? Very good, when Ambrose reached 400 Test wickets by removing both our openers, to leave England 10–2. Not so good, when Nasser and Thorpey took us to 80 without further mishap. The West Indies were back as favourites when they grabbed three late wickets. Caddie went in as night watchman and we closed at 105–5. Nasser made only 22, but it was probably his best knock of the year. His broken thumb was obviously still bothering him, but our skipper gutsed it out as best he could.

Friday at Lord's or Friday at Leeds. Both were remarkable, but I'd go for Leeds. England were on top for the whole of a remarkable day, and there was no unfinished business by the close. We had the luck of the weather. Batting is a much simpler process when the sun shines in Leeds. Vaughanie and Hickie made full use of the easier conditions and the sloppiest West Indies bowling and fielding performance I have ever seen. The ball was sprayed everywhere by some bowlers, sitters were dropped, misfields were followed by overthrows . . . it was dreadful. I hope England at our worst have never been that bad. The Windies had lost any stomach for the fight and it was reflected in the careless, cavalier manner in which the tourists batted for a second time, exactly 100 runs adrift. The key to our success was Vaughanie and Hickie's 98-run seventh-wicket stand. With Caddie as night watchman, Hickie actually came in at No. 8. The pair were partly responsible for the Windies' problems in the field, pressuring them, pushing for quick singles and generally exposing the tourists' lack of fight. Vaughanie continued the good work in a 45-run partnership with Corkie. I hardly troubled the scorers, but I was already thinking about getting the new ball in my hands.

I've often been accused of getting too pumped up on my home ground and too carried away in front of my own supporters. On this occasion I tried to have a few moments to myself in the dressing-room. Not that I didn't want to be high. I did. I had to make sure that all the adrenalin was pumping in the right direction. There are some days when you know that, no matter who is up the other end, you can do anything with the ball. It was ten minutes to three when I ran in to bowl my first delivery to Griffith. It was full, swung in late and removed his off-stump as he tried to attack. It was a hell of a delivery, but he should not have been trying to play that sort of shot. The Windies were 3–1. Hinds received a similar delivery for his first ball and didn't get forward, and umpire Doug Cowie had no hesitation in raising his finger – 3–2. Lara did well to keep out my hat-trick ball, but he was gone a few minutes later when he wandered across his stumps and shouldered arms again – 11–3. I set him up perfectly. I went wide of the crease so he was expecting the ball to swing away. It didn't. I got my fourth wicket when Hickie picked up a great two-handed catch to his right at second slip off Sherwin Campbell – 21–4, and we hadn't taken tea yet.

During the break, we chatted about finishing it off today. The Windies had 'gone'. The tourists were there for the taking. Trying to smash their way out of trouble was little more than a gesture. I felt great and was looking for a big haul, the biggest of my Test career. I didn't get another wicket. No matter. Corkie got Adams to drag the ball on for the second time in the match – 49–5 – before Caddie decided to grab a share of the action in an incredible over. Jacobs went first ball, l.b.w. – 52–6. Two balls later, Nixon

McLean's off-stump was removed and Ambrose's went the next delivery. King survived a dot ball, a no-ball, then his off-stump was knocked back – 53–9. When the over had started, I was thinking about taking seven or eight wickets. Now there was only one wicket left, and I needed that for my five-for. I didn't get it. Caddie bowled Walsh for his, and I was left with 4–30.

Caddie had sneaked in again. This time he was not crowing, having learnt his lesson at Lord's. In that diplomatic way of his, Caddie had often told me that, if he couldn't get a five-for, I wasn't getting one either. That might sound a strange thing to say. It's just Caddie; he doesn't mean anything by it. We think he is trying to be funny; he is not. Of course, there is an element of competition between us. That's great. That's healthy. There are just times when Caddie opens his mouth without engaging his brain. I turned up for the second morning of the Lord's Test with four wickets and one West Indies wicket left to fall. Caddie got his first of the match with the first of the day. He just laughed when he saw me. It meant that Caddie had stopped me getting another five-for. He carried on that theme as the lads were getting padded up. I think he was probably relieved at finally getting a wicket after a couple of bad Tests. Only really close mates can take the mick out of each other like that. Caddie and I do not have that sort of relationship. The dressing-room went quiet and I told him what a twat he was. He realized then that he had stepped over the mark. The management called him outside and had a word with him. Later he apologized. Later he went out, took five wickets and got on the Lord's honours board. Maybe he will shut up now he's on that. It only bothered me at the time. Caddie's harmless. He tries so hard to be involved, but sometimes he just puts his foot in it. He knew not to gloat after another of his five-fors had left me stranded on four again at Headingley. I am not as concerned about five-fors as Caddie. All I want is my name on that Lord's board!

The Windies had been dismissed in less than 27 overs. We were all rather bemused because events had moved so quickly, quicker than I've ever known on a cricket field. Craig, bowling hero of Thursday, had not even got on this time. Man of the Match –

Michael Vaughan. I told you it was a batters' game. Only joking.
No complaints from me. Michael's had a torrid time with injuries,
but he played his part in us beating the Windies. Our summer
might have turned out differently but for two crucial partnerships:
Atherton/Vaughan at Lord's and Vaughan/Hick at Leeds. This
time I felt well enough to partake of the champagne as we celebrated
on the balcony. Those celebrations carried on into the night, and
several of us turned up at Headingley the next morning for the
Channel 4 Roadshow rather the worse for wear.

We could not lose the series now. But nobody wanted to go to
the Oval in a defensive mood, trying to hang on to what we had.
Those tactics usually backfire. Anyway, we had shown ourselves
more determined, committed, tougher and together than the
Windies. I would never write off a side that contained three
world-class players like Lara, Walsh and Ambrose; that would be
more than foolish. But that Headingley performance suggested to
me that Adams's team were never going to come to terms with
throwing away the series at Lord's.

Not that everyone was made ecstatic by England's new-found
cricketing success. Old ways die hard. The new central contracts
scheme could not have made a better start in 2000. But our absence
from the county scene was too big a price to pay for some. That
was the downside to our new England commitment. There has
always been resentment on the county circuit for those who play
for England. A few clever-clogs thought it was funny to award
Darren Gough the OBE: that's 'Only Bowls for England'. Those
sort of remarks had gone the rounds, even before central contracts.
My view has been that what I achieve for England brings credit to
Yorkshire. Surely spectators must be proud that a Yorkshire fast
bowler, born and bred, has led the England attack for several years.
I still hear the odd 'But he never plays for Yorkshire.' I have even
received poison-pen letters calling for me to be sacked. One even
arrived on the final morning of the Oval Test. There was no name
or address; what a surprise!

I play when I can and when I'm allowed to. Me in person, my
name, my picture are always a prominent part of any Yorkshire

marketing campaigns. I'm always there on the open days for the youngsters. When they're asked who's their favourite cricketer, it is usually 'Darren Gough.' I get very angry when it's claimed I don't care about Yorkshire or my county career. How many England players would represent their county academy as I did in the summer of 2000? How many youngsters, not only in Yorkshire, have taken up cricket because they want to be Darren Gough? That's not being big-headed. Why has the club got so many young seamers? The crowd don't often get on my back. Most of the abusive and offensive remarks are passed on to me by team-mates. Occasionally I bite back when a voice comes from the terraces. 'Pitch it up, Gough!' usually gets a thoughtful and profound: 'Shut up. Who are you supporting?' Yorkshire people are plain and simple folk. They like their language the same way. They are like me: proud. Sometimes their mouths open without engaging the brain. Often I've heard that I don't want to play for Yorkshire, I don't try for Yorkshire, I only want to play for England, I only bowl fast when I bowl for England. I've heard some belters. The only answer I've got is to give one hundred per cent on the field. I realize deep down that over 90 per cent of the fans support me and are proud of what I've achieved for Yorkshire and for England.

There was more fun and games during the National League Roses Match on our patch before the Test. The central contracts issue had led to plenty of argument concerning the unavailability and resting of England players. For a scheme that was primarily devised to help look after us hard-working bowlers, the batsmen seemed to be the ones who rarely missed an opportunity to put their feet up. Athers had told the Lancie lads that I'd probably be missing from this clash. I wasn't, but he was. Freddie told me England's opening bat had gone fishing. 'No, he has not. Athers is in the south of France at St Tropez.' They didn't believe me. Athers wasn't happy, either, that I'd let his secret out of the bag. There was more general county unrest when it was decided that we would be sitting out the remaining fortnight of the season at the end of the West Indies series. Fletcher wanted us to rest before heading for the I.C.C. Trophy in Nairobi at the end of September. Many counties had consoled themselves with the prospect of getting their stars back for the final couple of championship games. The increasing international schedule put an end to that.

English cricket's money problems still continued, even when we started winning. Our success had come so quickly at Leeds, it cost the E.C.B. money. Three Tests against the Windies had finished early, and the other had been disrupted by the weather. The Zimbabwe series had not been well attended. A loss of £4 million was mentioned. On top of that, we had not heard who was replacing Test sponsor Cornhill. The early finishes were not what Channel 4 or its advertisers wanted, either. It didn't matter to us, as long as we won. There was a £215,000 bonus from team sponsors Vodafone if England took this series. The E.C.B. must have been pleased, though, with our form. The first four days of the Oval Test were sold out.

Traditionally, an England spinner appears at the Oval. Several times in the 1990s that spinner was Phil Tufnell, who put in match-winning displays against the West Indies (1991) and Australia (1997). He was edged out by Ashley Giles this time, although I never imagined he would play. I did not see how England could do anything but walk out with the same 11 players who had triumphed at Headingley. Yorkshire had had no game before the Leeds Test, or before the Oval. What I did find strange in the domestic schedule was the lack of full county programmes between Tests. My last first-class game for Yorkshire had been way back at the start of June. I certainly felt fresh but couldn't really say whether I was fresher than normal. Appearing at the Oval was going to mean that, for the first time in my England career, Darren Gough would have played a full international summer.

All the England squad were in unfamiliar territory. The last time England turned up for the final Test of a home series ahead was way back in 1985 against Australia. Such was England's confident mood that the winter tour squad was announced before this final Test. There were no surprises: Ian Salisbury joined Giles in the spinning department, Paul Nixon was Stewie's understudy, Hoggard the support fast bowler, and Flintoff was brought back. The selection was of only passing interest, with the Oval three days away.

Forgetting the drama of Lord's and Leeds, for sheer sentimental emotion I've never experienced anything like the Oval in 2000. The match was a personal triumph for Athers. Without his dogged determination, England might have struggled. The Oval crowd tried to match the Old Trafford ovation given to Stewie when Athers reached his second-innings century; it came close, but not quite. In one of those great sporting ironies, Ambrose's distinguished career came to an end when Athers took a catch in the slips. After all that had gone on between them over a decade, Athers was pleased to have the final word. Only winning the Ashes will compare with the moment when England took the series on a day when thousands were locked outside on the Monday. But the Oval's goodbye to Courtney Walsh and Curtly Ambrose, the bowlers, on Sunday came very close. It was difficult to prevent the tears welling up as the pair, arm in arm, walked off and said their goodbyes to a packed Oval that was on its feet in appreciation. Whatever problems cricket may have had in 2000 – and there were plenty – there can't be too much wrong with a game which gives two fearsome adversaries such a genuine emotional farewell.

This Test was unique in the summer of 2000: it lasted five days and the weather was good. From the moment Adams asked England to bat, we took control and never let go. Athers and Trescothick put on 159 for the first wicket. If a final total of 281 was a disappointment after that, then the England bowlers – for the third time in the series – took the game to the Windies and found them wanting. Once again Craig White stole the show with another five-wicket haul. The pick of them was the round-the-wicket delivery that bowled Lara round his legs, first ball. Our fielding and catching had been superior to the tourists' all summer. The half-chances were sticking. We knew on the Saturday, when the Windies were bowled out for 125, that we could not slip up now. Athers's 15th century comprised half our second-innings total. More crucially, it helped set the West Indies a target of 374 to win. I never thought for a second the tourists would get close. By Sunday night, the Windies' openers had reduced that target by 33 runs.

Tickets were only £10 for the final day, with schoolkids charged £5. The gates were closed at 11.30 a.m. Apparently, 5,000 were still outside, unable to join the capacity 18,500 inside. Even the empty hospitality boxes were used as an overflow. The initial exchanges were not without the odd moment of frustration. I could not believe it when Hickie dropped a straightforward chance when I got Campbell to nick one. Hickie looked distraught. Was it a bad omen? Any discussions on that matter ended with the next ball, when Campbell chose Hickie for more catching practice. This time, it stuck. Mind you, he grounded another chance when I found the end of Hinds's bat. Any last lingering West Indies hopes ended when I removed Lara for the fifth time in the series. I was pleased to get him out in every Test. Caddie got stuck in, and Corkie, as he has a habit of doing, wrapped up the tail. The final wicket to fall was that of Walsh, undone by Corkie's slower ball. Victory by 158 runs and our fifth win in eight Tests. The celebrations began. It was only later in the highlights that I saw Nasser sink to his knees in the moment of victory. That's the strain our England captain was under.

If there was a setback in this triumph, it was the way our skipper's miserable year with the bat continued. I remember Nasser coming up to me at the Oval after his pair: 'What do you think I should do?' I didn't know what he was on about. 'The captaincy and that. What do you think?'

'What do I think! For Christ's sake, Nas. Don't be so stupid. You're the best captain we've had for ages. We're winning. I think you should carry on, you dozy twat.' I told him straight as that. That's why, when I was interviewed after being named England's Man of the Series, I mentioned Nasser's captaincy. I wasn't brown-nosing or being diplomatic. His captaincy was a major factor in our success that summer, and he led from the front without the benefit of runs or being in form. That took some doing. He was pretty down. That's the first time I've ever seen Nasser emotional and unsure of what to do. Nasser averaged 40 in Test cricket, then he becomes captain. In his first full calendar year in the job, scoring over 200 runs at an average of less than 15, you have to wonder whether the job is part of the reason. His injury didn't help and, outside international cricket, Nasser had few opportunities to recapture his form. I think his worst moment of the whole summer came when the *Sun* published a baby picture of him as he was in 1969 when England last beat the West Indies. Nasser had perked up by the time our skipper went out to collect the Wisden Trophy: the first Englishman to get his hands on the trophy since Ray Illingworth, 31 years earlier. More significantly, Nasser was being cheered to the rafters on the very spot where a year earlier he'd been booed off the park.

I felt sorry for Curtly and Courtney, who'd both been given guards of honour by us as they came to the wicket on their final appearance. The pair had bowled their hearts out. But, Lara at Old Trafford apart, they battled alone. Adams was in a Catch 22 situation, caught between bowling them in tandem or splitting them up. There was no support, with bat or ball. We did bowl well – Caddick and I jointly opened the attack the entire series, the first time that had happened since Trueman and Statham (the latter sadly died during the summer) in 1960, and we took 47 wickets to Walsh/Ambrose's 51 – but the Windies batsmen showed no appetite for a fight and very little technique. One big plus was that Chanderpaul did not play after Lord's because of that problem with his forearm. He was badly missed. Campbell never got going after Lord's. Hinds has talent but he tried to hit every ball for four. Lara was out of sorts, but we also bowled well to him. Old Trafford showed his brilliance. But that spirit and flair were in short supply. The West Indies' nightmare continued in Australia.

29. Charge of the Light Brigade

Would England actually make its first tour of Pakistan for 13 years? Would Wasim Akram, named and shamed in Pakistan's match-fixing report, be banned before the Test series? There was plenty of discussion on both topics for most of the English summer in 2000. I never doubted we would go, and I never doubted that Wasim Akram would be a member of the opposition. Our tour was a goodwill mission to repair the damage caused by various squabbles over umpires and ball-tampering that had afflicted recent England–Pakistan series.

Before we flew to Karachi, England joined the challenge for the I.C.C. Trophy in Nairobi. We prepared for this straight knock-out with a friendly against Australia, if there can be such a thing. The media speculated about Nasser dropping down to No. 6 after his poor summer. I gave that idea the same consideration as the two questions above. It is claimed that you can get statistics to prove anything. You would have struggled with Nasser's to prove anything other than a horror trot. A total of 166 runs in ten first-class matches during the summer at an average of just over 11. Nasser had opened in the World Cup, but the emergence of Marcus Trescothick and his successful opening partnership with Stewie left no vacancy there. We should have beaten Australia but lost wickets to the last two balls with the scores level at 236.

Our participation in the I.C.C. Challenge lasted as long as the form book predicted. We disposed comfortably of Bangladesh, who had just joined the Test-playing circuit. South Africa removed us with similar ease. The Nairobi Gymkhana Club ground is another place for batsmen: the wicket is good and the boundaries are short. The Bangladesh total of 232 looked well short, especially when Hasibul Hossain's opening over produced six no-balls and 17 runs. We eased home by eight wickets, with more than six overs to spare. Nasser batted beautifully, falling five short of his century. Our captain had answered his critics in the only way he knows.

Shaun Pollock was South Africa's new captain in place of the disgraced Cronje. I can't explain our poor showing. This was a real chance for us to show off to the rest of the cricket world at close quarters our summer improvement. We went into the South Africa game ready for a real scrap. We never got started. The South Africa bowlers took control and did not let go. We got a Nasser rollocking as only he can give them after our defeat by South Africa. 'We were outplayed. If you can't do the basics, you are going to lose. We didn't even come second,' was the skipper's verdict on our eight-wicket defeat. Our total of 182 was woefully short; we even failed to use up six of our overs. Pollock's team did not need even 40 overs to get past us. It was still a memorable day for my old mate, P.G., who had flown out as cover for the injured Ashley Giles. P.G. had a Gavin Hamilton sort of debut – a duck and no wickets. At least, he's an England player now. One small consolation: we lasted longer than the Aussies. They went out at the hands of India, who then beat South Africa before losing to New Zealand in the final.

We decided to stay and practise in Nairobi rather than fly, a few days early, to Pakistan. Two months there would be long enough. Pakistan is a tough tour. The hotels are fine and the people are very friendly. The big drawback is that there is not a lot to do. If we were not at the cricket ground or in our hotels, it is a safe bet we would be at one of the British Embassy clubs, enjoying some English grub and beer. The absence of alcohol in the hotels does affect you. Not that we are winos, but hotel bars are great meeting-places for the lads, and meals tend to take half the time without the odd glass of wine. Play generally ends a lot earlier than back home. The light goes at around five o'clock, as we discovered in Karachi! Back at our hotel by six, there's a lot of time to kill. If you are having a tough time on the field, you are left with a lot of thinking time.

We had little time to draw breath during the one-day day/night series. The bowlers took a real hammering in Karachi's National

Stadium. The Yorkshire pacemen, Gough and White, went for 140 runs in 19 overs. That was certainly not part of the game-plan. The National Stadium was packed and the 30,000 spectators gave us a hard time as the ball disappeared to all parts. The noise was deafening. The atmosphere was about as intimidating as you can get. Fortunately, we had discussed that beforehand, as well as the dangers of losing the plot if we got distracted. The crowd thought they were home and dry when their heroes came off with 304—9 on the scoreboard. On only three occasions had a side made 300-plus to win. Now it was four. Despite losing both openers cheaply, despite the oppressive heat and the intimidating atmosphere, we 'walked it' with 16 balls and five wickets to spare. The result was never in doubt. Nasser and Hickie made the start, Thorpey and Freddie finished the job. The night was a personal triumph for Freddie. He was unable to bowl because of his back and knew he was going to be replaced by Alex Tudor at the end of the one-dayers. Freddie made his point with 84. His controlled power hitting included sixes off Wasim and Waqar. Nigel Stockdill, our physiologist, weighed us after our three hours in the field. Most of us had lost 2—3 kilos in the stifling heat.

That was the best of our one-day form. We had peaked too early. England made a hash of the other two games. We weren't helped when attacked by millions of flies in Lahore or by the insecticide, tear-gas and flying water-bottles in Rawalpindi. The simple truth was, we could not cope with the Pakistan spinners. I had to wear my dark glasses to protect myself from the flies, but I couldn't stop them getting up my nose and in my mouth. I tried to hold my breath for the entire run-up but couldn't do it. The timing of the final game in Rawalpindi was brought forward to prevent a repeat. The media tried to make the umpiring an issue — remember Gatt — but Nasser played it down, even though our skipper received a shocking l.b.w. in Rawalpindi that pitched about a foot outside leg stump. The glass door on our dressing-room fridge got the sharp end of Nasser's boot for that one. A new one was brought in the next day and all fridge doors were strengthened for the rest of the series. It was not the last time that Nasser was to make his way back to the dressing-room in Pakistan with a grievance.

Spin had reared its ugly head. We knew it would. The general consensus was that England would crumble under the spell of top-class spin again and that it was hardly worth us bothering to turn up. At Lahore, the trio of Saqlain, Mushtaq and Afridi had taken 8–108 in 30 overs in the one-day eight-wicket win. As our one-day specialists headed for home and the Test boys joined us, spin was no longer the main topic of discussion. Stewie was named in the Indian C.B.I. report on match-fixing and all hell broke loose. A bookie claimed he had paid Stewie £5,000 for team, pitch and weather information, adding that he had refused to fix further matches for him. Stewie's alleged 'crime' was the same as Warne's and Waugh's, which again showed the authorities' folly in linking the giving of information with match-fixing. Stewie was not alone. The bookie, Gupta, also named Lara, Mark Waugh, Martin Crowe, Aravinda de Silva, Arjuna Ranatunga, Asif Iqbal, Salim Malik and Cronje, as well as Azharuddin. Suddenly, there were lots of meetings behind closed doors, conference calls and press statements. Stewie denied all charges and saw no reason for coming home. Neither did we.

Ever since we had left England there had been much speculation about whether several Pakistan players should have been banned by the I.C.C. after the Pakistan Qayyum Report had fined them. Even Lord MacLaurin got into hot water, claiming England would have taken stronger action. Now Pakistan wanted the same treatment for Stewie. That was ridiculous. The Pakistan players had been fined by a judicial inquiry. Stewie was the object of unsubstantiated allegations from a bookie. There was no way that Indian report could have been published in England. By releasing several foreign names, India made sure everyone appreciated this was a worldwide rather than a sub-continental problem. Stewie's a tough sort, but this attack on his integrity hit him hard. I was astonished when it was reported that the anti-corruption unit would like to see his bank statements. Whatever happened to innocent before being proved guilty? If anyone speaks up against what the cricket authorities are doing, it looks like he might have something to hide. But there is a lot the players are not happy with. Fortunately, Stewie was sitting this latest tour game out when the story broke. However focused you like to pretend you are, it is impossible to shut something like this out of your thoughts. In the circumstances, I thought Stewie performed brilliantly during the rest of the tour.

We won the two warm-up games before the opening Test in Lahore. The opposition in these matches were not great and the wickets were green and juicy and absolutely nothing like the tracks we would see in the Test series. More fun and games in Pakistan. Those two wins actually doubled the number of first-class games won by England in six tours of Pakistan. Oggie bowled well against the Patron's XI, taking a career-best 9–102, while Craig White, who had not managed a single run in the one-day series for twice out, hit his first century for England.

The final warm-up game at Peshawar was my first first-class action since the Oval Test, two months earlier. I was still sharp enough to send Governor's XI opener Wasti back to the dressing-room with a broken hand the day after his wedding; he had been on my hit-list for a while. The lads had gone up the Khyber Pass earlier in the week, but I preferred to stay by the Peshawar pool, working on this book. Caddie tried to liven up a dull game on the third evening by starting another international incident with a Pakistan umpire. Caddie had claimed a regulation caught-behind, but Akhtar Sarfraz refused to go. Umpire Sajjad Asghar was in no hurry to send him on his way, either. Caddie lost it and had a word with both. It was a storm in a tea-cup, but any confrontation between an England cricketer and a Pakistan umpire was likely to grab the headlines. That's Caddie. Wrong toys out of wrong pram at the wrong time. Not the week before England's first Test in Pakistan for 13 years.

Caddie was obviously fired up. I felt in good nick after our eight-wicket win as we headed back to Lahore and the best hotel in Pakistan. I was really up for the Test series. A week later I was in deep depression, wondering how I would get through the final three weeks. Why I got so down, I don't know. Looking back, my reaction seems silly and extreme. I have been wicketless in Tests before. From the team's point of view, we had come out of the contest with great credit, especially as injuries kept Corkie and Vaughanie out of consideration for the whole series. Freddie was rushed back from England and dripping blood in his first net session when a ball hit him in the face. The selectors took a chance with Craig's hamstring, and we went in with two spinners.

Key man on the first morning was Nasser. He called correctly and England were still batting on the third day. Saqlain took all eight wickets to fall, but our opening stand, Thorpey's century and Craig's 93 gave us a great start. I thought I had, too, when one nipped back into Saeed Anwar – just what I needed. Well, it would have been if the Pakistan umpire had made any sort of a move. To be fair, apart from one or two schoolboy howlers, the umpiring in the series was good. The only problem for us fast bowlers was that any umpiring mistakes favoured the batsmen. This was definitely a 'not out' series. On those slow and dead pitches that made life doubly difficult. We almost got Pakistan to follow on. Once safely past that target, the Test fizzled out to a draw.

With so few distractions in Pakistan, how exactly do you spend your time? The days are tiring, I can tell you. I spent most of the early evenings in the hotel gym. Most of the lads were working there or in the pool. Our reserve wicket-keeper, Paul Nixon, is as strong as an ox. Hickie is fairly impressive, too. I have dipped in and out of fitness regimes in the past, but now I am a dedicated follower of lifestyle management. I see it as an important part of extending my England career, or at least coping with the current hectic international schedule.

There's been a big emphasis on fitness in the England set-up in the past few years. It started with Dean Riddle and carried on with Nigel Stockdill. I was brought up with Dean at Yorkshire. When this Kiwi came to cricket from the rugby league environment with Leeds and England, our lads didn't know what hit them. My brief Y.T.S. time at Rotherham had prepared me for the way soccer coaches snap at players, and I had watched Dean at Leeds. His style is very aggressive. He expects you to do what you are told, not start a discussion. Cricketers were used to being treated gently and Dean had a tough time at first, with never-ending arguments. Fitness and training were not seen as a high priority, whether at county or national level.

As soon as the England side focused on training, the traditionalists moaned that this time would be better spent in the nets. England has had to fight harder against the traditions of the gifted amateur than anywhere else in the world, not just at cricket. Take a typical session: roll up, run round the ground a couple of times, take a few catches, then wander back to the pavilion for bacon sandwiches. That wasn't quite Dean's style. I was lucky because I worked with him at Yorkshire and England. I've always been a moaner, but I do what I'm told. The moaning helps me get through it. Dean did a good job. Towards the end of his time, our fitness became better, and so did our fielding. It was almost as if we had to wait to see the benefit (i.e. better fielding) before his role was grudgingly accepted. That's the cricket culture we're always fighting against, I'm afraid.

Fitness and diet have been two of the biggest changes in the England set-up over the past few years. Fletch let it be known that if Nigel Stockdill wants us to do something, we have to comply. Fletch is big on fitness. After the Pakistan tour, the word went out that we had to be fitter and stronger than ever, before the trip to Sri Lanka. He was right; it was hot, steamy and hard work out there, even before all the nonsense started.

Dean eventually decided to move from cricket into soccer. I'm sure it was a good move, financially speaking. England have been lucky to replace him with Nigel, who's highly qualified. Nigel produced a paper and study on the injuries to fast bowlers. Lifestyle has certainly played a part in that. Cricket has traditionally been a game for bending your arm – well, in the bar anyway – and I appreciate the importance of the social side of the game. Professional rugby, too, has abandoned the beer-swilling image for those at the very top. The demands are greater.

I'd love to have shared a dressing-room with Denis Compton after he slept off a late night in his dinner jacket before going out to hit a century. That's then. This is now. To compete for an

England place, to compete on the world stage these days, there's a price to pay. One of the most talented Yorkshire players in the era before me was Graham Stevenson. But he enjoyed the social side as much as playing cricket, and he never fulfilled his potential. I never saw him play, but I was brought up on his phenomenal exploits off the field. I remember when Paul Jarvis had become an England player and one of his main challenges for the next season was to see if he could drink 1,000 pints. Every pint of lager was marked down and the target was reached by the end of July. I thought that was amazing, but nobody batted an eye. When I saw him last winter, he informed me the total had passed 1,500 by the end of the summer.

That was the sporting environment I came into: half a dozen pints every night. I was with my Yorkshire heroes. I was a young lad, had a few bob in my pocket and you don't want to be judged as a Goody Two-shoes. Not that I was. I liked a drink, but when I was in the company of Arnie, Fergie, Bluey and Jarvo it was impossible to stop at times. All my mates were still at school or on the Y.T.S. I was a professional sportsman. The problem is, you're not behaving professionally. Sponsored car, good hotels, good money and a few pints. That's the comfort zone of county cricket, and the lifestyle that held England back for decades. Hopefully now, the drinking culture is dying.

I certainly drink a hell of a lot less than I did up to 1997. It was after that New Zealand tour that many of us began to see the light. Although I didn't play much in my early seasons with Yorkshire, I was twelfth man a lot. That's the worst of both worlds: all the social side with none of the actual cricket. As I got older and more mature, I realized that I had to make sacrifices if I wanted to stay at the top. To be honest, the boozy lifestyle had long since lost its attraction and I had better things to do with my time. I was lucky: I had an England place to consider. What about those 250-plus professional cricketers who don't have that carrot? Where's the incentive for them to stop going to the hotel bar and the curry house? It's easy for me to say that I would have found a way out. Some counties are a lot more professional in their approach, but there's an awful lot of players marking time for a benefit because they have nothing else to do.

I wish I had known then what I know now. But we probably all do. I was never one for seeking advice. I found out things the hard way. That's probably the best way, because you don't forget. I'm over 30 now and I'm still learning. I also appreciated that I have to set an example, the way the likes of Gussie, Judgey and Goochie did when I came into the England team. That applies off the field as well as on it. People do look at me. The coach says they look at Darren Gough and how he reacts to situations. If I, one of the best bowlers, am down, how will others react?

I was certainly down after the Lahore Test. Pakistan is a hard place to tour as well as to bowl fast. I wasn't going out much. I was bored. I had built myself up for the first Test, then found myself bowling on the ultimate flat track. Afterwards I took stock. What was I bitching about? I was not experiencing anything I had not expected or had not been told about. Get on with it, Gough. Not just for the sake of myself, but also for the team.

Our next Test was in Faisalabad, scene of the famous Gatting–Shakoor clash in 1987. We stayed at the same Serena hotel which had been open only a few weeks when England toured last time. We kept the same team, even though Ian Salisbury had struggled on his return to Test cricket after more than two years away. I saw no reason to change. There were supposedly two potential pitches at the Stadium; one was green, the other looked like the flat track at Lahore. The sponsors' logos had been painted directly behind the second one, so we made a correct guess: another flat one.

Moin Khan got the chance to bat first this time. We did well to keep them to 316. At one stage Pakistan were 271–5. Mind you, they had been 151–5. Ashley Giles was the pick of our bowlers, going one better than at Lahore and taking 5–75. I got three and felt much happier. Bowling was not any easier than Lahore had been; it was just that I had come to terms with the conditions and what was expected of me. There was also a growing feeling within the squad that England could come away from this tour with something.

One person definitely hoping that that was true was our skipper. Nasser's bad trot continued. This time, he was sent on his way by West Indian umpire Steve Bucknor, adjudged l.b.w. The TV replays showed a big nick first. Television captured a great close-up of Nasser's reaction. I rate his keeping his cool that day as one of the greatest achievements of his career. His eyes showed all his pain. You can imagine what the England dressing-room was like. 'That looked close.' 'Let's see the replay.' 'Bloody hell.' Nobody had to say anything. Nasser just sat down. Half an hour later, his pads were still on. Bucknor had made a genuine mistake, no one doubted that. What upset Fletch and the rest of us was that the technology is available to eradicate such mistakes.

This dead pitch was killing the game. The match entered its fourth day and we were still in our first innings. That was a shame, because Faisalabad was the only time the crowds came to watch Test cricket in Pakistan. I could not get over how cold it was in the evening. Just as well there was nowhere to go outside the hotel. We had been away nine weeks and were at last entering the home straight. Now we knew we could come home with a draw and, if Karachi went our way, who knows . . .

Fletch had really come into his own on this trip. The professional job England were doing on the park was the result of the set-up off it. Fletch is the first coach to come in and draw up the lines of demarcation: 'We're management, you're the players. You'll do what we say.' That might sound dictatorial. Indeed it is, but Fletch is not going to ask you to do something just to make him look good. When he speaks, it's for a purpose. That purpose is to make us better cricketers and a better team. Fletch wants to hear about anyone who demurs, and he'll sort it out.

It's not all hard work. When we have a night out with the team, such as at Islamabad British Club, Fletch comes along and gets hammered along with the rest of us. That policy had been established in South Africa. So had his policy of 'look and learn'. He still doesn't say much but he watches carefully. Fletch likes to know what makes an individual tick so that he can treat them individually. That's his man-management style. It's obvious he doesn't like small groups or cliques developing within the team environment. That doesn't mean Fletch doesn't want strong personalities in his team. He does, but he wants that individuality to work for the good of the team.

After two winters and one summer under him, I know Fletch stands no nonsense. During the Northern Transvaal game at Centurion, Fletch had us doing crossover fielding, chasing in one direction, then back, throwing the ball back over the stumps. Tuffers was not a great one for practice, throwing poor throws back in order to try and get out of it. Fletch's expression hardly changed but he started making Tuffers run that bit further each time. Tuffers didn't work it out. We were laughing on the balcony because we could see what was happening. Fletch will not give in; you won't beat him. Tuffers started throwing the ball harder and harder into Fletch's baseball mitt. Fletch kept pushing the ball further and further. Fletch had achieved his aim; Tuffers, for once, was working hard. There was much less need for Fletch to crack the whip in Pakistan. The boys understand now.

I have no problems with a foreigner coaching England. That's what we needed. Fletch came with no baggage. He had not been sucked into the comfort zone or indoctrinated by an English county system that fails to produce tough Test players. He listens but refuses to be intimidated by players, blazers or tradition. Fletch does things his way. Our fielding now is twice as good as it was. Fletch doesn't make a song and dance about it. We've probably just about reached a 'pass' mark in his view. He simply wants us better. Nasser's the same. We have three groups when we go out in the morning: Phil Neale's, Bob Cottam's and Fletch's. He normally has the best fielders. Then, one day, Fletch will say: 'I'm having Gough, Caddick, White,' and he runs us into the ground. The squad was genuinely pleased when Fletch's England contract was extended at the start of the Pakistan tour to the end of 2003.

We wobbled, batting out the final day in Faisalabad after Nasser received another 'bad one' and another error of judgement from Hickie. That man Athers was not for moving, though. Wasim cracked one into his jaw. That is just the sort of wake-up call Athers loves. He batted almost three and a half hours for his undefeated 65. It's strange but I never really feel we are in trouble while Athers is at the crease. The England party was in buoyant mood as we packed to leave the Serena. Two Tests, two draws, was part of the reason. The other was, the next time we got on a plane after this journey we would be heading back to England.

It was back to Karachi and the Pearl Continental where the tour had started. Time for shopping, Christmas gifts and leather jackets and carpets. The cricket had been hard work, but our hosts could not do enough for us off the field. A few of the tour journalists had also been on Gatt's trip, but it was hard to understand how relationships could have deteriorated so badly that we had stayed away for so long. If we had any complaints this time, it was those 'dead' pitches. If anything is going to kill Test cricket, it is surfaces like these. Another two wickets were prepared at the National Stadium. Spot the Test strip!

Despite our two fighting draws, the knives were out for Hickie and Salisbury. When we got to Karachi, the management stated that changes might be made for the Sri Lanka leg. I never thought for a second that Hickie was under threat. Soals was a different matter; the Surrey leg-spinner was struggling. This was about his fifth go at Test cricket, having earned this latest chance after his spinning partnership with Saqlain had brought Surrey two championship titles. But the Test stage was a step too far. Soals never got the early breakthrough that might have kick-started his return. Like Athers and Stewie before him, Nasser felt he could bowl our leg-spinner only at certain times in short spells. I was not surprised when Soals was released from the second half of the winter schedule. Not that he did not play a significant part in our Pakistan success, twice contributing valuably with the bat, in Faisalabad and Karachi.

England fielded an unchanged side for Karachi. Our black arm-bands this time were a mark of respect for Lord Colin Cowdrey, who had died at 67. On the same day that his death was announced, Azharuddin was banned for life by the Indian Cricket Board, leaving him permanently stuck on 99 Tests. Waqar Younis, named and fined in the Pakistan match-fixing report, was back. His old sparring partner, Wasim Akram, was not in the final line-up after playing his hundredth Test at Faisalabad. Wasim had been complaining about the quality of Test pitches. The official reason was, Wasim had a bad back. Most thought he had either decided another poor wicket was not for him or the selectors had dumped him for his public comments. As usual, I am not sure how near the truth we got. Wasim did have a point. The way he bowled with the new ball at Faisalabad and Waqar performed at Karachi, we could have had a great contest if the pitches had been livelier. I, for one, would not have complained about that.

Another umpiring blunder cost us dear on the first day after Nasser lost the toss. Inzamam finished the day on 123 not out. Our occasional seamer Trescothick had already removed opener Elahi when he hit Inzamam plumb in front on four. Official Nazir Junior did not move. Tresco could not believe it, like the rest of us. Maybe, just maybe, there had been a little inside nick. Junior confirmed there wasn't. His negative verdict was because the ball was going down the leg side! We were looking down the barrel at the end of the first day with Pakistan 292–3. Another day like that, and England were in trouble. We knew we had to rattle them early on. That showed the new confidence of this England. In recent years we have felt helpless, not strong enough to fight the forces against us and would have accepted our fate rather too willingly and easily. Now Fletch and Nasser had given us the belief that we have the ability and strength to influence events.

That is what happened that second morning. Our recovery all started with a magnificent caught-and-bowled by Ash. Our left-arm spinner had really come into his own, but hanging on to Youhana's smashing of a full toss back at him was something else. Ash finished with four wickets, Craig got rid of Inzamam and I took a couple at the end. I felt that Pakistan came out that morning as though the series was now safe; it would have been if they had batted all day. I sensed they felt we would not attack, be positive and that we would settle for trying to bat out the game. Certainly Test cricket is very much cat and mouse, long periods of little happening, yet matches can be lost in a few overs out there. It is much easier to throw away a match out in Pakistan than grab it by the scruff of the neck.

You almost have to lull the opposition into a false sense of security, convince them that you are more concerned about losing than they are. It was all about getting into a position on the final day that would allow us a chance of victory. Who better to lull Pakistan into a state of switch-off than Athers? Our veteran opener was in seventh heaven out there. No clock-watching, no frantic run-chases, just a licence to do what he enjoys most and does best . . . bat all day. This time he batted Friday afternoon, all day Saturday and for over an hour on Sunday morning. The going was slow, but we had to get near to Pakistan's 405. We didn't want to spend the last two sessions of the series with all the home fielders round the bat. Nasser managed his first Test fifty of the year, and my more sensible batting approach added 30 for the final wicket with Soals to get us to within 17 of Pakistan.

The odds were still heavily on the draw that fourth night, even when Ash produced a Warnie-type wonder ball that removed Inzamam at the end of the day. Pakistan were 88 runs ahead with three wickets down. Many of the press corps had written off the series as a draw, criticizing Athers's slow vigil at the crease. Back at the hotel, we felt a win for either side was on. At the ground, you could see that the Pakistan players were feeling the strain. They had never lost a Test in 34 contests at Karachi, they had lost the three previous home series and their media were getting stuck in. For whatever reason, Moin Khan and his team decided to go for the draw: forget the win, let's hang on. It was incredible. Maybe they thought England felt the same way. They were wrong.

In a year of amazing days of cricket – at Centurion Park, Lord's, Headingley – that day at the Lahore National Stadium took its place. We bowled Pakistan out for 158, three-quarters of an hour before tea. The victory target was 176 in 44 overs. The problem was not the runs or overs; it was time and the light. We had bowled and fielded positively and were determined to bat the same way. There was no prediction from Nasser this time about me hitting the winning runs; that would have been too close for comfort. Our dressing-room was buzzing. I could not get over the way Pakistan had batted. Moin Khan was the worst offender. Two or three overs from the attacking Pakistan skipper could have finished us. Once our target got near 200 and five per over, the match would be over. Instead, Moin scratched around, trying to waste time instead of going for runs. Every minute was vital, and I rate trapping No. 11 Danish Kaneria for a duck as one of the most important wickets of my career.

Moin's day went from bad to worse. He started wasting time in the short session before tea and got right up umpire Bucknor's nose. A five-run penalty for time-wasting was not part of the regulations for this series, so Bucknor's powers were limited. I understand that he chatted with the match referee at the tea interval. The message came back to the England dressing-room that we would be given every chance to go for victory. If we wanted to stay out there, we could, however bad the light was. Athers and Tresco gave us a flying start, before Thorpey and Hickie edged us towards the winning target. I did not think we would make it. A couple of times, I felt those two should have taken more of a chance, as it seemed as if the light would fail completely before we got there. But what do I know? Hickie answered his critics, but the light was going when Nasser went out to join Thorpey. Pakistan were far from happy and Moin was not the only Pakistan player appealing to Bucknor.

There was no stopping us now. An inside edge from Thorpey went for the two runs needed for victory and our dressing-room erupted. Nasser gave it everything. Who can blame him? A few months after beating the West Indies for the first time in 31 years, we had ended a 39-year wait for success in Pakistan. How dark was it? Pitch black by the time we went out for the presentation, ten minutes later. Nasser had his hands on another trophy. Athers got Man of the Match. He should have got Man of the Series, but that went to Youhana.

It might have been Ramadan, but we found some beer and wine for a short party, back at the hotel, before heading for the airport. Most of our celebrations took place in an Irish pub in Dubai. The first leg of our flight back that night was dry on P.I.A., before we switched to B.A. What a finish! What a year! Since losing the series in Cape Town, England had won five Tests out of 11 and lost one, winning three series on the trot. More significantly, England were unearthing their next generation of cricketers, as well as discovering that some of those discarded were not so bad after all. Ash, for over two years a one-cap, one-wicket wonder, took 17 wickets in the series. Vaughanie, despite his injury problem in Pakistan, and Tresco have great futures. Caddie's found confidence and comfort in the new set-up. So has Thorpey. So has Craig. His emergence last year was just about the most pleasing aspect for me. And as for Darren Gough, I am just glad to be part of a winning England team at last.

30. Going South

I finally moved home from Yorkshire in January 2001, in between the Pakistan and Sri Lanka tours. It was a wrench leaving Yorkshire and our house, called the Ashes, which Anna and I had helped design in 1996. Our new home in Buckingham (the deep soft south) is the sort of place I have always dreamed of living in. With the new central contracts, being based more centrally means a lot less long-haul travelling. Sadly, I was not the only person who left Yorkshire after the Pakistan trip. Martyn Moxon had finally had enough and joined Durham as coach. Yorkshire will miss him. I shall miss him. The final straw came when the county kept some of the wages the E.C.B. paid him during our one-day series in Pakistan. Like most of the arguments in my time, it boiled down to money and the counties' reluctance to part with it, even for the good of Yorkshire cricket.

As well as being in Ashes year, 2001 is my benefit season. Even that nearly led to a bust-up with the club. I approached the end of 1999 with my contract up for renewal, but I had not decided what I was doing. The view from the county was typical. You can't want to leave Yorkshire. That's when I was told that I was being awarded a benefit in 2001. Most players know roughly when they are going to get one, but it's the club who makes the final decision and announcement. It hadn't been worrying me. I knew I'd get one eventually and I was delighted it was going to be an Ashes year. Australia has always been special for me. We shook hands. That was good enough for me. County chairman Bob Platt, Keith Moss and Chris Hassell, the chief executive, were involved in the discussion. I thought no more about it. The club did not want to make it public until David Byas had got his benefit season underway. I was getting rather twitchy by the start of the 2000 summer. Before the game with Leicester at

Headingley, I collared Bob Platt on the field. I couldn't believe his response 'We've tried our best, but we couldn't get it through the general committee. The club want a benefit in 2001 – we're knocking you back a year.'

'You taking the mick?' I said. I lost it totally and told him I wanted a meeting that day. It took place between innings and I told them straight. 'You've gone back on your word. How can you treat players like this?' I also made it clear that I was not going to let the matter rest. I know a cricketer has no right to a benefit, it's granted by the club, but it had been promised. Martyn Moxon also came in on my behalf, unhappy that one of his players had been upset like this on the morning of the match. It didn't help Darren Maddy either. I was in such a rage the Leicester opener went first ball. Eventually the club agreed after three weeks that I could have my benefit in 2001 – but the county were also going to have one as well. Was I happy with that? I went ahead. It was typical Yorkshire. At least I've been lucky with my benefit chairman, Colin Graves of Costcutter. He and Ian Bishop have done a great job in organizing a variety of events. You are very much in the hands of others during a benefit season, but they have been terrific and left me to worry only about my cricket.

One of the big events is a Rest of the World game scheduled for the end of summer 2001. My bat and ball, my benefit. At last I'm a cricket captain. It says a lot for my powers of leadership that the only means by which I can get a game in charge of ten other cricketers is to organize my own. Fletch is the first person in the England set-up to recognize my qualities in that direction. I do not imagine it will go much beyond having me on his management team. I have enjoyed that responsibility. Having a small group of players to discuss various matters was something he did at Glamorgan. I am also sure he saw that as a way of getting to know us. Tuffers was part of the team with me in South Africa. Tuffers likes the role of rebel, but he also enjoyed being one of the senior professionals on that trip. It worked, too. Tuffers has a good cricket brain which he manages to keep well concealed most of the time. Fletch likes to hear from us about what's happening in the squad.

We are not spies. If there is a problem that could develop into something serious, our coach wants to know about it early. In South Africa we were asked about replacement players. Fletch genuinely wants our views. This is not to say that the captain and coach do not take the final decision. They do, but at least we have been consulted. Marcus Trescothick joined the management team in Pakistan as Fletch has started to bring the younger players in. It is another way of seeing how we react under pressure and what we are thinking about the game.

I have hardly ever seen Fletch get upset. He was not happy at the Oval when we lost to Zimbabwe, a week after overcoming the West Indies at Lord's. He was certainly very angry about the way we played our cricket at Edgbaston at the start of the West Indies series. After a three-day defeat, all I wanted to do was head for home that Saturday night and lick my wounds. Fletch has made it a rule that we stay together and celebrate as a team. He insisted on us staying for a post mortem on this particular Sunday morning, adding that he did not think it was appropriate to chat straight after the game. After breakfast, he told us that this sort of performance was not acceptable and that we had let ourselves down in all aspects of play. Nasser talked after him, then Fletch asked what everyone thought. I have been at countless team meetings at which players have been asked when it is obvious that those at the head of the table do not care a damn. Not Fletch; he involves everyone. It is not always the same people and he likes to get players who are rather quiet, like Craig White, to open up.

At the end of Pakistan, Fletch told us that we had to be much fitter for the second half of our winter cricket. He was not wrong there. The heat in Sri Lanka was stifling. A Test and a one-day series in a five-week spell was quite a physical ordeal, even without worrying about the cricket.

What a tour! Outside the Tests, I twice found myself in the middle of controversy. The first time was against a Colts team in Colombo, when I was accused of threatening their players with my bat. The second time came against another Colts team in Kurunegala after a clash with one of their batsmen. The first time I was

given out to a pad-bat catch that wasn't. I was last man out and the
fielders were laughing as I came off. I told them to show some
respect, but they carried on, so I told them more forcibly. Only
two days later it was revealed that I had been reported. It was a fuss
about nothing. The second time I was deliberately tripped up as I
tried to field my own bowling as the home side went for a run. I
gave the batsman a mouthful and then told the umpire that was the
second time a Sri Lankan batsman had done that to me. I left
the field straight after because of a bad back, but the press got very
excited because they thought Nasser had sent me off. Nonsense.
Another storm in a teacup.

The same couldn't be said about the Test series, which grabbed
headlines because of the umpiring – in some cases, the lack of
it. There was mayhem at Galle in the first Test when we were
on the receiving end of half a dozen bad decisions. Stewie got
the worse l.b.w. I've ever seen and Craig White's wasn't far
behind. Worse than that was all the running on the wicket, appealing, and just general nonsense. Our failure to save the follow-on
cost us the Test. There was more trouble at Kandy, where we
levelled the series. Probably, the Sri Lankans got the worst of
the decisions here, but we still had to battle hard to win. Nasser
got his first century since Durban in 1999 and I was delighted
for our skipper. I took four wickets in each innings. (I've kept a
list of England's leading wicket-takers in my cricket coffin for a
long time and ticked them off as I've gone past. It was about four
years ago that I put a mark by John Snow's 202 total as my special
target. I'll have to reassess that now – which took me to sixth place
in the P.C.W. world rankings, my highest-ever position), and I
claimed Man of the Match. Just as important was my first innings
last-wicket stand with Croftie. We edged home by three wickets
to set up the decider in Colombo, where I went past Jim Laker's
193 Test wickets. At the same time Australia's match-winning run
of 16 Tests was coming to an end in Calcutta. That was a shame in
a way. There is no denying that all eyes were beginning to focus
on the 2001 Ashes summer towards the end of Sri Lanka. That is
the big prize.

These cricket life stories normally end with the author picking his favourite England team against the Rest. I, as ever, would like to be slightly different. I have picked a squad of cricketers whom I have played Test and one-day cricket with and against. These are the guys I would love to have in the dressing-room with me for a Test or a one-day international. This way I am guaranteed a place. I do not need to explain my selections; if you've read this book carefully enough, you will know why. And, for good luck, I have picked the next England generation. I am definitely not in that one.

Gough's Test squad:

Mike Atherton (England)
Michael Slater (Australia)
Brian Lara (West Indies)
Martin Crowe (New Zealand)
Steve Waugh (captain, Australia)
Alec Stewart (wicket-keeper, England)
Shane Warne (Australia)
Wasim Akram (Pakistan)
Glenn McGrath (Australia)
Allan Donald (South Africa)
Courtney Walsh (West Indies)
Gough. Come to think of it, I might be twelfth man here.

Gough's one-day squad:

Adam Gilchrist (wicket-keeper, Australia)
Sanath Jayasuriya (Sri Lanka)
Sachin Tendulkar (India)
Jacques Kallis (South Africa)
Neil Fairbrother (England)
Michael Bevan (Australia)
Lance Klusener (South Africa)
Wasim Akram (Pakistan)
Shane Warne (captain, Australia)
Shaun Pollock (South Africa)
Glenn McGrath (Australia)
Gough

Gough's (Star Trek) Next Generation England Cricketers:

Michael Powell (Warwickshire)
Marcus Trescothick (Somerset)
Michael Vaughan (Yorkshire)
Vikram Solanki (Worcestershire)
James Foster (Essex)
Matthew Hoggard (Yorkshire)
Ryan Sidebottom (Yorkshire)
Graeme Swann (Northamptonshire)

David Sales (Northampton)   Chris Schofield (Lancashire)
Ben Hollioake (Surrey)   A. Tudor (Surrey)
A. Flintoff (Lancs)   M. Lamb (Yorkshire)

I am not sure how long I will continue. There was a lot of soul-searching during the winter of 2000/1 in Pakistan and Sri Lanka. Thorpey's form in Pakistan showed the value of a long break. The tough decision is – when? The winter before the Ashes tour and World Cup (2002/3) to India and New Zealand would seem to be obvious time. Hand back my England place and I might never gain possession again; that is the risk. The other route is to decide between Test and one-day cricket. If you play in both teams, the schedule is suicidal now. Other countries play as much international cricket as England, it's true. They do not have England's domestic programme. We have no opportunities for the sort of decent break required to recover properly from a sustained period of top-class cricket. I will need to be fresh if I head for Australia in October 2002 and do not come home until after the World Cup in South Africa in March 2003.

I know we moan and ruck about the length of tours and the intense pressures of a seven Tests, ten one-dayers summer. Sometimes I wonder what keeps me going. Then I think back to the great life and experiences cricket has given me. The highs and lows. The fun. The private and public moments of triumph and despair. The camaraderie. There are always new targets. Only seven England bowlers – Ian Botham, Bob Willis, Fred Trueman, Derek Underwood, Brian Statham, Sir Alec Bedser and John Snow – have taken 200 Test wickets. In Sri Lanka I got close. And entering the millennium, I am part of that generation of England cricketers which has been humbled by Australia; we have not had as much as a sniff of the Ashes. The six series since 1989 have not even been close. Our exploits in 2000 certainly raised expectations for 2001, although watching, from Pakistan, Australia's demolition of the West Indies in the winter of 2000/1 left us in no doubt as to the scale of our task. So, if we win, I will probably be smiling for the rest of my life.

A STATISTICAL APPENDIX

by Paul Dyson

Brief Chronology

Birth: 18 September 1970, Barnsley

First day in first-class cricket: 20 April 1989, Yorkshire *v*. Middlesex, Lord's

First limited-overs match: 22 April 1990, Yorkshire *v*. Nottinghamshire, Trent Bridge

Awarded county cap: 9 September 1993, Yorkshire *v*. Sussex, Scarborough

First one-day international: 19 May 1994, England *v*. New Zealand, Edgbaston

First day in Test cricket: 30 June 1994, England *v*. New Zealand, Old Trafford

One of Five Cricketers of the Year, *Wisden Cricketers' Almanack*, 1999

Awarded E.C.B. contract, March 2000

NOTE: All figures in the following pages are correct as at 5 February 2002.

For the latest updated statistics please check Darren's official website at: www.darrengough.com

First-class Cricket

BOWLING

In each season

	Mtchs	Ovrs	Mdns	Runs	Wkts	Avge	BB	5wi	10wm
1989	2	65	13	173	6	28.83	3-44	–	–
1990	14	279.4	49	1037	28	37.03	4-68	–	–
1991	13	270	55	945	18	52.50	5-41	1	–
1991/2	1	18	5	40	2	20.00	1-20	–	–
1992	11	255.1	53	910	25	36.40	4-43	–	–
1992/3	1	26	8	66	2	33.00	1-18	–	–
1993	16	507.3	115	1517	57	26.61	7-42	3	1
1993/4	5	192.1	34	589	23	25.60	5-81	1	–
1994	13	479.2	100	1526	62	24.61	6-66	3	–
1994/5	5	222.5	44	688	26	26.46	6-49	2	–
1995	14	414.5	89	1365	51	26.76	7-28	1	1
1995/6	5	88.4	18	283	9	31.44	3-30	–	–
1996	16	573.3	142	1535	67	22.91	6-36	2	–
1996/7	8	276.3	63	802	44	18.22	6-64	3	1
1997	12	334.4	70	1149	43	26.72	5-56	3	–
1998	11	340.3	65	1067	42	25.40	6-42	2	–
1998/9	7	266.2	56	873	31	28.16	5-96	1	–
1999	3	96.5	20	319	17	18.76	4-27	–	–
1999/2000	8	264.1	56	849	27	31.44	5-70	1	–
2000	10	324.1	62	949	50	18.98	6-63	2	–
2000/1	8	242.1	47	733	36	20.36	4-47	–	–
2001	9	321.4	55	1212	39	31.07	5-61	2	–
TOTALS	192	5859.4	1219	18627	705	26.42	7-28	27	3

For each team

	Mtchs	Ovrs	Mdns	Runs	Wkts	Avge	BB	5wi	10wm
Yorkshire (Championship)	104	3021.1	652	9573	351	27.27	7-42	12	1
Yorkshire (Other Matches)	12	285.3	80	774	35	22.11	7-28	2	1
England 'A'	5	192.1	34	589	23	25.61	5-81	1	–
England XI	15	443.4	93	1403	68	20.63	6-64	3	1
England (Tests)	56	1917.1	360	6288	228	27.57	6-42	9	–
TOTALS	192	5859.4	1219	18627	705	26.42	7-28	27	3

Against each opponent

(minimum two matches, excluding Test matches)

	Mtchs	Ovrs	Mdns	Runs	Wkts	Avge	BB	5wi	10wm
Derbyshire	8	191.5	33	707	22	32.14	4-24	–	–
Durham	5	205.2	51	504	31	16.26	6-63	2	–
Essex	5	141.1	20	554	19	29.16	5-74	1	–
Glamorgan	6	177	41	533	17	31.35	5-56	1	–
Gloucestershire	5	155.1	39	443	13	34.08	4-27	–	–
Hampshire	8	251.2	56	791	31	25.52	6-70	2	–
Kent	6	139.2	28	475	11	43.18	4-43	–	–
Lancashire	11	335.2	77	1065	45	23.66	7-28	3	1
Leicestershire	6	181.4	39	580	17	34.12	3-46	–	–
Middlesex	8	189.3	42	561	20	28.05	4-68	–	–
Northamptonshire	5	141	23	481	12	40.08	3-62	–	–
Nottinghamshire	4	113.5	22	329	18	18.28	6-36	1	–
Somerset	8	258.5	60	863	31	27.84	7-42	1	1
Surrey	5	115.2	34	292	19	15.37	6-66	2	–
Sussex	5	149.1	36	518	19	27.26	4-69	–	–
Warwickshire	9	275.2	57	826	28	29.50	4-62	–	–
Worcestershire	4	114.5	30	336	14	24.00	5-36	1	–
Cambridge University	2	47.4	17	100	4	25.00	2-37	–	–
Oxford University	2	29	4	95	4	23.75	2-40	–	–
Australian teams	4	134.5	27	449	16	28.06	5-143	1	–

Against each opponent (*cont.*)

	Mtchs	Ovrs	Mdns	Runs	Wkts	Avge	BB	5wi	10wm
South Africa 'A'	2	88.1	19	263	11	23.91	5-81	1	–
Western Province	3	82.5	18	210	11	19.09	4-57	–	–
Other South African teams	8	220	46	715	27	26.48	4-60	–	–
Zimbabwean teams	3	83.2	16	249	16	15.56	6-64	2	1
Other overseas teams	4	120.4	24	400	21	19.05	4-47	–	–

Summary

	Mtchs	Ovrs	Mdns	Runs	Wkts	Avge	BB	5wi	10wm
English teams	112	3212.4	709	10053	375	26.81	7-28	14	2
Overseas teams	24	729.5	150	2286	102	22.41	6-64	4	1
Tests	56	1917.1	360	6288	228	27.57	6-42	9	–
TOTALS	192	5859.4	1219	18627	705	26.42	7-28	27	3

On each ground

(minimum two matches)

(a) In England, listed by county

	Mtchs	Ovrs	Mdns	Runs	Wkts	Avge	BB	5wi	10wm
Chesterfield	2	52	8	194	5	38.80	3-38	–	–
Chester-le-Street	2	76.2	16	184	12	15.33	6-63	1	–
Chelmsford	2	60.1	4	279	9	31.00	4-94	–	–
Cardiff	3	93	19	284	8	35.50	3-57	–	–
Southampton	2	58.3	7	226	7	32.29	5-50	1	–
Old Trafford	9	332.1	59	1086	32	33.94	5-75	1	–
Leicester	2	78.4	17	245	11	22.27	3-44	–	–
Lord's	10	322.4	60	1027	48	21.40	5-61	1	–
Northampton	4	124	20	431	12	35.92	3-62	–	–
Trent Bridge	4	131.4	25	450	13	34.62	4-116	–	–
Taunton	3	100.1	24	332	13	25.54	7-42	1	1
The Oval	6	161.2	27	557	15	37.13	3-64	–	–
Edgbaston	10	280.1	53	998	32	31.19	5-109	1	–
Worcester	3	104.5	23	322	14	23.00	5-36	1	–

On each ground (*cont.*)

	Mtchs	Ovrs	Mdns	Runs	Wkts	Avge	BB	5wi	10wm
Bradford	3	74	17	217	4	54.25	2-32	–	–
Harrogate	6	141	43	339	16	21.19	4-57	–	–
Headingley	37	1150.4	262	3479	142	24.50	7-28	7	1
Middlesbrough	5	117	29	343	12	28.58	5-36	1	–
Scarborough	13	355.2	79	1155	55	21.00	6-36	3	–
Sheffield	7	171.5	35	563	15	37.53	4-24	–	–
The Parks	2	29	4	95	4	23.75	2-40	–	–
Others	9	248.2	57	898	26	34.54	5-74	1	–

Summary

	Mtchs	Ovrs	Mdns	Runs	Wkts	Avge	BB	5wi	10wm
In Yorkshire	71	2009.5	465	6096	244	24.98	7-28	11	1
In Rest of England	73	2253	423	7608	261	29.15	7-42	8	1
TOTALS	144	4262.5	888	13704	505	27.14	7-28	19	2

(b) overseas, listed by country

	Mtchs	Ovrs	Mdns	Runs	Wkts	Avge	BB	5wi	10wm
Adelaide	2	98.5	15	341	10	34.10	5-143	1	–
Brisbane	2	95	14	370	7	52.86	4-107	–	–
Melbourne	2	94.4	24	269	14	19.21	5-96	1	–
Perth	2	69.5	24	177	8	22.13	4-74	–	–
Sydney	2	78.5	15	233	11	21.18	6-49	1	–
Others in Australia	2	52	8	171	7	24.43	3-29	–	–
In New Zealand	4	152.1	37	435	25	17.40	5-40	1	–
In Pakistan	4	129.1	25	373	16	23.31	3-30	–	–
In Sri Lanka	4	113	22	360	20	18.00	4-47	–	–
Bloemfontein	2	85.5	18	238	11	21.64	4-60	–	–
Cape Town	4	119.5	24	298	13	22.92	4-57	–	–
Centurion Park	3	49.1	6	230	7	32.86	3-69	–	–
Durban	2	75.4	13	252	4	63.00	2-36	–	–
East London	2	45	14	111	7	15.86	3-30	–	–
Johannesburg	3	81.3	19	262	8	32.75	5-70	1	–
Port Elizabeth	2	91.2	20	304	9	33.77	5-81	1	–
Others in South Africa	2	40.4	7	132	4	33.00	3-30	–	–
In Zimbabwe	4	124.2	26	367	19	19.32	6-64	2	1

Overall summary

In England	144	4262.5	888	13704	505	27.14	7-28	19	2
Overseas	48	1596.5	331	4923	200	25.18	6-49	8	1
TOTALS	192	5859.4	1219	18627	705	26.42	7-28	27	3

Six wickets in an innings

7-28	Yorkshire *v.* Lancashire	Headingley	1995
7-42	Yorkshire *v.* Somerset	Taunton	1993
6-36	Yorkshire *v.* Nottinghamshire	Scarborough	1996
6-42	ENGLAND *v.* SOUTH AFRICA	Headingley	1998
6-49	ENGLAND *v.* AUSTRALIA	Sydney	1994/5
6-63	Yorkshire *v.* Durham	Chester-le-Street	2000
6-64	England XI *v.* Matabeleland	Bulawayo	1996/7
6-66	Yorkshire *v.* Surrey	Scarborough	1994
6-70	Yorkshire *v.* Hampshire	Headingley	1994

Ten wickets in a match

11-139	England XI *v.* Matabeleland	Bulawayo	1996/7
10-80	Yorkshire *v.* Lancashire	Headingley	1995
10-96	Yorkshire *v.* Somerset	Taunton	1993

Hat-tricks

Yorkshire *v.* Kent	Headingley	1995
ENGLAND *v.* AUSTRALIA	Sydney	1998/9

NOTE: The hat-trick against Kent came in a spell of four wickets in five balls.

Conceding less than one run per over in an innings (minimum ten overs)

14-7-12-3	Yorkshire *v.* Essex	Headingley	1992
12-5-11-0	Yorkshire *v.* Middlesex	Lord's	1996

500th Wicket

D. J. Cullinan l.b.w. b. Gough 0　ENGLAND *v.*　　Headingley 9 August 1998
　　　　　　　　　　　　　　　　SOUTH AFRICA

Batsmen most frequently dismissed

8　R. T. Ponting, M. J. Slater (both Australia)
　　N. J. Speak (Lancashire & Durham)

7　S. L. Campbell (Durham & West Indies),
　　G. F. J. Liebenberg (Orange Free State & South Africa)

6　D. J. Cullinan (Border & South Africa)
　　B. C. Lara (West Indies)
　　M. A. Taylor (Australia)

Most fielding dismissals		Methods of dismissals		
77	R. J. Blakey	caught	386	54.8%
47	A. J. Stewart	bowled	163	23.1%
31	D. Byas	l.b.w.	155	22.0%
15	G. A. Hick	hit wkt	1	0.1%
14	G. P. Thorpe, S. J. Rhodes,	TOTAL	705	100.0%
	M. P. Vaughan			

BATTING AND FIELDING

Full career record for each team

	Mtchs	Inns	NO	Runs	HS	Avge	100	50	Ct
Yorkshire in Championship	104	139	24	2196	121	19.10	1	10	20
Yorkshire in other matches	12	13	2	160	43	14.55	–	–	3
England XI	15	19	4	142	26	9.47	–	–	4
England 'A'	5	6	2	75	24	18.75	–	–	2
England (Tests)	56	83	18	806	65	12.40	–	2	12
TOTALS	192	260	50	3379	121	16.09	1	12	41

Best seasons

(a) by average: 27.90 (307 runs) – 1991   (b) by aggregate: 501 runs
                                               (average 22.77) – 1996

Century

121   Yorkshire *v.* Warwickshire   Headingley   1996

Two consecutive half-centuries

(a) 72 Yorkshire *v.* Northamptonshire,   60* Yorkshire *v.* Lancashire,
    Northampton;   Scarborough, 1991

(b) 121 Yorkshire *v.* Warwickshire,   50 Yorkshire *v.* Leicestershire,
    Headingley;   Bradford, 1996

NOTE: There was a period of 68 innings between the 11th and 12th half-centuries.

Making highest score in a completed innings

Own score (Batting position)	Next highest score	Team Total			
72 (8)	55 (M. D. Moxon)	325	Yorkshire *v.* Northamptonshire	Northampton	1991
24 (8)	16 (H. Morris)	116	England 'A' *v.* Natal	Durban	1993/4
58 (9)	49 (R. J. Blakey)	288	Yorkshire *v.* Northamptonshire	Northampton	1998
39*(10)	34 (A. J. Stewart)	184	England *v.* Australia	The Oval	2001

Century partnerships

130	8th	P. A. J. DeFreitas	ENGLAND *v.* NEW ZEALAND	Old Trafford	1994
117	7th	D. S. Lehmann	Yorkshire *v.* Kent	Headingley	1997
110	8th	R. J. Blakey	Yorkshire *v.* Somerset	Headingley	1998

Pairs

ENGLAND *v.* AUSTRALIA   Headingley   1997
ENGLAND *v.* AUSTRALIA   Edgbaston   2001

ALL-ROUND FEATS

A half-century and five wickets in an innings in the same match

60*	5-41	Yorkshire *v.* Lancashire	Scarborough	1991
51	6-49	ENGLAND *v.* AUSTRALIA	Sydney	1994/5

500 runs and 50 wickets in a season

501 runs (avge 22.77); 67 wickets (avge 22.91)   1996

Test Cricket

BOWLING

In each series

		Tests	Ovrs	Mdns	Runs	Wkts	Avge	BpW	BB	5wi
1994	New Zealand	1	47.5	7	152	6	25.33	47.83	4-47	–
1994	South Africa	3	122.3	21	414	11	37.64	66.82	4-46	–
1994/5	Australia	3	152.5	33	425	20	21.25	45.85	6-49	1
1995	West Indies	3	70	6	255	6	42.50	70.00	3-79	–
1995/6	South Africa	2	27	4	112	0	–	–	–	–
1996/7	Zimbabwe	2	64	16	171	7	24.42	54.86	4-40	–
1996/7	New Zealand	3	127.3	31	361	19	19.00	40.26	5-40	1
1997	Australia	4	142	27	511	16	31.93	53.25	5-149	1
1998	South Africa	4	130.5	26	388	17	22.82	46.18	6-42	1
1998	Sri Lanka	1	30	5	102	2	51.00	90.00	2-102	–
1998/9	Australia	5	201.3	40	687	21	32.71	57.57	5-96	1
1999/2000	South Africa	5	171	34	527	14	37.64	73.29	5-70	1
2000	Zimbabwe	2	49.3	6	174	9	19.33	33.00	4-57	–
2000	West Indies	5	173.5	34	530	25	21.20	41.72	5-109	1
2000/1	Pakistan	3	91.1	18	268	10	26.80	54.70	3-30	–
2000/1	Sri Lanka	3	82	15	274	14	19.57	35.14	4-50	–
2001	Pakistan	2	78.3	13	280	14	20.00	33.64	5-61	1
2001	Australia	5	155.1	24	657	17	38.64	54.76	5-103	1
TOTALS		56	1917.1	360	6288	228	27.57	50.45	6-42	9

Against each opponent

	Tests	Ovrs	Mdns	Runs	Wkts	Avge	BpW	BB	5wi
Australia	17	651.3	124	2280	74	30.81	52.82	6-49	4
New Zealand	4	175.2	38	513	25	20.52	42.08	5-40	1
Pakistan	5	169.4	31	548	24	22.83	42.42	5-61	1
South Africa	14	451.2	85	1441	42	34.31	64.48	6-42	2
Sri Lanka	4	112	20	376	16	23.50	42.00	4-50	—
West Indies	8	243.5	40	785	31	25.32	47.19	5-109	1
Zimbabwe	4	113.3	22	345	16	21.56	42.56	4-40	—
TOTALS	56	1917.1	360	6288	228	27.57	50.45	6-42	9

On each ground in England

	Tests	Ovrs	Mdns	Runs	Wkts	Avge	BpW	BB	5wi
Edgbaston	5	132.5	24	495	14	35.36	56.93	5-109	1
Headingley	6	204.4	39	701	31	22.61	39.61	6-42	3
Lord's	7	230	41	770	39	19.74	35.38	5-61	1
Old Trafford	5	220.2	34	715	21	34.05	62.95	4-47	—
The Oval	4	120	17	428	8	53.50	90.00	3-64	—
Trent Bridge	3	92.2	14	354	10	35.40	55.40	4-116	—
TOTALS	30	1000.1	169	3463	123	28.15	48.79	6-42	5

In each country overseas

	Tests	Ovrs	Mdns	Runs	Wkts	Avge	BpW	BB	5wi
Australia	8	354.2	73	1112	41	27.12	51.85	6-49	2
New Zealand	3	127.3	31	361	19	19.00	40.26	5-40	1
Pakistan	3	91.1	18	268	10	26.80	54.70	3-30	—
South Africa	7	198	38	639	14	45.64	84.86	5-70	1
Sri Lanka	3	82	15	274	14	19.57	35.14	4-50	—
Zimbabwe	2	64	16	171	7	24.42	54.86	4-40	—
TOTALS	26	917	191	2825	105	26.90	52.40	6-49	4

Five wickets in an innings

6–49	Australia	Sydney	1994/5
5–40	New Zealand	Wellington	1996/7
5–149	Australia	Headingley	1997
6–42	South Africa	Headingley	1998
5–96	Australia	Melbourne	1998/9
5–70	South Africa	Johannesburg	1999/2000
5–109	West Indies	Edgbaston	2000
5–61	Pakistan	Lord's	2001
5–103	Australia	Headingley	2001

100th wicket

J. N. Rhodes c. Flintoff b. Gough 85 *v.* South Africa Headingley 9 August 1998

200th wicket

Rashid Latif   c. Stewart   b. Gough   18 *v.* Pakistan   Lord's   20 May 2001

Batsmen most frequently dismissed

8 R. T. Ponting, M. J. Slater (Australia)
6 M. A. Taylor (Australia), S. L. Campbell, B. C. Lara (West Indies)
5 J. N. Rhodes (South Africa), S. K. Warne, M. E. Waugh, S. R. Waugh (Australia)
4 S. B. Doull (New Zealand), D. J. Cullinan, J. H. Kallis, G. Kirsten, G. F. J. Liebenberg (South Africa), G. W. Flower (Zimbabwe), Saqlain Mushtaq (Pakistan)

Numbers of batsmen dismissed by batting order

	Australia	New Zealand	Pakistan	South Africa	Sri Lanka	West Indies	Zimbabwe	TOTALS
1	7	3	3	6	3	7	4	33
2	9	2	3	4	2	4	2	26
3	13	4	1	5	1	4	1	29
4	5	1	–	4	1	4	3	18
5	8	1	4	5	1	2	2	23
6	8	4	–	4	2	2	2	22
7	4	1	–	4	1	1	1	12
8	4	1	2	2	2	3	–	14

9	7	3	5	4	1	2	–	22
10	6	3	3	2	2	2	1	19
11	3	2	3	2	–	–	–	10
TOTALS	74	25	24	42	16	31	16	228

Most fielding dismissals	
41	A. J. Stewart
15	G. A. Hick
11	G. P. Thorpe
9	M. A. Atherton
7	S. J. Rhodes
6	N. V. Knight

Methods of dismissals		
caught	134	58.8%
bowled	49	21.5%
l.b.w.	45	19.7%
TOTAL	228	100.0%

BATTING AND FIELDING

Full career record by venue

	Tests	Inns	NO	Runs	HS	Avge	50	Ct
In England	30	39	8	511	65	16.48	1	4
Overseas	26	44	10	295	51	8.68	1	8
TOTALS	56	83	18	806	65	12.40	2	12

Half-centuries

65	*v.* New Zealand	Old Trafford 1994
51	*v.* Australia	Sydney	1994/5

NOTE: The score of 65 was his first innings in Test cricket and remains his highest total.

AWARDS

Man of the Match	*v.* Australia	Sydney	1994/5
Man of the Match	*v.* Sri Lanka	Kandy	2000/01
Man of the Series	*v.* West Indies	Five Tests	2000
Man of the Series	*v.* Sri Lanka	Three Tests	2000/01

One-day Internationals

BOWLING

In each season

	Mtchs	Ovrs	Mdns	Runs	Wkts	Avge	RpO	BB	4wi
1994	3	32	4	115	4	28.75	3.59	2-36	–
1994/5	4	28.4	3	112	8	14.00	3.91	5-44	1
1995	3	32	1	123	5	24.60	3.84	2-30	–
1995/6	12	110	8	439	15	29.26	3.99	4-33	1
1996	5	46	3	193	6	32.16	4.20	3-39	–
1996/7	8	74.4	5	337	13	25.92	4.51	4-43	1
1997	3	30	5	119	7	17.00	3.97	5-44	1
1998	6	60	4	274	13	21.07	4.57	4-35	1
1998/9	16	144	15	676	26	26.00	4.69	4-28	1
1999	5	48.4	4	192	11	17.45	3.95	4-34	1
1999/2000	9	84	11	290	16	18.12	3.45	4-29	1
2000	7	56	5	213	9	23.66	3.80	3-20	–
2000/1	8	74	7	334	5	66.80	4.51	2-71	–
2001	6	54	5	243	9	27.00	4.50	2-31	–
2001/02	6	55.4	1	302	8	37.75	5.43	3-46	–
TOTALS	101	929.4	81	3962	155	25.56	4.26	5-44	8

Against each opponent

	Mtchs	Ovrs	Mdns	Runs	Wkts	Avge	RpO	BB	4wi
Australia	15	124	10	592	20	29.60	4.77	5-44	1
Bangladesh	1	10	1	38	0	–	3.80	–	–
Holland	1	3	0	23	0	–	7.66	–	–
India	11	103.4	5	511	15	34.07	4.93	3-46	–
Kenya	1	10	1	34	4	8.50	3.40	4-34	1
New Zealand	7	66.5	2	320	8	40.00	4.79	2-29	–
Pakistan	12	114	8	541	16	33.81	4.75	3-39	–
South Africa	19	188	17	706	37	19.08	3.76	4-29	3
Sri Lanka	12	111.4	11	476	19	25.05	4.26	4-28	1

Against each opponent (*cont.*)

	Mtchs	Ovrs	Mdns	Runs	Wkts	Avge	RpO	BB	4wi
United Arab Emirates	1	8	3	23	1	23.00	2.88	1-23	–
West Indies	6	52	2	195	9	21.66	3.75	2-30	–
Zimbabwe	15	138.3	21	503	26	19.34	3.63	5-44	2
TOTALS	101	929.4	81	3962	155	25.56	4.26	5-44	8

On each ground in England

	Mtchs	Ovrs	Mdns	Runs	Wkts	Avge	RpO	BB	4wi
Bristol	1	10	2	44	2	22.00	4.40	2-44	–
Canterbury	1	10	1	34	4	8.50	3.40	4-34	1
Chester-le-Street	1	10	1	38	2	19.00	3.80	2-38	–
Edgbaston	7	68	5	305	12	25.42	4.49	3-39	–
Headingley	4	38	7	153	5	30.60	4.03	2-33	–
Lord's	8	68.4	3	283	18	15.72	4.12	5-44	1
Old Trafford	6	57	3	223	10	22.30	3.91	4-35	1
The Oval	6	56	5	261	4	65.25	4.66	2-33	–
Trent Bridge	4	41	4	131	7	18.71	3.20	2-24	–
TOTALS	38	358.4	31	1472	64	23.00	4.10	5-44	3

In each overseas country

	Mtchs	Ovrs	Mdns	Runs	Wkts	Avge	RpO	BB	4wi
Australia	16	134.4	14	603	26	23.19	4.48	5-44	2
India	7	65.4	1	365	8	45.63	5.56	3-46	–
Kenya	2	19	3	81	1	81.00	4.26	1-43	–
New Zealand	5	45.5	1	221	6	36.83	4.53	2-29	–
Pakistan	8	69	6	322	6	53.66	4.67	2-48	–
South Africa	12	118	10	403	25	16.12	3.42	4-29	2
Sri Lanka	3	27	2	106	2	53.00	3.93	1-24	–
United Arab Emirates	4	38	4	185	8	23.12	4.87	3-55	–
Zimbabwe	6	53.5	9	204	9	22.66	3.79	4-43	1
TOTALS	63	571	50	2490	91	27.36	4.36	5-44	5

Five wickets in an innings

5-44	*v.* Zimbabwe	Sydney	1994/5
5-44	*v.* Australia	Lord's	1997

Most economical 10-over analyses

10-2-20-3	*v.* Zimbabwe	Lord's	NatWest Series	2000
10-2-24-2	*v.* Zimbabwe	Trent Bridge	World Cup	1999
10-2-24-1	*v.* Sri Lanka	Dambulla	ODI	2000/1
10-1-25-3	*v.* South Africa	East London	ODI	1995/6

Most expensive 10-over analyses

10-0-71-2	*v.* Pakistan	Karachi	ODI	2000/1
10-1-68-2	*v.* Sri Lanka	Adelaide	Carlton & Utd Series	1998/9
10-0-65-1	*v.* New Zealand	Auckland	ODI	1996/7

100th wicket

M. O. Odumbe b. Gough 6 *v.* Kenya World Cup Canterbury 18 May 1999

Batsmen most frequently dismissed

6   S. T. Jayasuria (Sri Lanka), G. Kirsten (South Africa)
5   A. C. Gilchrist (Australia)

Most fielding dismissals

25	A. J. Stewart
8	G. A. Hick
7	N. Hussain
6	N. V. Knight

Methods of dismissals

caught	94	60.6%
bowled	46	29.7%
l.b.w.	15	9.7%
TOTAL	155	100.0%

BATTING AND FIELDING

Full career record by venue

	Mtchs	Inns	NO	Runs	HS	Avge	Ct
In England	38	21	7	127	40*	9.07	5
Overseas	63	44	18	311	45	11.96	9
TOTALS	101	65	25	438	45	10.95	14

Highest score

45 *v.* Australia   Melbourne   1994/5

AWARDS

Man of the Match	Australia	Lord's	1997
Man of the Series	South Africa	Texaco Trophy (3 matches)	1998
Man of the Match	Sri Lanka	Melbourne	1998/9
Man of the Match	South Africa	Bloemfontein	1999/2000

Domestic limited-overs Matches

(all for Yorkshire – main competitions only)

BOWLING

Season by season

	Mtchs	Ovrs	Mdns	Runs	Wkts	Avge	RpO	BB	4wi
1990	8	51	3	240	6	40.00	4.71	2–22	–
1991	12	76.2	3	375	9	41.66	4.91	2–32	–
1992	19	148	16	614	25	24.56	4.15	3–30	–
1993	20	179.4	25	668	27	24.74	3.72	4–25	1
1994	13	109.3	7	444	19	23.37	4.05	5–13	2
1995	18	143.4	15	542	19	28.53	3.77	4–35	1

Season by season (*contd.*)

	Mtchs	Ovrs	Mdns	Runs	Wkts	Avge	RpO	BB	4wi
1996	25	206.2	20	838	33	25.39	4.06	3-31	–
1997	18	146.5	7	633	34	18.62	4.31	7-27	2
1998	13	104.2	9	417	29	14.38	4.00	5-25	3
1999	3	23.1	2	80	2	40.00	3.45	2-29	–
2000	14	110.5	19	334	24	13.92	3.01	5-30	3
2001	8	75	7	290	7	41.43	3.86	3-15	–
TOTALS	171	1374.4	133	5475	234	23.40	3.98	7-27	12

In each competition

	Mtchs	Ovrs	Mdns	Runs	Wkts	Avge	RpO	BB	4wi
Chelt & Glos Trophy	26	273.5	40	939	54	17.39	3.43	7-27	5
Sunday League	95	674.2	41	3022	122	24.77	4.48	5-13	6
Benson & Hedges Cup	39	340.2	39	1245	45	27.66	3.66	4-17	1
National League	11	86.1	13	269	13	20.69	3.12	3-15	–
TOTALS	171	1374.4	133	5475	234	23.40	3.98	7-27	12

Against each opponent

	Mtchs	Ovrs	Mdns	Runs	Wkts	Avge	RpO	BB	4wi
Derbyshire	11	74	4	371	8	46.38	5.01	3-30	–
Durham	9	70	7	246	11	22.36	3.51	3-27	–
Essex	5	33.5	3	146	7	20.86	4.32	3-23	–
Glamorgan	7	59.1	6	238	13	18.31	4.02	4-20	2
Gloucestershire	9	70.1	11	282	12	23.50	3.98	3-15	–
Hampshire	9	64	3	280	13	21.54	4.38	4-25	1
Kent	6	48.2	3	217	8	27.13	4.49	2-29	–
Lancashire	14	124.4	11	495	21	23.57	3.97	4-50	1
Leicestershire	9	68.5	10	254	11	23.09	3.69	2-13	–
Middlesex	7	56.4	2	216	13	16.62	3.81	4-35	1
Northamptonshire	14	124.4	12	489	20	24.45	3.92	4-36	1
Nottinghamshire	9	64.4	8	270	12	22.50	4.18	4-17	1

Against each opponent (*cont.*)

	Mtchs	Ovrs	Mdns	Runs	Wkts	Avge	RpO	BB	4wi
Somerset	9	72	5	322	10	32.20	4.47	3-51	–
Surrey	11	83	5	412	12	34.33	4.96	5-25	1
Sussex	6	50.3	5	178	11	16.18	3.52	5-13	1
Warwickshire	12	97.3	10	368	16	23.00	3.77	3-31	–
Worcestershire	13	108	14	376	16	23.50	3.48	4-30	1
Ireland	3	30.5	4	88	7	12.57	2.85	7-27	1
Scotland	3	26	3	82	3	27.33	3.15	2-21	–
Others	5	47.5	7	145	10	14.50	3.03	5-30	1
TOTALS	171	1374.4	133	5475	234	23.40	3.98	7-27	12

On certain grounds (qualification: 8 wickets)

(a) in Yorkshire

	Mtchs	Ovrs	Mdns	Runs	Wkts	Avge	RpO	BB	4wi
Harrogate	2	16.5	2	60	8	7.50	3.56	5-30	1
Headingley	67	557.2	58	2095	86	24.36	3.76	7-27	3
Scarborough	15	105.2	10	466	17	27.41	4.42	3-15	–
Others	8	62	5	282	10	28.20	4.55	2-13	–

(b) in rest of United Kingdom

Cardiff	3	27.1	4	96	9	10.66	3.53	4-20	2
Northampton	6	54	6	218	12	18.16	4.04	4-36	1
Old Trafford	6	58.4	6	227	13	17.46	3.87	4-50	1
Others	64	493.2	42	2031	79	25.71	4.12	5-13	4

Summary

In Yorkshire	92	741.3	75	2903	121	23.99	3.92	7-27	4
In rest of UK	79	633.1	58	2572	113	22.76	4.06	5-13	8
TOTALS	171	1374.4	133	5475	234	23.40	3.98	7-27	12

NOTE: The least successful ground is Derby, where the combined figures for 3 matches are 28-1-159-0, the runs being conceded at a rate of 5.68.

Five wickets in an innings

5-13	AXA Equity & Law League (Sunday Lg)	*v.* Sussex	Hove	1994
7-27	NatWest Trophy	*v.* Ireland	Headingley	1997
5-25	AXA LIFE League (Sunday Lg)	*v.* Surrey	Headingley	1998
5-30	NatWest Trophy	*v.* Yorkshire Cricket Board	Harrogate	2000

Most economical full innings analyses

1.63	8-2-13-2	Leicestershire	Sheffield	Sunday League	1992
1.66	9-3-15-3	Gloucestershire	Scarborough	Norwich Union League	2001
1.80	10-1-18-1	Somerset	Taunton	Benson & Hedges Cup	2001

Most expensive full innings analyses

8.13	8-0-65-0	Derbyshire	Derby	AXA LIFE League	1997
7.75	8-0-55-0	Hampshire	Southampton	AXA Equity & Law League	1995
7.75	8-0-55-1	Lancashire	Headingley	AXA Equity & Law League	1996

100th wicket

K. M. Curran b. Gough 29 *v.* Northamptonshire NWT semi-final Headingley 1995

200th Wicket

W. K. Hegg c. Hamilton b. Gough 4 *v.* Lancashire AXA LIFE League Headingley (day/night) 1998

(the middle wicket of a hat-trick)

100th Wicket in Sunday League

M. R. Ramprakash c. Lehmann b. Gough 10 *v.* Middlesex Headingley 1997

Batsmen most frequently dismissed

6	W. K. Hegg (Lancashire)	4	A. J. Moles (Warwickshire)

Most fielding dismissals

33	R. J. Blakey
17	D. Byas
7	C. White
5	M. D. Moxon

Methods of dismissals

caught	90	38.5%
bowled	103	44.0%
l.b.w.	41	17.5%
TOTAL	234	100.0%

BATTING AND FIELDING

Full career record in each competition

	Mtchs	Inns	NO	Runs	HS	Avge	50	Ct
Chel & Glos Trophy	26	14	1	234	46	18.00	–	3
Sunday League	95	63	16	593	72*	12.62	1	18
Benson & Hedges Cup	39	19	6	177	48*	13.62	–	11
National League	11	7	4	80	16*	26.66	–	1
TOTALS	171	103	27	1084	72*	14.26	1	33

Half-century

72* *v.* Leicestershire Leicester 1991

Century Partnership

129* 7th D. Byas *v.* Leicestershire Leicester 1991

MATCH AWARDS

v. Sussex	Hove	NWT	1996
v. Ireland	Headingley	NWT	1997
v. Nottinghamshire	Trent Bridge	BHC	2000

Miscellaneous

Best strike rate (BpW) in Tests for England (qualification: 150 wickets)

	Tests	Balls	Runs	Wkts	Avge	BpW	BB	5wi	10wm
S. F. Barnes 1901/2–13/14	27	7873	3106	189	16.43	**41.65**	9-103	24	7
F. S. Trueman 1952–65	67	15178	6625	307	21.57	**49.44**	8-31	17	3
D. GOUGH 1994–2001	56	11503	6288	228	27.57	**50.45**	6-42	9	–
R. G. D. Willis 1970/71–84	90	17357	8190	325	25.20	**53.41**	8-43	16	–
I. T. Botham 1977–92	102	21815	10878	383	28.40	**56.96**	8-34	27	4
J. A. Snow 1965–76	49	12021	5387	202	26.66	**59.51**	7-40	8	1

NOTE: Other than the bowlers listed above, only D. L. Underwood (297), J. B. Statham (252) and A. V. Bedser (236) have taken more Test wickets for England than Gough's 228.

It is also interesting to compare the full career record with pace bowling contemporaries, as well as the leading Test bowlers from Yorkshire:

Test career figures for recent England pace bowlers
(qualification: 100 wickets)

	Tests	Balls	Runs	Wkts	Avge	BpW	BB	5wi	10wm
D. GOUGH 1994–2001	56	11503	6288	**228**	27.57	50.45	6-42	9	–
A. Caddick 1993–2001	50	10728	5392	**181**	29.79	59.27	7-46	10	–
A. R. C. Fraser 1989–98/99	46	10876	4836	**177**	27.32	61.45	8-53	13	2
P. A. J. DeFreitas 1986/7–95	44	9838	4700	**140**	33.57	70.27	7-70	4	–
D. E. Malcolm 1989–97	40	8480	4748	**128**	37.09	66.25	9-57	5	2
D. Cork 1995–2000	31	6622	3363	**118**	28.50	56.12	7-43	5	–

Most Test wickets by Yorkshire bowlers

	Tests	Balls	Runs	Wkts	Avge	BpW	BB	5wi	10wm
F. S. Trueman 1952–65	67	15178	6625	**307**	21.57	49.44	8-31	17	3
D. GOUGH 1994–2001	56	11503	6288	**228**	27.57	50.45	6-42	9	–
H. Verity 1931–9	40	11173	3510	**144**	24.37	77.59	8-43	5	2
C. M. Old 1972/3–81	46	8858	4020	**143**	28.11	61.94	7-50	4	–
W. Rhodes 1899–1929/30	58	8231	3425	**127**	26.96	64.81	8-68	6	1

Most Test wickets in a series against West Indies in England

	Tests	Ovrs	Mdns	Runs	Wkts	Avge	BpW	BB	5wi	10wm
F. S. Trueman	1963	5	236.4	53	594	**34**	17.47	41.76	7-44	4	2
D. G. Cork	1995	5	184.2	30	661	**26**	25.42	42.54	7-43	1	–
D. GOUGH	2000	5	173.5	34	530	**25**	21.20	41.72	5-109	1	–

NOTE: It is again interesting to note the comparable strike rates (BpW).

Test hat-tricks for England against Australia

W. Bates	Melbourne	1882/3
J. Briggs	Sydney	1891/2
J. T. Hearne	Headingley	1899
D. GOUGH	Sydney	1998/9

Test hat-tricks for England since 1945

P. J. Loader	*v.* West Indies	Headingley	1957
D. G. Cork	*v.* West Indies	Old Trafford	1995
D. GOUGH	*v.* Australia	Sydney	1998/9

NOTE: There have been a total of nine hat-tricks in Tests for England and 27 for all countries.

Test opening bowling partners

Bowled in 93 innings, opening on 79 occasions with seven different partners, as follows:

42 A. R. Caddick
 9 A. R. C. Fraser
 7 D. W. Headley
 5 D. G. Cork, P. A. J. DeFreitas, D. E. Malcolm, A. D. Mullally

Opened with Caddick in 37 consecutive innings, this being an England record, as the following shows:

Pairs of opening bowlers in most consecutive Test innings for England
(qualification: ten consecutive innings)

37 innings	A. R. Caddick & D. GOUGH	2 January 2000–27 August 2001	603 days
17 innings	H. Larwood & M. W. Tate	11 August 1928–19 July 1929	343 days
13 innings	J. B. Statham & F. S. Trueman	9 June 1960–26 June 1961	383 days
13 innings	S. F. Barnes & F. R. Foster	30 December 1911–10 July 1912	194 days
12 innings	D. E. Malcolm & G. S. Small	24 February–10 July 1990	137 days

NOTES: Opened with Caddick in 41 out of 42 consecutive England innings.

Acted as first-change bowler on eight occasions and second-change on six.

The world record is 44 consecutive innings (801 days) by Kapil Dev and K. D. Ghavri (India) at the turn of the 1970s–1980s.

Most ODI wickets for England (qualification: 100)

		Mtchs	Ovrs	Mdns	Runs	Wkts	Avge	RpO	BB	4wi
D. GOUGH	1994–2001/02	101	929.4	81	3962	155	25.56	4.26	5-44	8
I. T. Botham	1976–92	116	1045.1	109	4139	145	28.54	3.96	4-31	3
P. A. J. DeFreitas	1986/7–97	103	952	113	3775	115	32.82	3.96	4-35	1

Most ODI wickets for England by Yorkshire bowlers (qualification: 40)

		Mtchs	Ovrs	Mdns	Runs	Wkts	Avge	RpO	BB	4wi
D. GOUGH	1994–2001/02	101	929.4	81	3962	**155**	25.56	4.26	5-44	8
C. White	1994/5–2000/1	37	278	16	1208	**47**	25.70	4.35	5-21	2
C. M. Old	1973–80/81	32	292.3	42	999	**45**	22.20	3.41	4-8	2

Four wickets in five balls, including a hat-trick, for Yorkshire in first-class matches

A. Waddington	*v.* Northamptonshire	Northampton	1920
G. G. Macauley	*v.* Lancashire	Old Trafford	1933
P. J. Hartley	*v.* Derbyshire	Chesterfield	1995
D. GOUGH	*v.* Kent	Headingley	1995

Best bowling average for Yorkshire in limited-overs matches
(qualification: 200 wickets)

		Mtchs	Ovrs	Runs	Wkts	Avge	RpO	BB	4wi
C. M. Old	1967–82	218	1786.1	5817	306	**19.01**	3.26	5-33	13
P. W. Jarvis	1981–93	142	1159.4	4575	209	**21.89**	3.95	6-27	11
D. GOUGH	1990–2001	171	1374.4	5475	234	**23.40**	3.98	7-27	12
G. B. Stevenson	1973–86	216	1632.3	6820	290	**23.52**	4.18	5-27	12
P. J. Hartley	1985–97	216	1705.4	7425	280	**26.52**	4.35	5-36	7
A. Sidebottom	1974–91	233	1839	6841	258	**26.52**	3.72	5-27	11
P. Carrick	1970–92	302	1891.2	7361	236	**31.19**	3.89	5-22	6

Most wickets for Yorkshire in Cheltenham & Gloucester Trophy
(including Gillette Cup and NatWest Trophy – qualification: 40 wickets)

		Mtchs	Ovrs	Mdns	Runs	Wkts	Avge	RpO	BB	4wi
D. GOUGH	1990–2001	26	273.5	40	939	**54**	17.39	3.43	7-27	5
P. J. Hartley	1986–97	28	285.5	28	1108	**45**	24.62	3.88	5-46	1
C. M. Old	1967–82	28	286.1	59	799	**43**	18.58	2.79	4-9	2

Most wickets at Headingley in limited-overs matches
(qualification: 70 wickets)

.	Mtchs	Ovrs	Mdns	Runs	Wkts	Avge	RpO	BB	4wi
P. J. Hartley	74	617	69	2465	95	25.95	4.00	5-43	1
C. White	72	493.3	48	1961	88	22.28	3.97	5-25	5
D. GOUGH	67	557.2	58	2095	86	24.36	3.76	7-27	3
A. Sidebottom	51	443.5	64	1388	73	19.01	3.13	5-27	4
C. E. W. Silverwood	50	389	50	1532	73	20.99	3.94	5-28	2

Hat-tricks for Yorkshire in limited-overs matches

P. W. Jarvis	*v.* Derbyshire	Derby	John Player League	1982
D. GOUGH	*v.* Lancashire	Headingley	AXA LIFE League	1998
C. White	*v.* Kent	Headingley	CGU National League	2000

Best bowling performances for Yorkshire in limited-overs matches

7-15	R. A. Hutton *v.* Worcestershire	Headingley	John Player Sunday League	1969
7-27	D. GOUGH *v.* Ireland	Headingley	NatWest Trophy	1997

NOTE: These are the only two instances of Yorkshire players taking seven wickets in an innings in such matches.

Highest scores by Yorkshire players in first Test innings

107	J. H. Hampshire	*v.* West Indies	Lord's	1969
93	P. A. Gibb	*v.* South Africa	Johannesburg	1938/9
91	F. S. Jackson	*v.* Australia	Lord's	1893
74	M. D. Moxon	*v.* New Zealand	Lord's	1986
65	D. GOUGH	*v.* New Zealand	Old Trafford	1994

Briefs

First place in Yorkshire bowling averages:
    (a) first-class matches – 1994, 1996, 1999
    (b) limited-overs matches – 1993, 1998, 2000
Opened bowling in second innings of debut first-class match, with Paul Jarvis.
Took a wicket with sixth ball on Test debut *and* on one-day international debut.

And finally . . .

The first wicket to fall in the Benson & Hedges Cup match against Leicestershire at Headingley on 19 April 2000 was that of **Darren** Maddy, caught by **Darren** Lehmann off the bowling of **Darren** Gough for a duck.

Bibliography

Paul Dyson: *Benson and Hedges Cup Record Book*

Bill Frindall: *Limited-Overs International Cricket – The Complete Record*
    The Wisden Book of Test Cricket
    The Wisden Book of Cricket Records

Les Hatton: *Sunday League Record Book*

V. H. Isaacs and R. Isaacs: *Gillette Cup/NatWest Trophy Record Book*

V. H. Isaacs and R. K. Whitham: *One Day International Cricket Records*

H. M. Taufique: *150 Great Test Cricketers*

Jason Woolgar: *England's Test Cricketers*
    England – the Complete One-Day International Record

Also various editions of *ACS International Year Book*, *The Cricketer Quarterly*, *Playfair Cricket Annual*, *The Times*, *Wisden Cricketers' Almanack* and *Yorkshire C.C.C. Year Book*

Also www-uk.cricket.org (CricInfo)

Also the assistance of Rachel O'Halloran (Yorkshire C.C.C.) is gratefully acknowledged.

INDEX